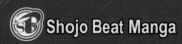
Shojo Beat Manga

Story & Art by
Yuki Kure

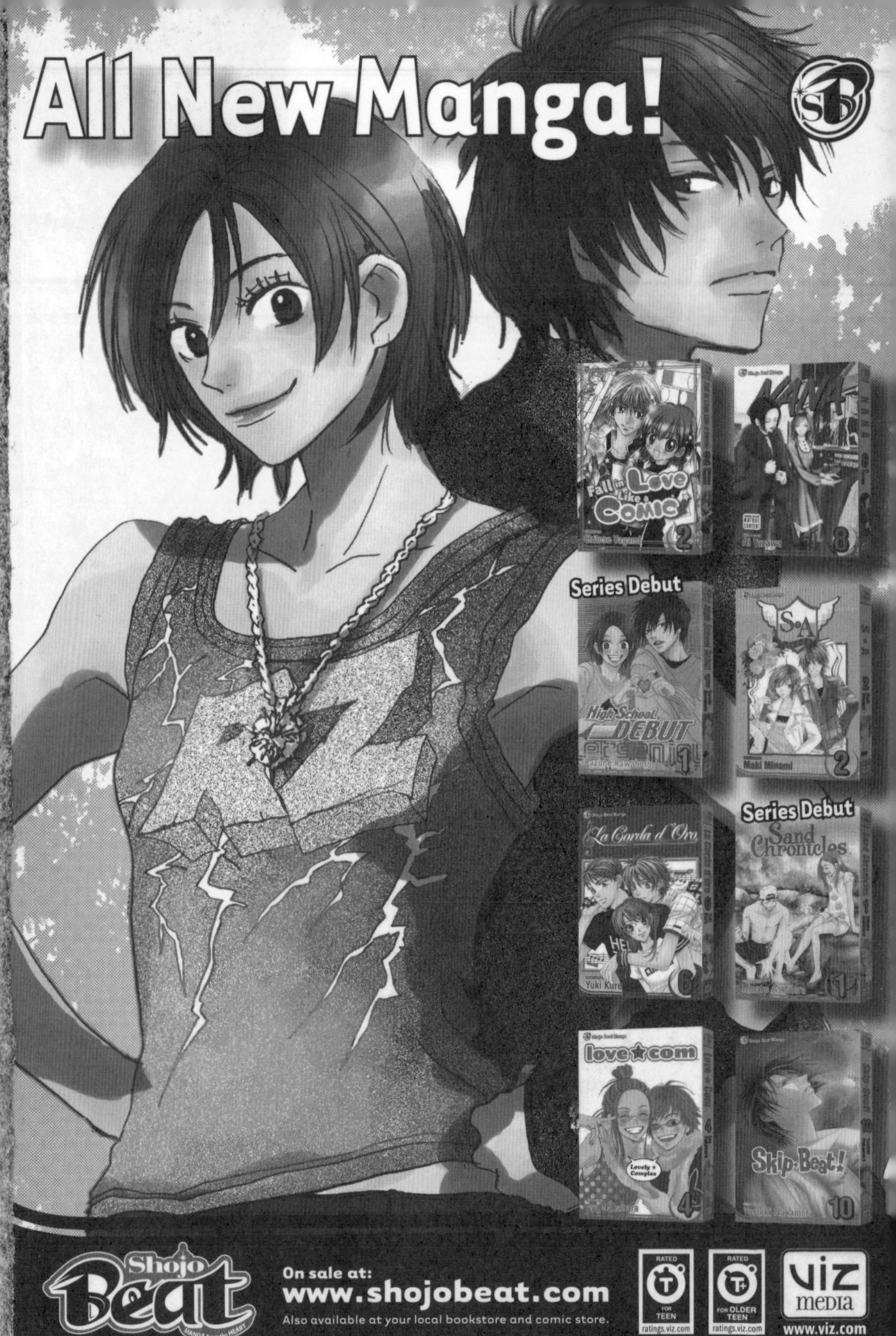
All New Manga!
Fall in Love Like a Comic
2
NANA
8
Series Debut
High School DEBUT
1
S·A
Maki Minami
2
La Corda d'Oro
Yuki Kure
6
Series Debut
Sand Chronicles
1
love★com
4
Skip·Beat!
10
Shojo Beat
MANGA from the HEART
On sale at:
www.shojobeat.com
Also available at your local bookstore and comic store.
RATED T FOR TEEN ratings.viz.com
RATED T+ FOR OLDER TEEN ratings.viz.com
VIZ media
www.viz.com

6
Story & Art by Yuki Kure

Characters

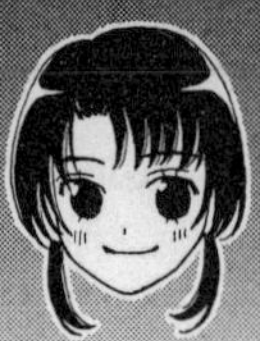

Kahoko Hino
(General Education School, 2nd year)

The heroine. She knows nothing about music, but she still finds herself participating in the music competition equipped with a magic violin.

Len Tsukimori
(Music School, 2nd year)

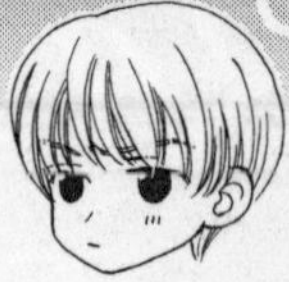

A violin major and a cold perfectionist from a musical family of unquestionable talent.

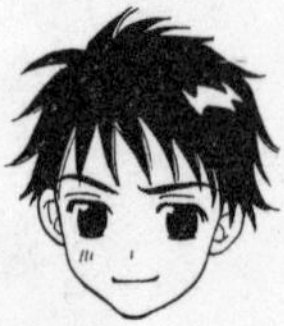

Ryotaro Tsuchiura
(General Education, 2nd year)

A member of the soccer team who seems to be looking after Kahoko as a fellow Gen Ed student.

Keiichi Shimizu
(Music school, 1st year)

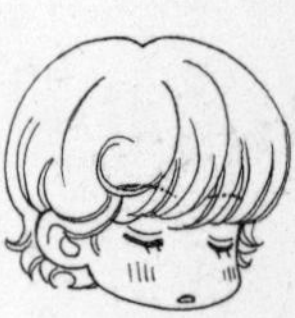

A student of the cello who walks to the beat of his own drum and is often lost in the world of music. He is also often asleep.

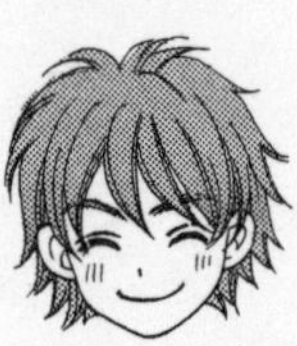

Kazuki Hihara
(Music school, 3rd year)

An energetic and friendly trumpet major and a fan of anything fun.

Azuma Yunoki
(Music school, 3rd year)

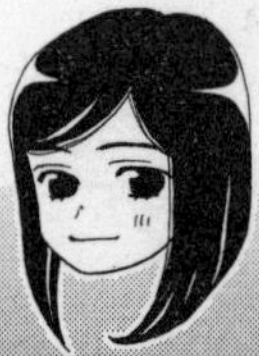

A flute major and the son of a graceful and kind traditional flower arrangement master. He even has a dedicated fan club called the "Yunoki Guard."

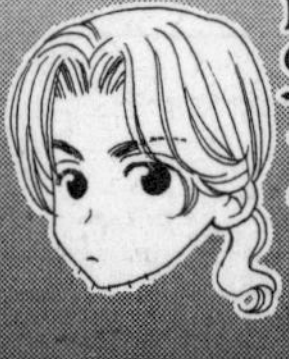

Hiroto Kanazawa
(Music teacher)

The contest coordinator whose lazy demeanor suggests he is avoiding any hassle.

Story

Our story is set at Seiso Academy, which is split into the General Education School and the Music School. Kahoko, a Gen Ed student, encounters a music fairy named Lili, who gives her a magic violin that anyone can play. Suddenly, Kahoko finds herself in the school's music competition, with good-looking, quirky Music School students as her fellow contestants! Kahoko comes to accept her daunting task and finds herself enjoying music. In the Second Selection, Len is kidnapped by jealous students and ends up having to withdraw. Kahoko places second, but begins to feel guilty about competing with a magic violin.

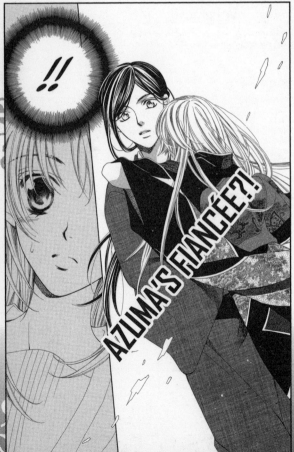

Previously ...

Azuma convinces Kahoko to pretend to be his fiancée in order to chase off an aggressive suitor. But when the girl, Ayano, is presented with the deception, she blindly professes her love for Azuma...

!!
AZUMA'S FIANCÉE?!

The music fairy Lili, who got Kahoko caught up in this affair. ↓

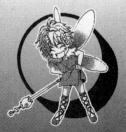

La Corda d'Oro

CONTENTS
Volume 6

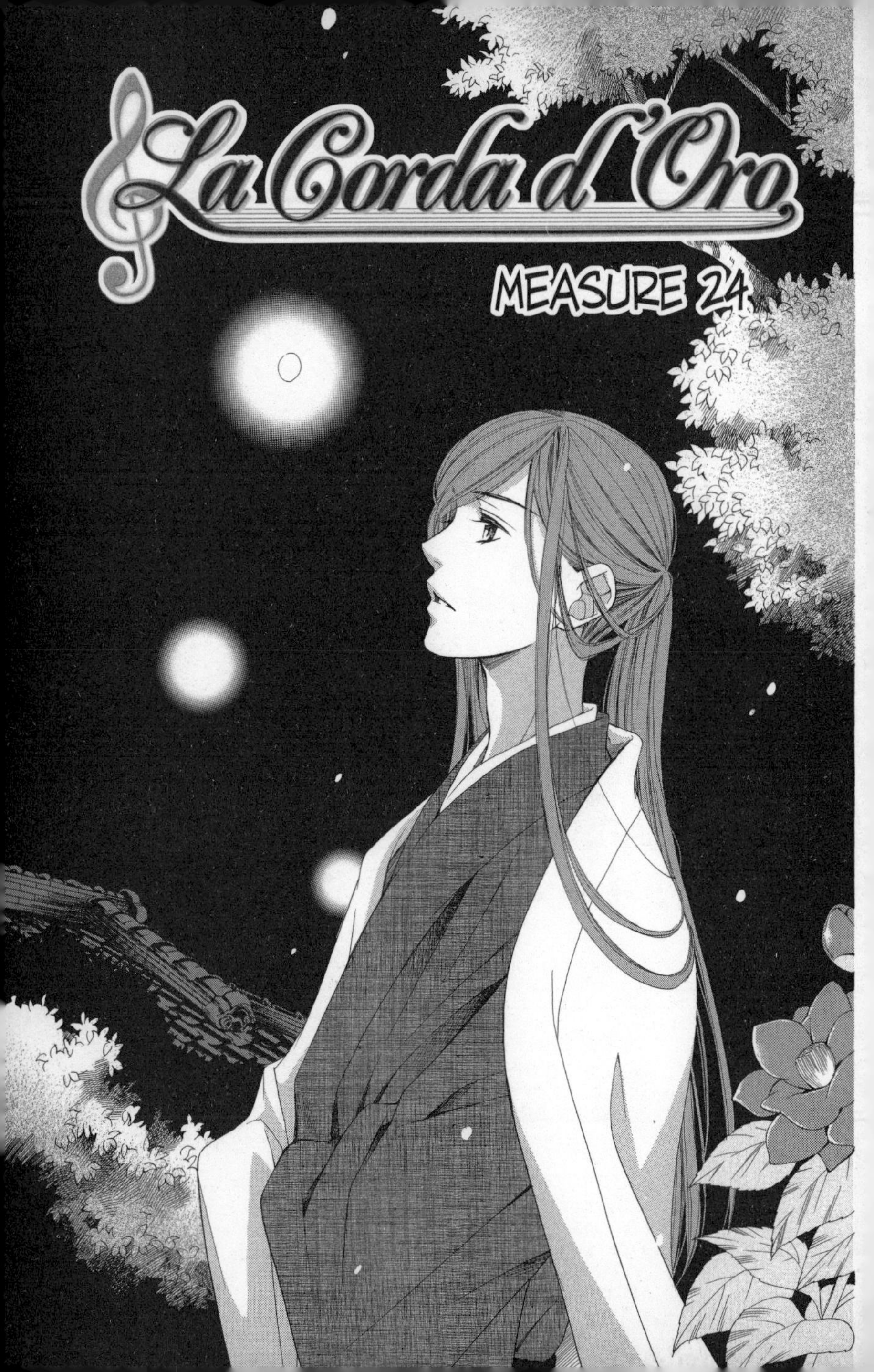
La Corda d'Oro
MEASURE 24

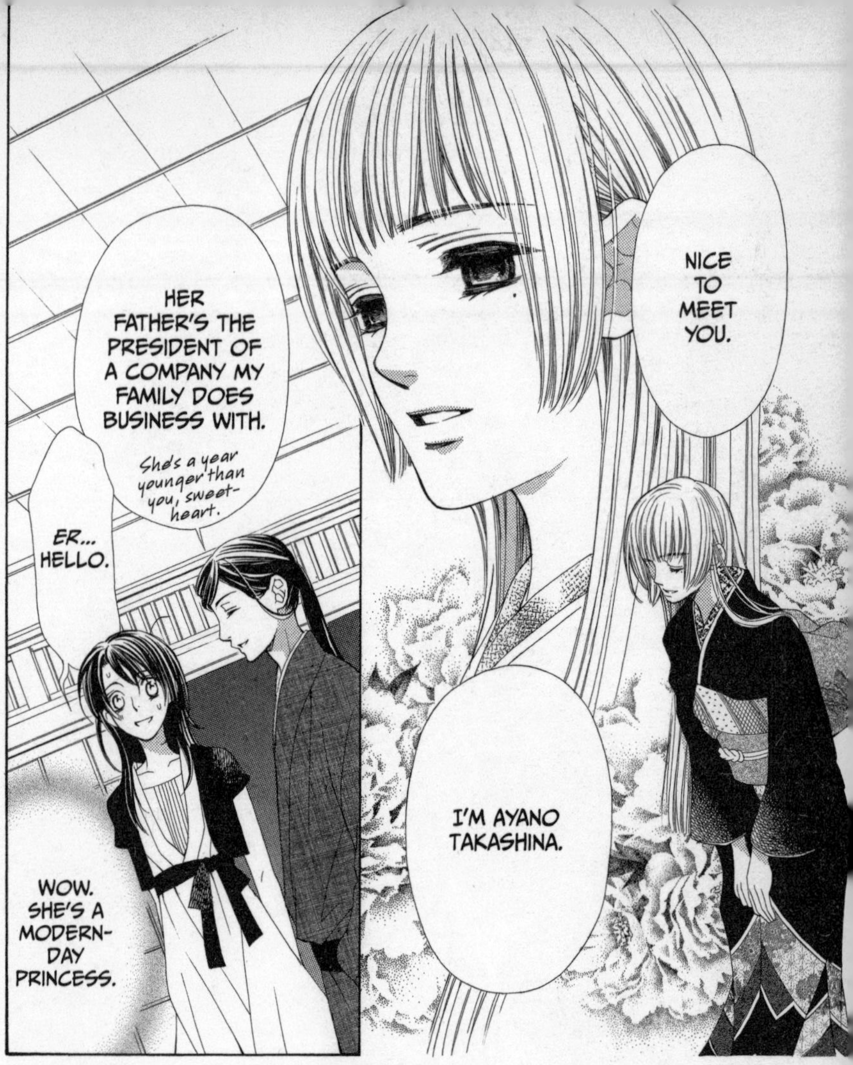
NICE TO MEET YOU.
I'M AYANO TAKASHINA.
HER FATHER'S THE PRESIDENT OF A COMPANY MY FAMILY DOES BUSINESS WITH.
She's a year younger than you, sweetheart.
ER... HELLO.
WOW. SHE'S A MODERN-DAY PRINCESS.

Daily Happenings 16

Art supplies (black and white)...

I've tried a lot of different stuff, but I feel like I'm finally settling on some favorites.

For the most part, I use a Zebra G-pen and a round nib pen from Nikko. The round nib pen tires out my hand, so I prefer the G-pen.

For black ink, I use Sumi no Hana. (It dries quickly. It's nice.) And I use a brush pen (for hair and adding shine) by COPIC called the Multiliner. I use a 0.7 Rotring pen for borders. Nothing groundbreaking, really...I have yet to break through into the digital age. Oh, yes, and the script paper I use is Muse.

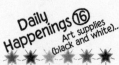

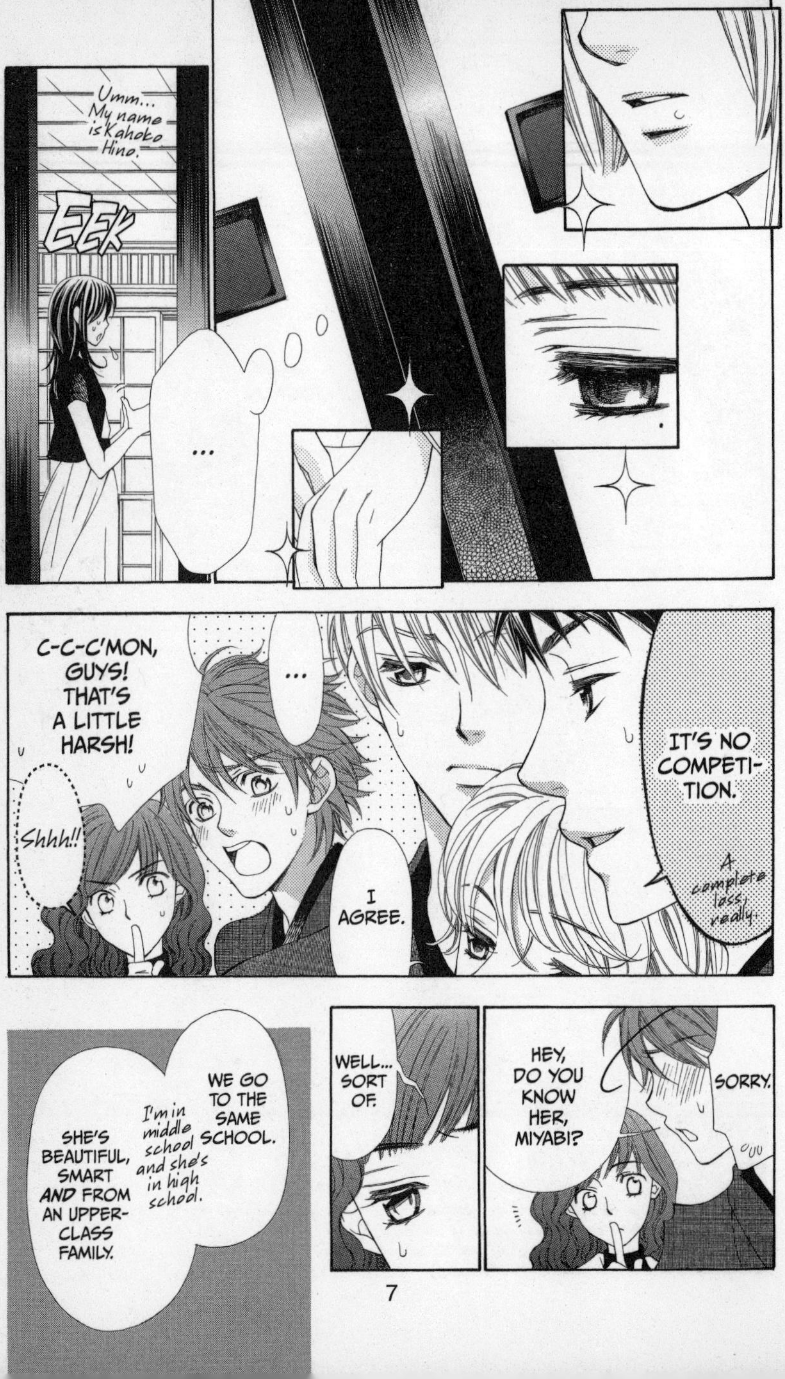
...
Umm... My name is Kahoko Hino.
EEK
IT'S NO COMPETITION.
A complete loss, really.
I AGREE.
...
C-C-C'MON, GUYS! THAT'S A LITTLE HARSH!
Shhh!!
SORRY.
HEY, DO YOU KNOW HER, MIYABI?
WELL... SORT OF.
WE GO TO THE SAME SCHOOL.
I'm in middle school and she's in high school.
SHE'S BEAUTIFUL, SMART AND FROM AN UPPER-CLASS FAMILY.

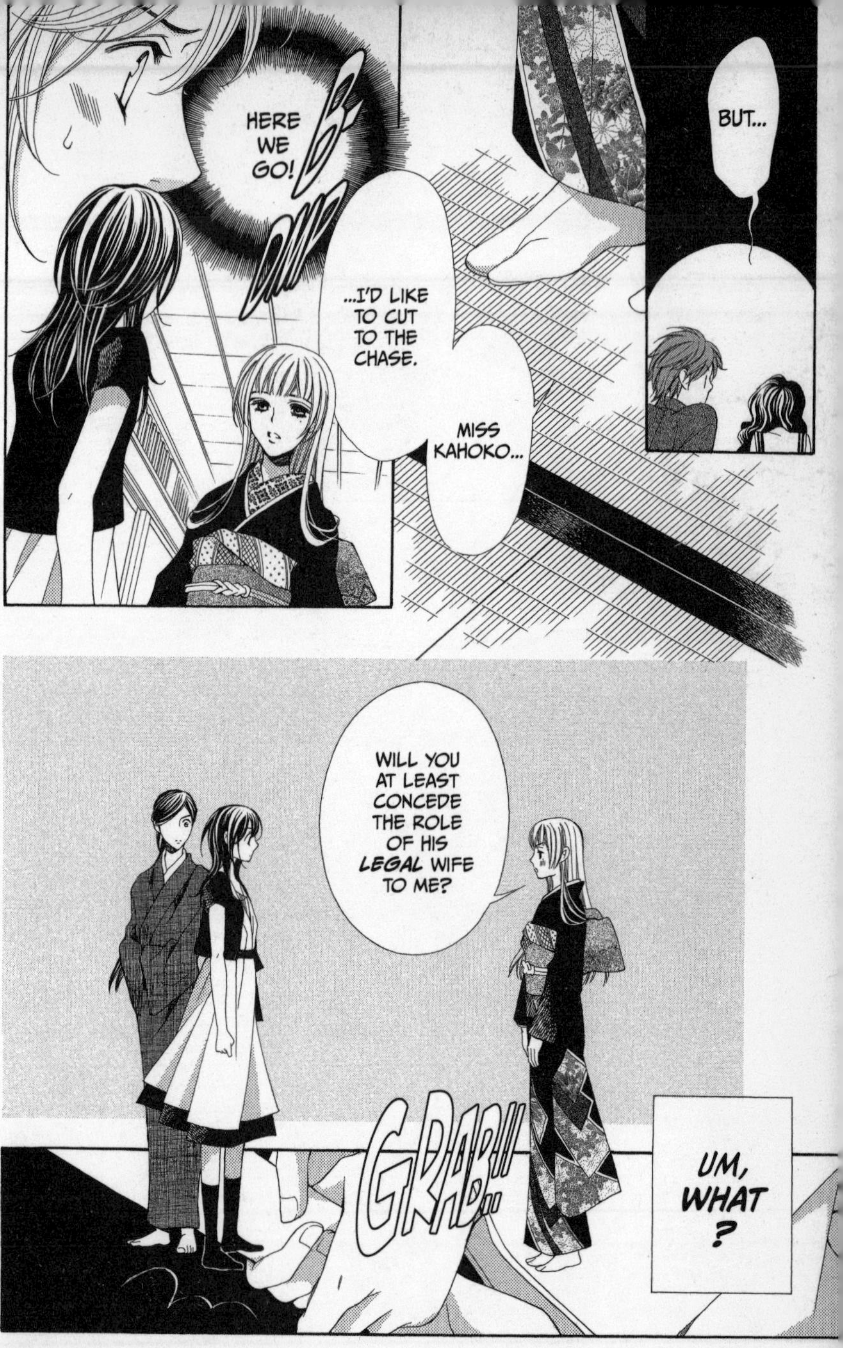
BUT...
MISS KAHOKO...
...I'D LIKE TO CUT TO THE CHASE.
HERE WE GO!
WILL YOU AT LEAST CONCEDE THE ROLE OF HIS *LEGAL* WIFE TO ME?
UM, WHAT?
GRAB!!

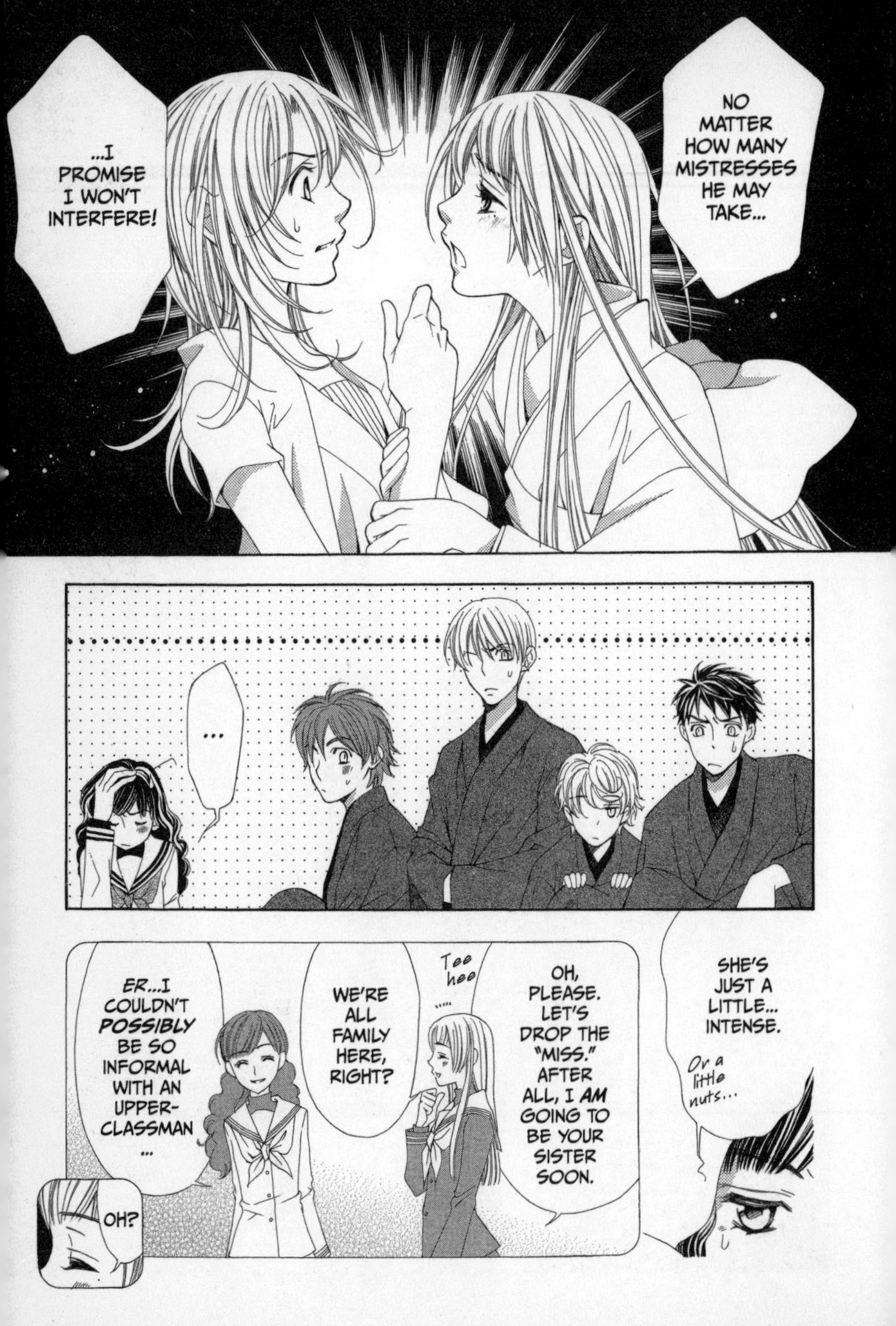
NO MATTER HOW MANY MISTRESSES HE MAY TAKE...
...I PROMISE I WON'T INTERFERE!
...
SHE'S JUST A LITTLE... INTENSE.
Or a little nuts...
OH, PLEASE. LET'S DROP THE "MISS." AFTER ALL, I *AM* GOING TO BE YOUR SISTER SOON.
Tee hee
WE'RE ALL FAMILY HERE, RIGHT?
ER...I COULDN'T *POSSIBLY* BE SO INFORMAL WITH AN UPPER-CLASSMAN...
OH?

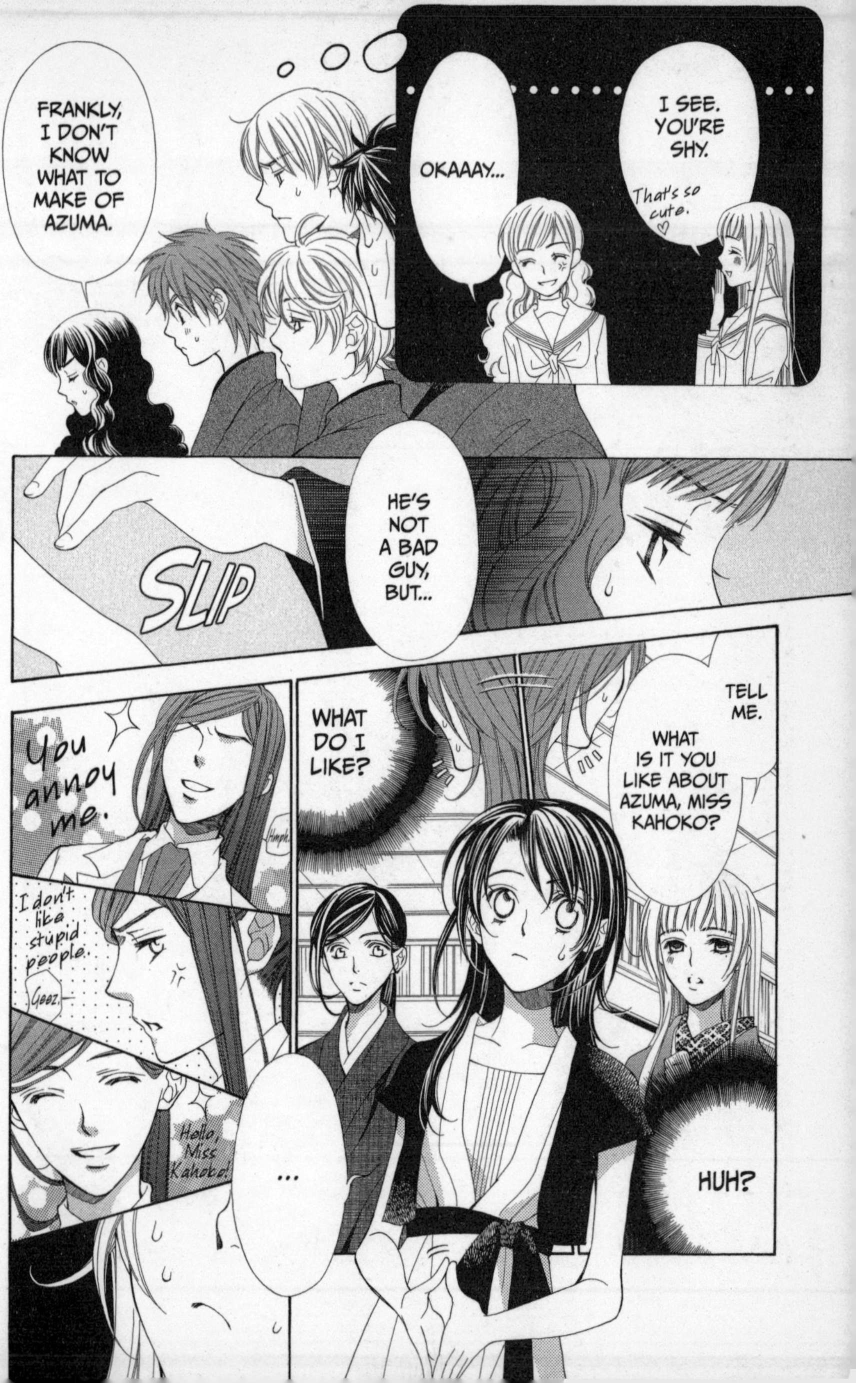
I SEE. YOU'RE SHY.
That's so cute. ♡
OKAAAY...
FRANKLY, I DON'T KNOW WHAT TO MAKE OF AZUMA.
HE'S NOT A BAD GUY, BUT...
SLIP
TELL ME.
WHAT IS IT YOU LIKE ABOUT AZUMA, MISS KAHOKO?
HUH?
WHAT DO I LIKE?
...
You annoy me.
Hmph.
I don't like stupid people.
Geez.
Hello, Miss Kahoko!

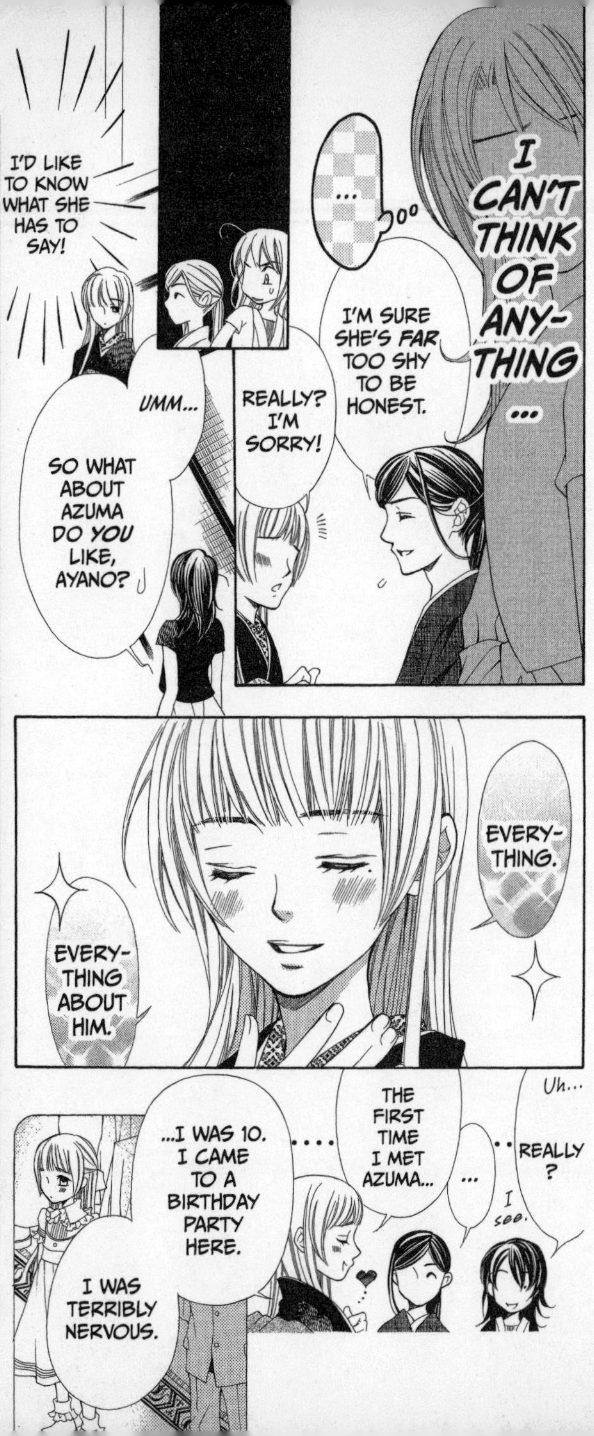
I CAN'T THINK OF ANY-THING...
...
I'M SURE SHE'S FAR TOO SHY TO BE HONEST.
REALLY? I'M SORRY!
I'D LIKE TO KNOW WHAT SHE HAS TO SAY!
UMM...
SO WHAT ABOUT AZUMA DO YOU LIKE, AYANO?
EVERY-THING.
EVERY-THING ABOUT HIM.
Uh...
REALLY?
I see.
...
THE FIRST TIME I MET AZUMA...
...I WAS 10. I CAME TO A BIRTHDAY PARTY HERE.
I WAS TERRIBLY NERVOUS.

ONE

Long time no see. Yuki here! Thank you very much for buying volume 6 of *La Corda!*

I can't believe it's already volume 6!

The cover for this volume... I know it's sort of implausible. Especially with Kazuki. But as my editor put it, "It's okay! You can think of the cover as a parody of sorts!" (lol) That's what I was told, anyway. It's fun for me, so I've got no complaints.

I think Kazuki's doing really well in the polls. He's always on the top of the request list for people to put on the cover. I wonder if it has something to do with how happy he is all the time... *Any insights?*

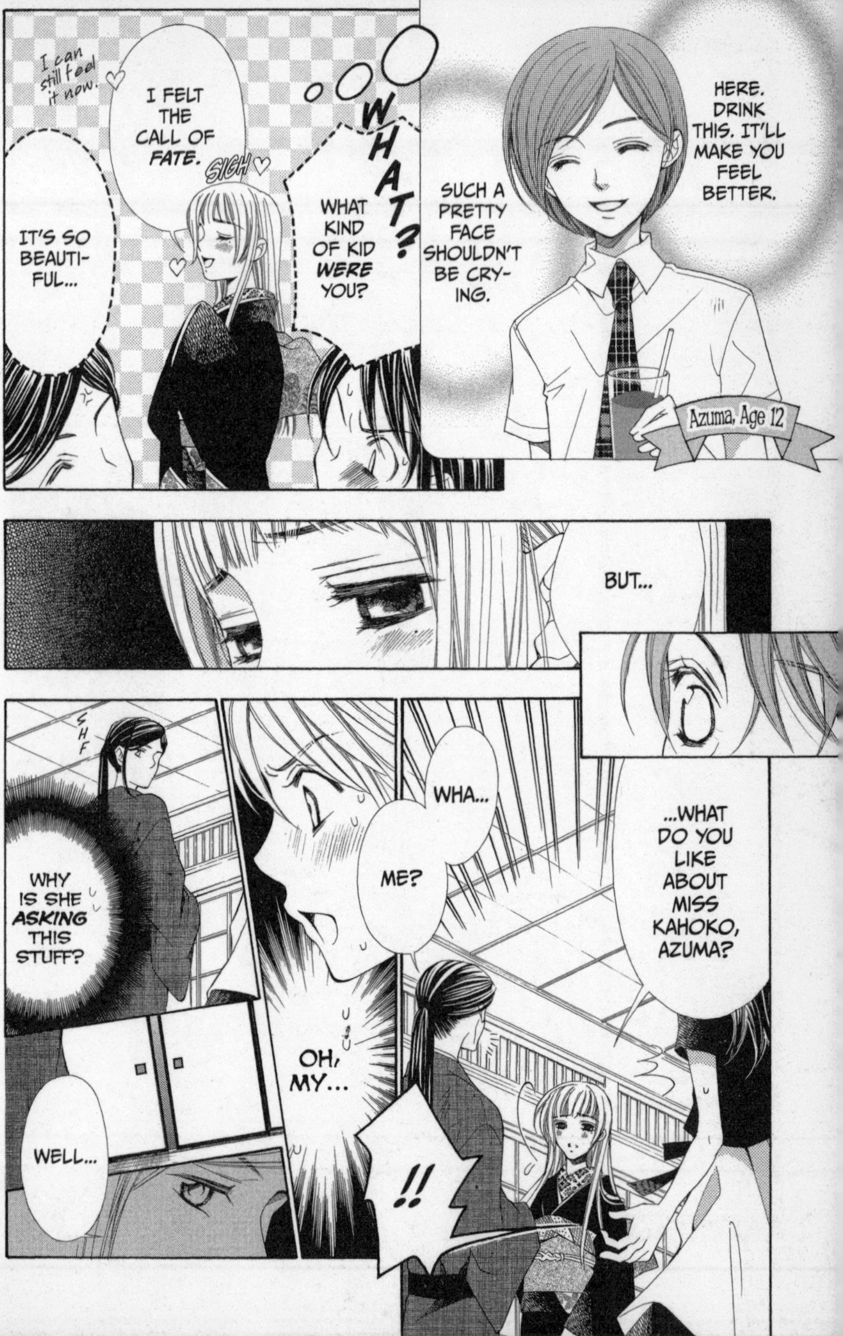
HERE. DRINK THIS. IT'LL MAKE YOU FEEL BETTER.
SUCH A PRETTY FACE SHOULDN'T BE CRY-ING.
Azuma, Age 12
OOO
WHAT?
WHAT KIND OF KID WERE YOU?
I FELT THE CALL OF FATE.
SIGH
I can still feel it now.
IT'S SO BEAUTI-FUL...
BUT...
...WHAT DO YOU LIKE ABOUT MISS KAHOKO, AZUMA?
!!
WHA...
ME?
OH, MY...
SHF
WHY IS SHE ASKING THIS STUFF?
WELL...

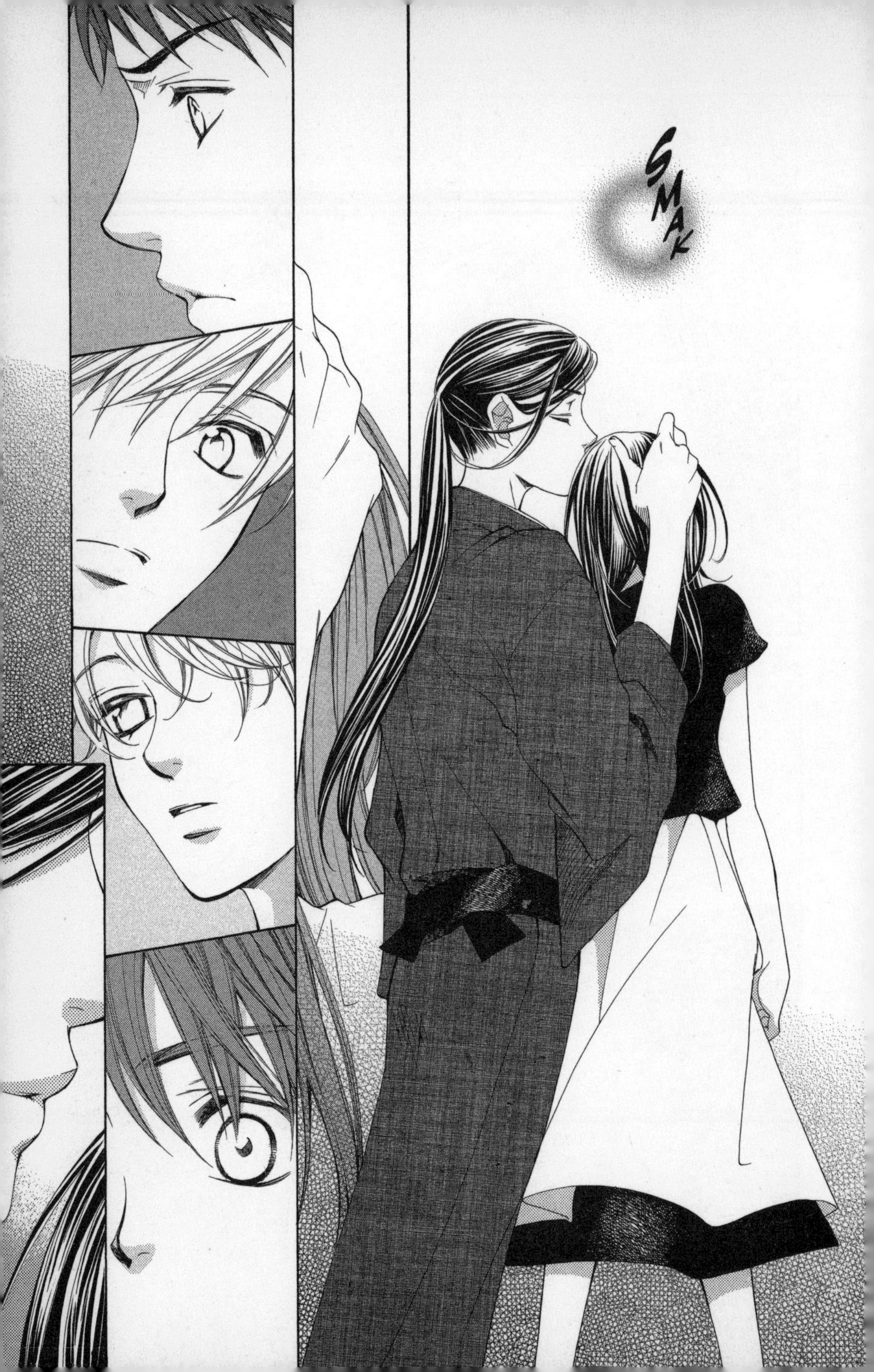
SMAK

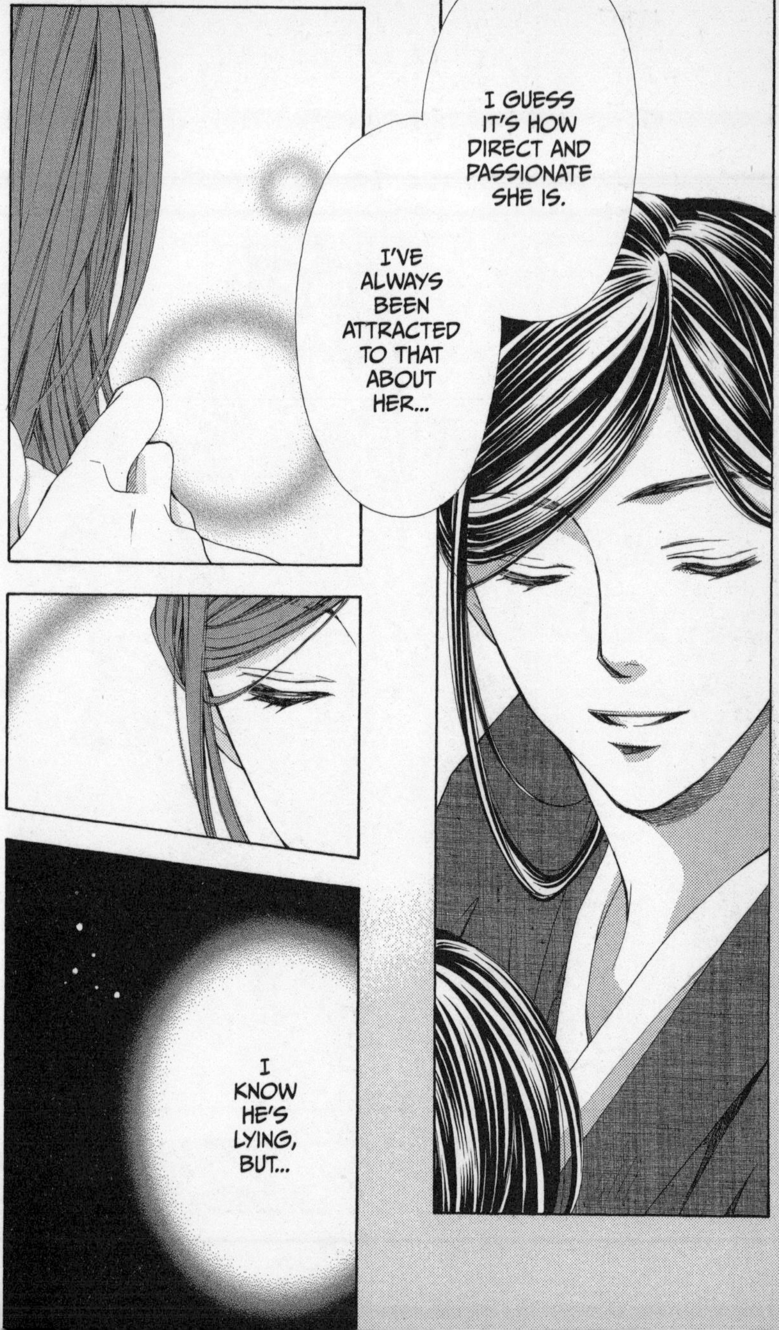
I GUESS IT'S HOW DIRECT AND PASSIONATE SHE IS.
I'VE ALWAYS BEEN ATTRACTED TO THAT ABOUT HER...
I KNOW HE'S LYING, BUT...

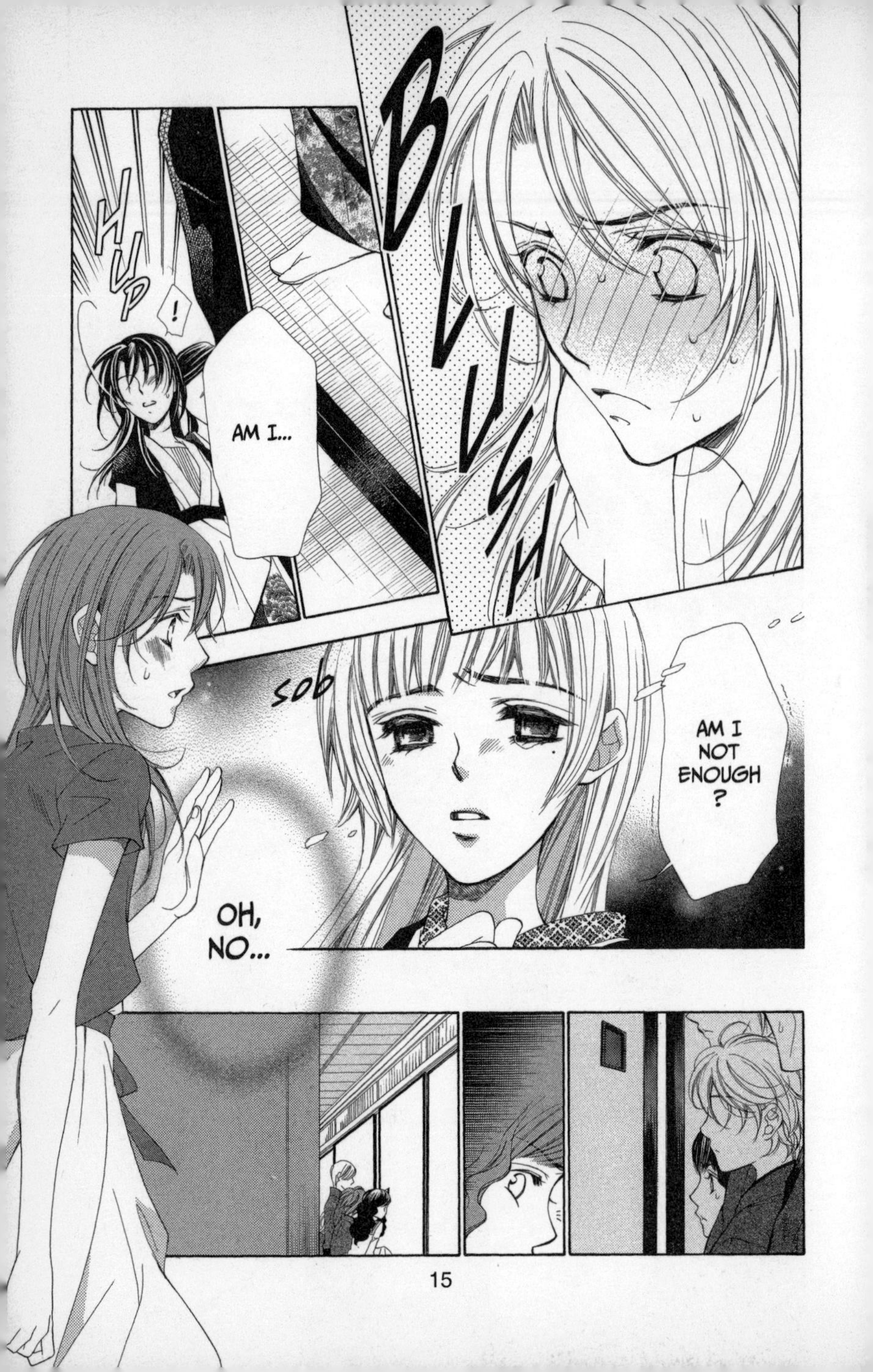
BLUSH
HUP
!
AM I...
AM I NOT ENOUGH ?
sob
OH, NO...

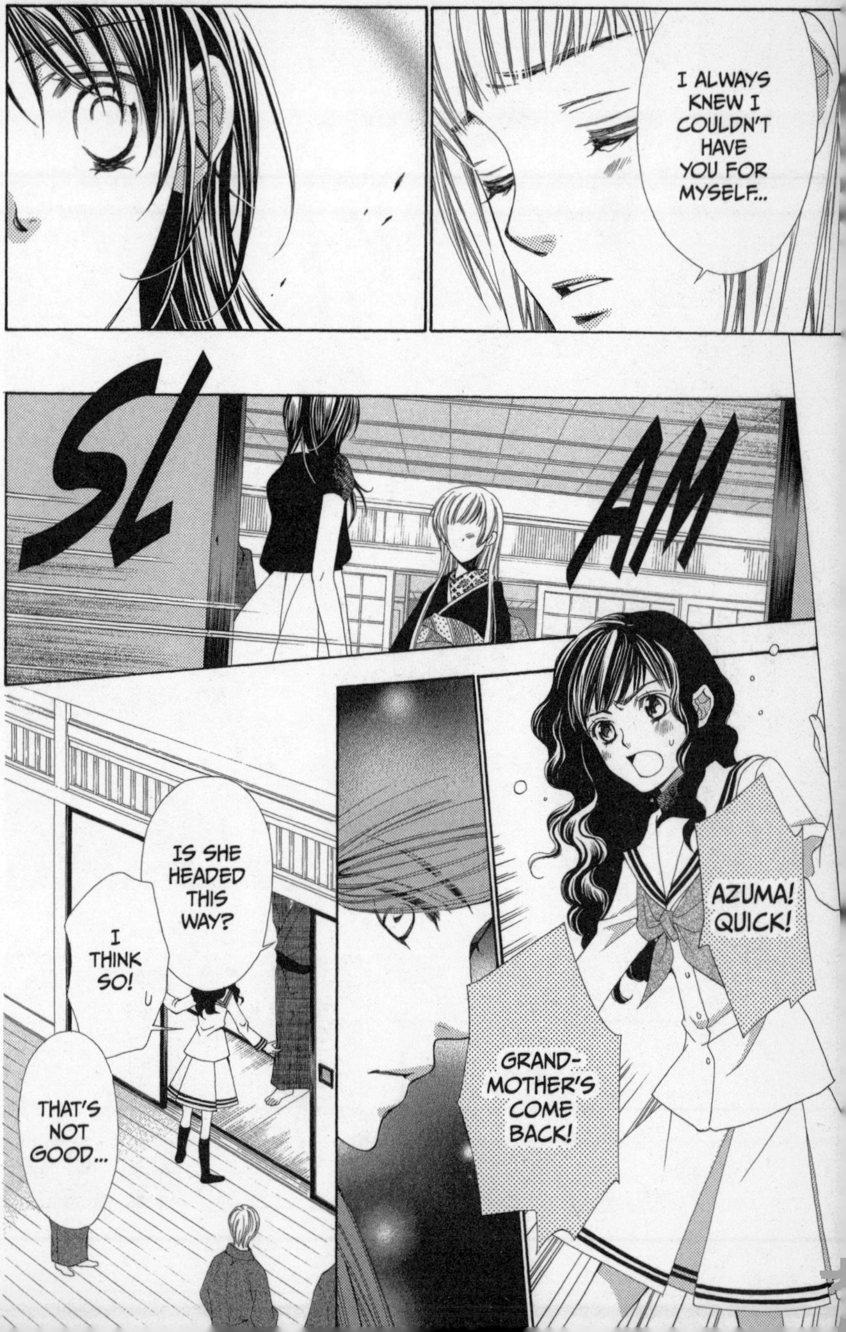
I ALWAYS KNEW I COULDN'T HAVE YOU FOR MYSELF...
SLAM
AZUMA! QUICK!
GRAND-MOTHER'S COME BACK!
IS SHE HEADED THIS WAY?
I THINK SO!
THAT'S NOT GOOD...

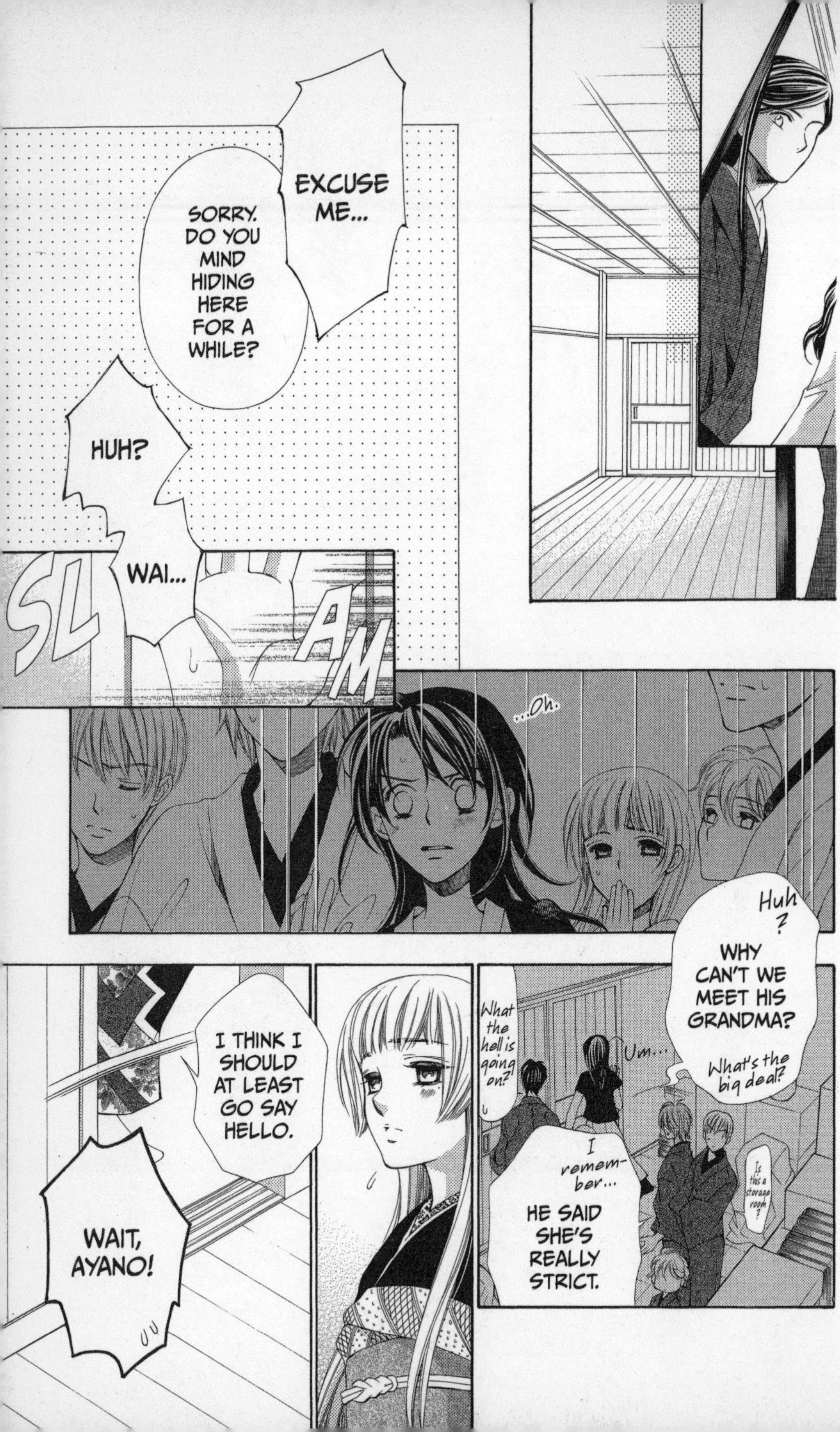
EXCUSE ME...
SORRY. DO YOU MIND HIDING HERE FOR A WHILE?
HUH?
WAI...
SLAM
...Oh.
Huh? WHY CAN'T WE MEET HIS GRANDMA?
What's the big deal?
Um...
What the hell is going on?
Is this a storage room?
I remember... HE SAID SHE'S REALLY STRICT.
I THINK I SHOULD AT LEAST GO SAY HELLO.
WAIT, AYANO!

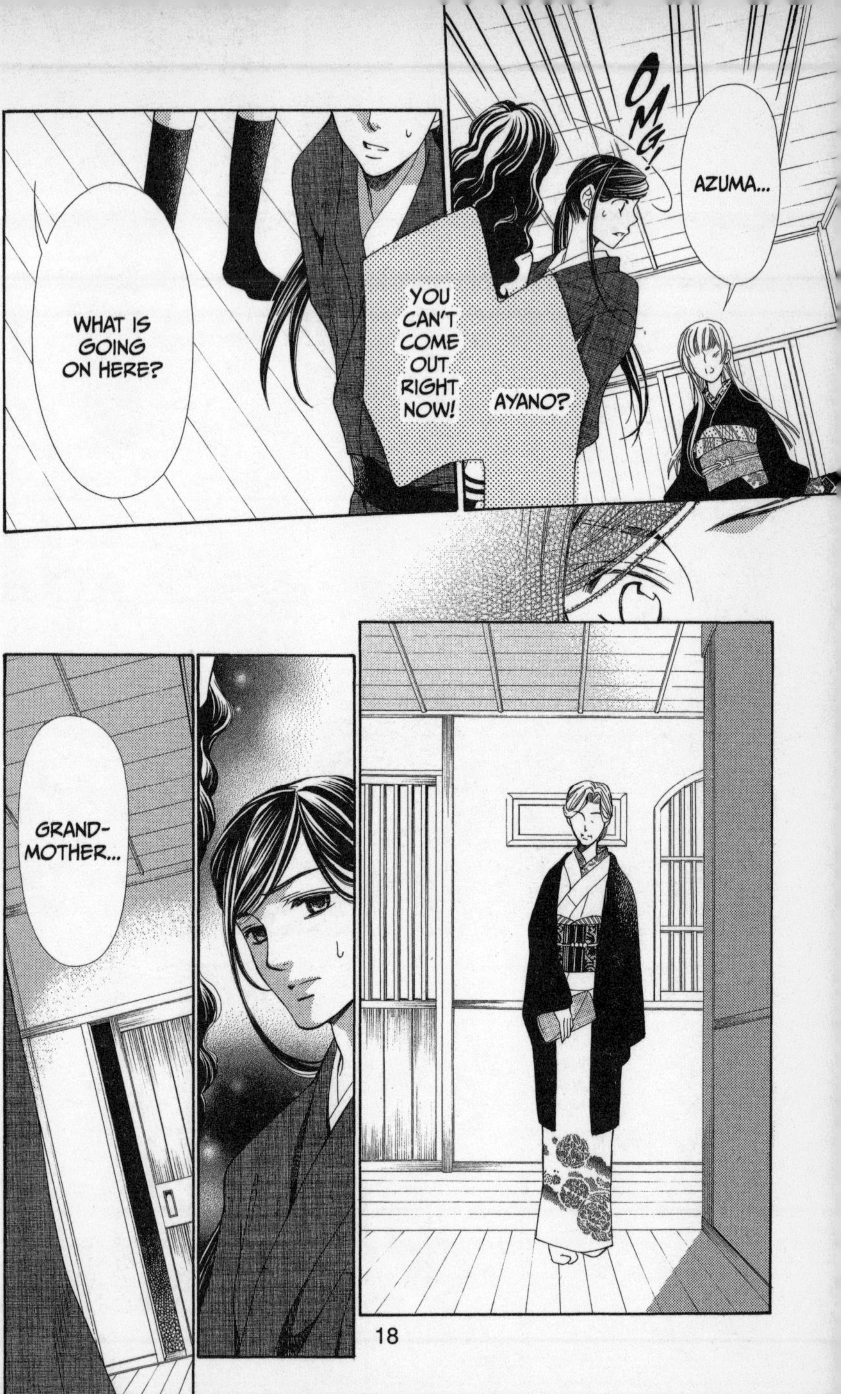
OMG!
AZUMA...
AYANO?
YOU CAN'T COME OUT RIGHT NOW!
WHAT IS GOING ON HERE?
GRAND-MOTHER...

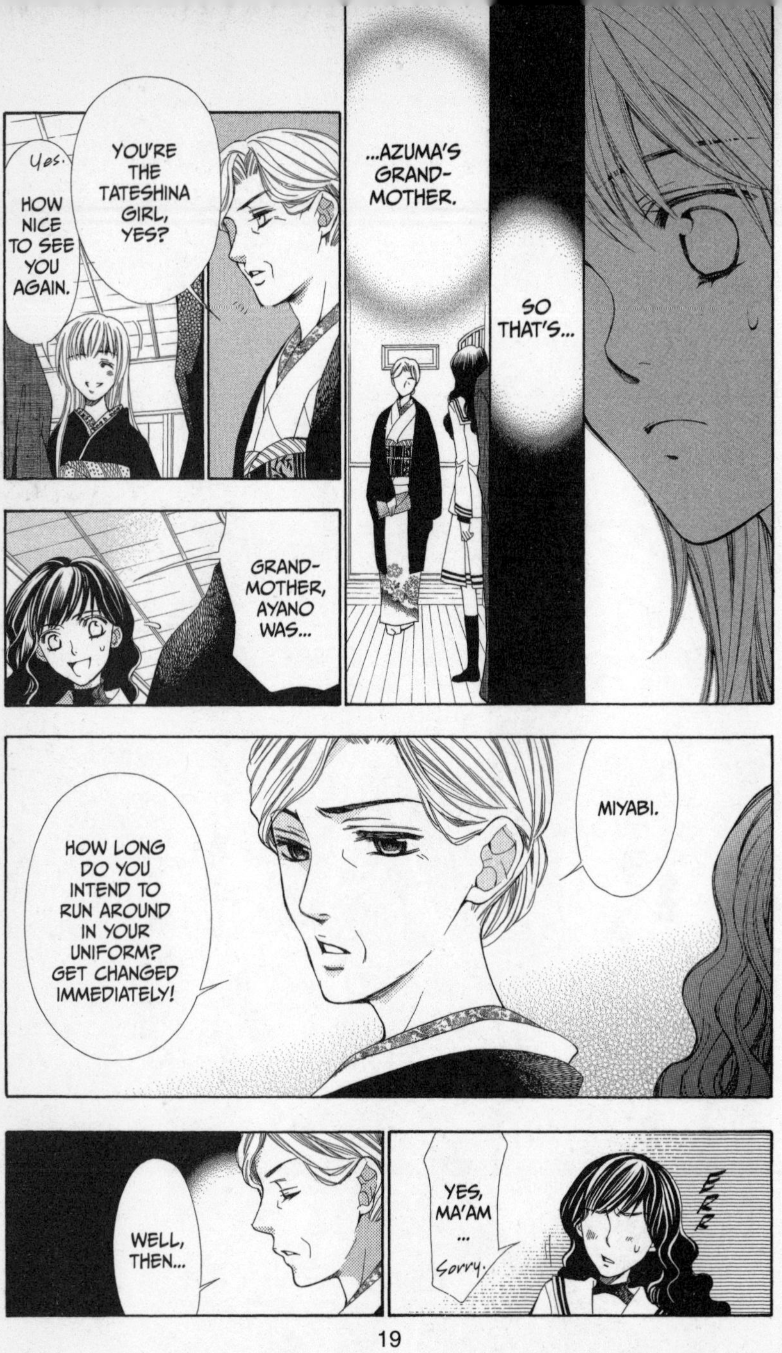
SO THAT'S...
...AZUMA'S GRAND-MOTHER.
YOU'RE THE TATESHINA GIRL, YES?
Yes.
HOW NICE TO SEE YOU AGAIN.
GRAND-MOTHER, AYANO WAS...
MIYABI.
HOW LONG DO YOU INTEND TO RUN AROUND IN YOUR UNIFORM? GET CHANGED IMMEDIATELY!
ERR
YES, MA'AM ...
Sorry.
WELL, THEN...

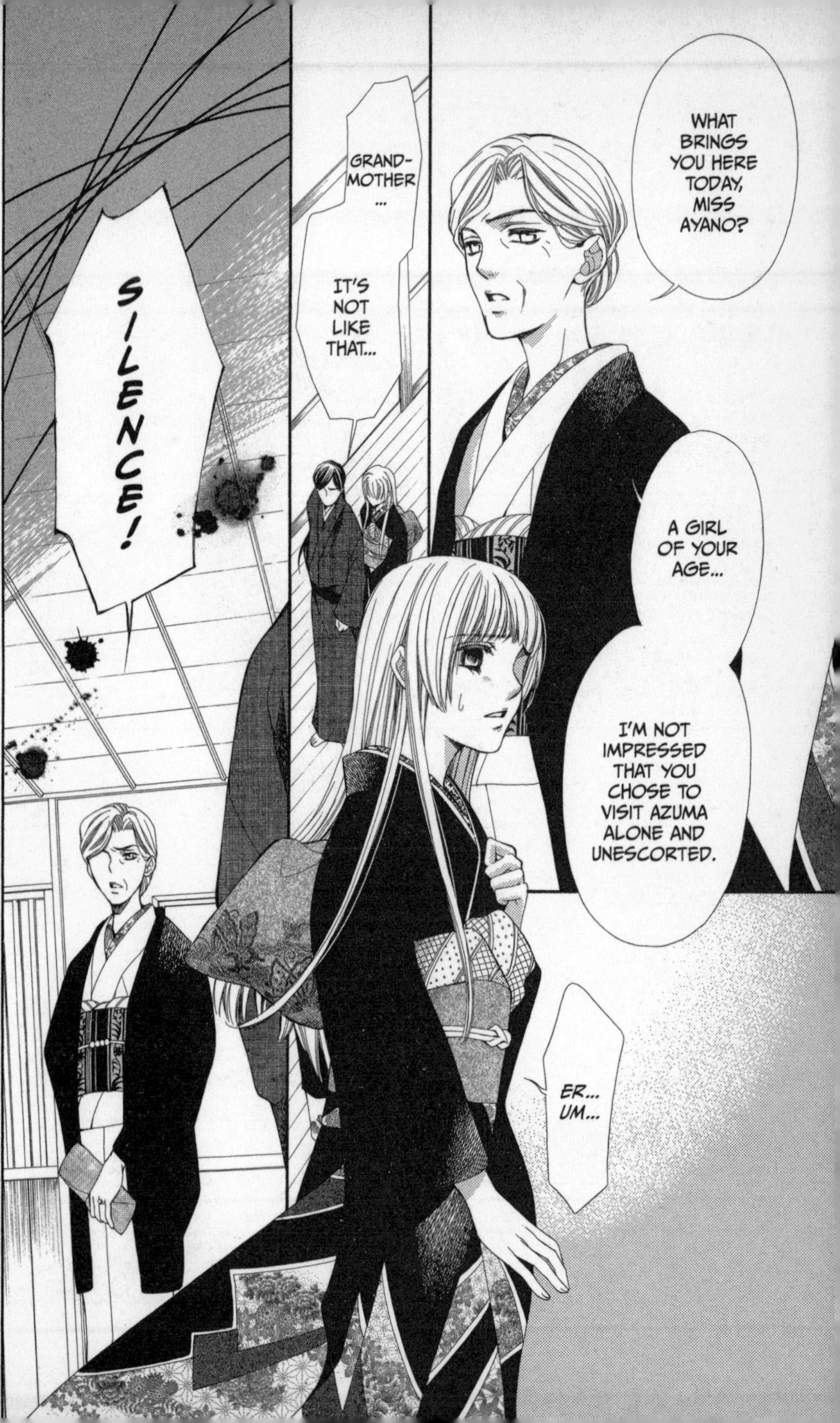
WHAT BRINGS YOU HERE TODAY, MISS AYANO?
A GIRL OF YOUR AGE...
I'M NOT IMPRESSED THAT YOU CHOSE TO VISIT AZUMA ALONE AND UNESCORTED.
ER... UM...
GRAND-MOTHER ...
IT'S NOT LIKE THAT...
SILENCE!

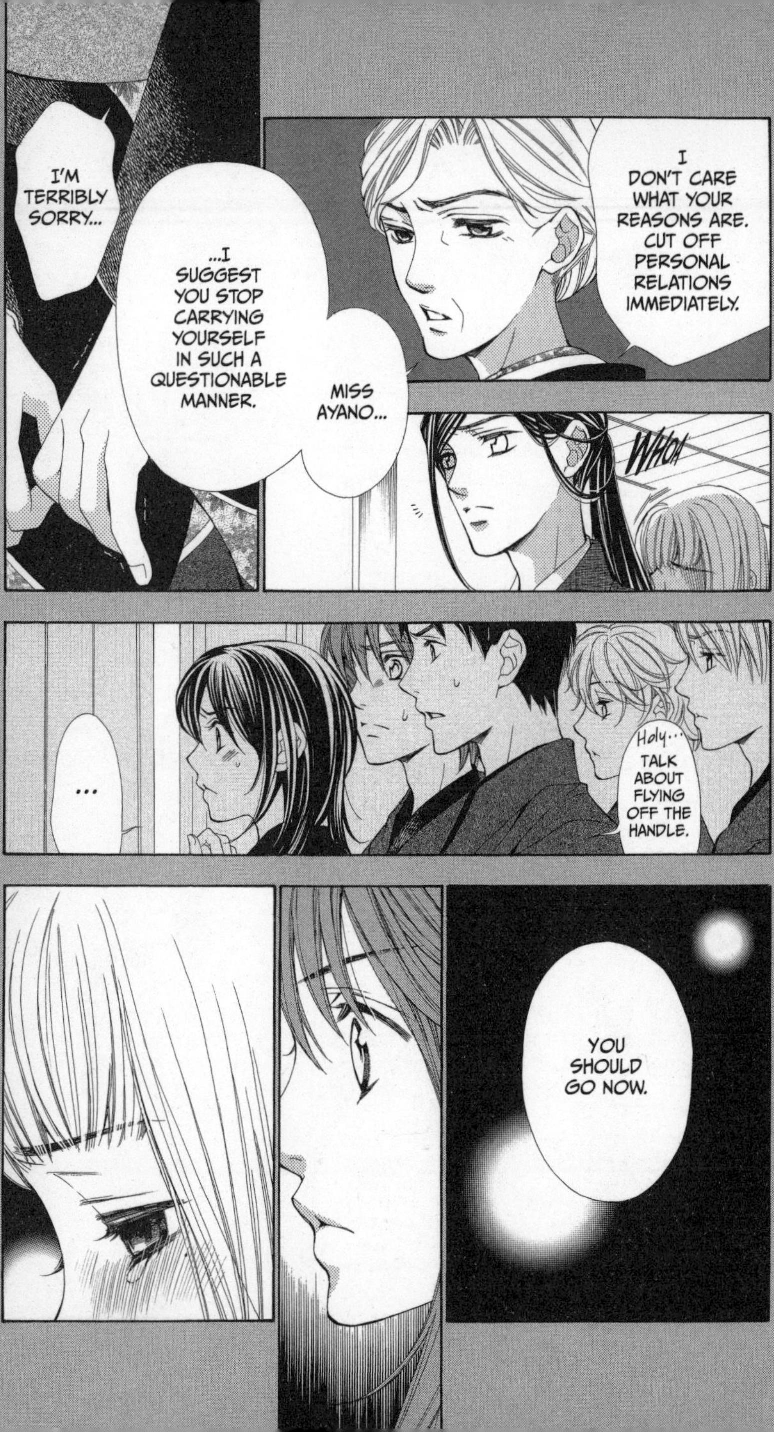
I DON'T CARE WHAT YOUR REASONS ARE. CUT OFF PERSONAL RELATIONS IMMEDIATELY.
WHOA
MISS AYANO...
...I SUGGEST YOU STOP CARRYING YOURSELF IN SUCH A QUESTIONABLE MANNER.
I'M TERRIBLY SORRY...
Holy... TALK ABOUT FLYING OFF THE HANDLE.
...
YOU SHOULD GO NOW.

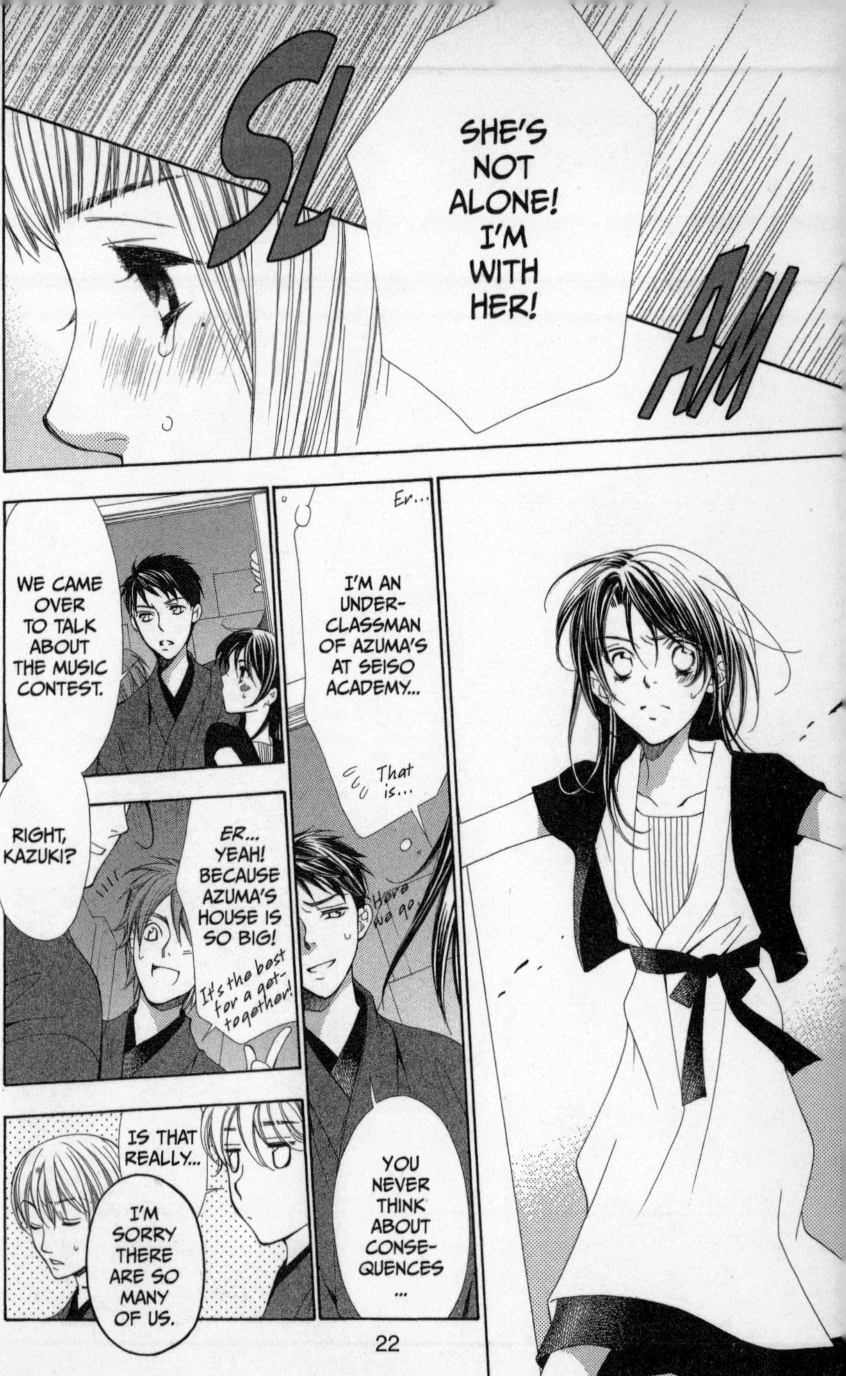
SL
AM
SHE'S NOT ALONE! I'M WITH HER!
Er...
I'M AN UNDER-CLASSMAN OF AZUMA'S AT SEISO ACADEMY...
That is...
Here we go...
YOU NEVER THINK ABOUT CONSE-QUENCES ...
WE CAME OVER TO TALK ABOUT THE MUSIC CONTEST.
RIGHT, KAZUKI?
ER... YEAH! BECAUSE AZUMA'S HOUSE IS SO BIG!
It's the best for a get-together!
IS THAT REALLY...
I'M SORRY THERE ARE SO MANY OF US.

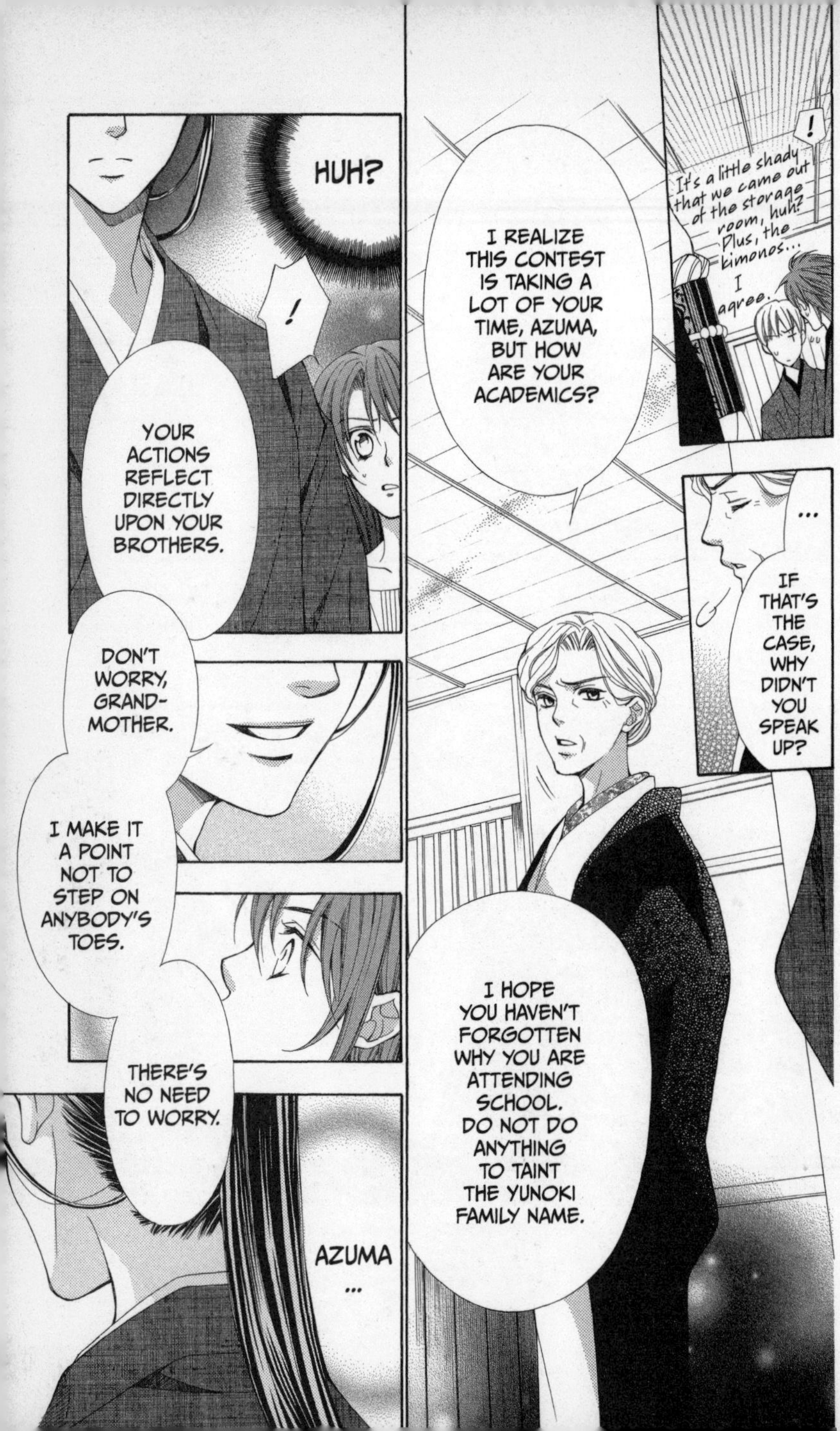
!
It's a little shady that we came out of the storage room, huh? Plus, the kimonos...
I agree.
...
IF THAT'S THE CASE, WHY DIDN'T YOU SPEAK UP?
I REALIZE THIS CONTEST IS TAKING A LOT OF YOUR TIME, AZUMA, BUT HOW ARE YOUR ACADEMICS?
I HOPE YOU HAVEN'T FORGOTTEN WHY YOU ARE ATTENDING SCHOOL. DO NOT DO ANYTHING TO TAINT THE YUNOKI FAMILY NAME.
HUH?
!
YOUR ACTIONS REFLECT DIRECTLY UPON YOUR BROTHERS.
DON'T WORRY, GRAND-MOTHER.
I MAKE IT A POINT NOT TO STEP ON ANYBODY'S TOES.
THERE'S NO NEED TO WORRY.
AZUMA ...

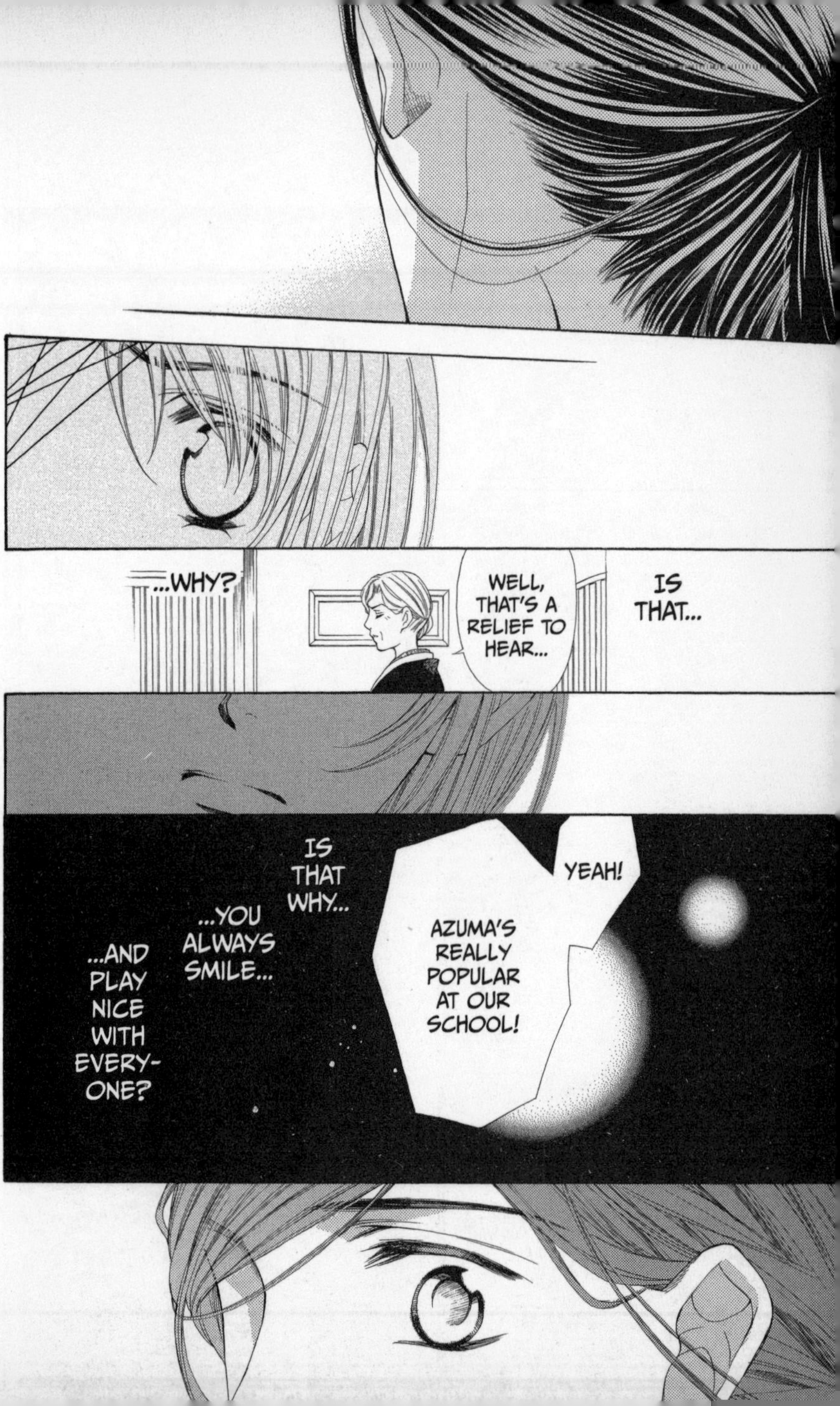
IS THAT...
WELL, THAT'S A RELIEF TO HEAR...
...WHY?
YEAH!
AZUMA'S REALLY POPULAR AT OUR SCHOOL!
IS THAT WHY...
...YOU ALWAYS SMILE...
...AND PLAY NICE WITH EVERY-ONE?

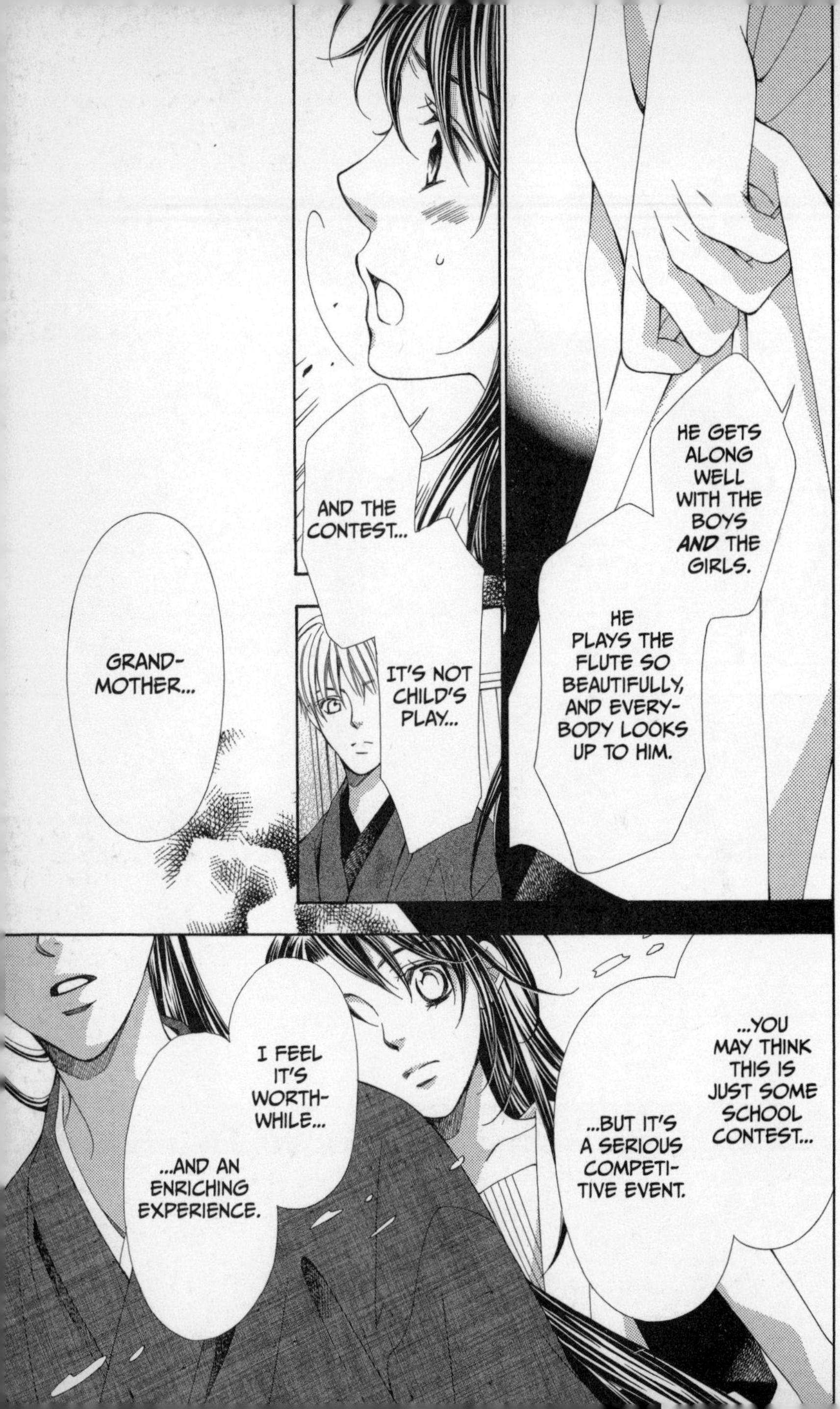
HE GETS ALONG WELL WITH THE BOYS *AND* THE GIRLS.
HE PLAYS THE FLUTE SO BEAUTIFULLY, AND EVERY-BODY LOOKS UP TO HIM.
AND THE CONTEST...
IT'S NOT CHILD'S PLAY...
GRAND-MOTHER...
...YOU MAY THINK THIS IS JUST SOME SCHOOL CONTEST...
...BUT IT'S A SERIOUS COMPETI-TIVE EVENT.
I FEEL IT'S WORTH-WHILE...
...AND AN ENRICHING EXPERIENCE.

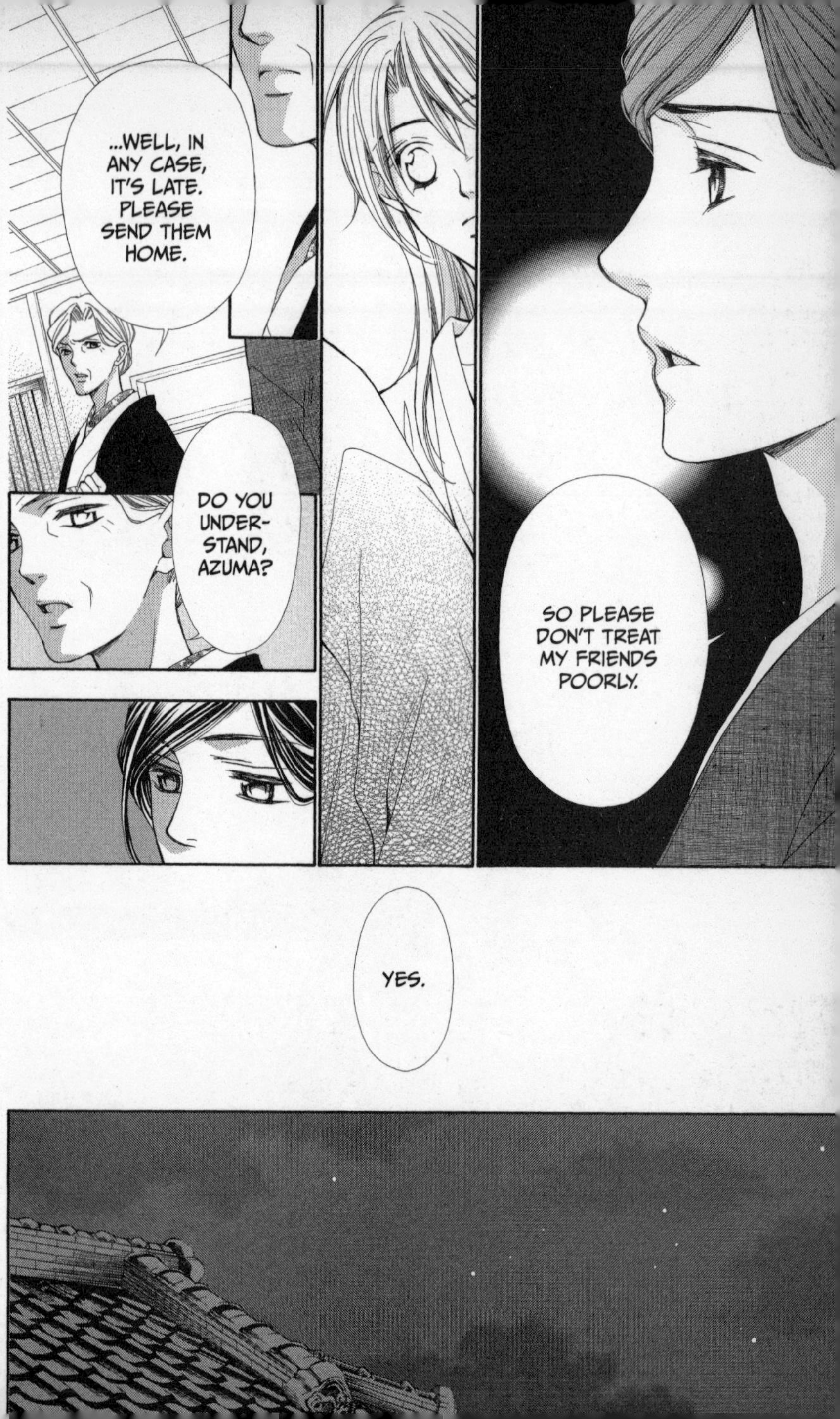
SO PLEASE DON'T TREAT MY FRIENDS POORLY.
...WELL, IN ANY CASE, IT'S LATE. PLEASE SEND THEM HOME.
DO YOU UNDER-STAND, AZUMA?
YES.

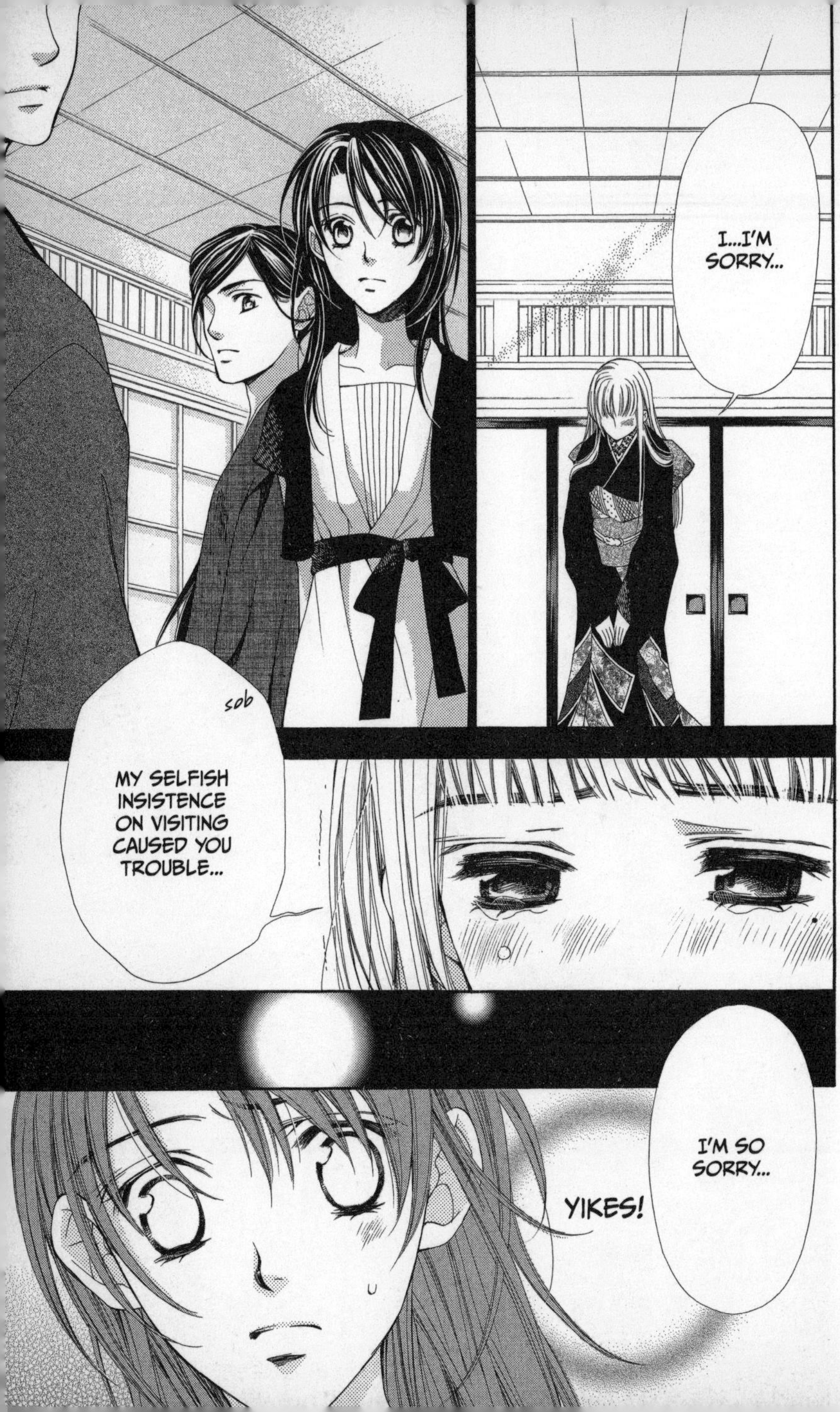

I...I'M SORRY...
sob
MY SELFISH INSISTENCE ON VISITING CAUSED YOU TROUBLE...
I'M SO SORRY...
YIKES!

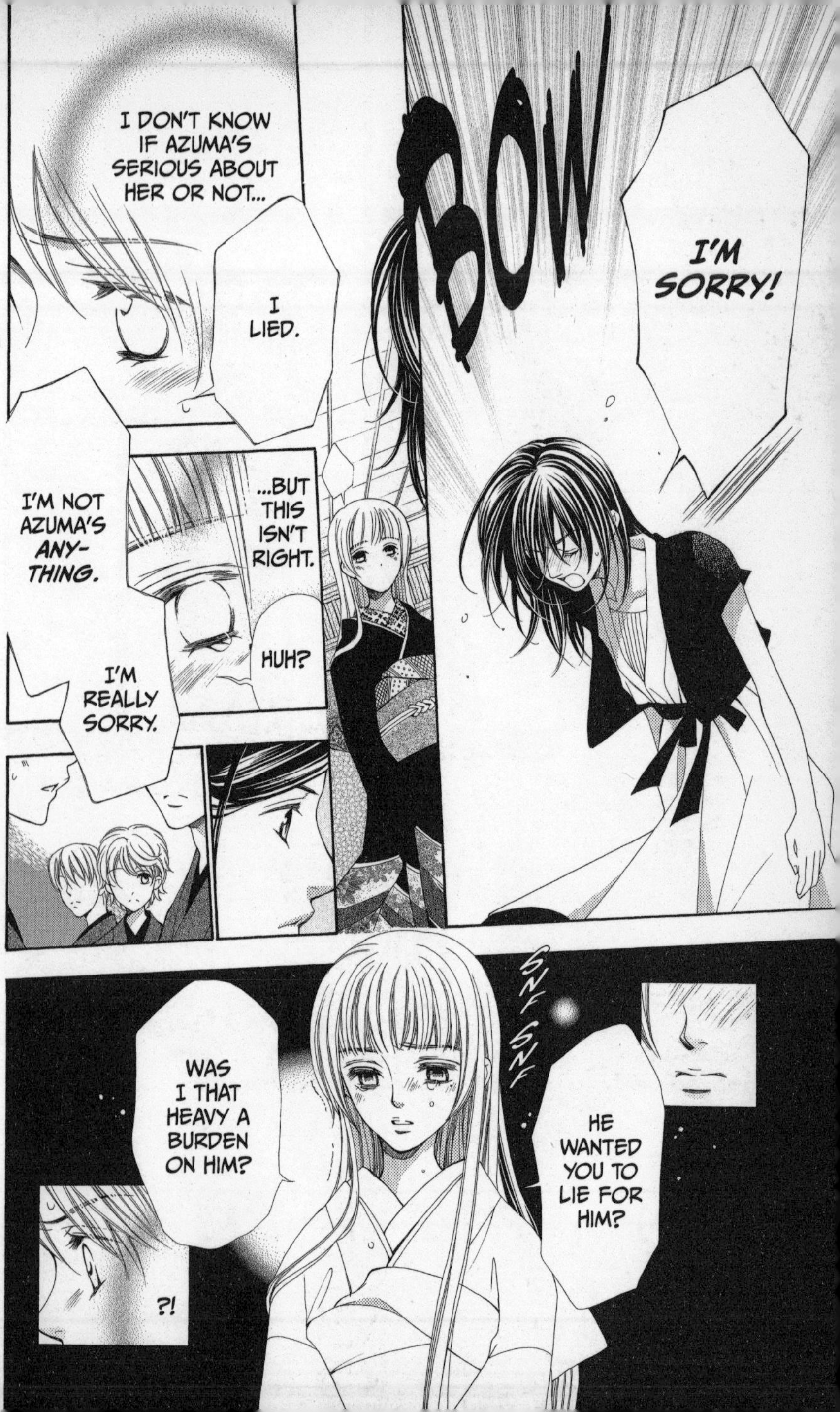
BOW
I'M SORRY!
I DON'T KNOW IF AZUMA'S SERIOUS ABOUT HER OR NOT...
I LIED.
...BUT THIS ISN'T RIGHT.
I'M NOT AZUMA'S ANY-THING.
HUH?
I'M REALLY SORRY.
SNF SNF
HE WANTED YOU TO LIE FOR HIM?
WAS I THAT HEAVY A BURDEN ON HIM?
?!

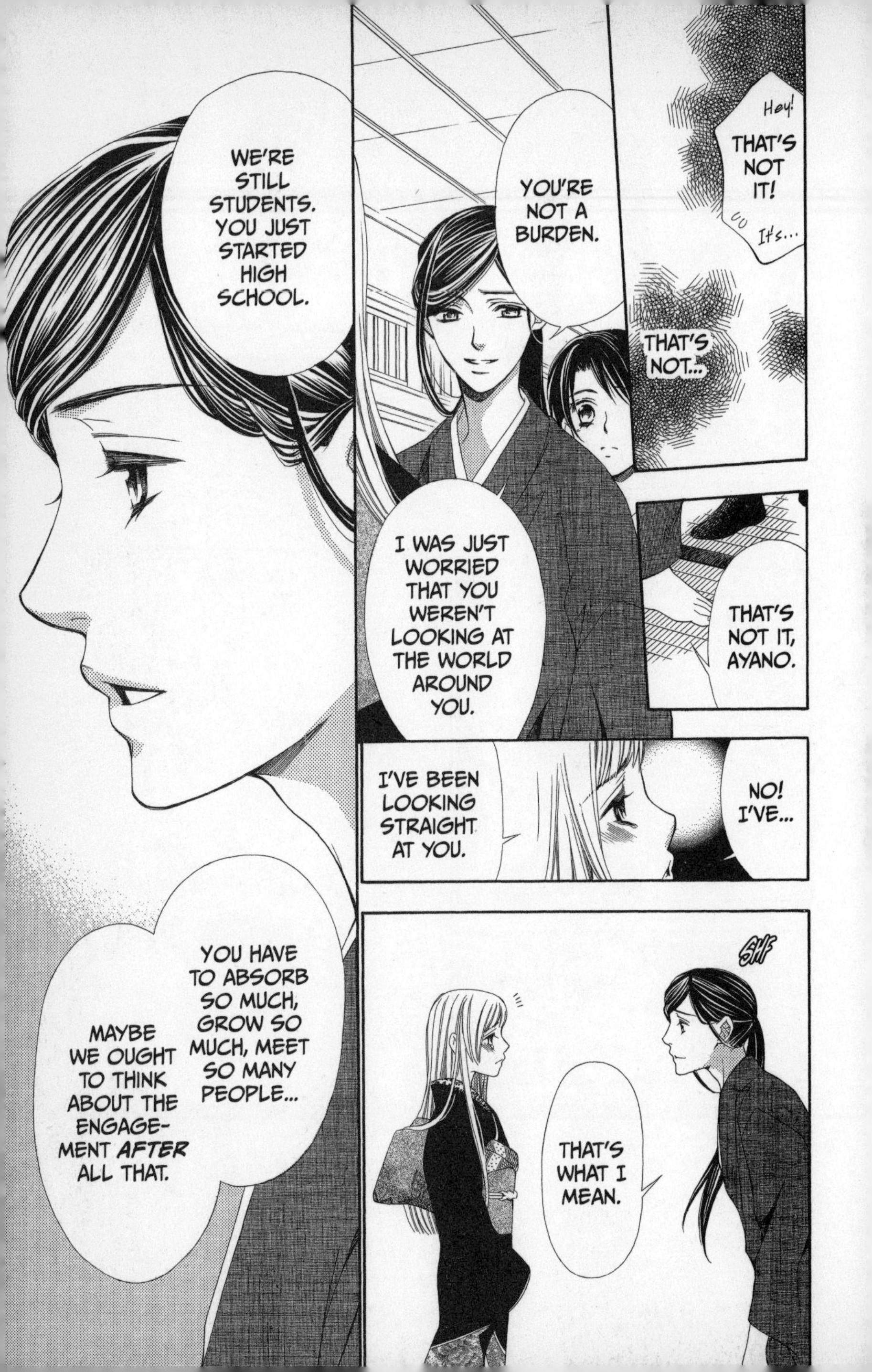
Hey!
THAT'S NOT IT!
It's...
THAT'S NOT...
THAT'S NOT IT, AYANO.
YOU'RE NOT A BURDEN.
I WAS JUST WORRIED THAT YOU WEREN'T LOOKING AT THE WORLD AROUND YOU.
NO! I'VE...
I'VE BEEN LOOKING STRAIGHT AT YOU.
SHF
THAT'S WHAT I MEAN.
WE'RE STILL STUDENTS. YOU JUST STARTED HIGH SCHOOL.
YOU HAVE TO ABSORB SO MUCH, GROW SO MUCH, MEET SO MANY PEOPLE...
MAYBE WE OUGHT TO THINK ABOUT THE ENGAGEMENT *AFTER* ALL THAT.

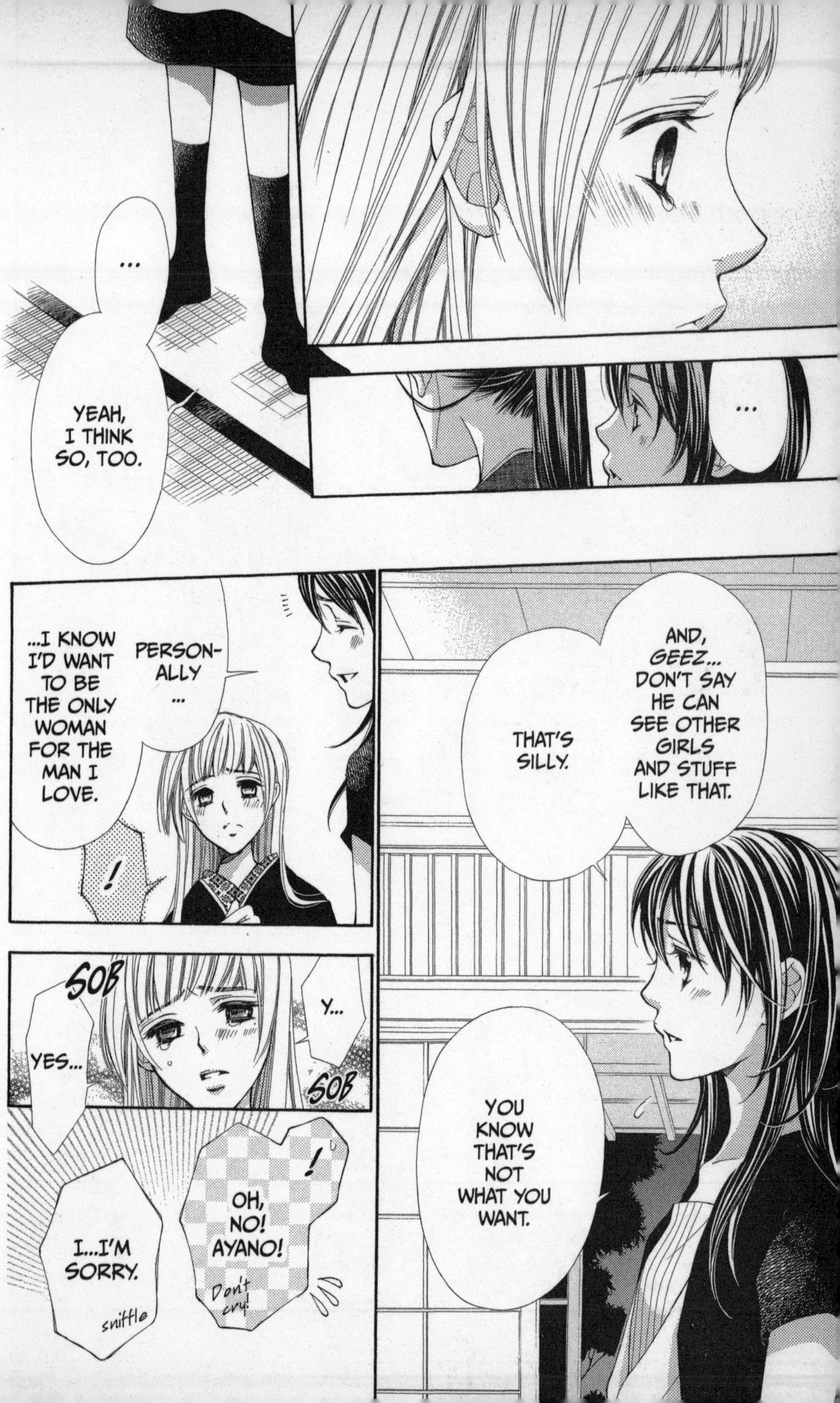
...
...
YEAH, I THINK SO, TOO.
AND, GEEZ... DON'T SAY HE CAN SEE OTHER GIRLS AND STUFF LIKE THAT.
THAT'S SILLY.
YOU KNOW THAT'S NOT WHAT YOU WANT.
PERSONALLY...
...I KNOW I'D WANT TO BE THE ONLY WOMAN FOR THE MAN I LOVE.
!
SOB
Y...
SOB
YES...
!
OH, NO! AYANO!
Don't cry.
I...I'M SORRY.
sniffle

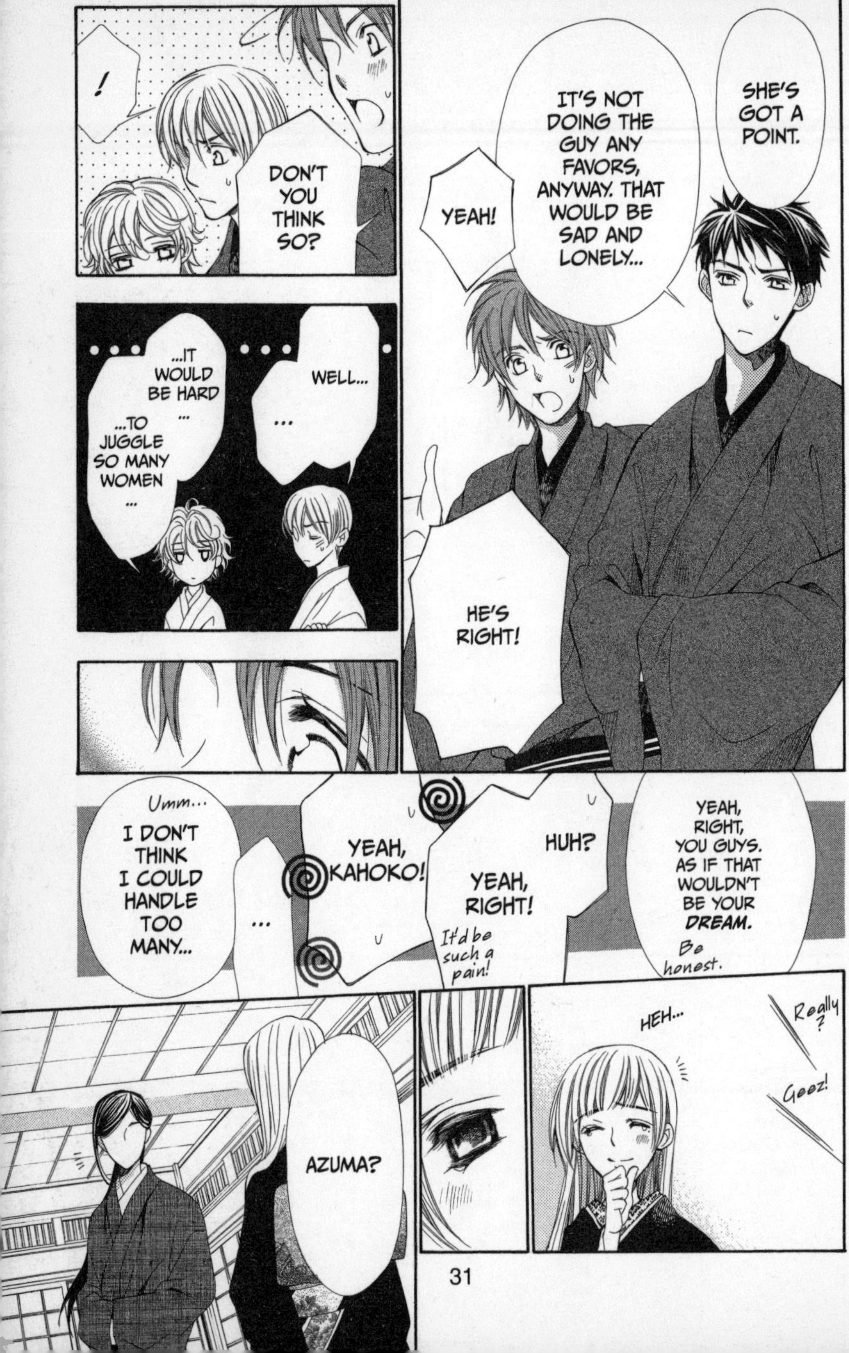
SHE'S GOT A POINT.
IT'S NOT DOING THE GUY ANY FAVORS, ANYWAY. THAT WOULD BE SAD AND LONELY...
YEAH!
HE'S RIGHT!
!
DON'T YOU THINK SO?
...
WELL...
...
...
...IT WOULD BE HARD...
...TO JUGGLE SO MANY WOMEN...
YEAH, RIGHT, YOU GUYS. AS IF THAT WOULDN'T BE YOUR DREAM.
Be honest.
HUH?
YEAH, RIGHT!
It'd be such a pain!
YEAH, KAHOKO!
...
Umm...
I DON'T THINK I COULD HANDLE TOO MANY...
HEH...
Really?
Geez!
AZUMA?

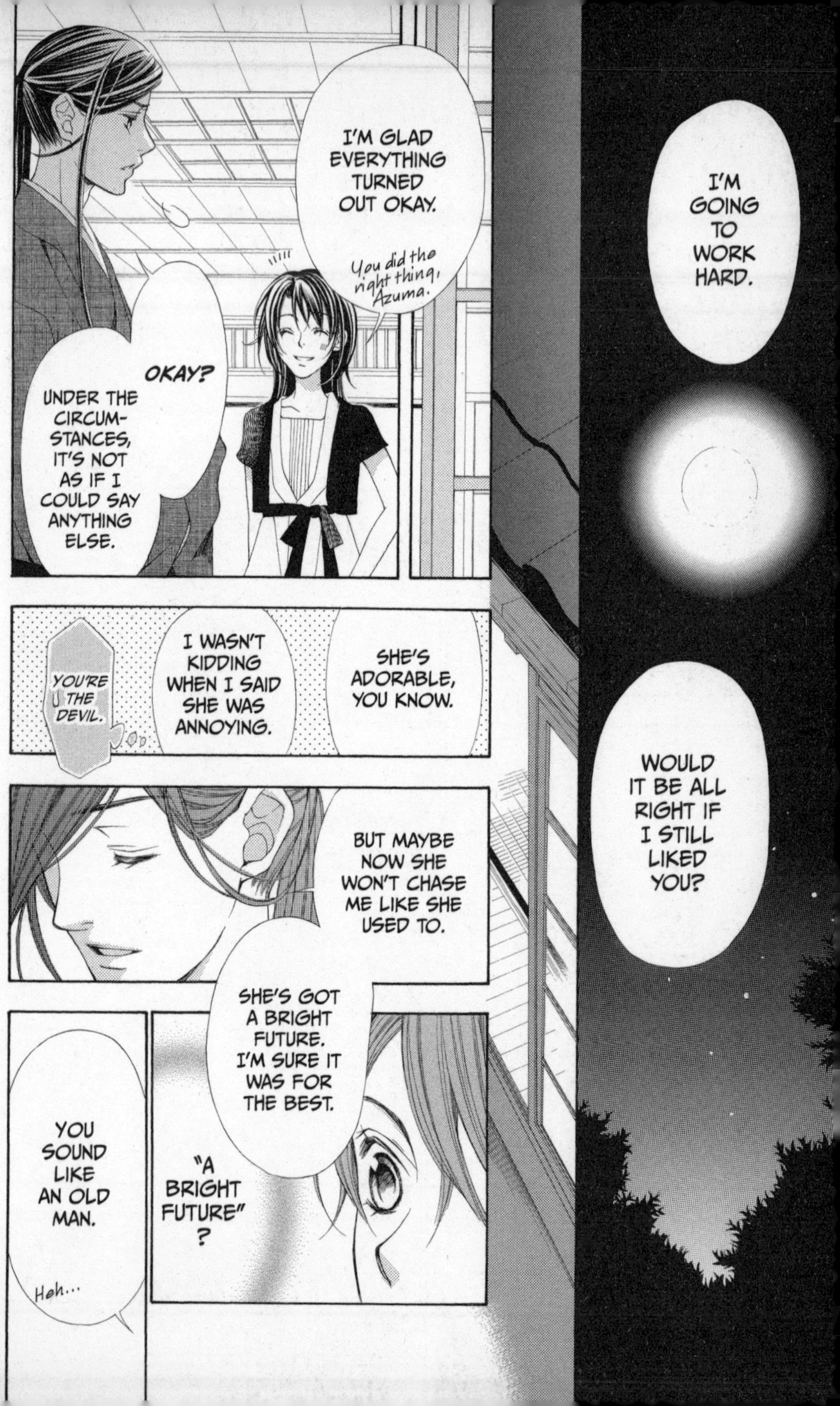
I'M GOING TO WORK HARD.
WOULD IT BE ALL RIGHT IF I STILL LIKED YOU?
I'M GLAD EVERYTHING TURNED OUT OKAY.
You did the right thing, Azuma.
OKAY?
UNDER THE CIRCUMSTANCES, IT'S NOT AS IF I COULD SAY ANYTHING ELSE.
SHE'S ADORABLE, YOU KNOW.
I WASN'T KIDDING WHEN I SAID SHE WAS ANNOYING.
YOU'RE THE DEVIL.
BUT MAYBE NOW SHE WON'T CHASE ME LIKE SHE USED TO.
SHE'S GOT A BRIGHT FUTURE. I'M SURE IT WAS FOR THE BEST.
"A BRIGHT FUTURE"?
YOU SOUND LIKE AN OLD MAN.
Heh...

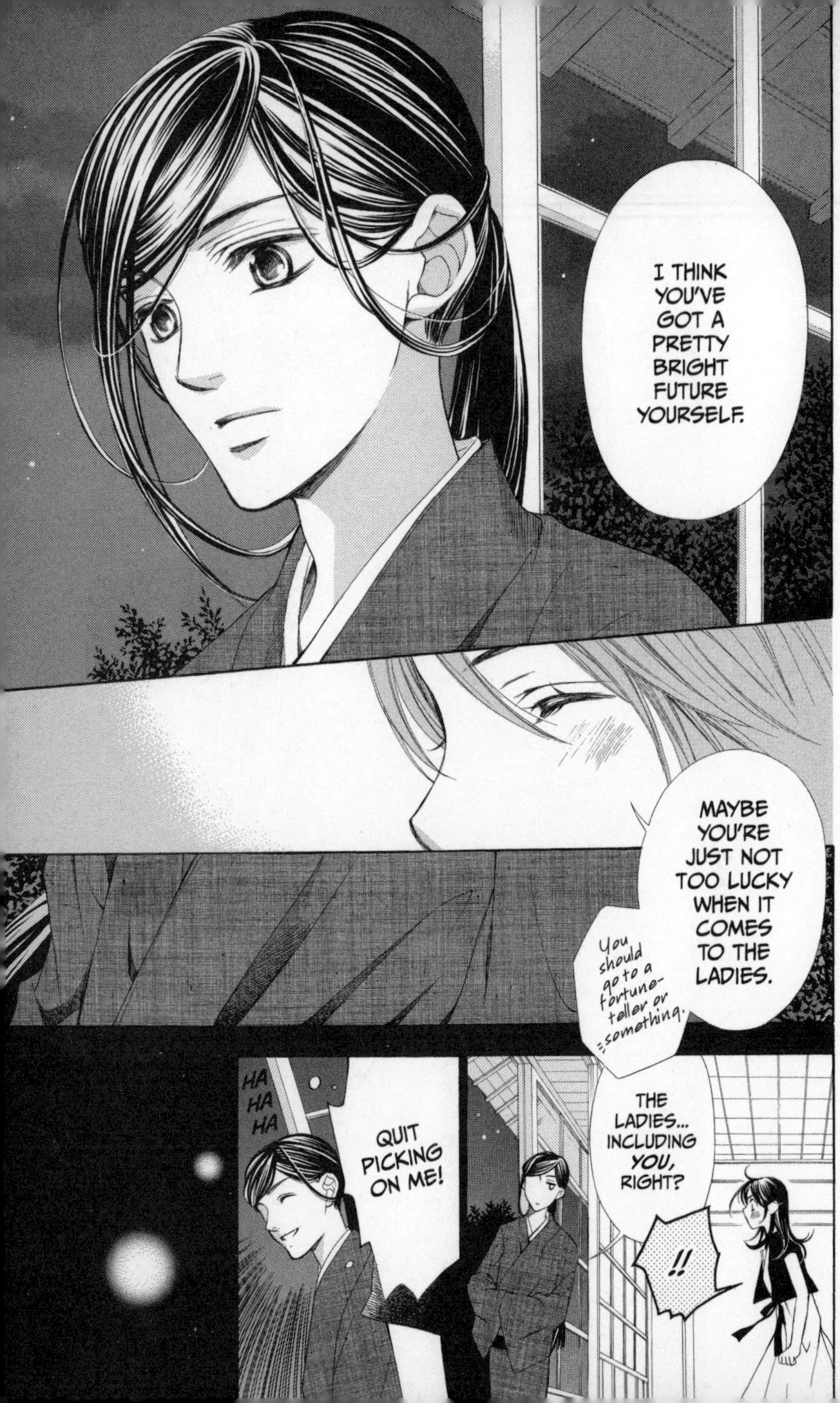
I THINK YOU'VE GOT A PRETTY BRIGHT FUTURE YOURSELF.
MAYBE YOU'RE JUST NOT TOO LUCKY WHEN IT COMES TO THE LADIES.
You should go to a fortune-teller or something.
THE LADIES... INCLUDING *YOU*, RIGHT?
!!
QUIT PICKING ON ME!
HA HA HA

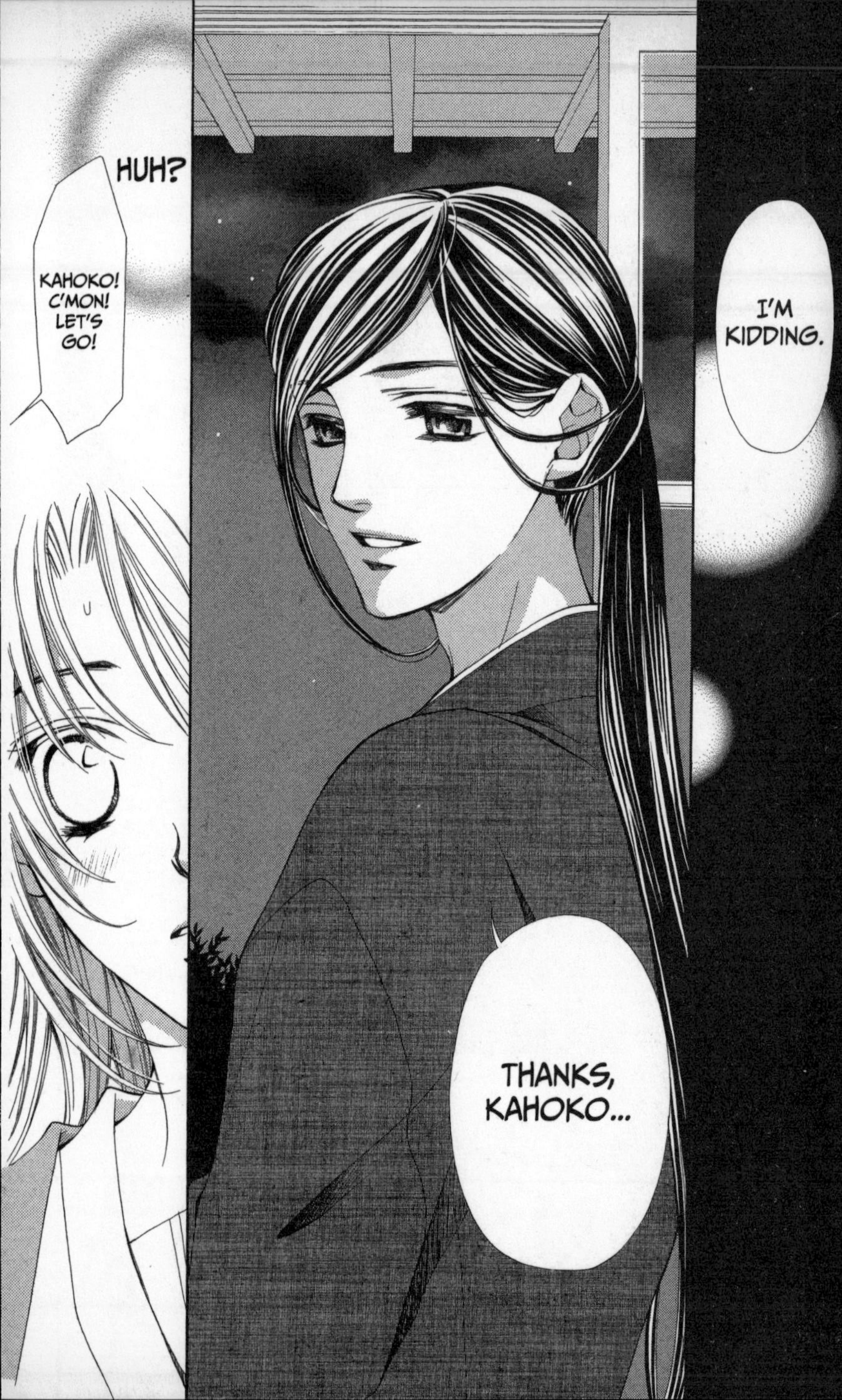
I'M KIDDING.
THANKS, KAHOKO...
HUH?
KAHOKO! C'MON! LET'S GO!

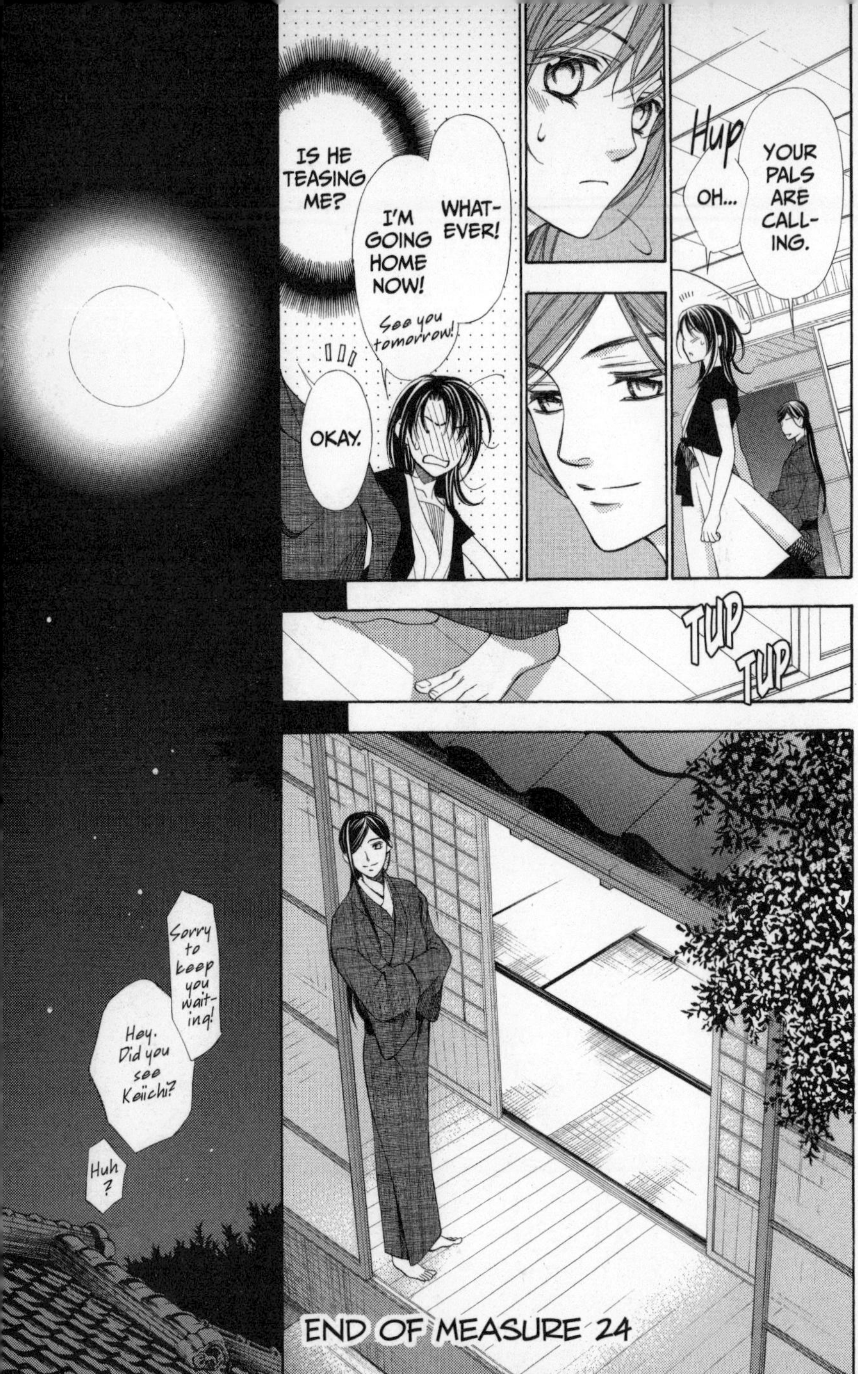
Hup
YOUR PALS ARE CALL-ING.
OH...
IS HE TEASING ME?
WHAT-EVER! I'M GOING HOME NOW!
See you tomorrow!
OKAY.
TUP TUP
END OF MEASURE 24
Sorry to keep you wait-ing!
Hey. Did you see Keiichi?
Huh?

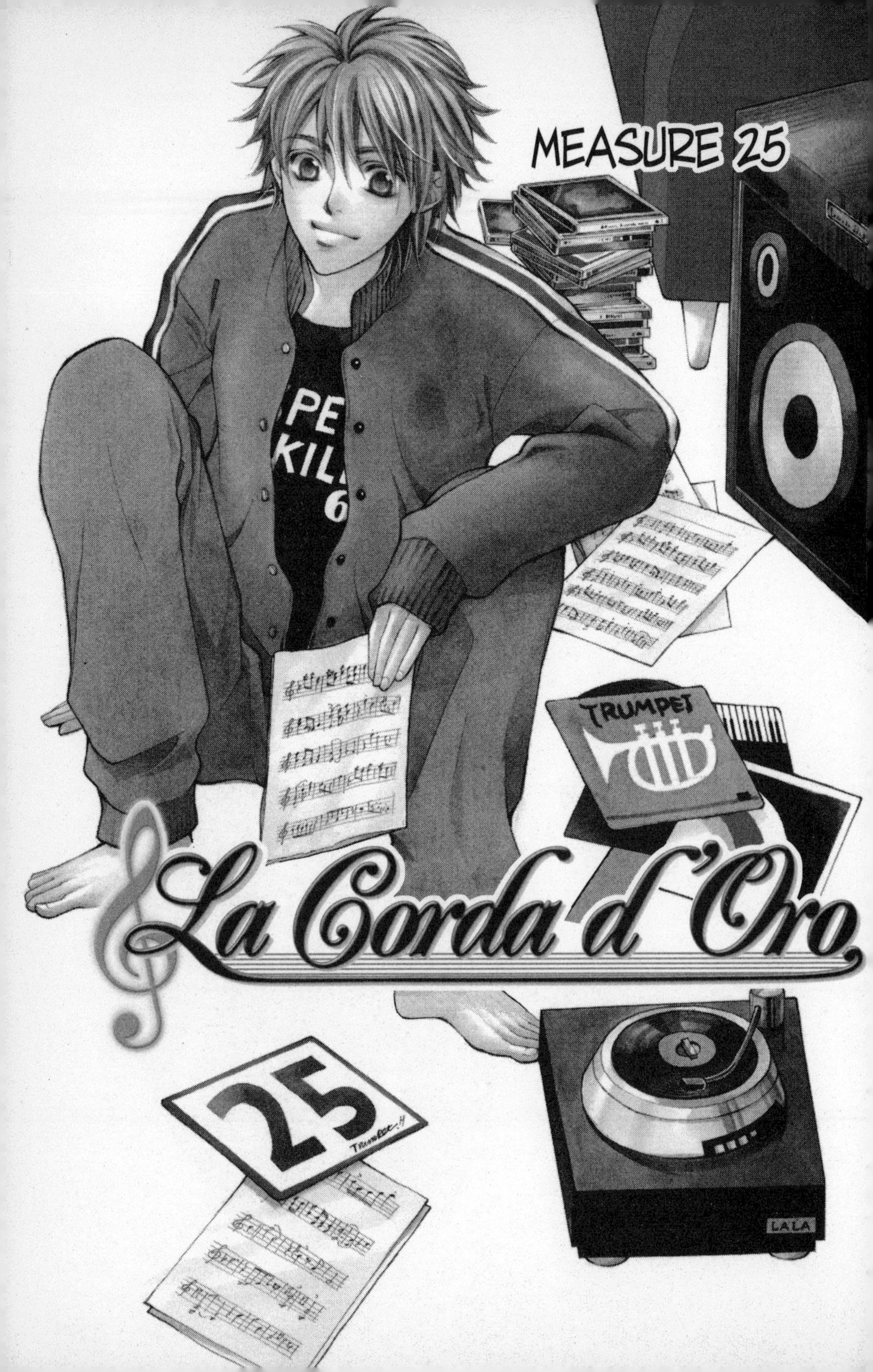
MEASURE 25
La Corda d'Oro
TRUMPET
25
LALA

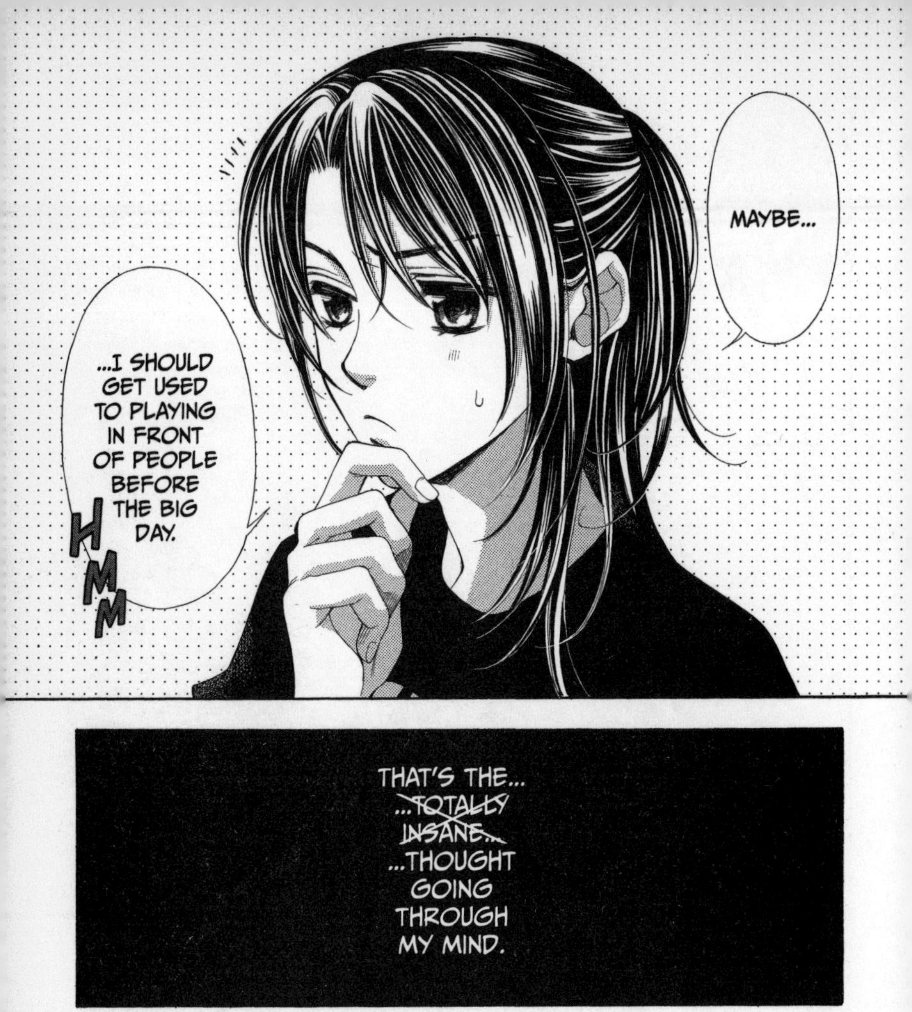
MAYBE...
...I SHOULD GET USED TO PLAYING IN FRONT OF PEOPLE BEFORE THE BIG DAY.
HMM
THAT'S THE... ...~~TOTALLY INSANE...~~ ...THOUGHT GOING THROUGH MY MIND.

Daily Happenings 17 Art supplies (color)...

Color...Color is difficult. It's always a struggle for me. I use cold press Arches paper with water for color ink. For the linework, I use the grey tones from Holbein. I also use Dr. Martin and ECOLINE, and others as well. Oh yes, I also use acrylic gouache...Again, very analog...

I actually can't use COPiCs. I'm hopeless with them. As an alternative, I use colored pencils. Yay colored pencils! (They're very inefficient, though...) But I love color art supplies. Colored inks...They're fun just to look at. Maybe that's why I keep buying stuff I don't even use...

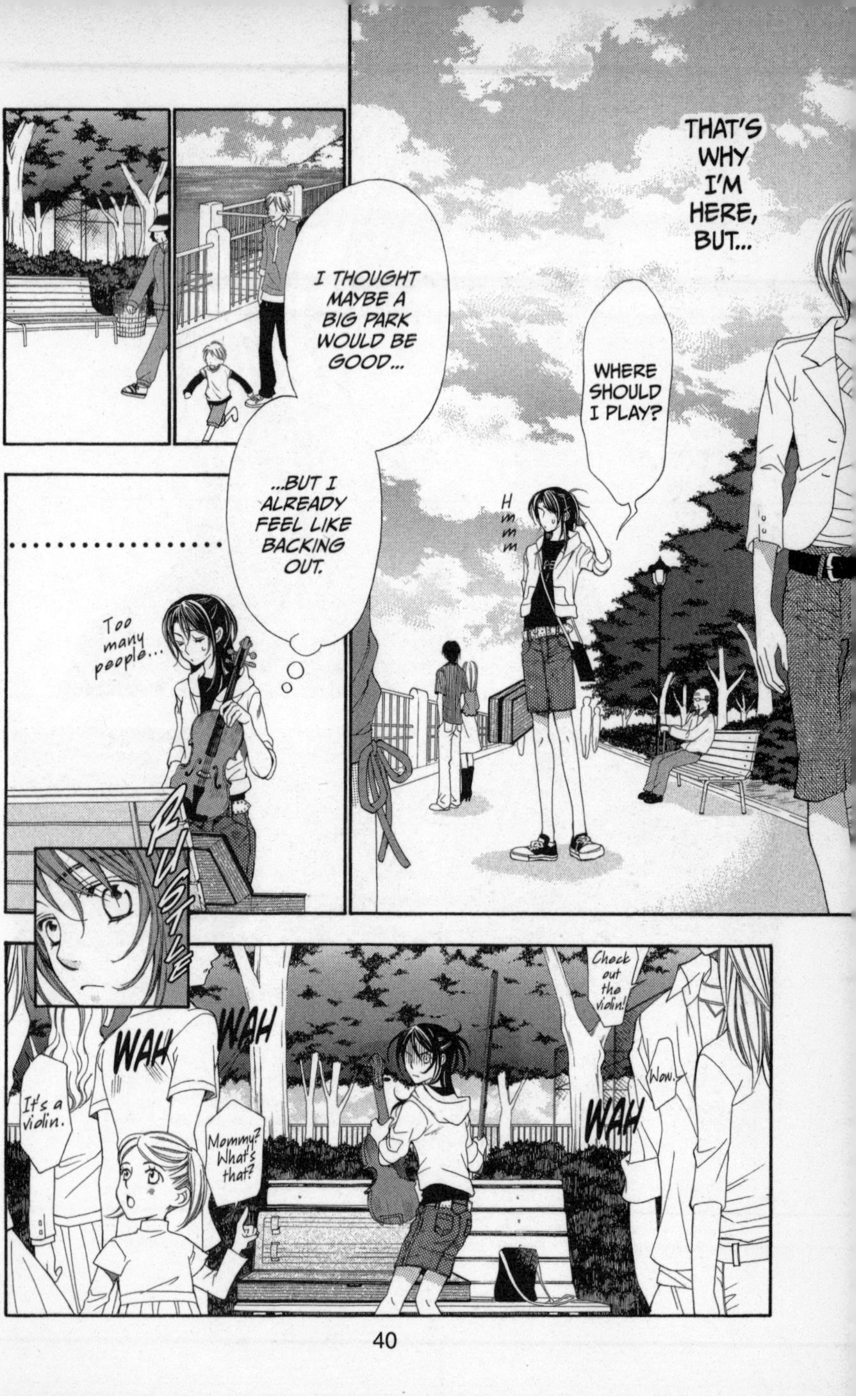
THAT'S WHY I'M HERE, BUT...
WHERE SHOULD I PLAY?
Hmmm
I THOUGHT MAYBE A BIG PARK WOULD BE GOOD...
...BUT I ALREADY FEEL LIKE BACKING OUT.
Too many people...
RUSTLE
Check out the violin!
Wow.
WAH
WAH
WAH
It's a violin.
Mommy? What's that?

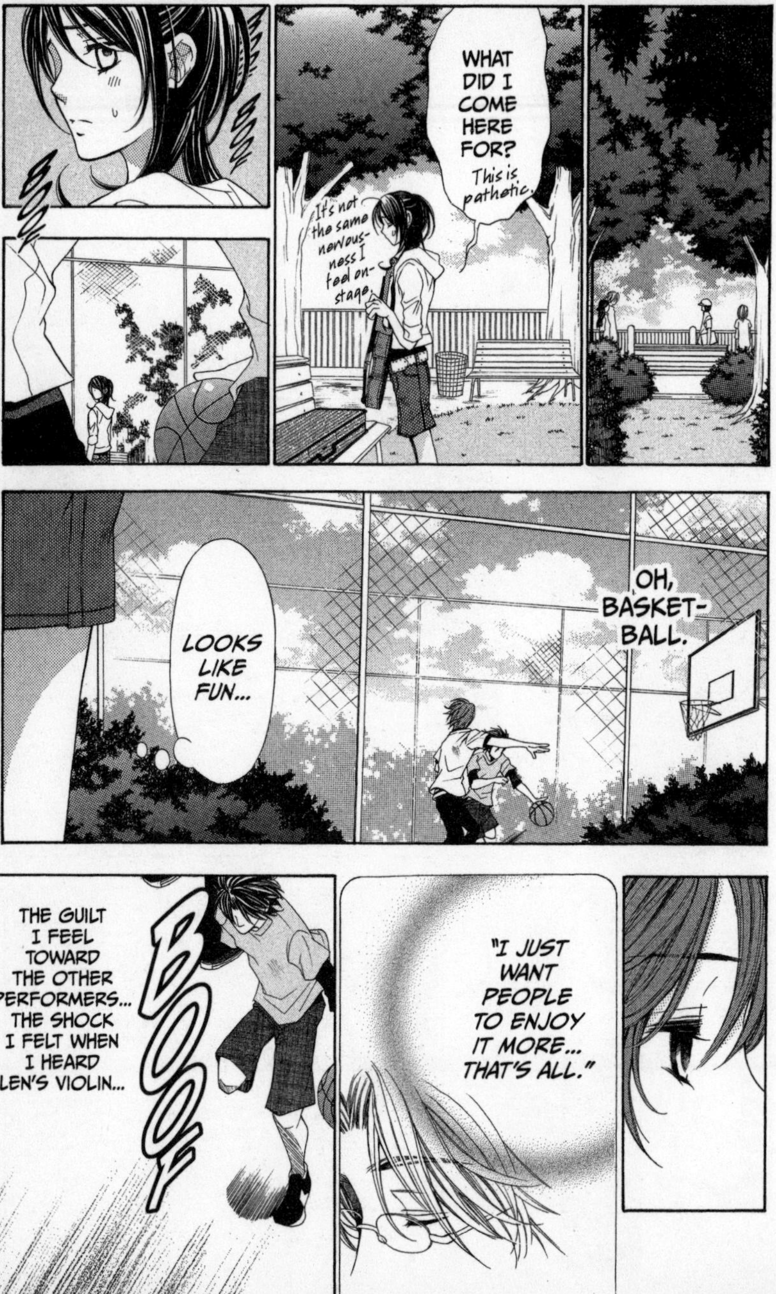
WHAT DID I COME HERE FOR?
This is pathetic.
It's not the same nervousness I feel on-stage.
OH, BASKET-BALL.
LOOKS LIKE FUN...
"I JUST WANT PEOPLE TO ENJOY IT MORE... THAT'S ALL."
THE GUILT I FEEL TOWARD THE OTHER PERFORMERS... THE SHOCK I FELT WHEN I HEARD LEN'S VIOLIN...

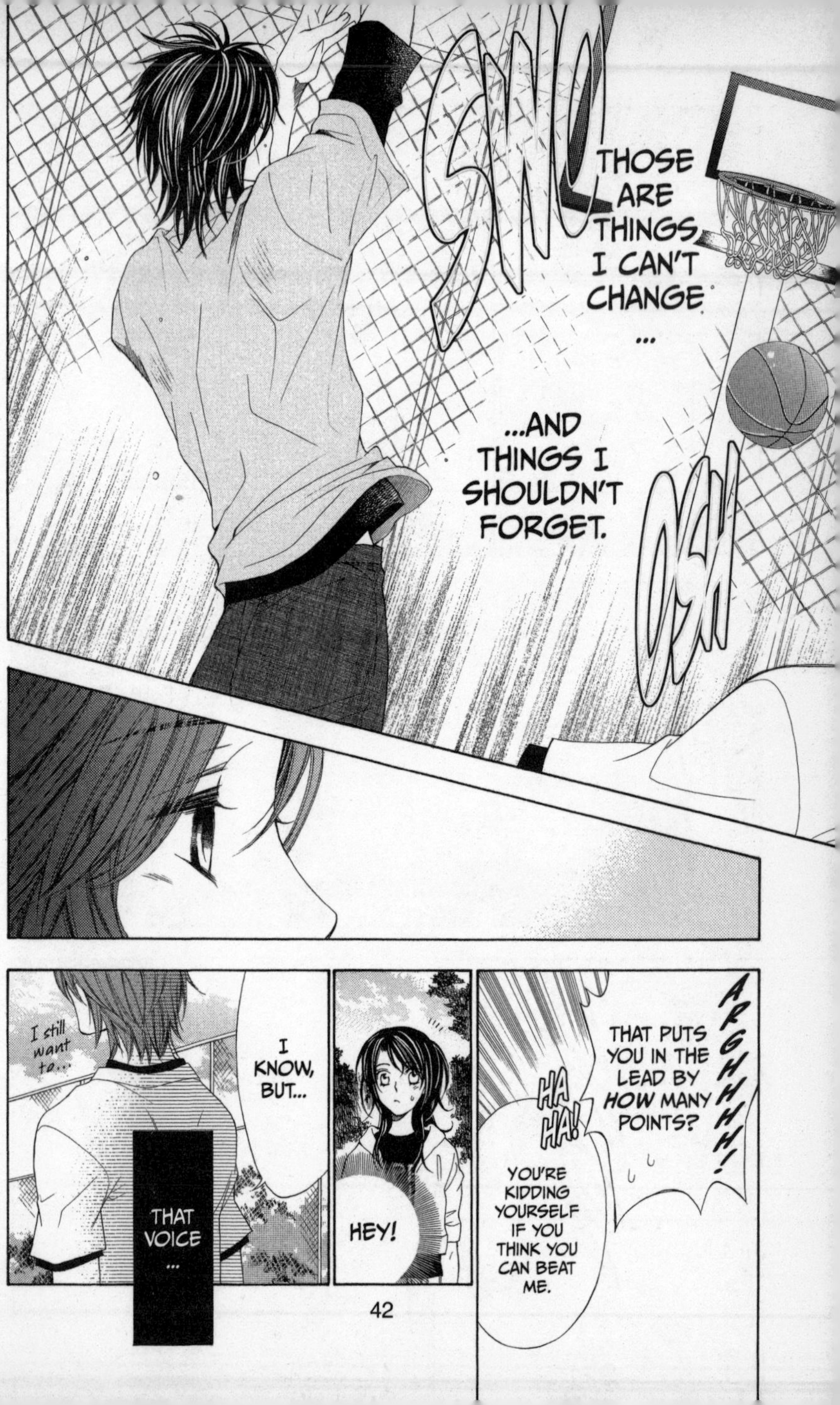
SWO
THOSE ARE THINGS I CAN'T CHANGE...
...AND THINGS I SHOULDN'T FORGET.
OSH
THAT PUTS YOU IN THE LEAD BY *HOW* MANY POINTS?
ARGHHHH!
HA HA!
YOU'RE KIDDING YOURSELF IF YOU THINK YOU CAN BEAT ME.
HEY!
I KNOW, BUT...
I still want to...
THAT VOICE...

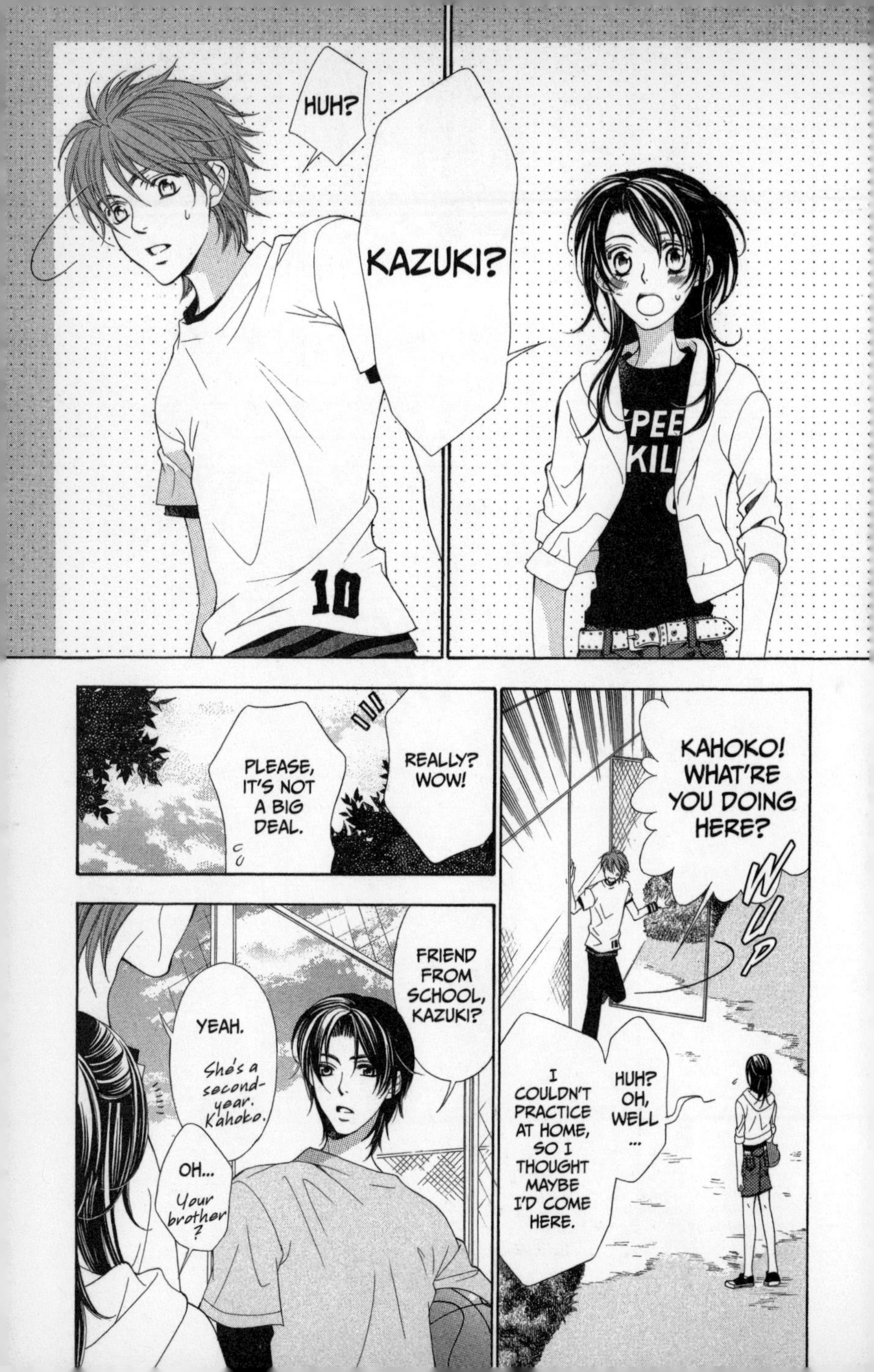
KAZUKI?
HUH?
KAHOKO! WHAT'RE YOU DOING HERE?
WHUP
HUH? OH, WELL ...
I COULDN'T PRACTICE AT HOME, SO I THOUGHT MAYBE I'D COME HERE.
REALLY? WOW!
PLEASE, IT'S NOT A BIG DEAL.
FRIEND FROM SCHOOL, KAZUKI?
YEAH.
She's a second-year. Kahoko.
OH...
Your brother?

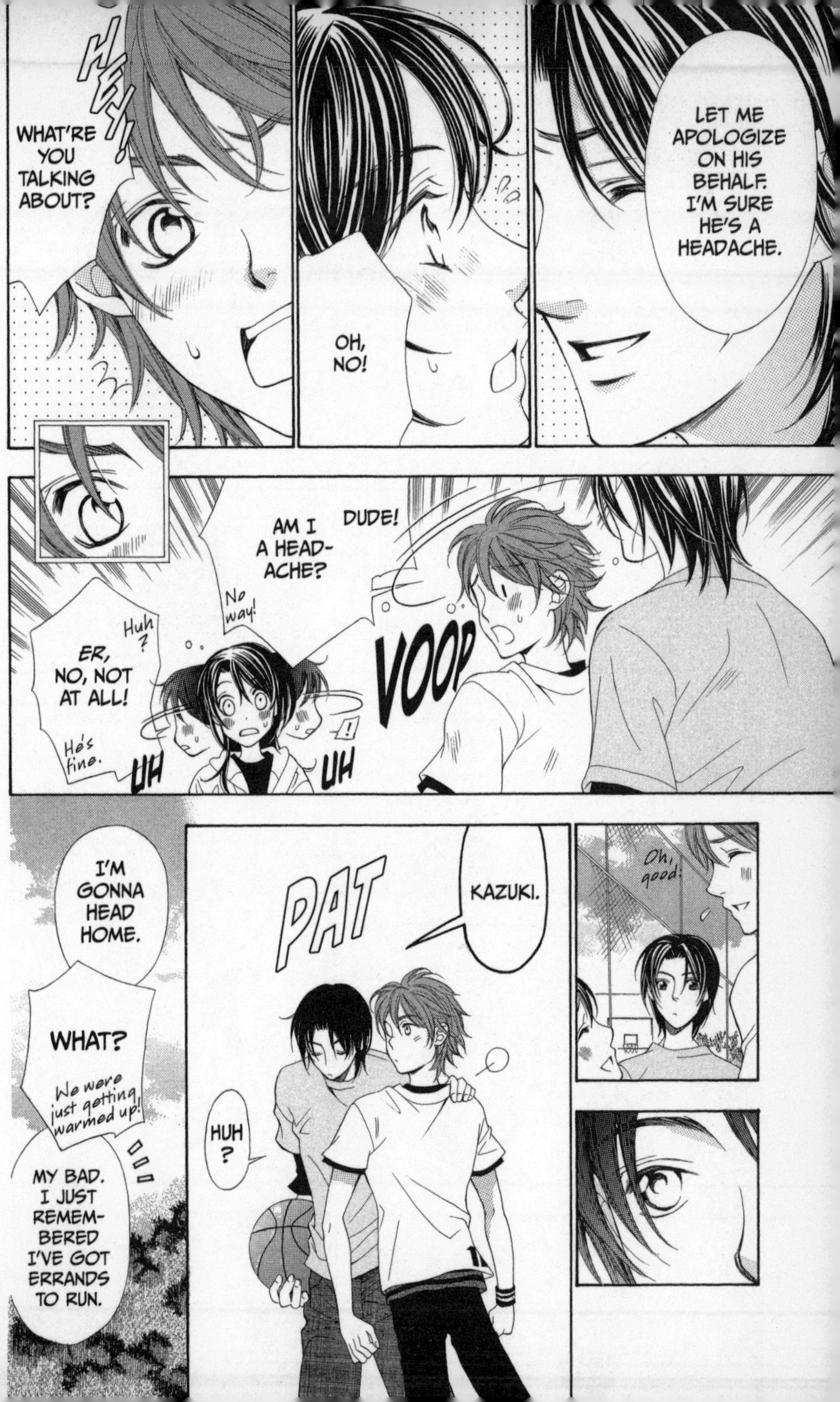
LET ME APOLOGIZE ON HIS BEHALF. I'M SURE HE'S A HEADACHE.
OH, NO!
HEY!
WHAT'RE YOU TALKING ABOUT?
DUDE!
AM I A HEADACHE?
VOOP
No way!
Huh?
ER, NO, NOT AT ALL!
He's fine.
UH
UH
Oh, good.
KAZUKI.
PAT
HUH?
I'M GONNA HEAD HOME.
WHAT?
We were just getting warmed up!
MY BAD. I JUST REMEMBERED I'VE GOT ERRANDS TO RUN.

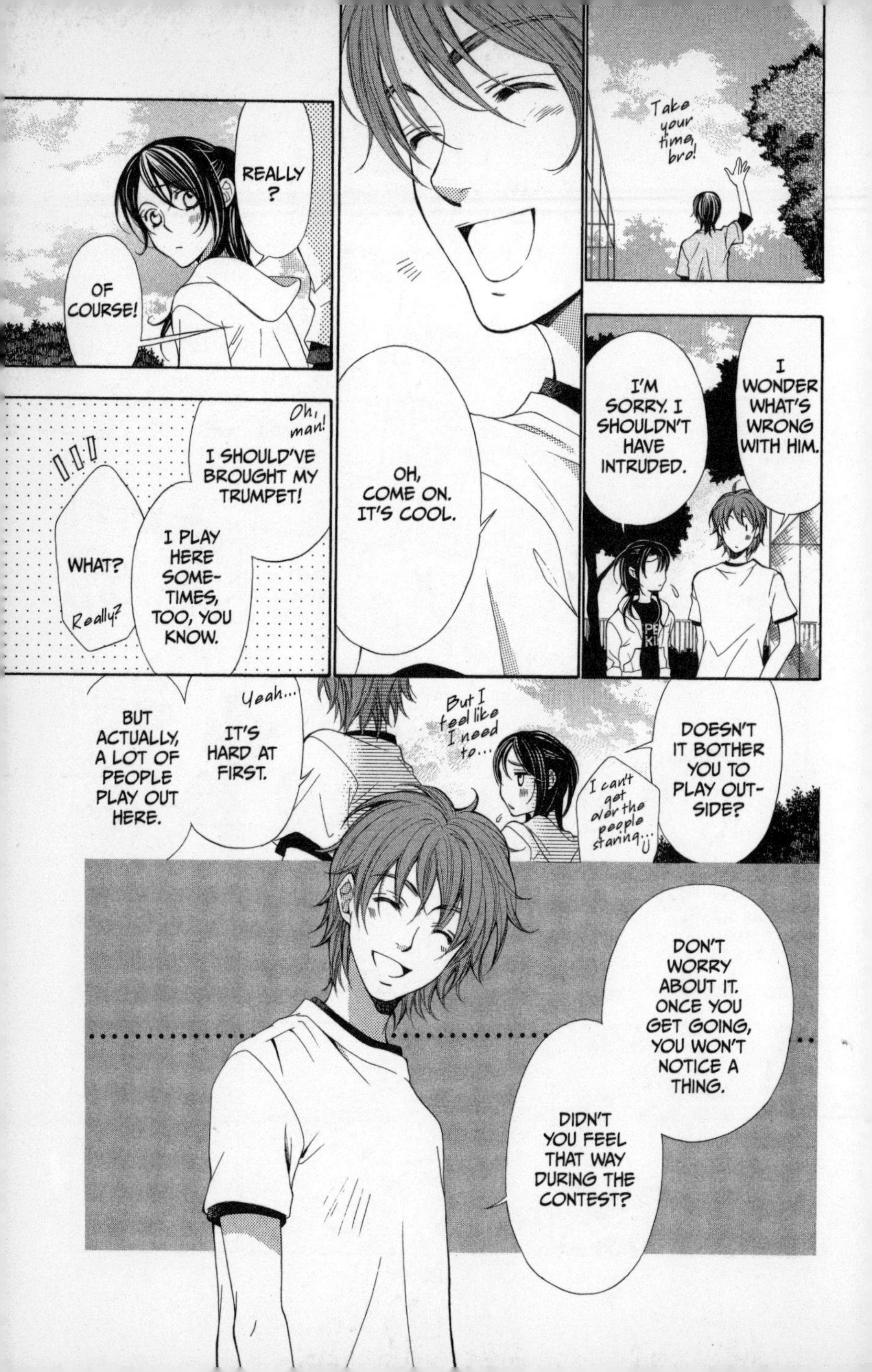
Take your time, bro!
I WONDER WHAT'S WRONG WITH HIM.
I'M SORRY. I SHOULDN'T HAVE INTRUDED.
OH, COME ON. IT'S COOL.
REALLY?
OF COURSE!
Oh, man!
I SHOULD'VE BROUGHT MY TRUMPET!
I PLAY HERE SOMETIMES, TOO, YOU KNOW.
WHAT?
Really?
DOESN'T IT BOTHER YOU TO PLAY OUTSIDE?
I can't get over the people staring...
But I feel like I need to...
Yeah...
IT'S HARD AT FIRST.
BUT ACTUALLY, A LOT OF PEOPLE PLAY OUT HERE.
DON'T WORRY ABOUT IT. ONCE YOU GET GOING, YOU WON'T NOTICE A THING.
DIDN'T YOU FEEL THAT WAY DURING THE CONTEST?

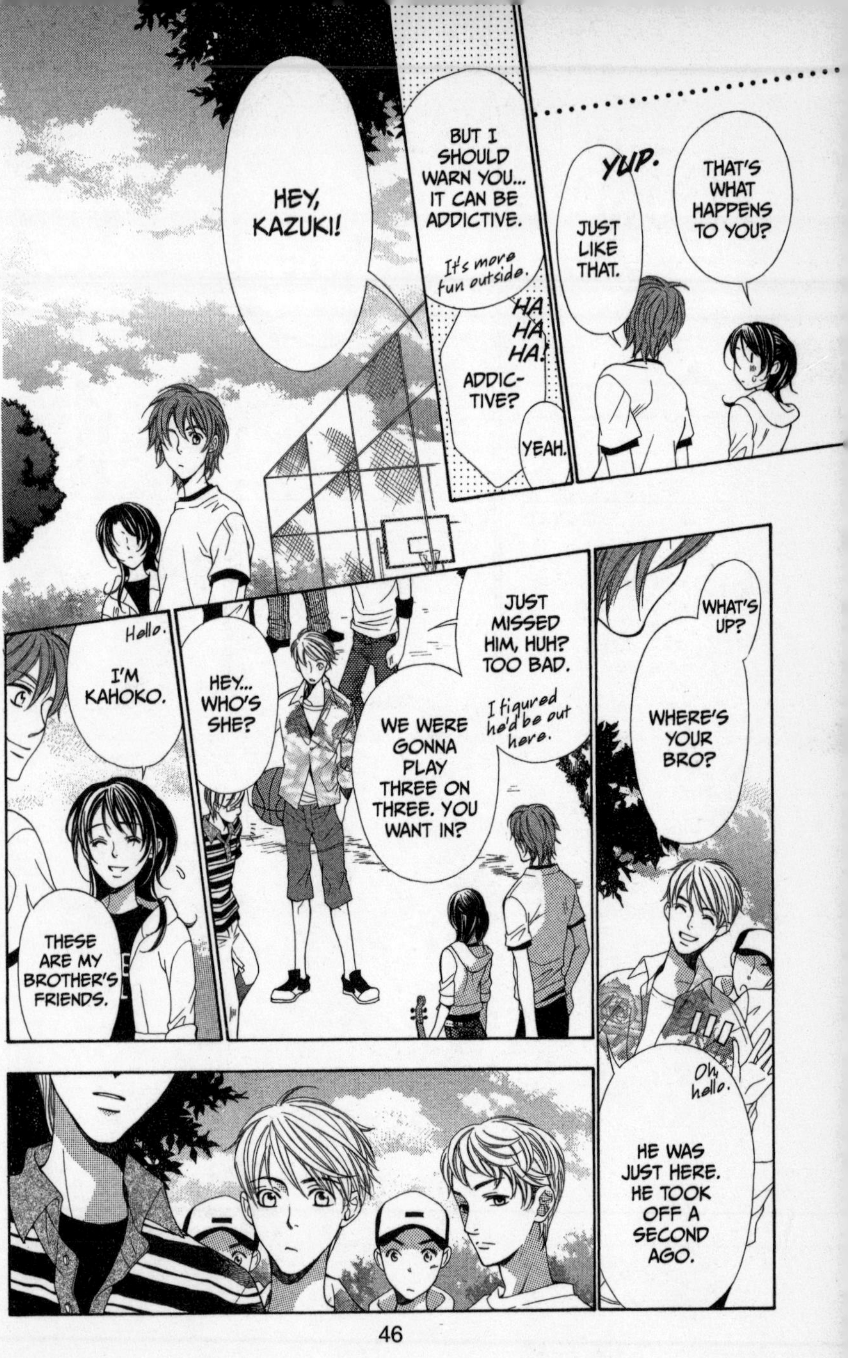
THAT'S WHAT HAPPENS TO YOU?
YUP.
JUST LIKE THAT.
BUT I SHOULD WARN YOU... IT CAN BE ADDICTIVE.
It's more fun outside.
HA HA HA!
ADDICTIVE?
YEAH.
HEY, KAZUKI!
WHAT'S UP?
WHERE'S YOUR BRO?
Oh hello.
HE WAS JUST HERE. HE TOOK OFF A SECOND AGO.
JUST MISSED HIM, HUH? TOO BAD.
I figured he'd be out here.
WE WERE GONNA PLAY THREE ON THREE. YOU WANT IN?
HEY... WHO'S SHE?
Hello.
I'M KAHOKO.
THESE ARE MY BROTHER'S FRIENDS.

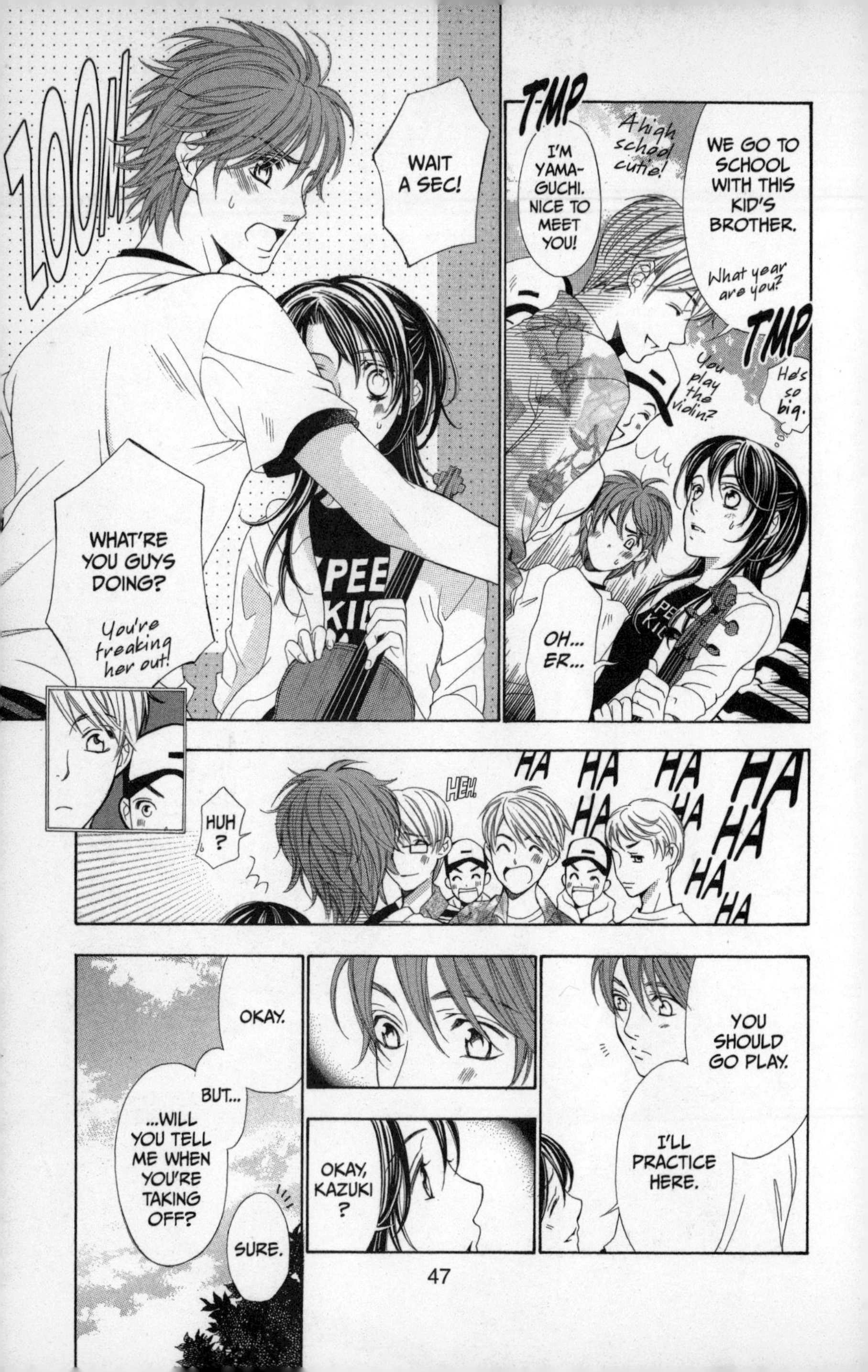
T-MP
WE GO TO SCHOOL WITH THIS KID'S BROTHER.
What year are you?
A high school cutie!
I'M YAMA-GUCHI. NICE TO MEET YOU!
TMP
He's so big.
You play the violin?
OH... ER...
ZOOM
WAIT A SEC!
WHAT'RE YOU GUYS DOING?
You're freaking her out!
HA HA HA HA HA HA HA HA HA HA HA
HEH
HUH?
YOU SHOULD GO PLAY.
I'LL PRACTICE HERE.
OKAY, KAZUKI?
OKAY.
BUT...
...WILL YOU TELL ME WHEN YOU'RE TAKING OFF?
SURE.

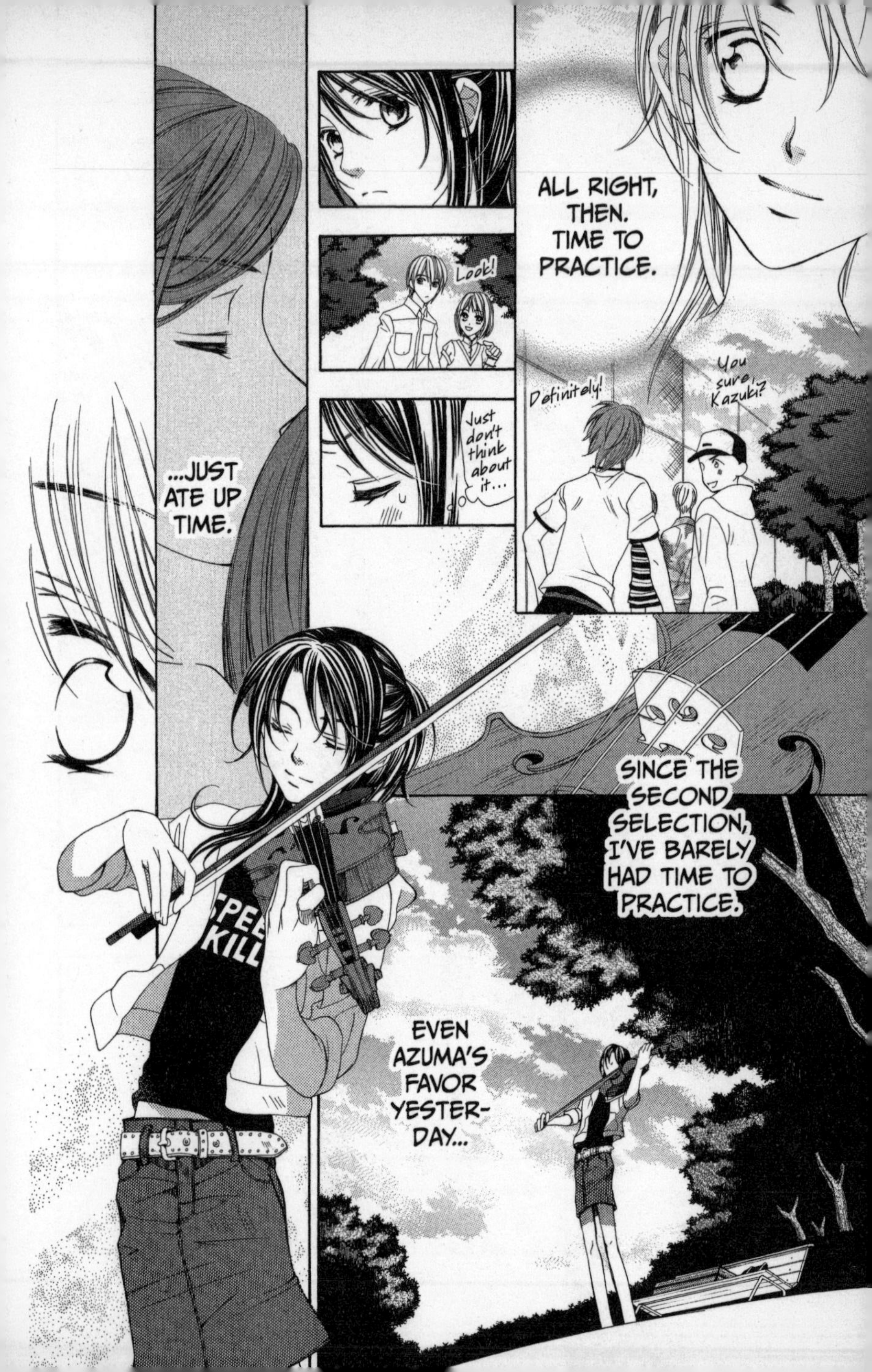
ALL RIGHT, THEN. TIME TO PRACTICE.
You sure, Kazuki?
Definitely!
Look!
Just don't think about it...
SINCE THE SECOND SELECTION, I'VE BARELY HAD TIME TO PRACTICE.
EVEN AZUMA'S FAVOR YESTER-DAY...
...JUST ATE UP TIME.
SPEE KILL

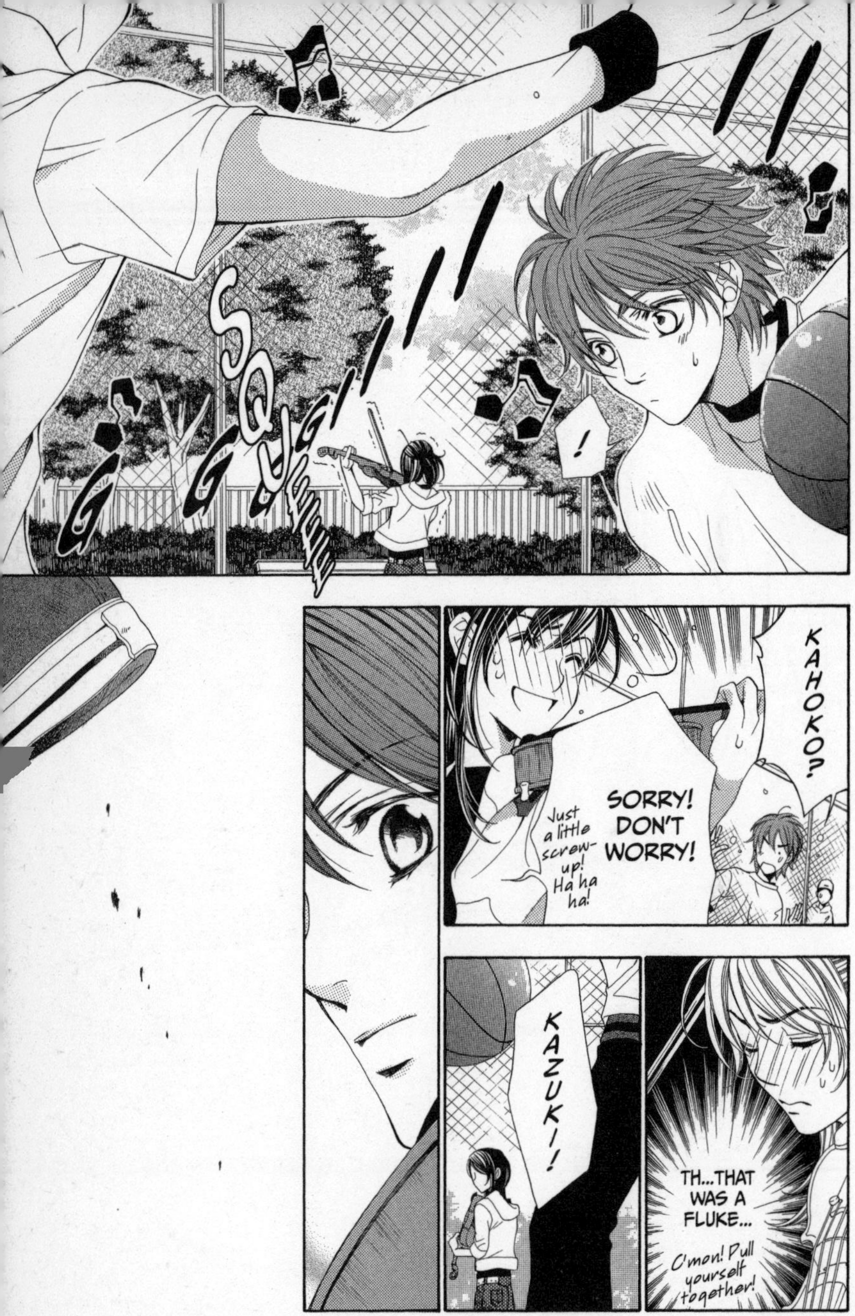
!
KAHOKO?
SORRY! DON'T WORRY!
Just a little screw-up! Ha ha ha!
TH...THAT WAS A FLUKE...
C'mon! Pull yourself together!
KAZUKI!

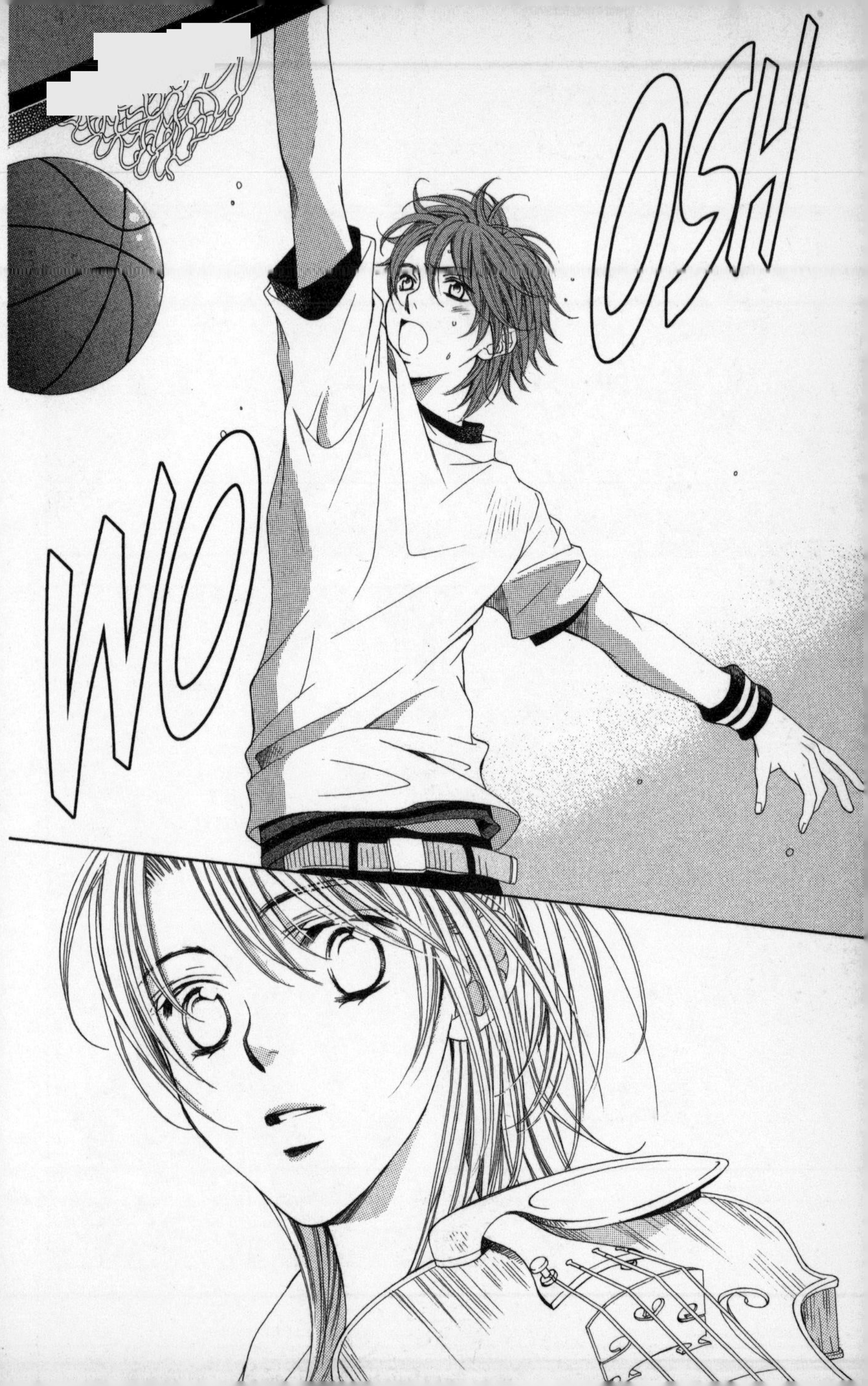
WOOSH

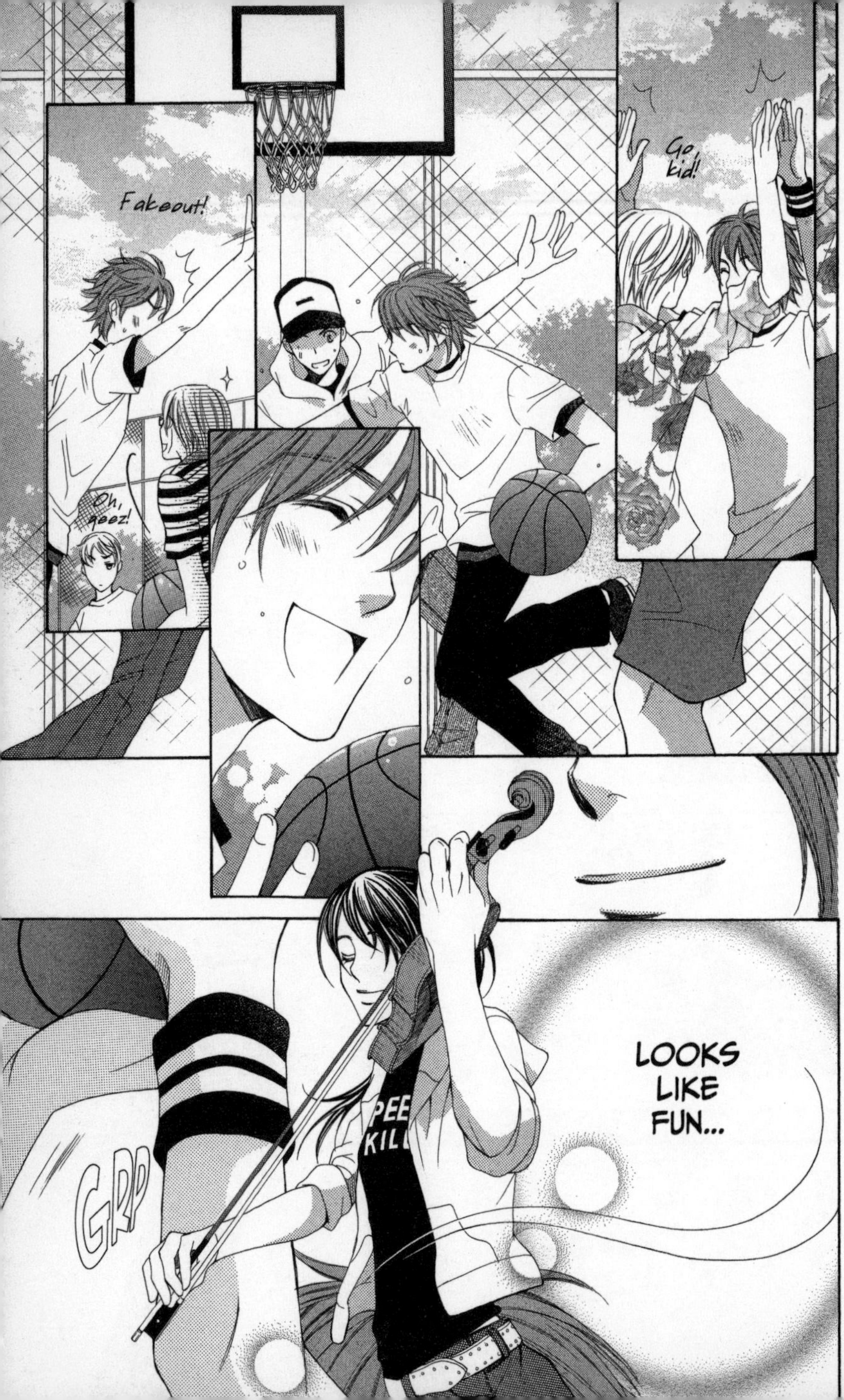
Go, kid!
Fakeout!
Oh, geez!
LOOKS LIKE FUN...
GRP

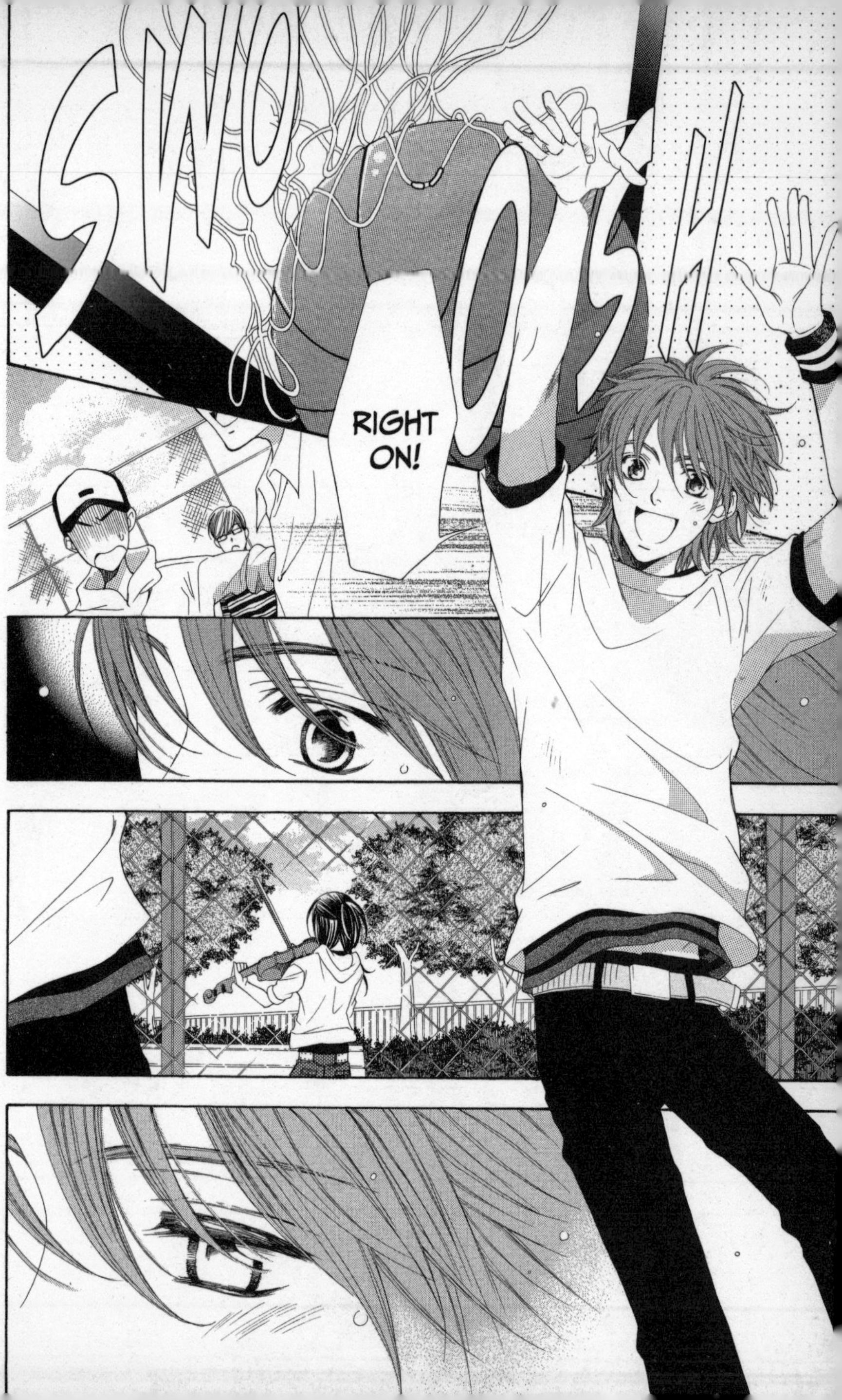
SWOOSH
RIGHT ON!

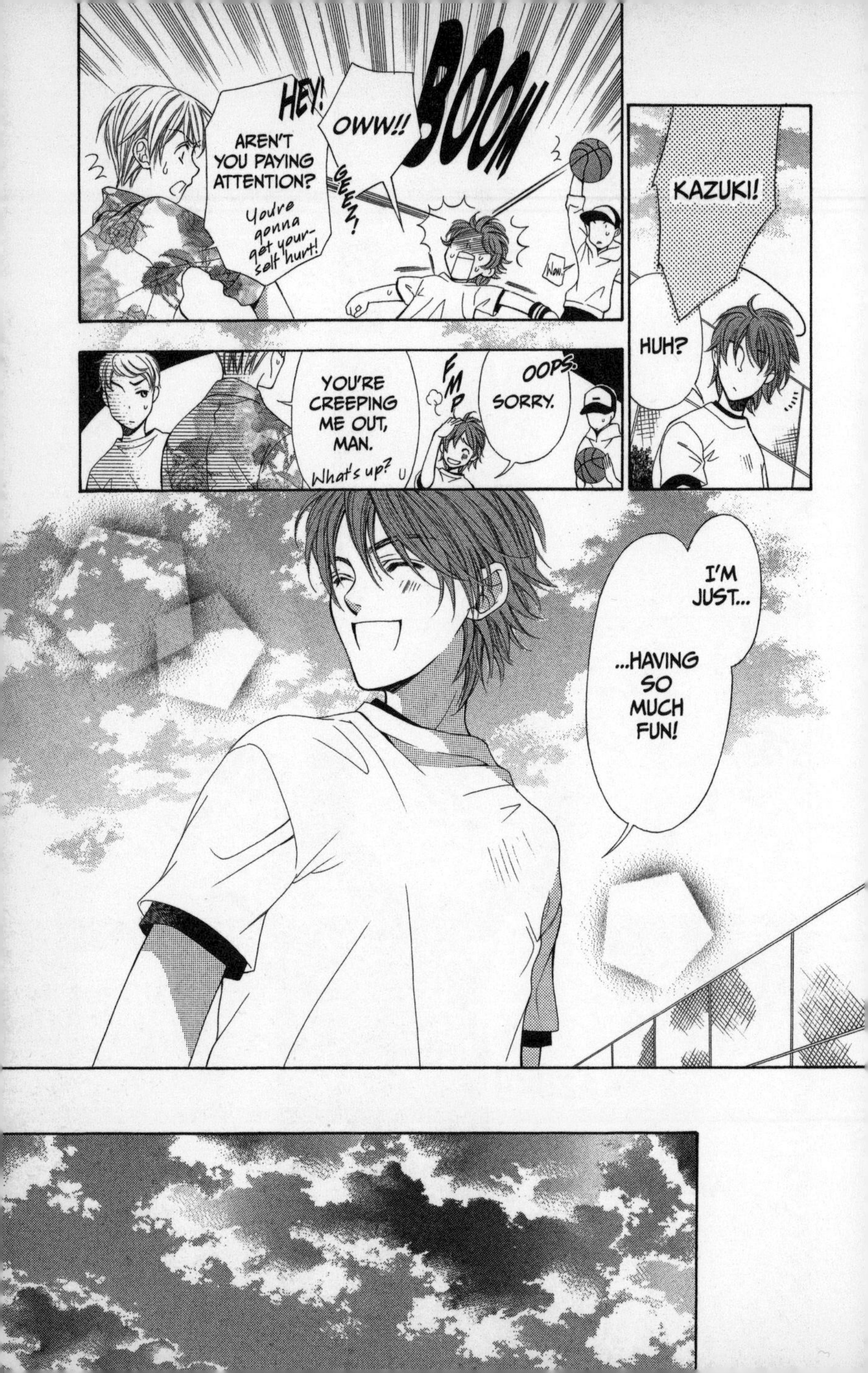
KAZUKI!
HUH?
BOOM
OWW!!
HEY!
AREN'T YOU PAYING ATTENTION?
You're gonna get yourself hurt!
GEEZ!
OOPS. SORRY.
FMP
YOU'RE CREEPING ME OUT, MAN.
What's up?
I'M JUST...
...HAVING SO MUCH FUN!

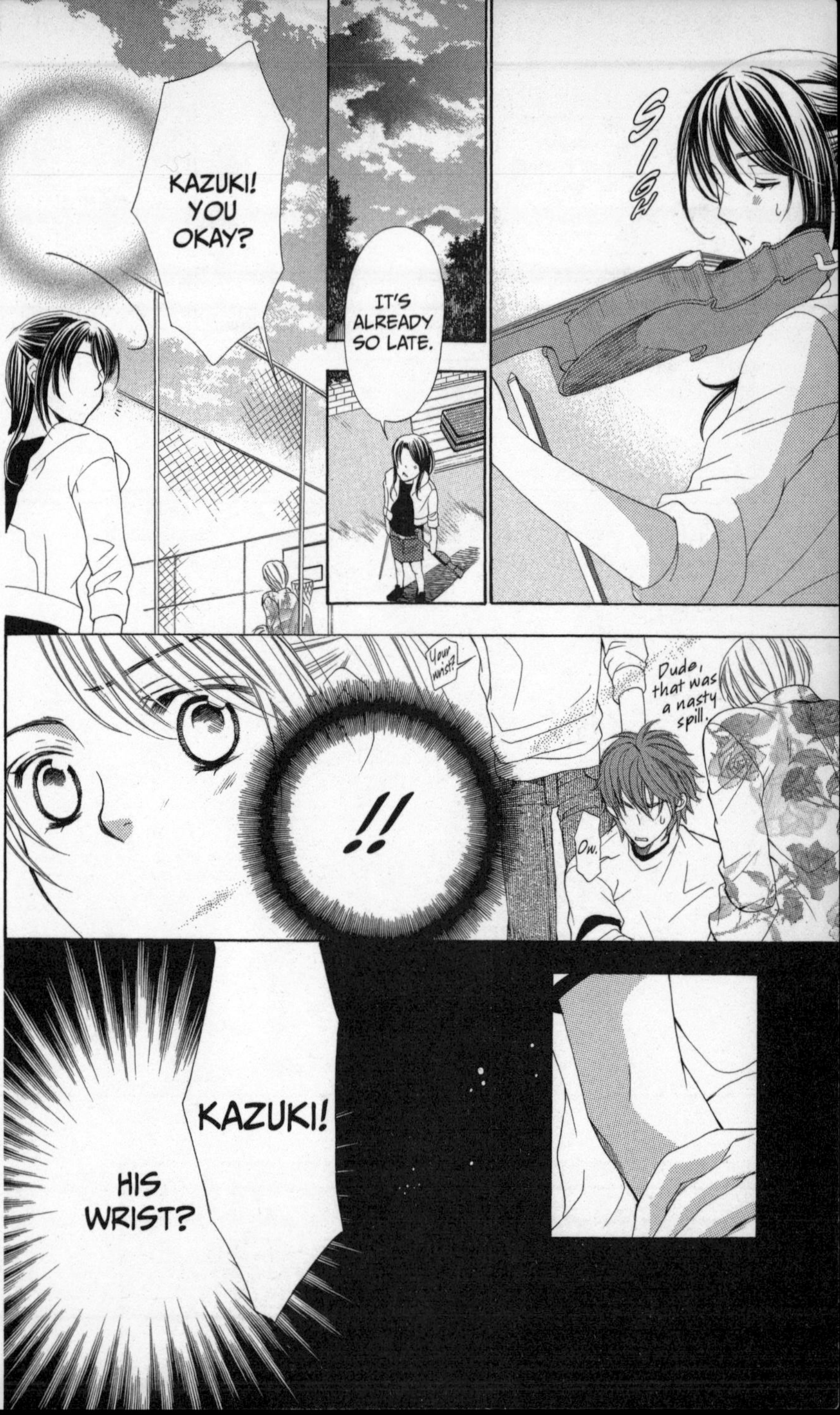
SIGH
IT'S ALREADY SO LATE.
KAZUKI! YOU OKAY?
Dude, that was a nasty spill.
Your wrist?
Ow.
!!
KAZUKI!
HIS WRIST?

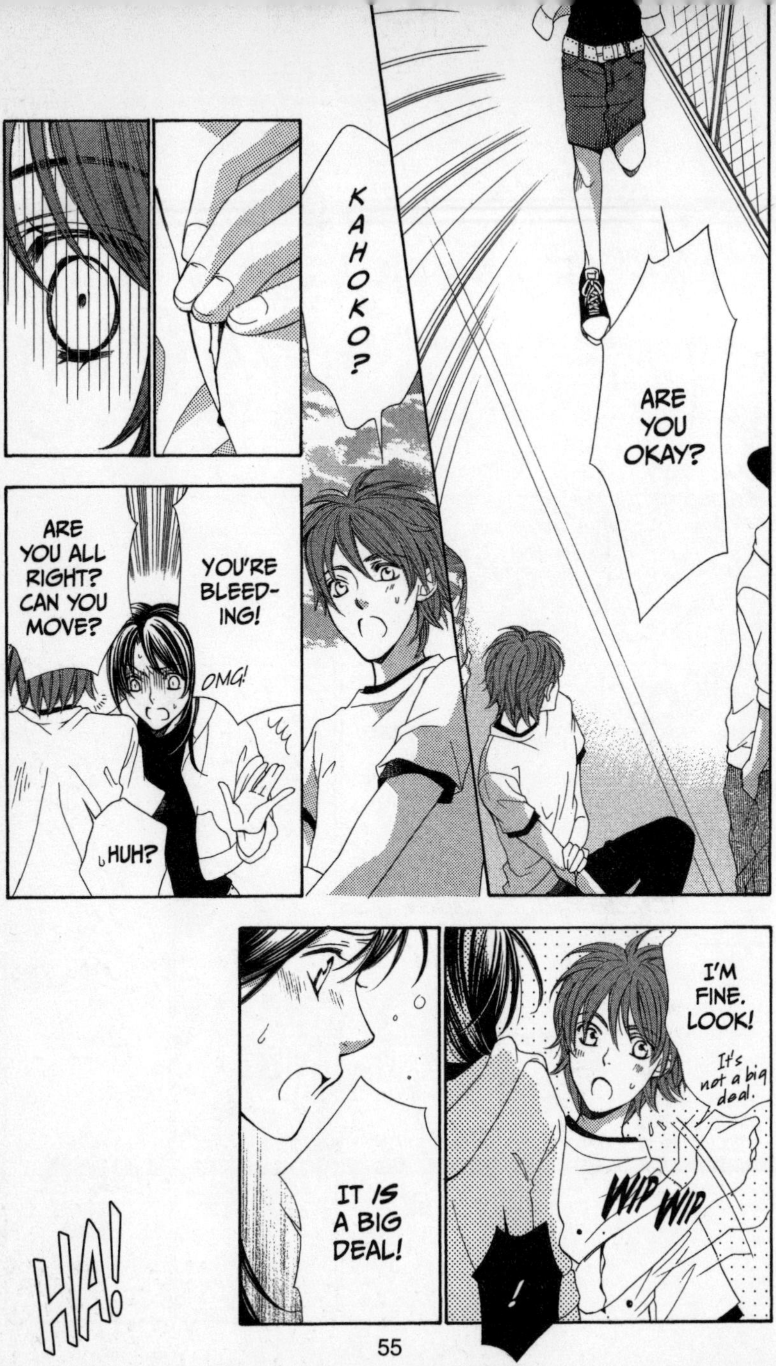
ARE YOU OKAY?
KAHOKO?
YOU'RE BLEEDING!
ARE YOU ALL RIGHT? CAN YOU MOVE?
OMG!
HUH?
I'M FINE. LOOK!
It's not a big deal.
WIP WIP
IT IS A BIG DEAL!
HA!

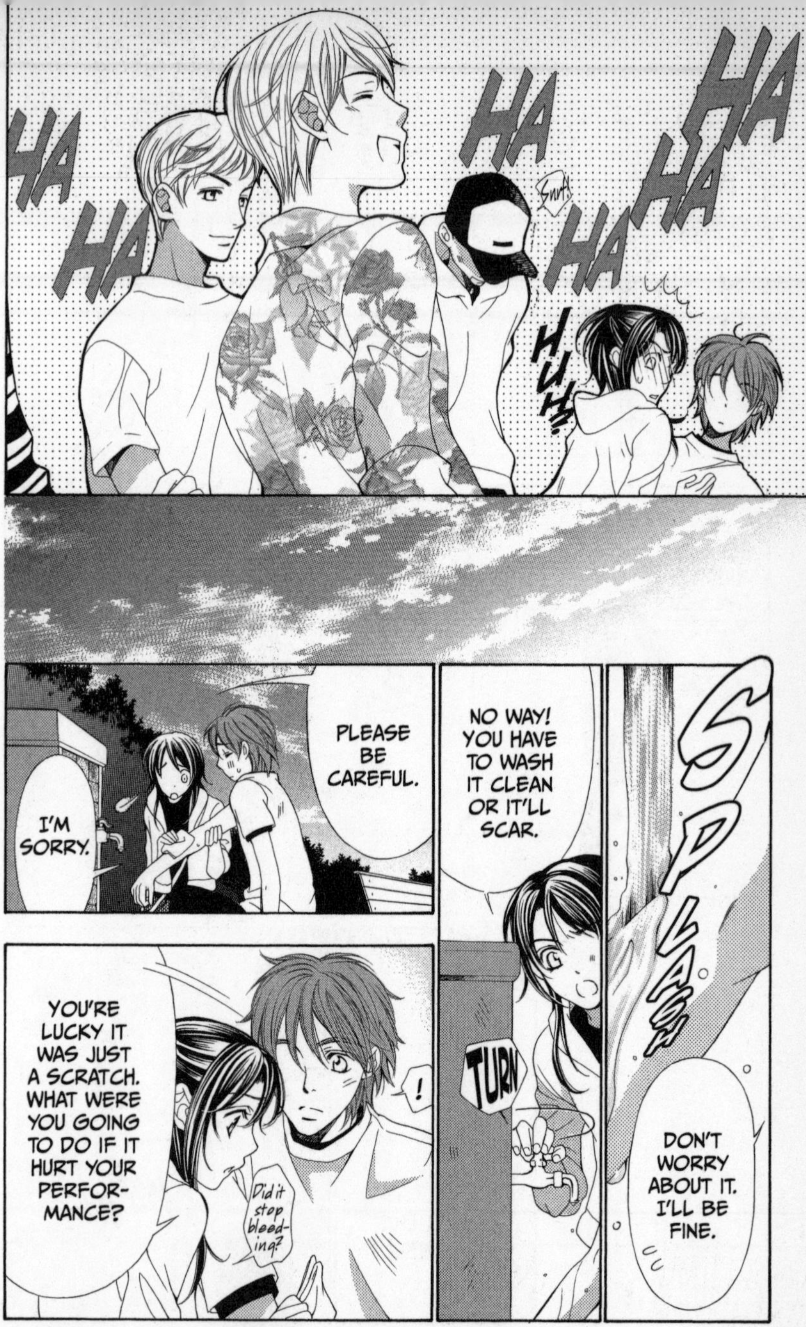
HA HA HA HA HA HA
HA HA
Snrf!
HA HA
HUH!?
SPLASH
DON'T WORRY ABOUT IT. I'LL BE FINE.
NO WAY! YOU HAVE TO WASH IT CLEAN OR IT'LL SCAR.
TURN
PLEASE BE CAREFUL.
I'M SORRY.
YOU'RE LUCKY IT WAS JUST A SCRATCH. WHAT WERE YOU GOING TO DO IF IT HURT YOUR PERFORMANCE?
!
Did it stop bleeding?

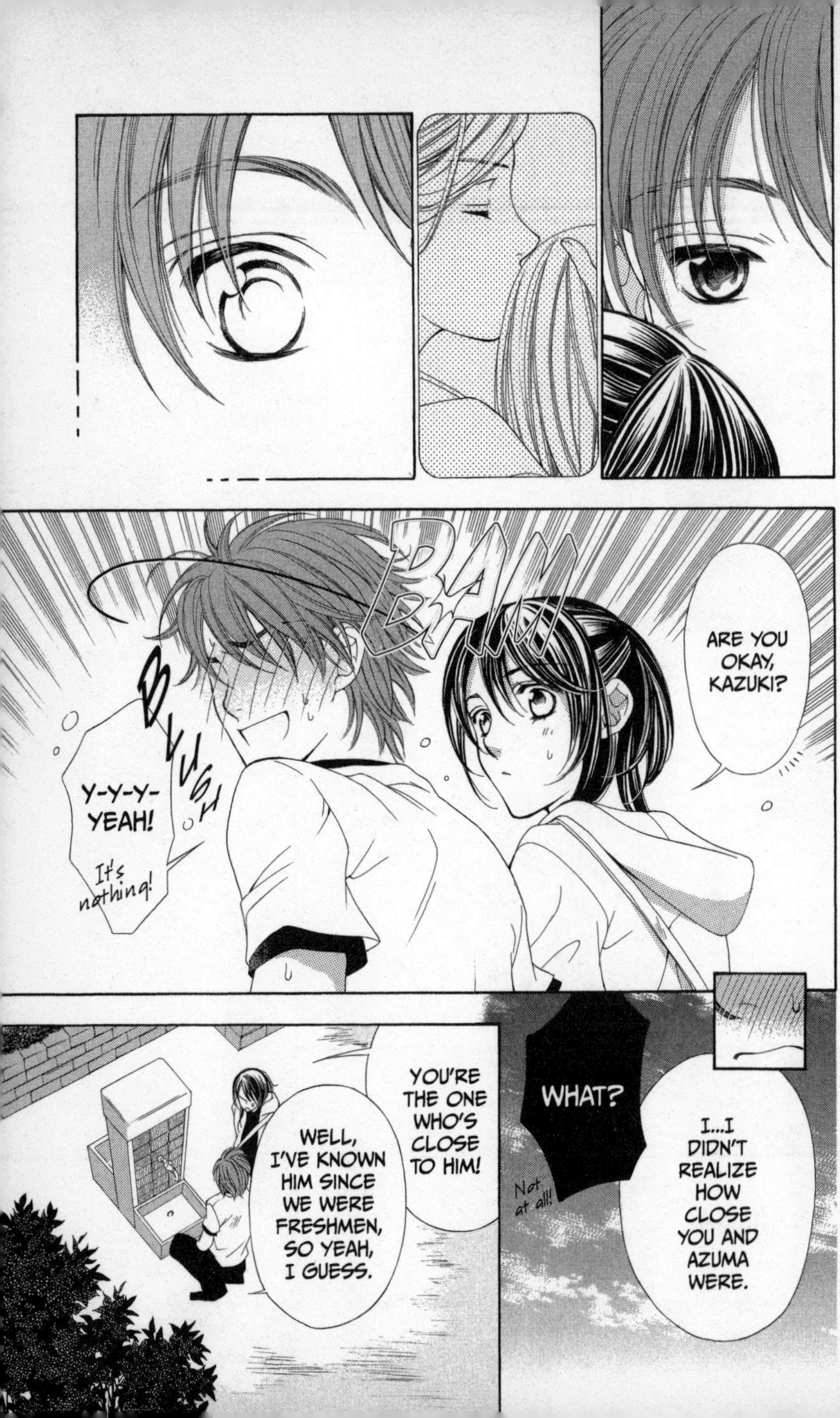
ARE YOU OKAY, KAZUKI?
BAM
BLUSH
Y-Y-Y-YEAH!
It's nothing!
I...I DIDN'T REALIZE HOW CLOSE YOU AND AZUMA WERE.
WHAT?
Not at all!
YOU'RE THE ONE WHO'S CLOSE TO HIM!
WELL, I'VE KNOWN HIM SINCE WE WERE FRESHMEN, SO YEAH, I GUESS.

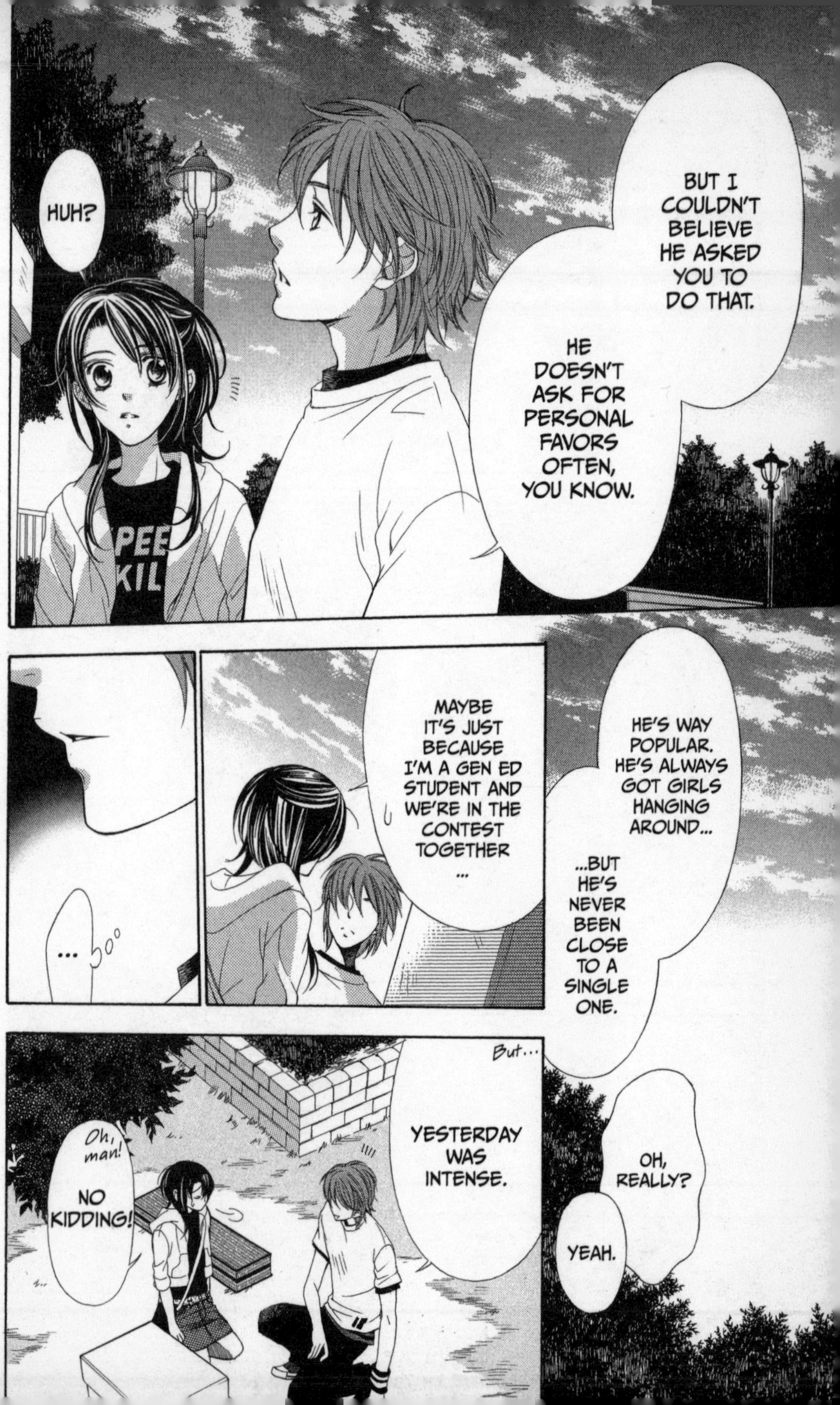
BUT I COULDN'T BELIEVE HE ASKED YOU TO DO THAT.
HE DOESN'T ASK FOR PERSONAL FAVORS OFTEN, YOU KNOW.
HUH?
HE'S WAY POPULAR. HE'S ALWAYS GOT GIRLS HANGING AROUND...
...BUT HE'S NEVER BEEN CLOSE TO A SINGLE ONE.
MAYBE IT'S JUST BECAUSE I'M A GEN ED STUDENT AND WE'RE IN THE CONTEST TOGETHER...
...
OH, REALLY?
YEAH.
But...
YESTERDAY WAS INTENSE.
Oh, man!
NO KIDDING!

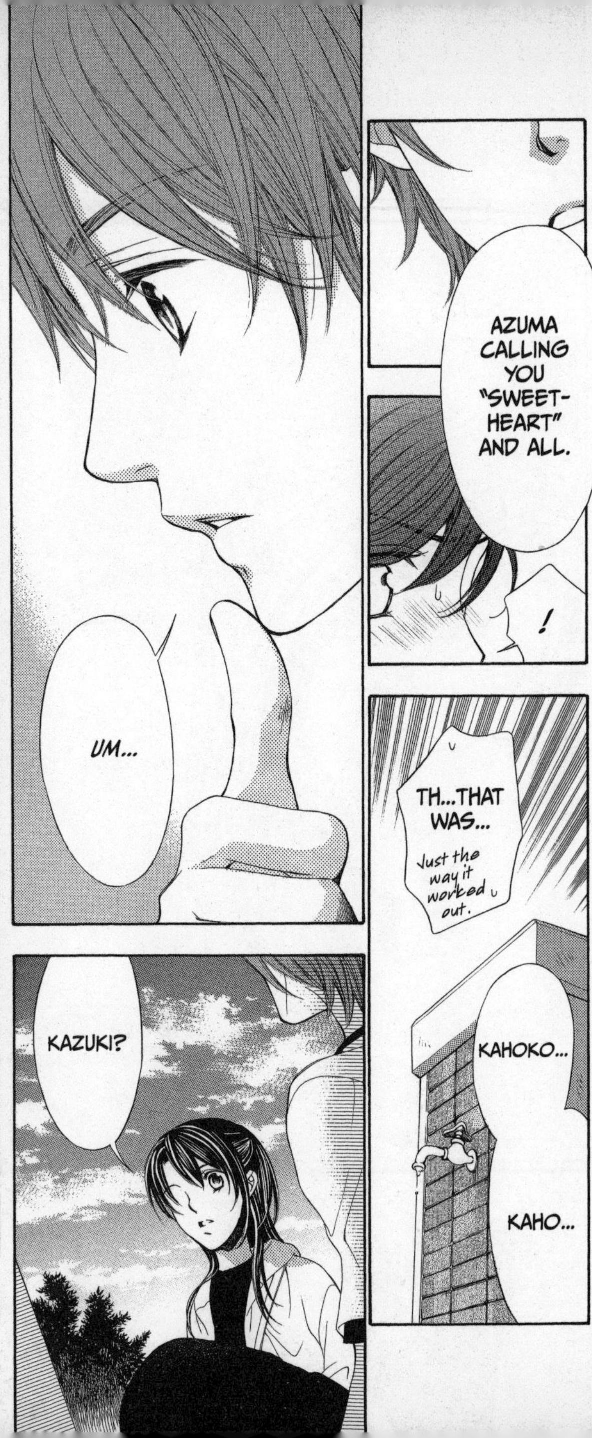
AZUMA CALLING YOU "SWEET-HEART" AND ALL.
!
TH...THAT WAS...
Just the way it worked out.
KAHOKO...
KAHO...
UM...
KAZUKI?

TWO

Measure 24 picks things up from volume 5. The theme of the title page is "like light snow..."

The Yunoki household story is pretty far removed from music. I thought it might be sort of refreshing.

Measure 25 is definitely an ode to Kazuki. He's the only male contestant in the entire chapter. (I think this is a first, even counting the side stories!)

I was also able to sneak in Kazuki's brother. I really like drawing him. I haven't given him a name yet, though...just "Kazuki's bro." (lol)

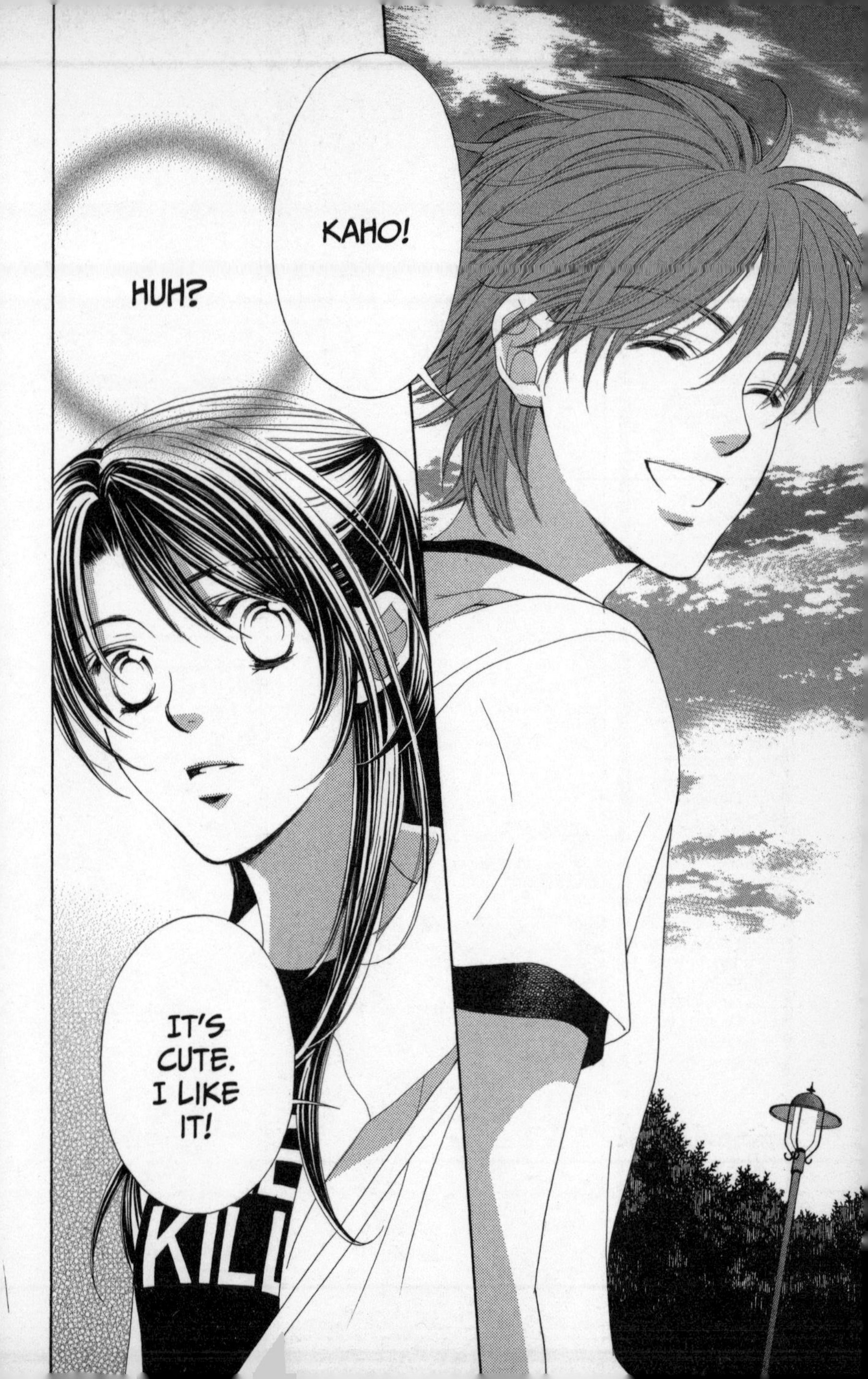
KAHO!
HUH?
IT'S CUTE. I LIKE IT!

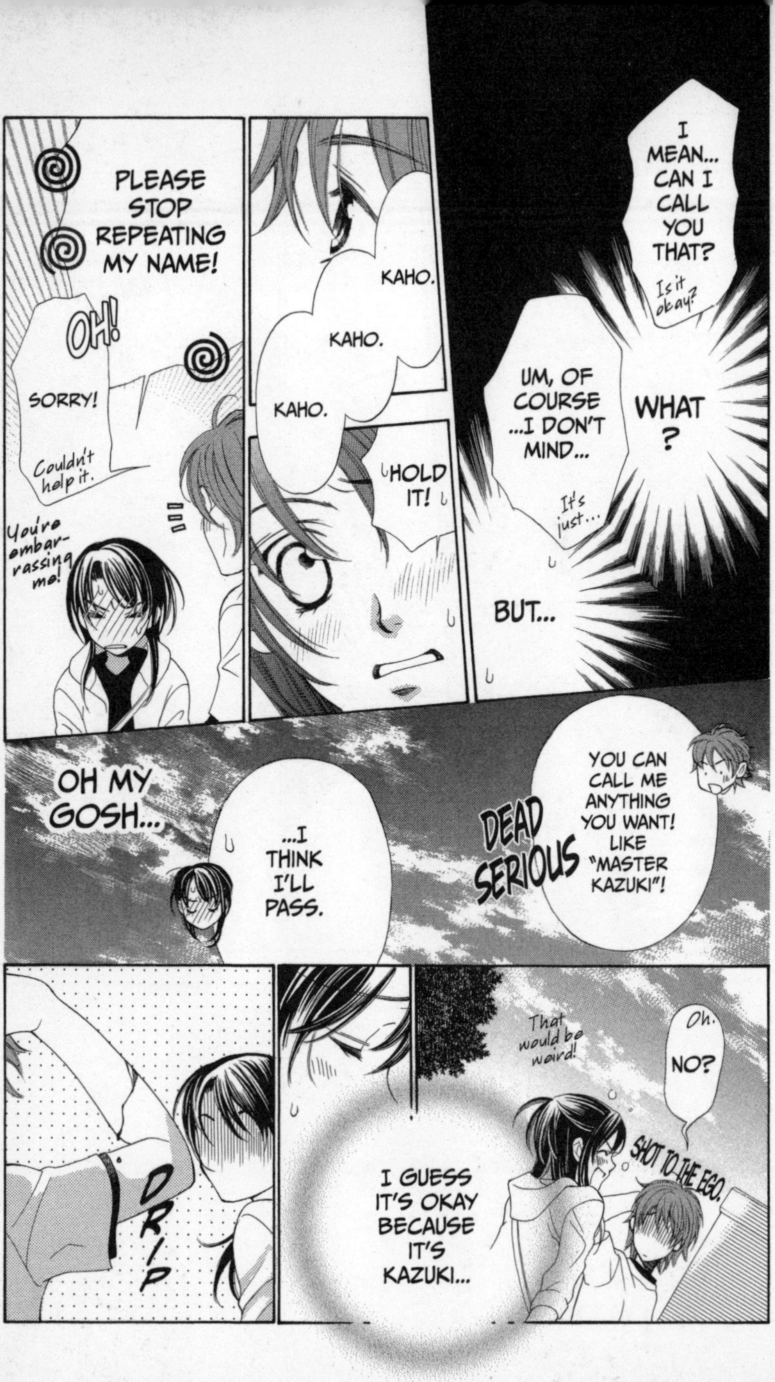
I MEAN... CAN I CALL YOU THAT?
Is it okay?
WHAT?
UM, OF COURSE ...I DON'T MIND...
It's just...
BUT...
KAHO.
KAHO.
KAHO.
HOLD IT!
PLEASE STOP REPEATING MY NAME!
OH!
SORRY!
Couldn't help it.
You're embarrassing me!
YOU CAN CALL ME ANYTHING YOU WANT! LIKE "MASTER KAZUKI"!
DEAD SERIOUS
...I THINK I'LL PASS.
OH MY GOSH...
Oh.
NO?
SHOT TO THE EGO.
That would be weird!
I GUESS IT'S OKAY BECAUSE IT'S KAZUKI...
DRIP

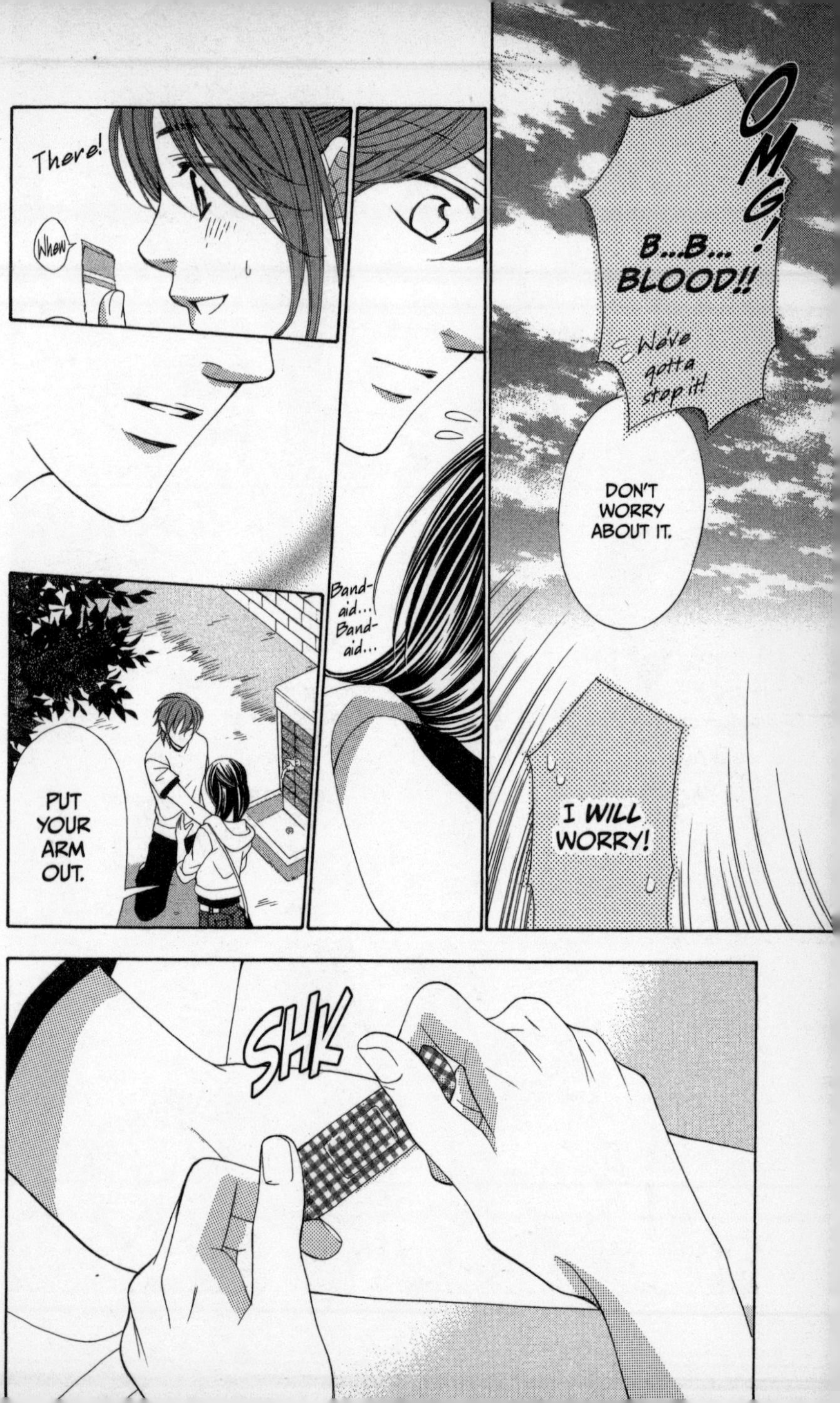
OMG!
B...B... BLOOD!!
We've gotta stop it!
DON'T WORRY ABOUT IT.
I WILL WORRY!
Band-aid... Band-aid...
There!
Whew
PUT YOUR ARM OUT.
SHK

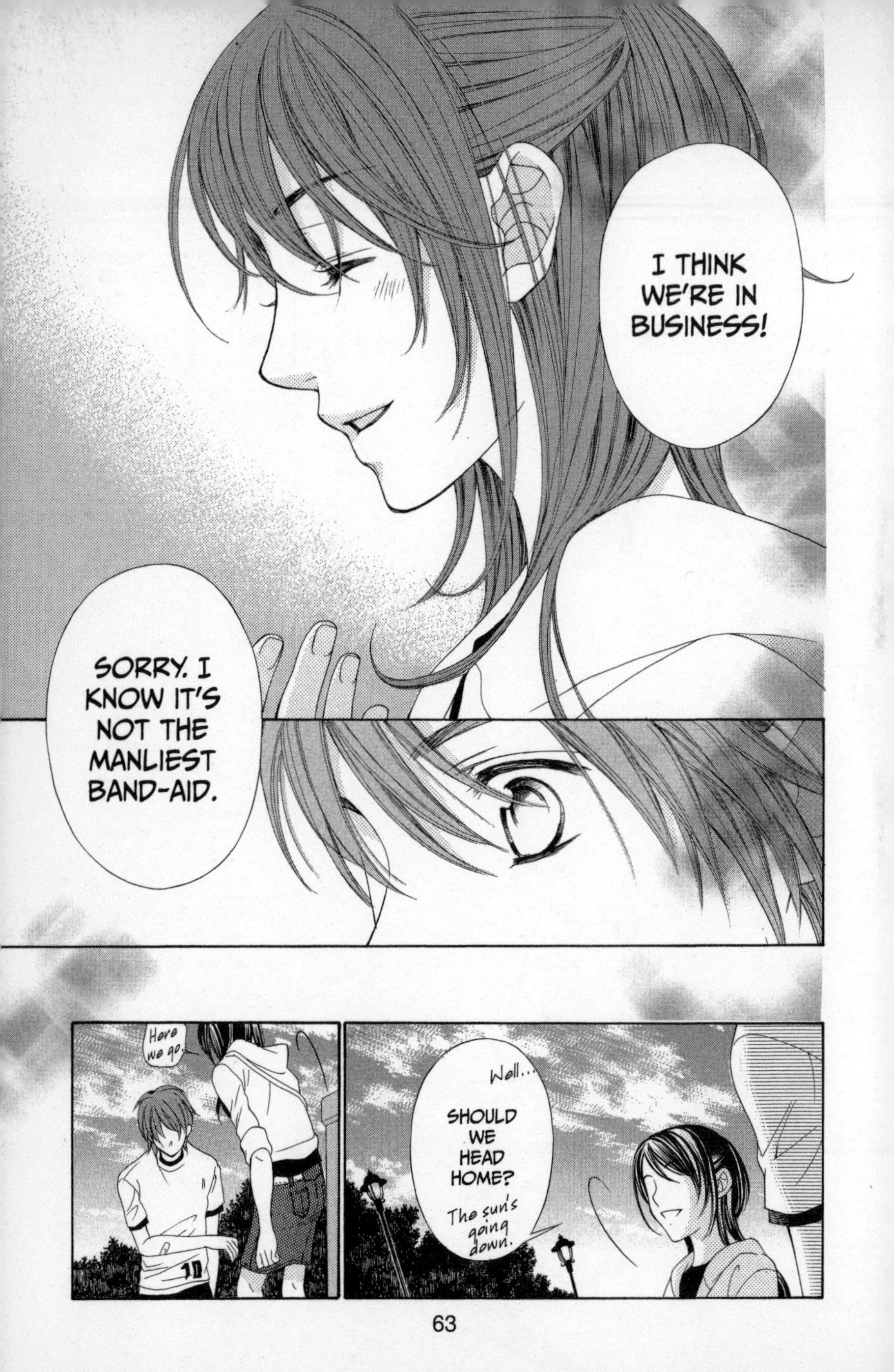
I THINK WE'RE IN BUSINESS!
SORRY. I KNOW IT'S NOT THE MANLIEST BAND-AID.
Well...
SHOULD WE HEAD HOME?
The sun's going down.
Here we go.

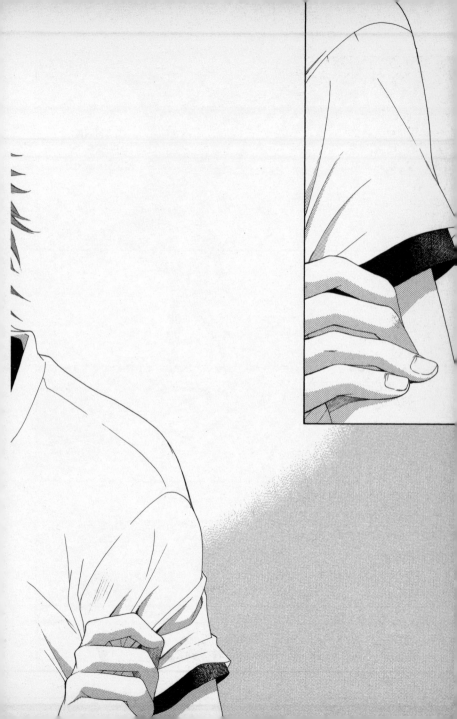

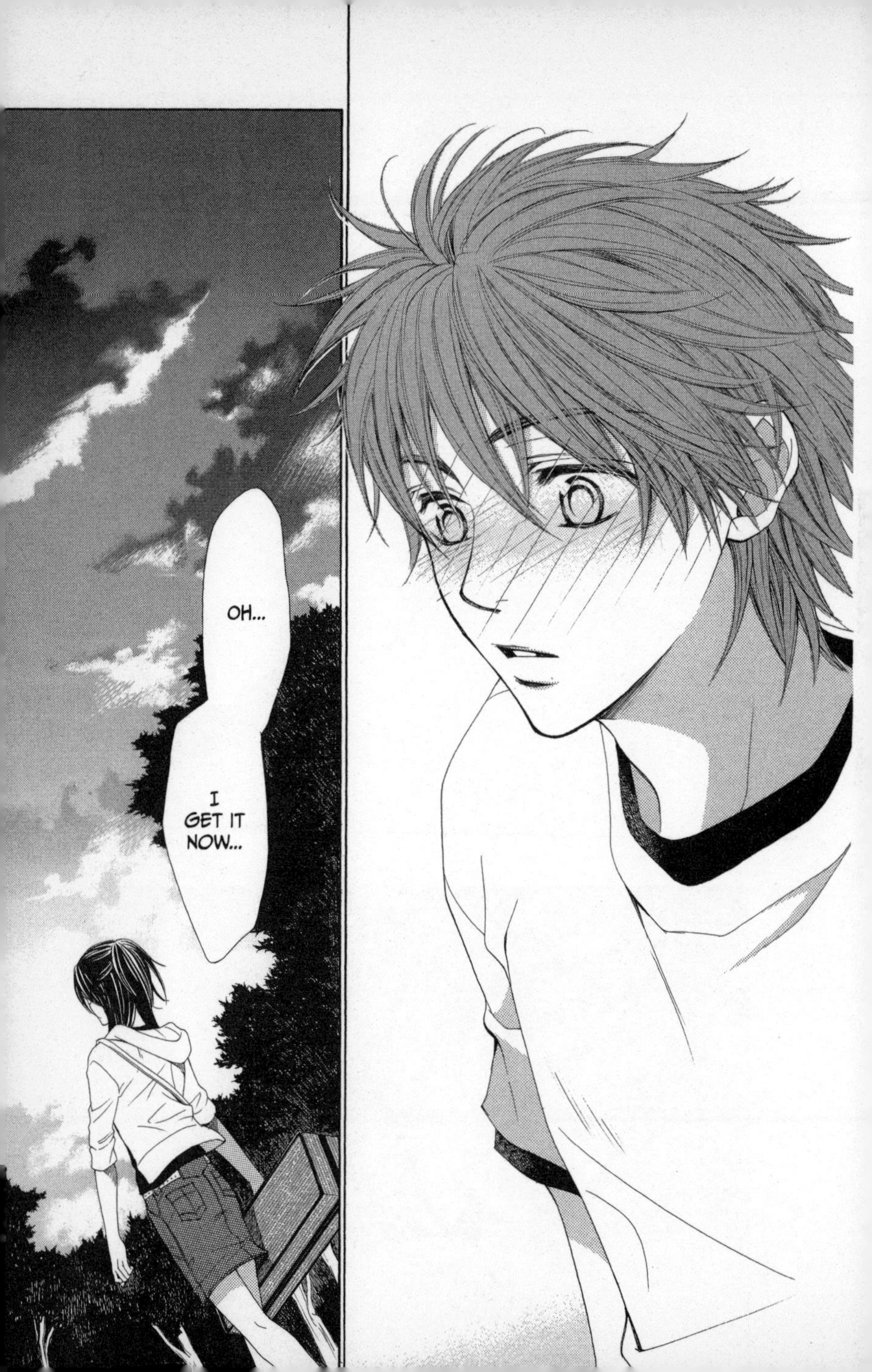
OH...
I GET IT NOW...

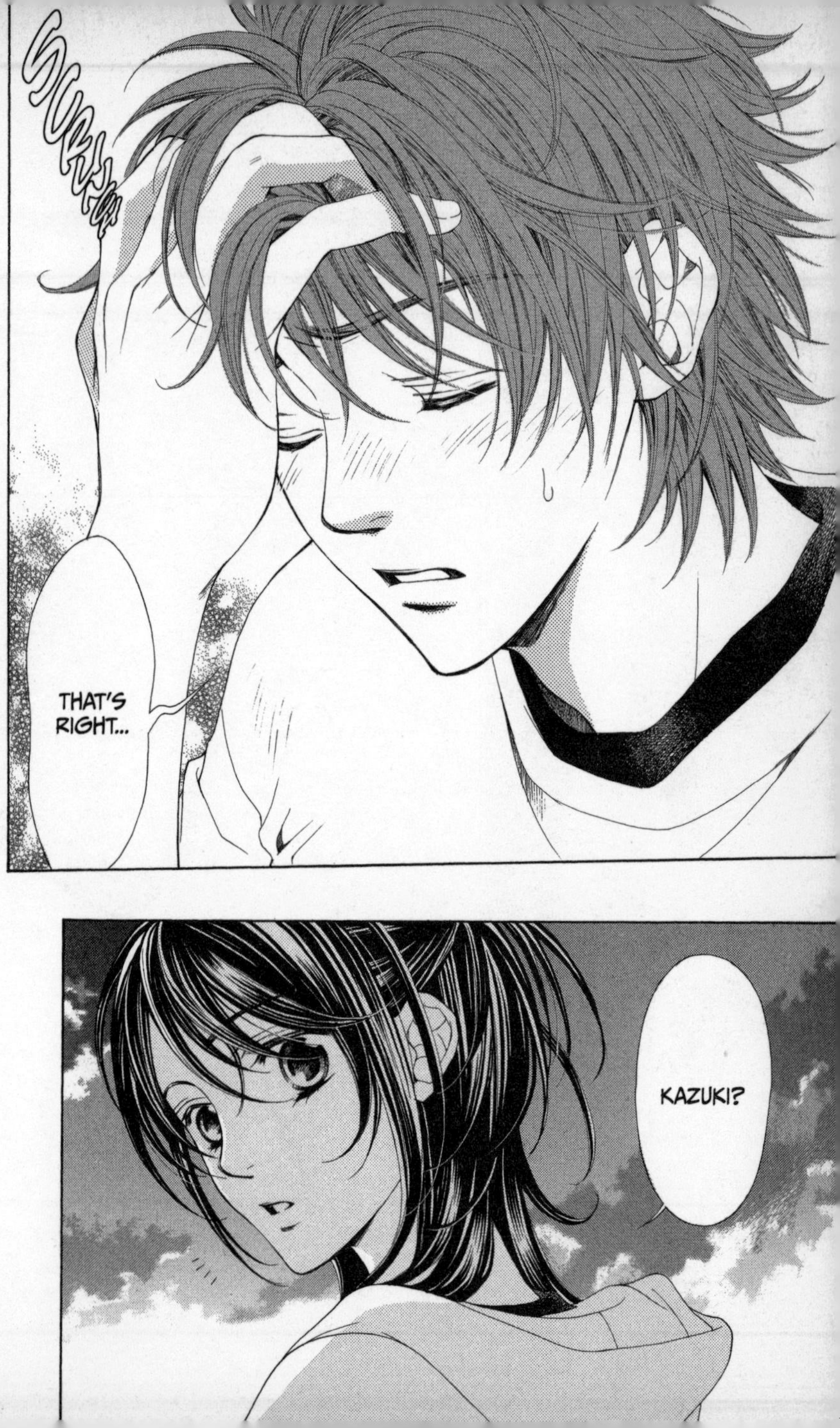
THAT'S RIGHT...
KAZUKI?

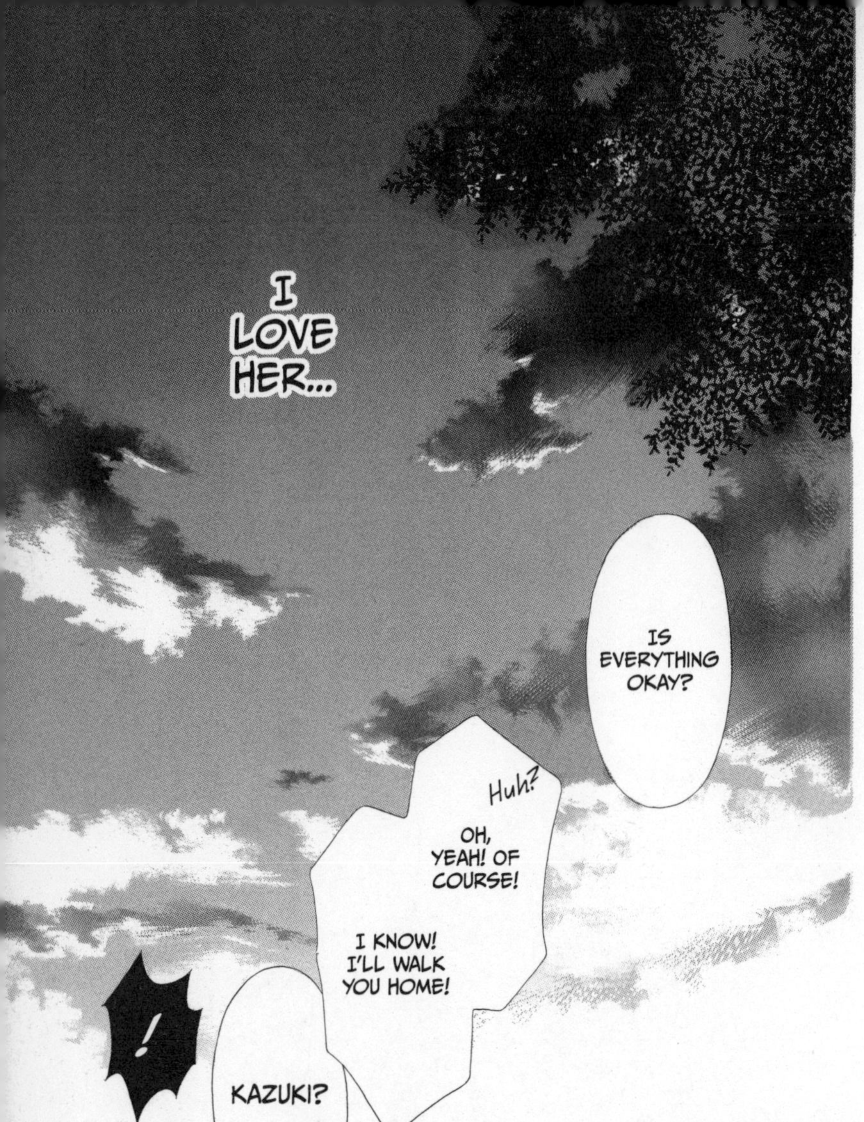
I LOVE HER...
IS EVERYTHING OKAY?
Huh?
OH, YEAH! OF COURSE!
I KNOW! I'LL WALK YOU HOME!
KAZUKI?
Your face is beet red...
!

END OF MEASURE 25

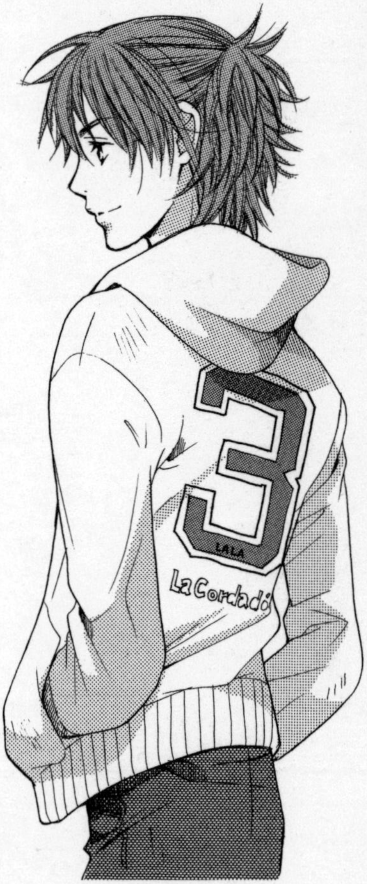
3
LALA
La Cordadó

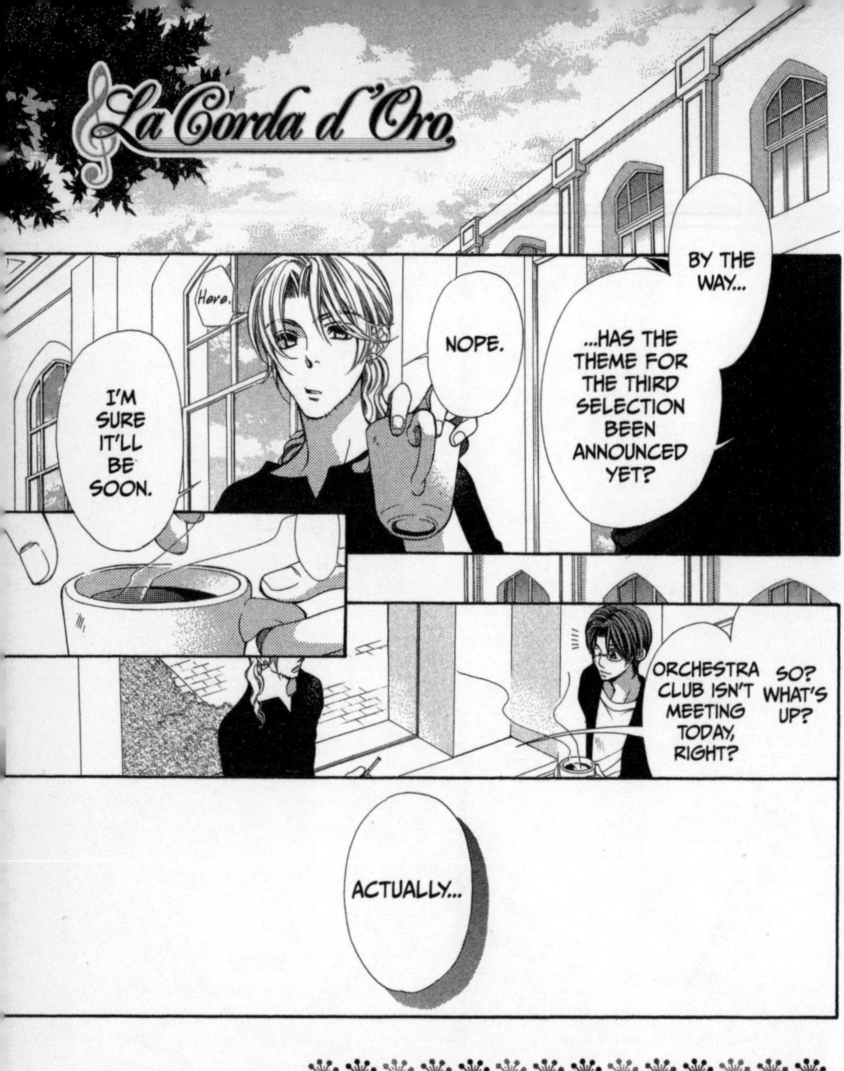
La Corda d'Oro
BY THE WAY...
...HAS THE THEME FOR THE THIRD SELECTION BEEN ANNOUNCED YET?
NOPE.
Here.
I'M SURE IT'LL BE SOON.
SO? WHAT'S UP?
ORCHESTRA CLUB ISN'T MEETING TODAY, RIGHT?
ACTUALLY...

Daily Happenings ⑱ Things I hate...

Slugs.
I remember writing something about hating cicadas the most, but slugs are just as bad...Actually, worse.

In Guam, I saw an entire sluggy swarm of them and vowed I would never go back...It's true...

La Corda d'Oro

MEASURE 26

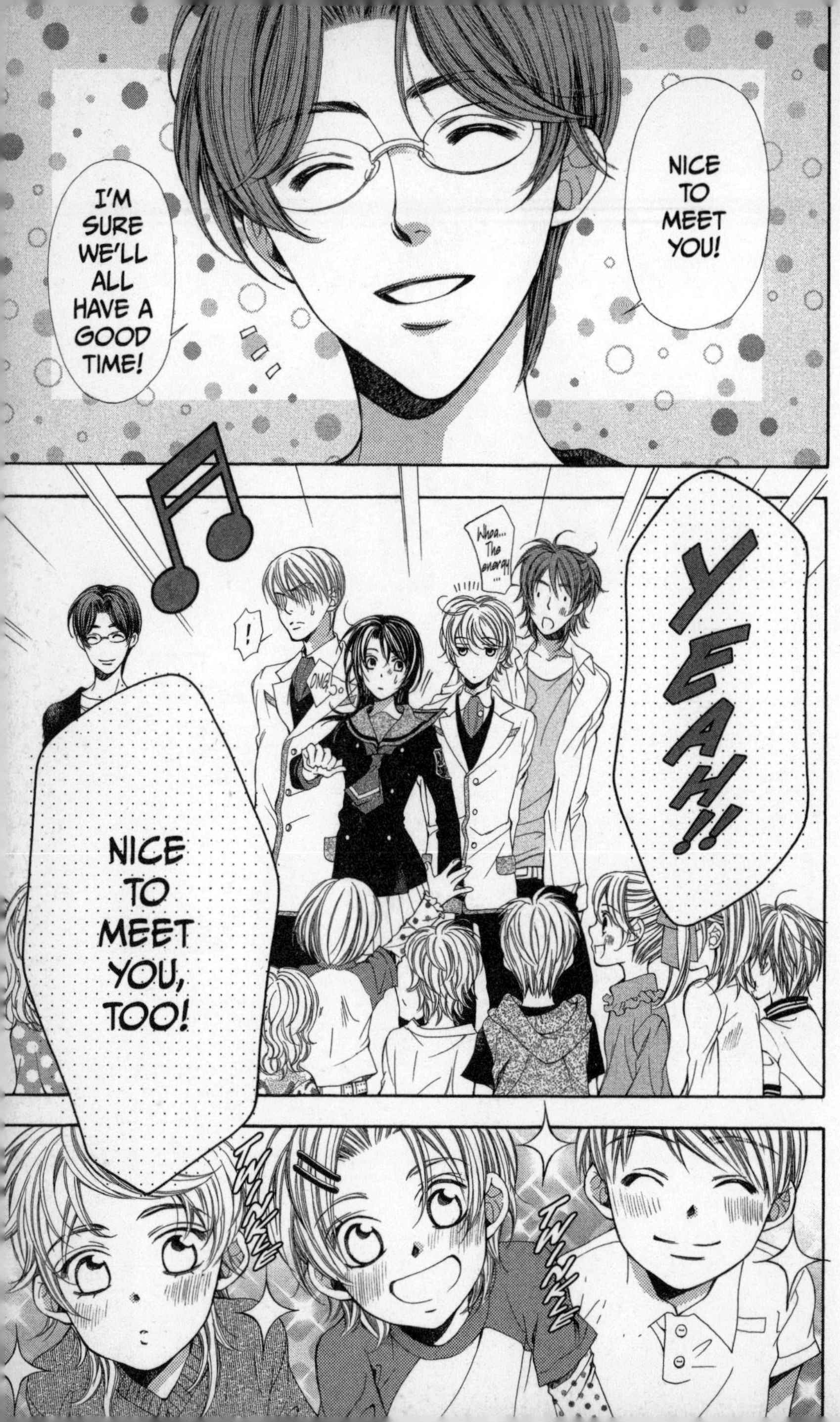
NICE TO MEET YOU!
I'M SURE WE'LL ALL HAVE A GOOD TIME!
YEAH!!
Whoa... The energy...
!
OMG!
NICE TO MEET YOU, TOO!
TWINKLE
TWINKLE

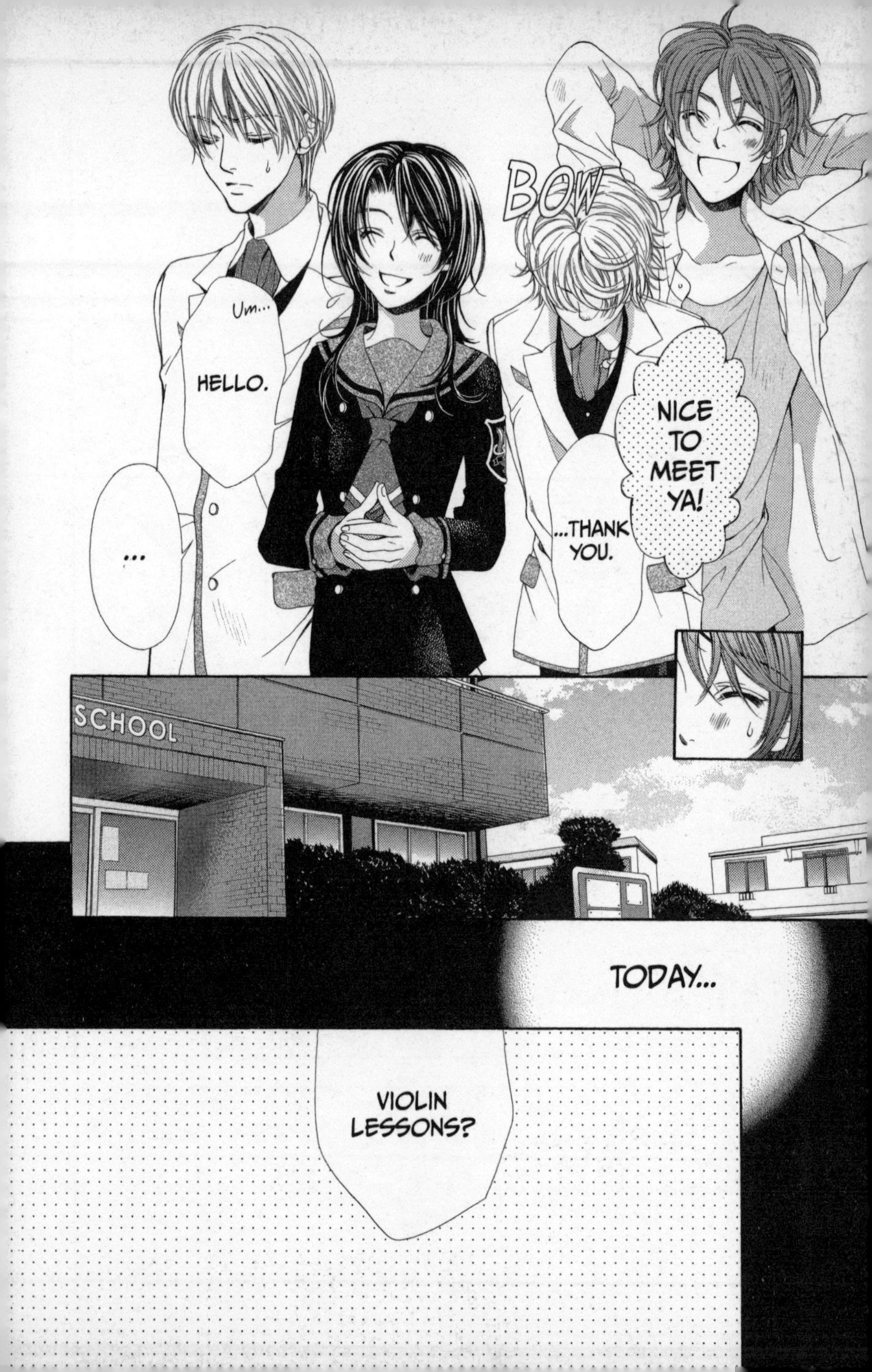
NICE TO MEET YA!
...THANK YOU.
BOW
Um... HELLO.
...
SCHOOL
TODAY...
VIOLIN LESSONS?

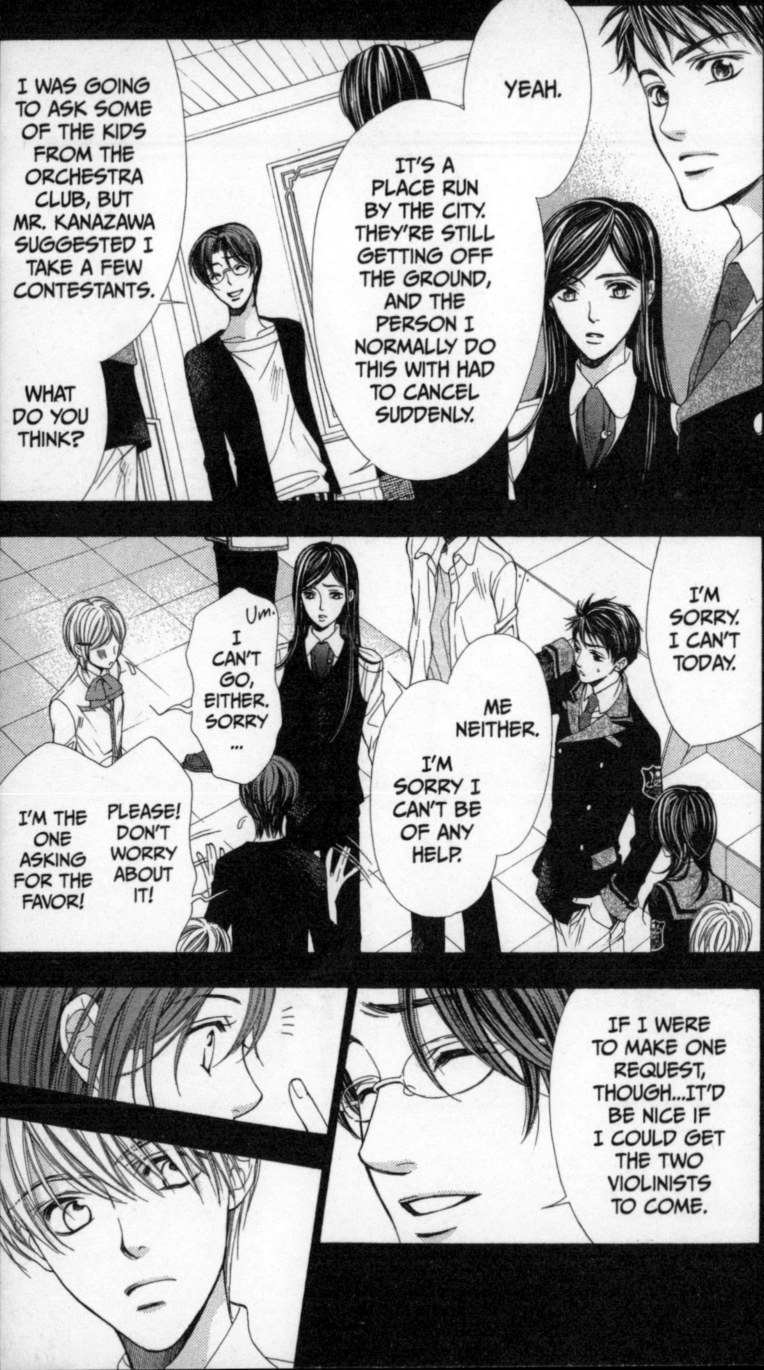
YEAH.
IT'S A PLACE RUN BY THE CITY. THEY'RE STILL GETTING OFF THE GROUND, AND THE PERSON I NORMALLY DO THIS WITH HAD TO CANCEL SUDDENLY.
I WAS GOING TO ASK SOME OF THE KIDS FROM THE ORCHESTRA CLUB, BUT MR. KANAZAWA SUGGESTED I TAKE A FEW CONTESTANTS.
WHAT DO YOU THINK?
I'M SORRY. I CAN'T TODAY.
ME NEITHER.
I'M SORRY I CAN'T BE OF ANY HELP.
Um.
I CAN'T GO, EITHER. SORRY...
PLEASE! DON'T WORRY ABOUT IT!
I'M THE ONE ASKING FOR THE FAVOR!
IF I WERE TO MAKE ONE REQUEST, THOUGH...IT'D BE NICE IF I COULD GET THE TWO VIOLINISTS TO COME.

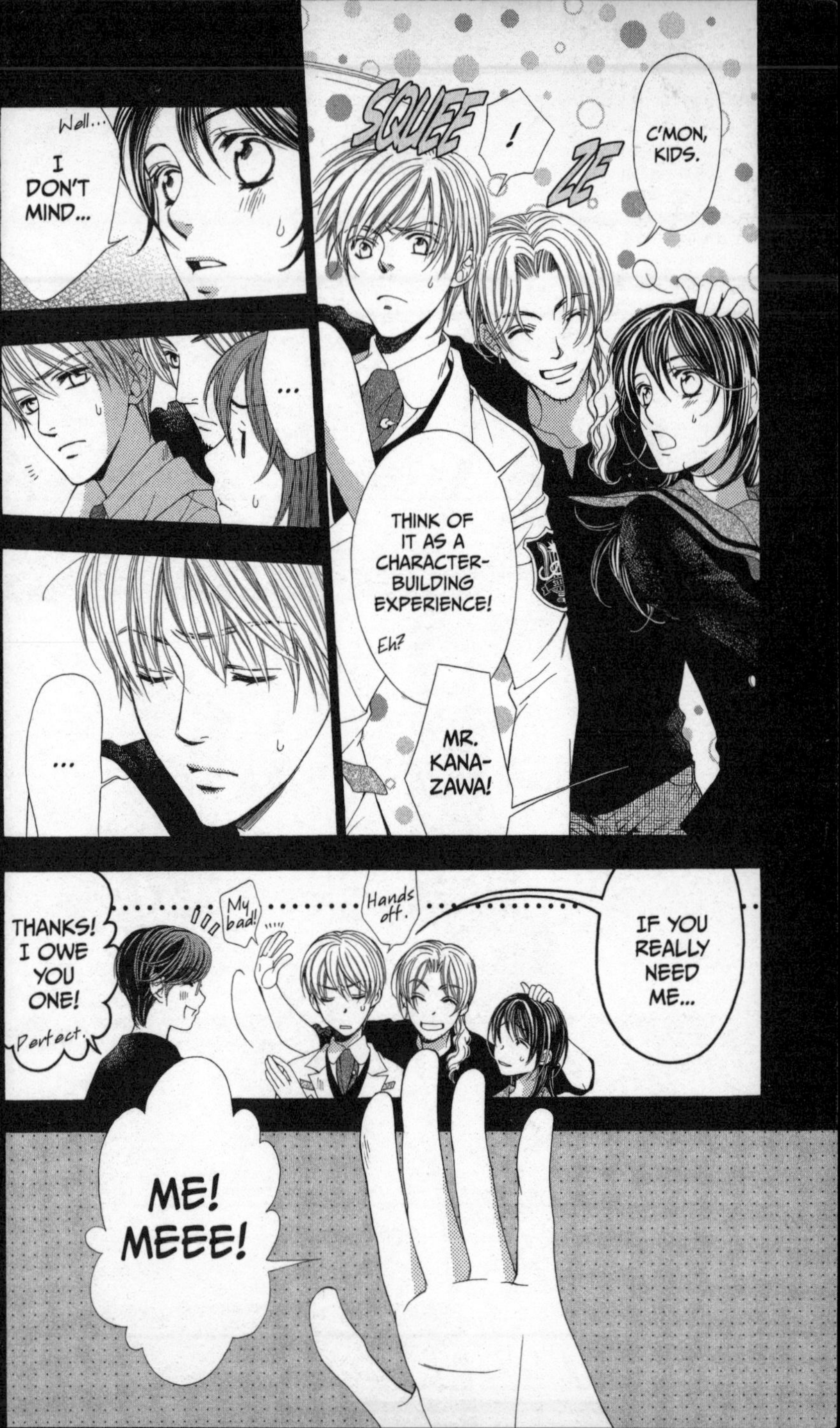
C'MON, KIDS.
SQUEEZE
!
THINK OF IT AS A CHARACTER-BUILDING EXPERIENCE!
Eh?
MR. KANAZAWA!
Well...
I DON'T MIND...
...
...
IF YOU REALLY NEED ME...
Hands off.
My bad!
THANKS! I OWE YOU ONE!
Perfect.
ME! MEEE!

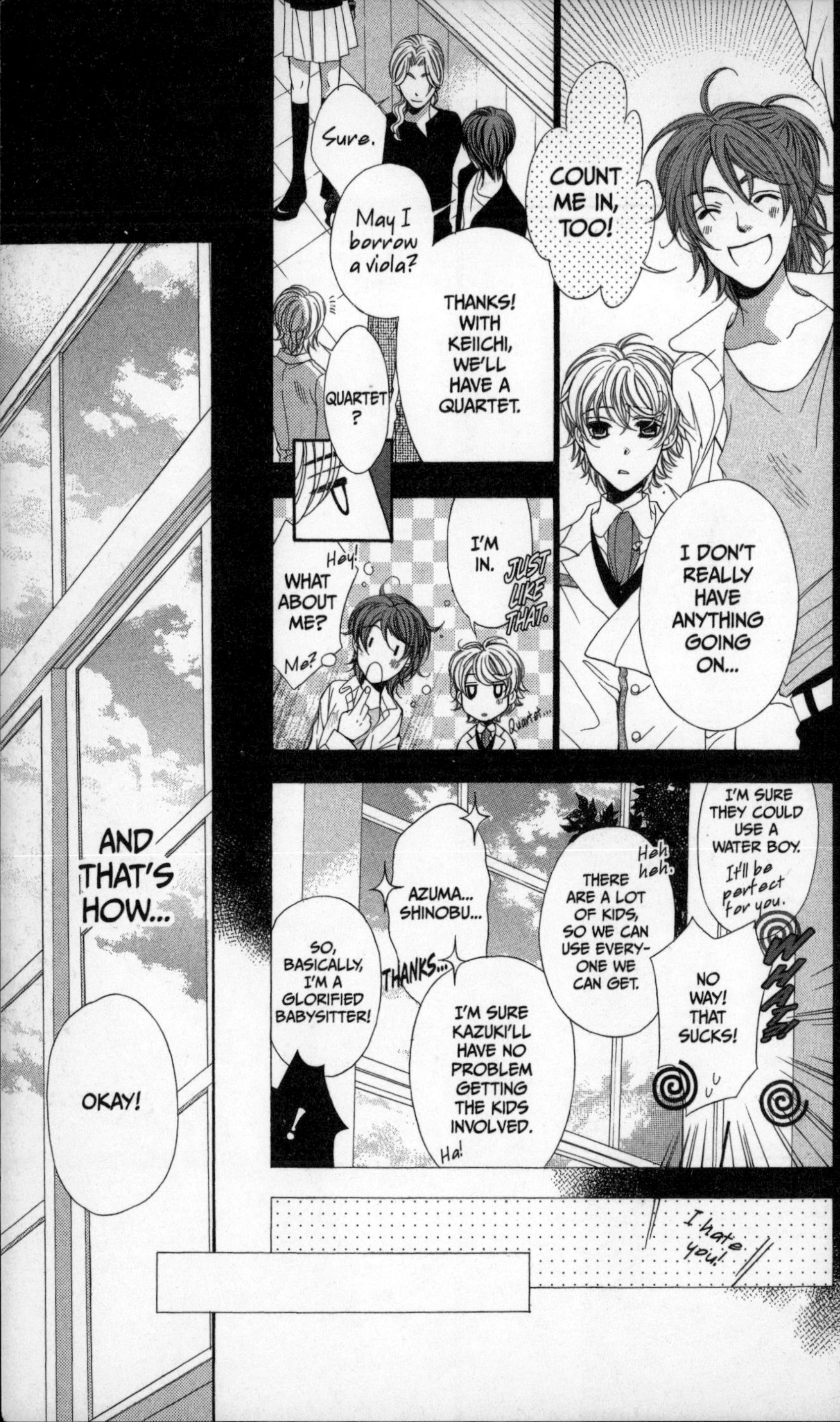
COUNT ME IN, TOO!
I DON'T REALLY HAVE ANYTHING GOING ON...
Sure.
May I borrow a viola?
THANKS! WITH KEIICHI, WE'LL HAVE A QUARTET.
QUARTET?
I'M IN.
JUST LIKE THAT.
Hey!
WHAT ABOUT ME?
Me?
Quartet...
I'M SURE THEY COULD USE A WATER BOY.
It'll be perfect for you.
NO WAY! THAT SUCKS!
WHAM!!
Heh heh.
THERE ARE A LOT OF KIDS, SO WE CAN USE EVERY-ONE WE CAN GET.
AZUMA... SHINOBU...
THANKS...
I'M SURE KAZUKI'LL HAVE NO PROBLEM GETTING THE KIDS INVOLVED.
Ha!
SO, BASICALLY, I'M A GLORIFIED BABYSITTER!
I hate you!
AND THAT'S HOW...
OKAY!

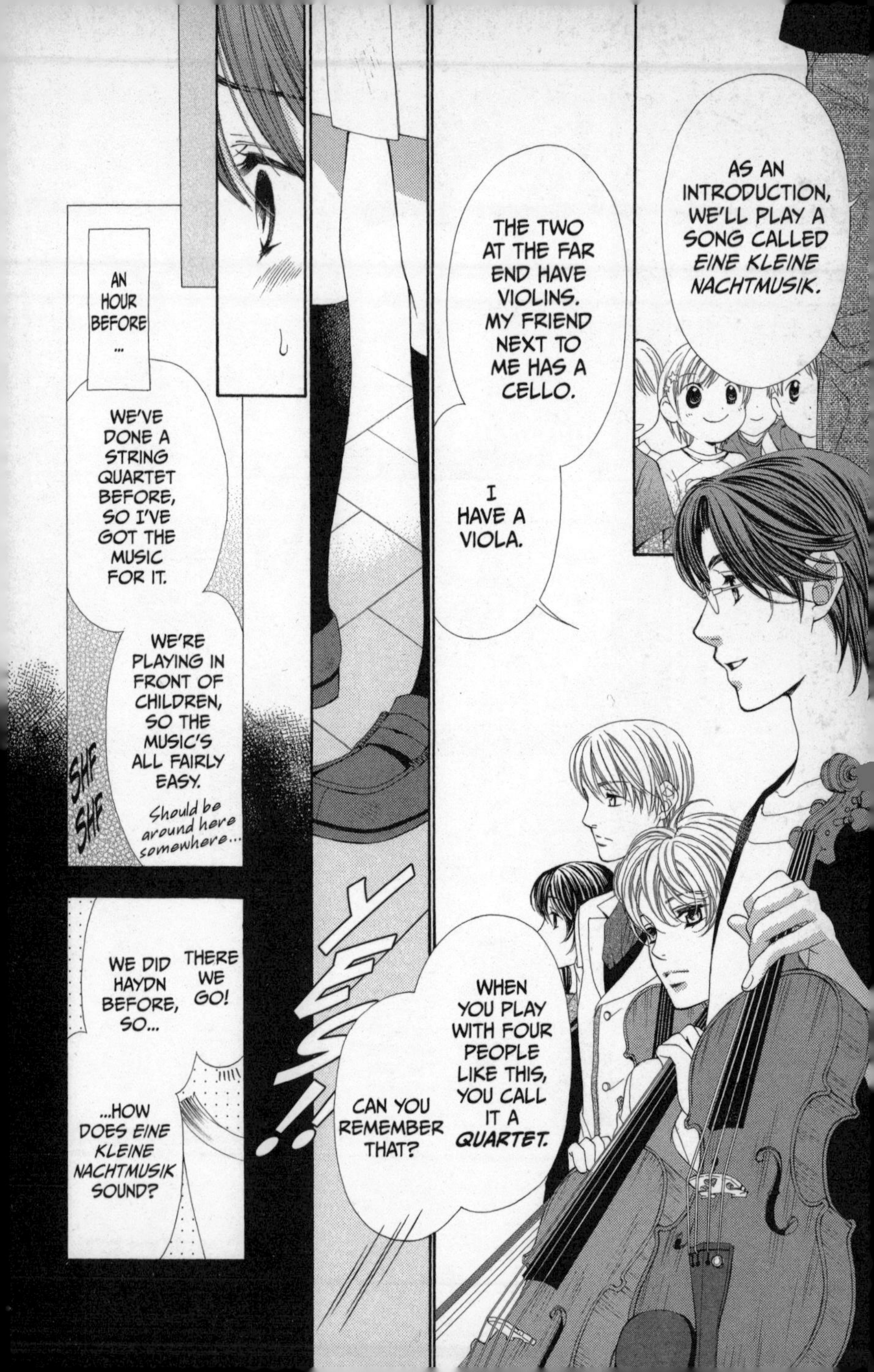
AS AN INTRODUCTION, WE'LL PLAY A SONG CALLED *EINE KLEINE NACHTMUSIK.*
THE TWO AT THE FAR END HAVE VIOLINS. MY FRIEND NEXT TO ME HAS A CELLO.
I HAVE A VIOLA.
WHEN YOU PLAY WITH FOUR PEOPLE LIKE THIS, YOU CALL IT A ***QUARTET.***
CAN YOU REMEMBER THAT?
YES!!
AN HOUR BEFORE...
WE'VE DONE A STRING QUARTET BEFORE, SO I'VE GOT THE MUSIC FOR IT.
WE'RE PLAYING IN FRONT OF CHILDREN, SO THE MUSIC'S ALL FAIRLY EASY.
SHF SHF
Should be around here somewhere...
THERE WE GO!
WE DID HAYDN BEFORE, SO...
...HOW DOES *EINE KLEINE NACHTMUSIK* SOUND?

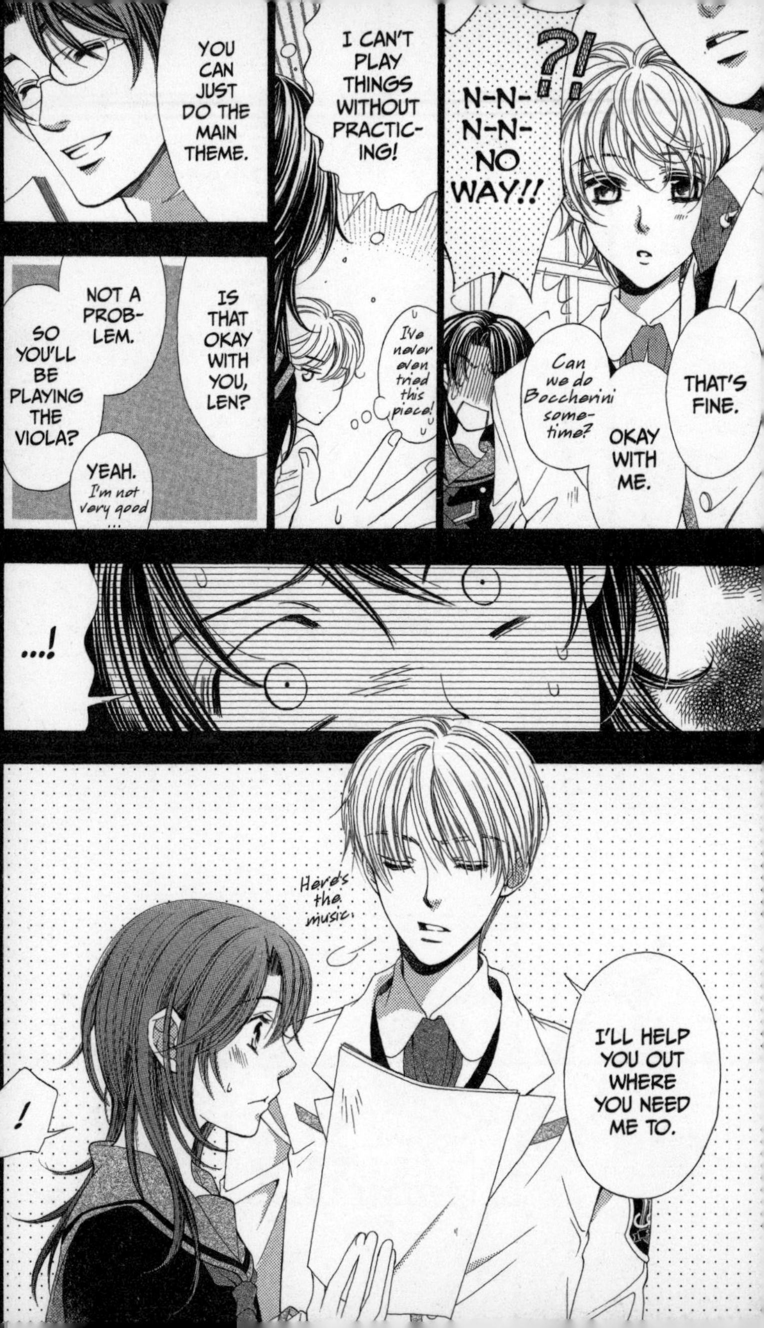
?!
N-N-N-N-NO WAY!!
THAT'S FINE.
OKAY WITH ME.
Can we do Boccherini sometime?
I CAN'T PLAY THINGS WITHOUT PRACTICING!
I've never even tried this piece!
YOU CAN JUST DO THE MAIN THEME.
IS THAT OKAY WITH YOU, LEN?
NOT A PROBLEM.
SO YOU'LL BE PLAYING THE VIOLA?
YEAH. I'm not very good...
...!
I'LL HELP YOU OUT WHERE YOU NEED ME TO.
Here's the music.
!

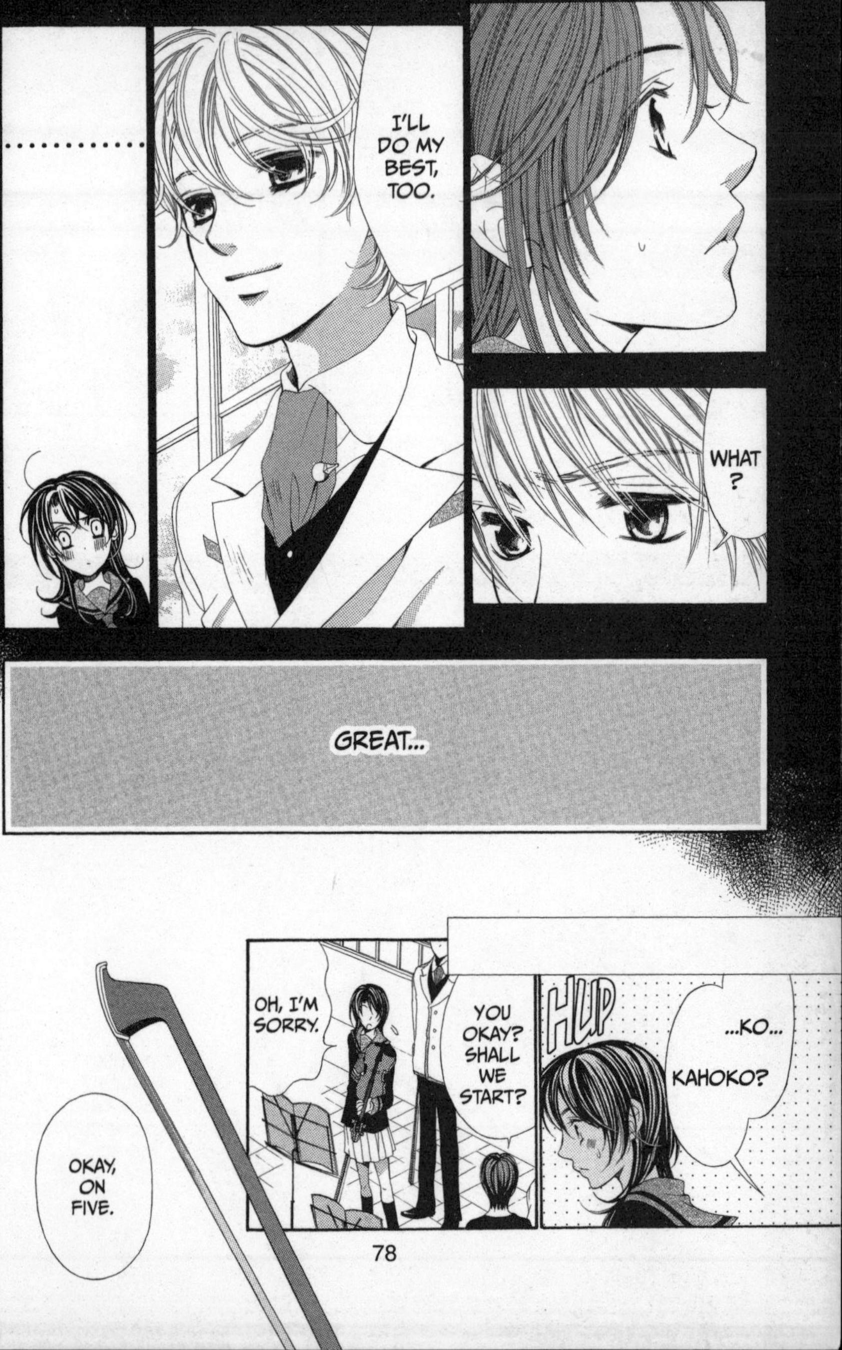
WHAT?
I'LL DO MY BEST, TOO.
....
GREAT...
...KO...
KAHOKO?
HUP
YOU OKAY? SHALL WE START?
OH, I'M SORRY.
OKAY, ON FIVE.

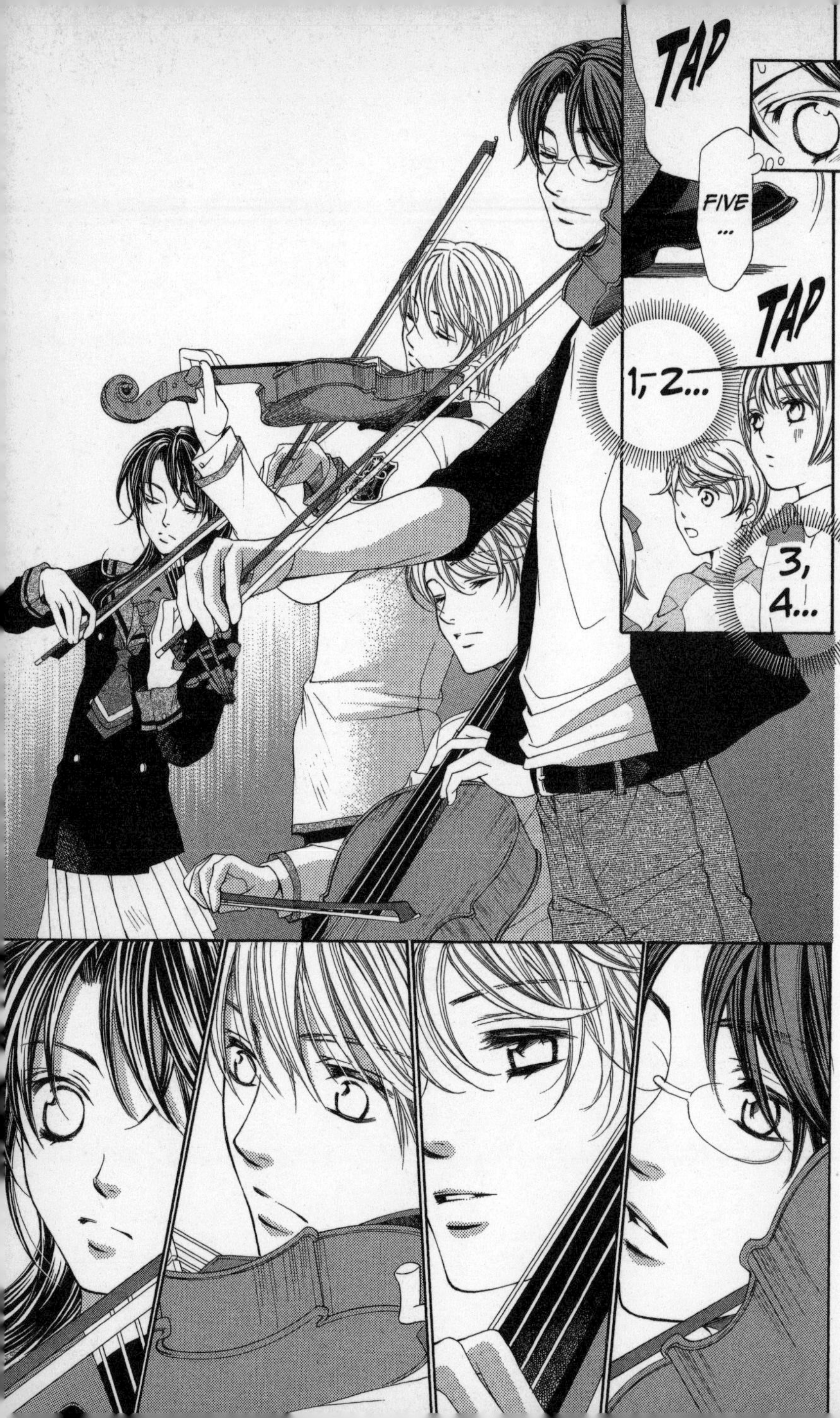
TAP
FIVE ...
TAP
1, 2...
3, 4...

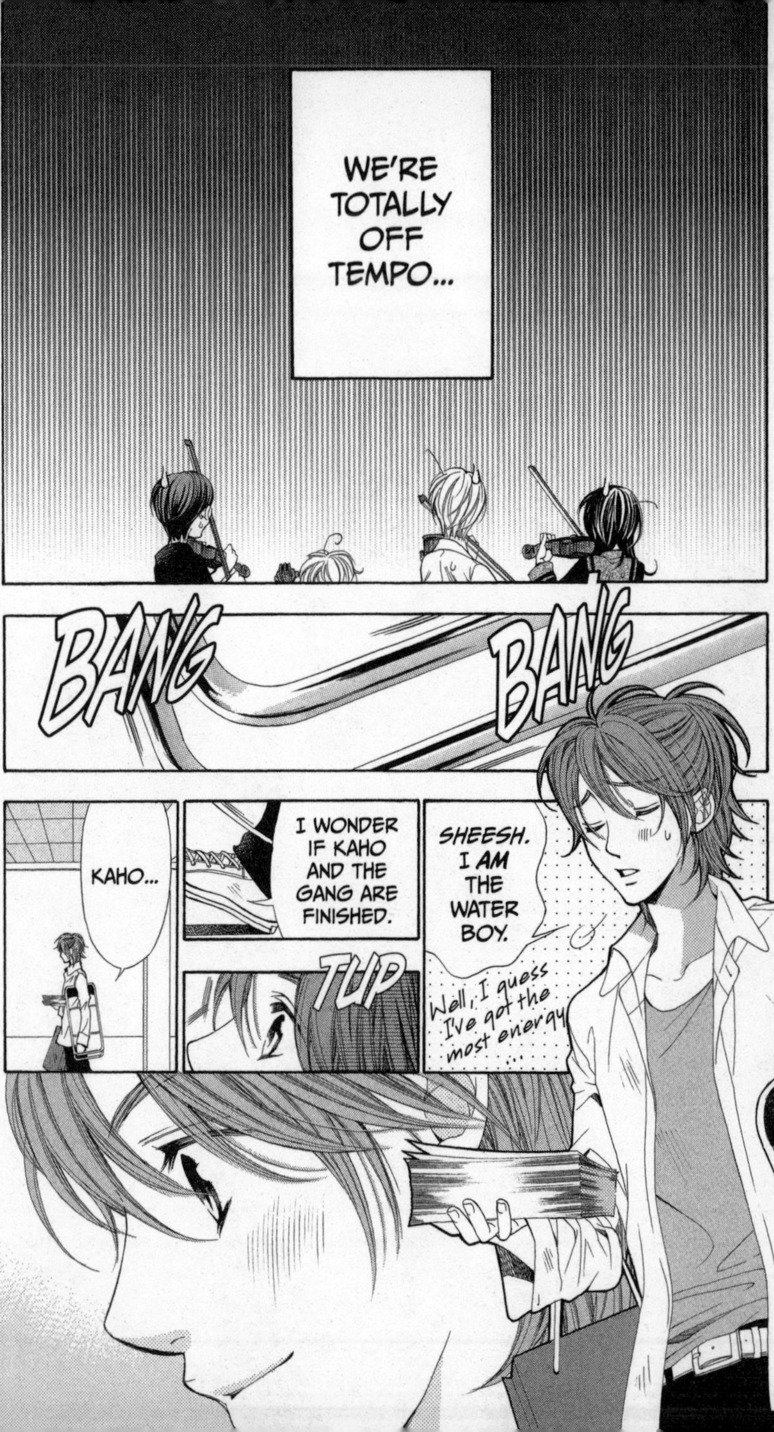
WE'RE TOTALLY OFF TEMPO...
BANG
BANG
SHEESH. I *AM* THE WATER BOY.
Well, I guess I've got the most energy...
I WONDER IF KAHO AND THE GANG ARE FINISHED.
TUP
KAHO...

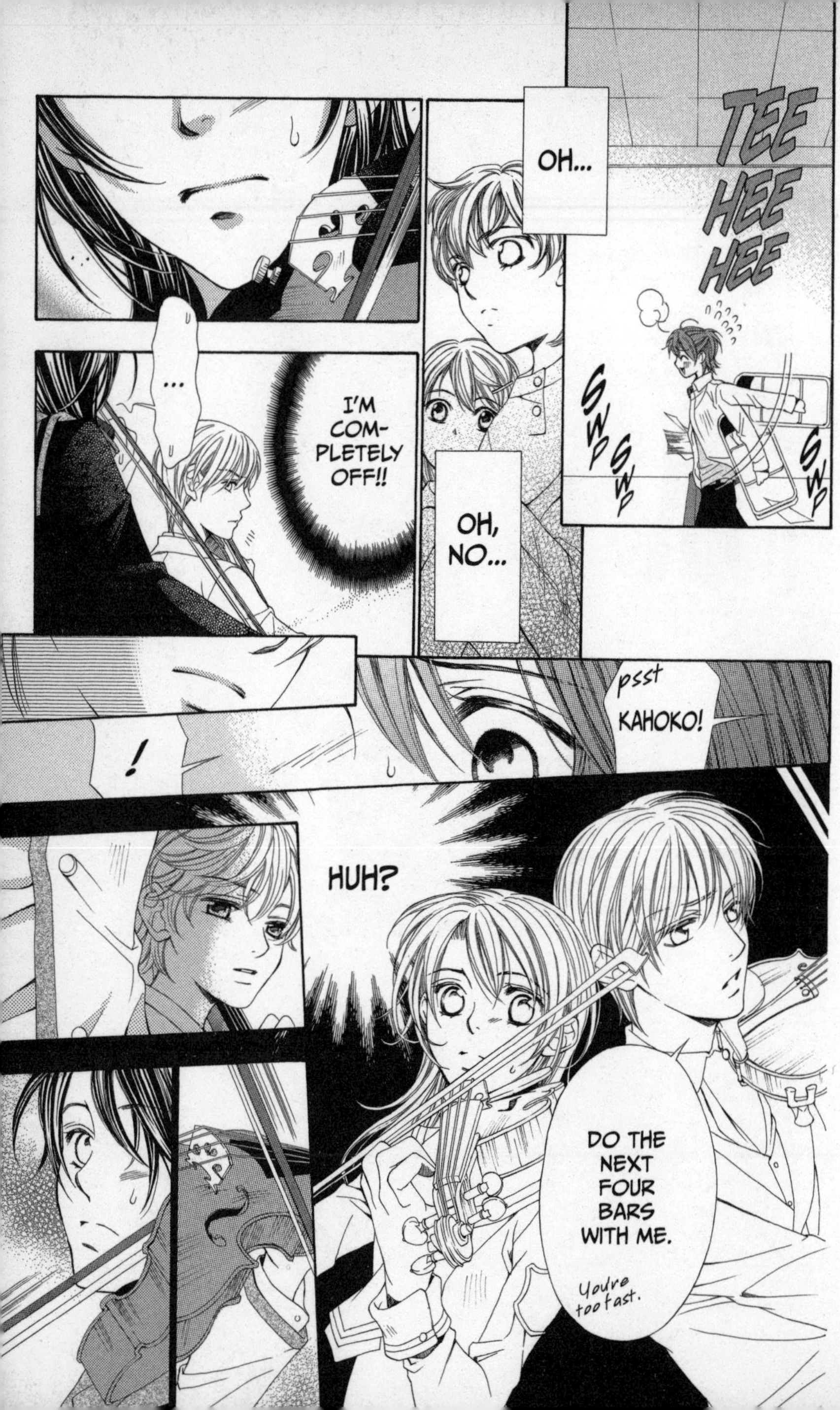
TEE HEE HEE
SWP SWP SWP SWP
OH...
OH, NO...
...
I'M COMPLETELY OFF!!
psst KAHOKO!
!
HUH?
DO THE NEXT FOUR BARS WITH ME.
You're too fast.

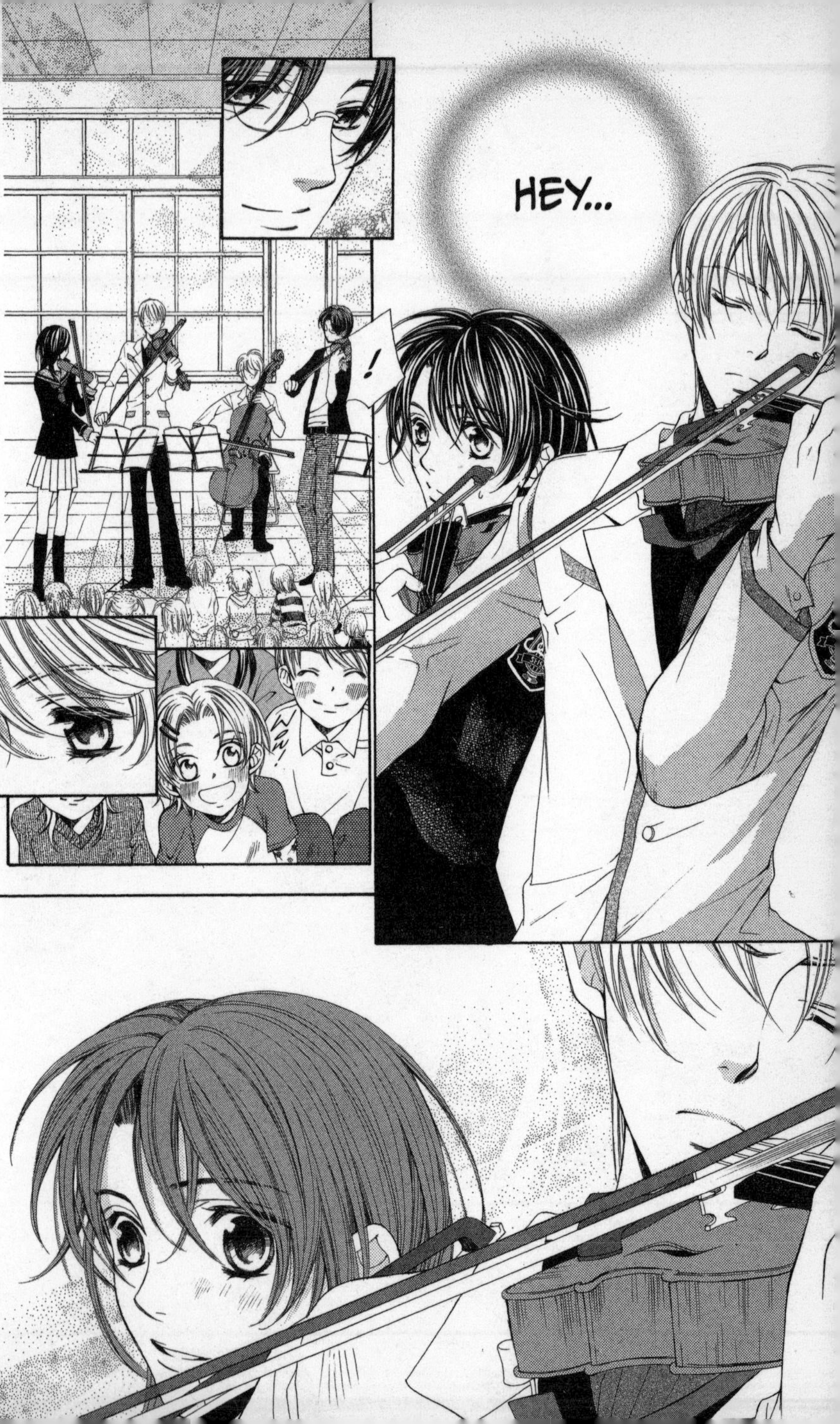
HEY...
!
WOW!

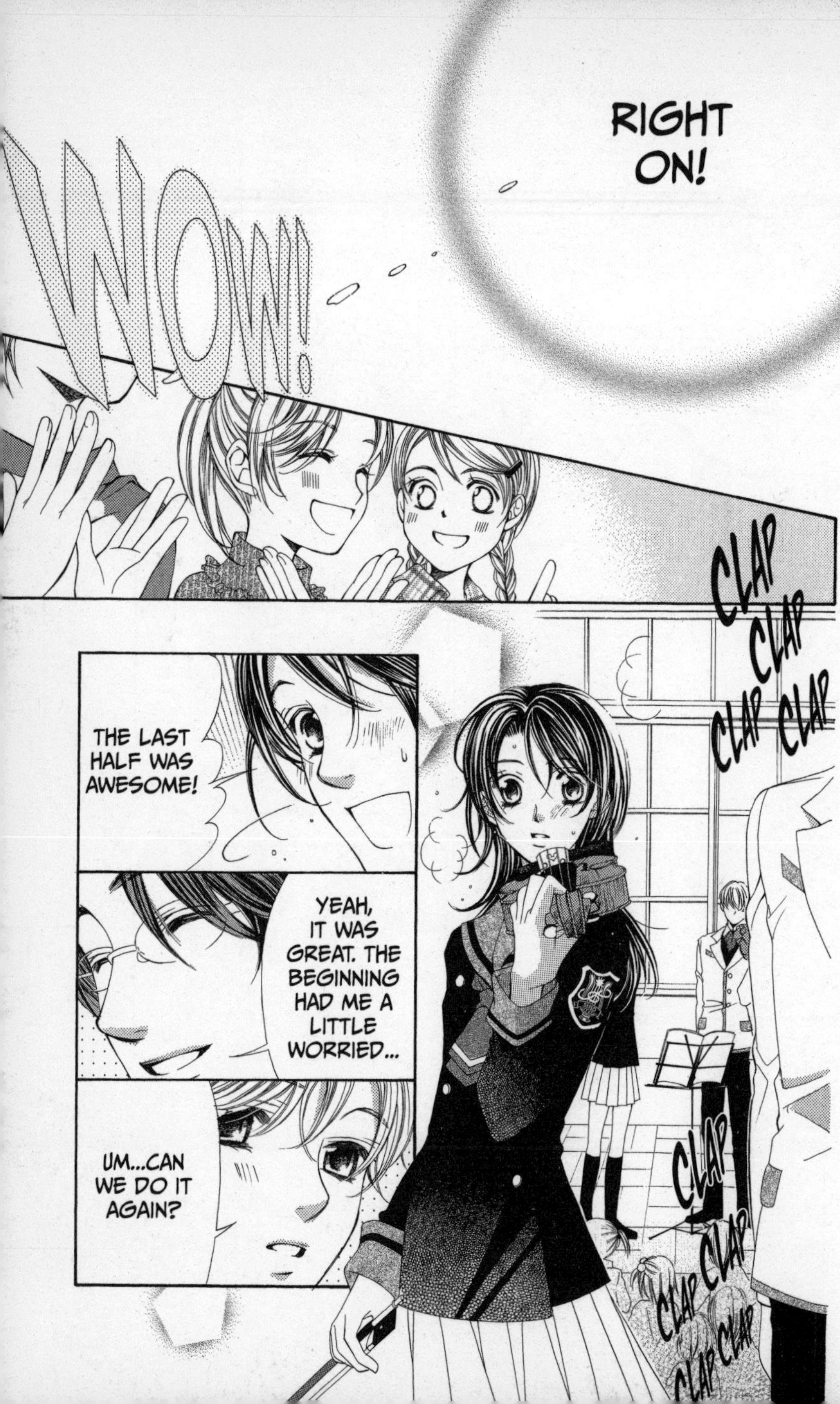
RIGHT ON!
WOW!!
CLAP CLAP CLAP CLAP
CLAP CLAP CLAP CLAP CLAP CLAP
THE LAST HALF WAS AWESOME!
YEAH, IT WAS GREAT. THE BEGINNING HAD ME A LITTLE WORRIED...
UM...CAN WE DO IT AGAIN?

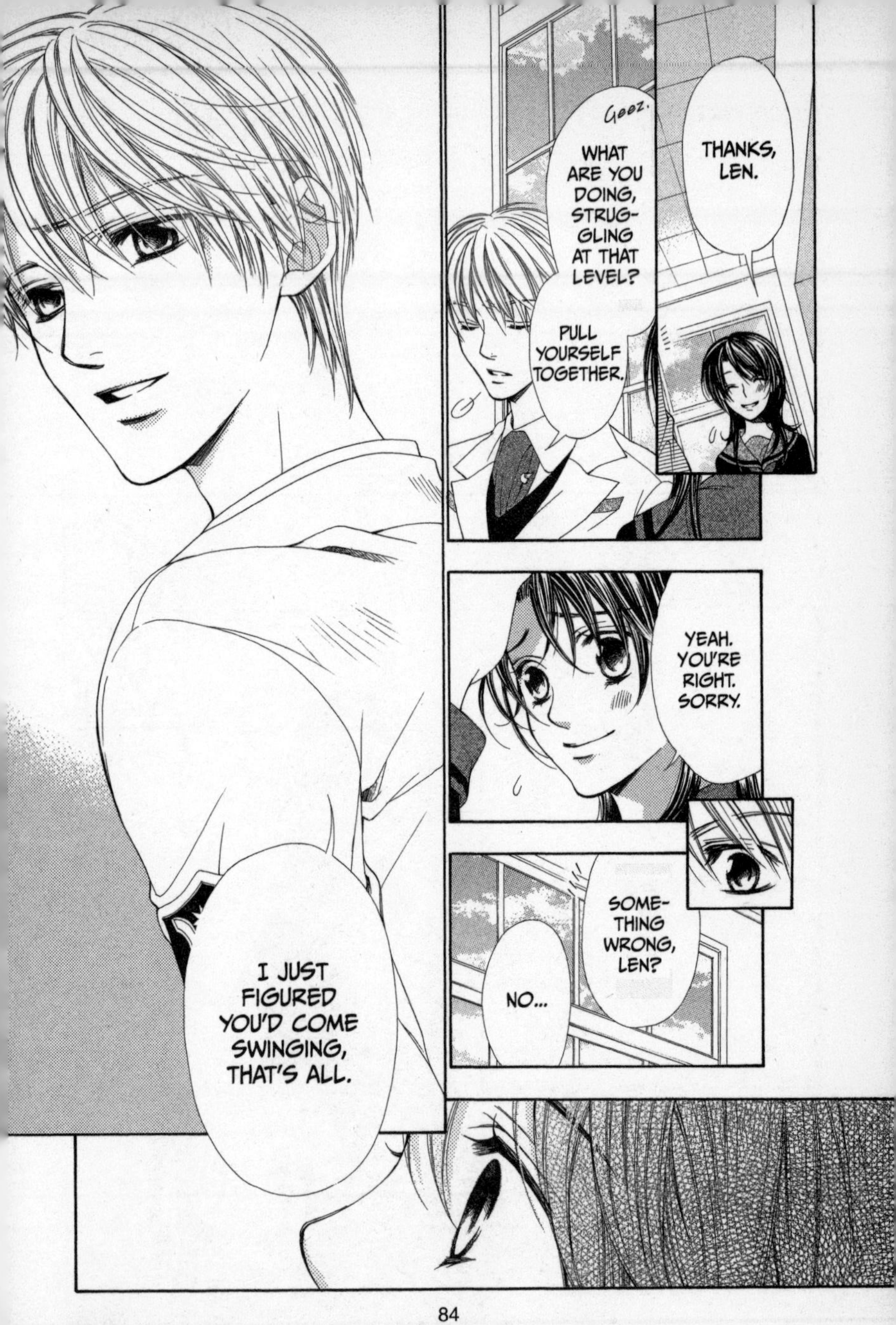
THANKS, LEN.
Geez.
WHAT ARE YOU DOING, STRUGGLING AT THAT LEVEL?
PULL YOURSELF TOGETHER.
YEAH. YOU'RE RIGHT. SORRY.
SOMETHING WRONG, LEN?
NO...
I JUST FIGURED YOU'D COME SWINGING, THAT'S ALL.

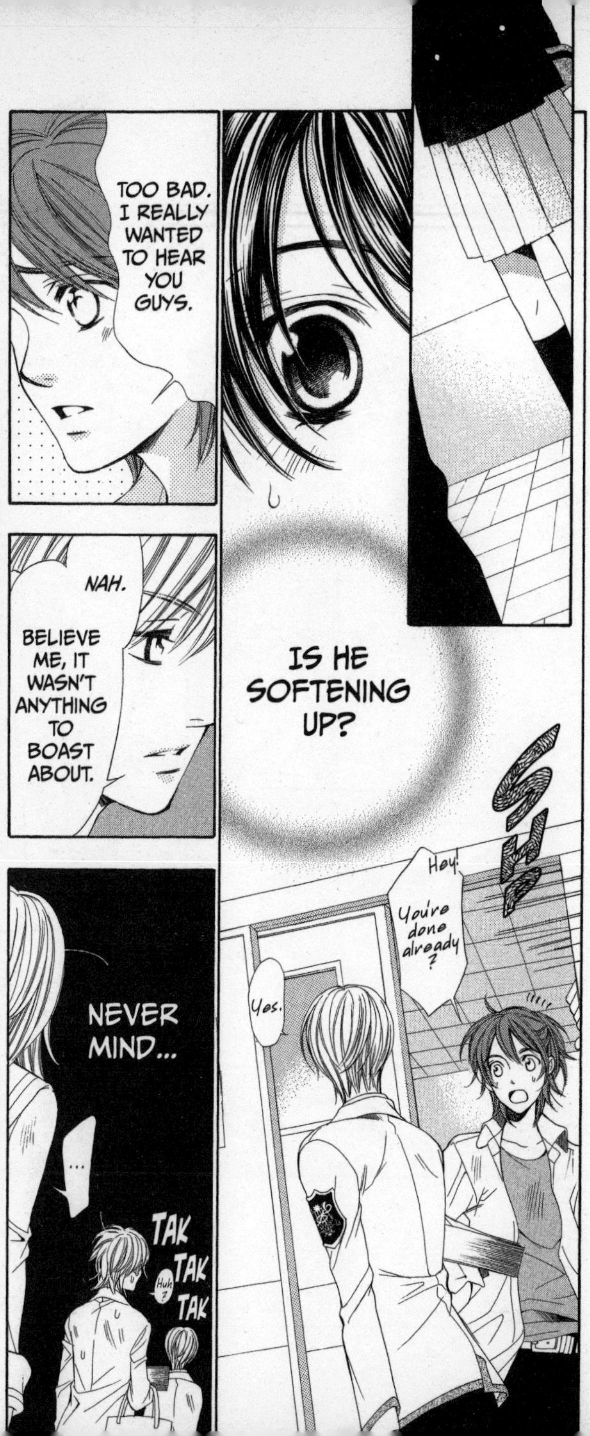
IS HE SOFTENING UP?
SHH
Hey!
You're done already?
Yes.
TOO BAD. I REALLY WANTED TO HEAR YOU GUYS.
NAH.
BELIEVE ME, IT WASN'T ANYTHING TO BOAST ABOUT.
NEVER MIND...
...
TAK TAK TAK
Huh?

THREE

I almost didn't make the deadline for Measure 26. It's true. (lol) It's not that I was given less time, but I didn't take into account how many violins I'd have to draw. Even my assistants commented on what a close call it was... I owe them big time.

Thank you!

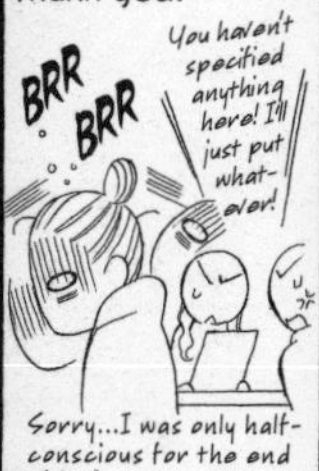
You haven't specified anything here! I'll just put whatever!
BRR BRR
Sorry...I was only half-conscious for the end of it.

Actually, I'm always cutting it pretty close with the deadlines. I keep telling myself I'll get better. I'm sorry to always keep you on the edge of your seat, Mr. Editor!

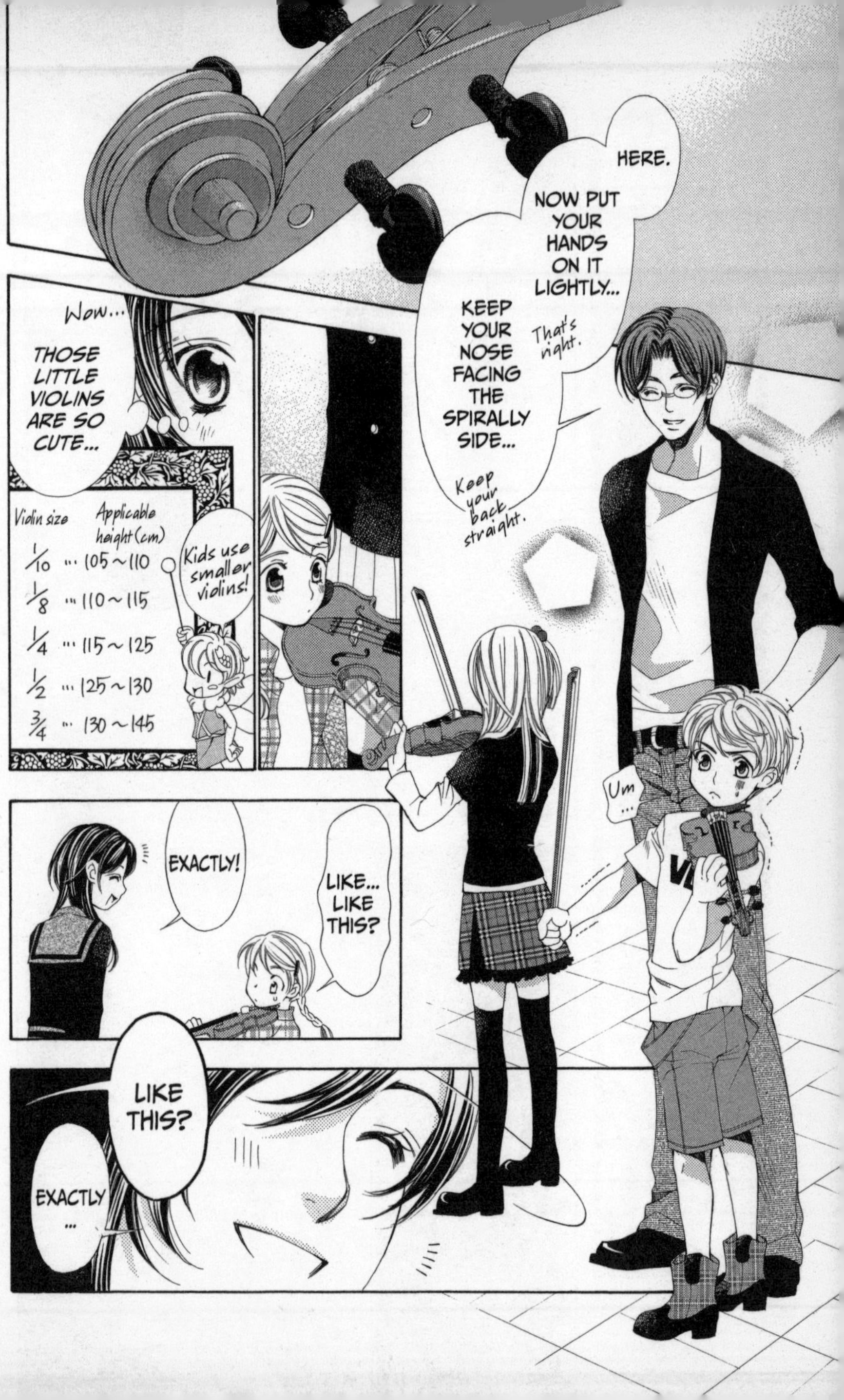

HERE.
NOW PUT YOUR HANDS ON IT LIGHTLY...
KEEP YOUR NOSE FACING THE SPIRALLY SIDE...
That's right.
Keep your back straight.
Um ...
Violin size
Applicable height (cm)
1/10 ... 105~110
1/8 ... 110~115
1/4 ... 115~125
1/2 ... 125~130
3/4 ... 130~145
Kids use smaller violins!
Wow...
THOSE LITTLE VIOLINS ARE SO CUTE...
LIKE... LIKE THIS?
EXACTLY!
LIKE THIS?
EXACTLY ...

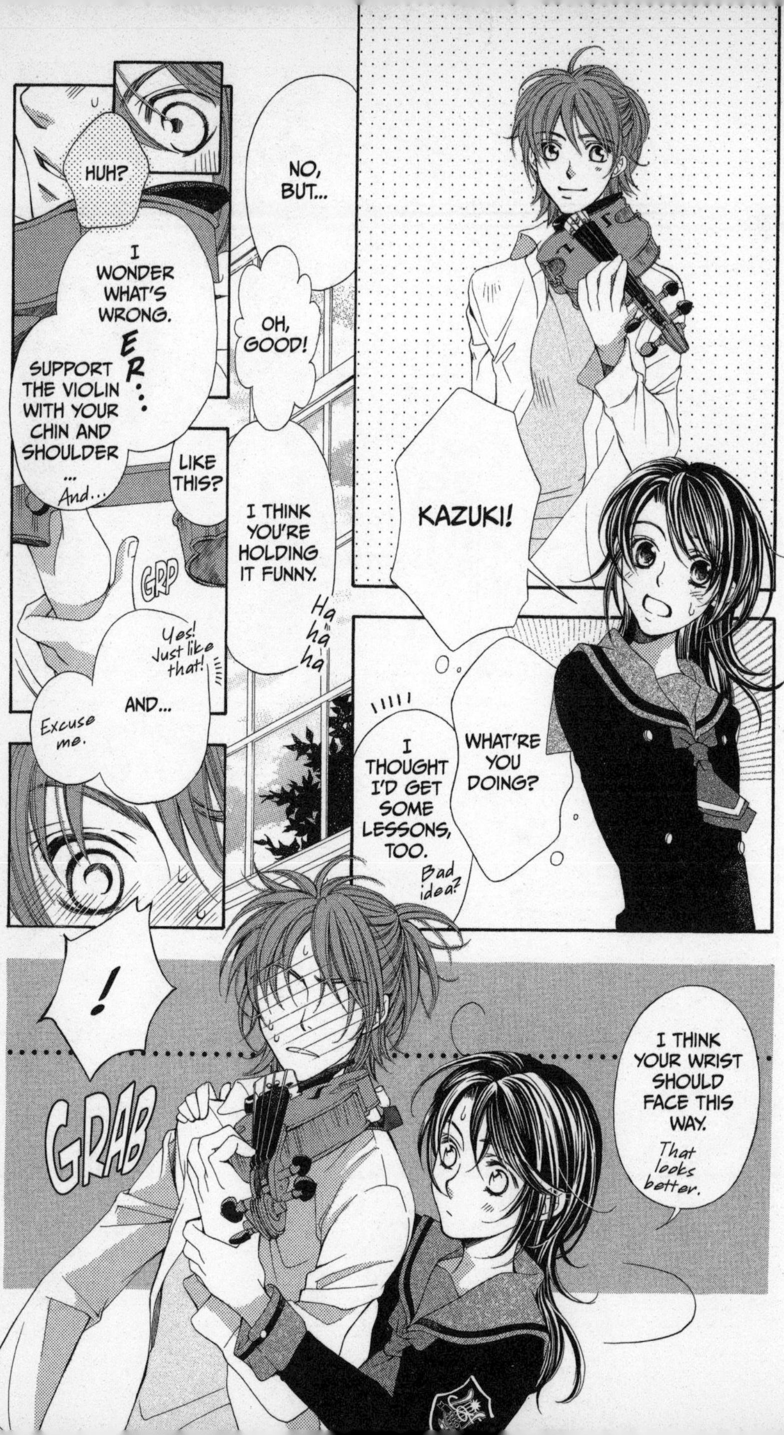
KAZUKI!
WHAT'RE YOU DOING?
I THOUGHT I'D GET SOME LESSONS, TOO.
Bad idea?
NO, BUT...
OH, GOOD!
I THINK YOU'RE HOLDING IT FUNNY.
Ha ha ha
HUH?
I WONDER WHAT'S WRONG.
ER...
SUPPORT THE VIOLIN WITH YOUR CHIN AND SHOULDER...
And...
LIKE THIS?
GRP
Yes! Just like that!
AND...
Excuse me.
!
I THINK YOUR WRIST SHOULD FACE THIS WAY.
That looks better.
GRAB

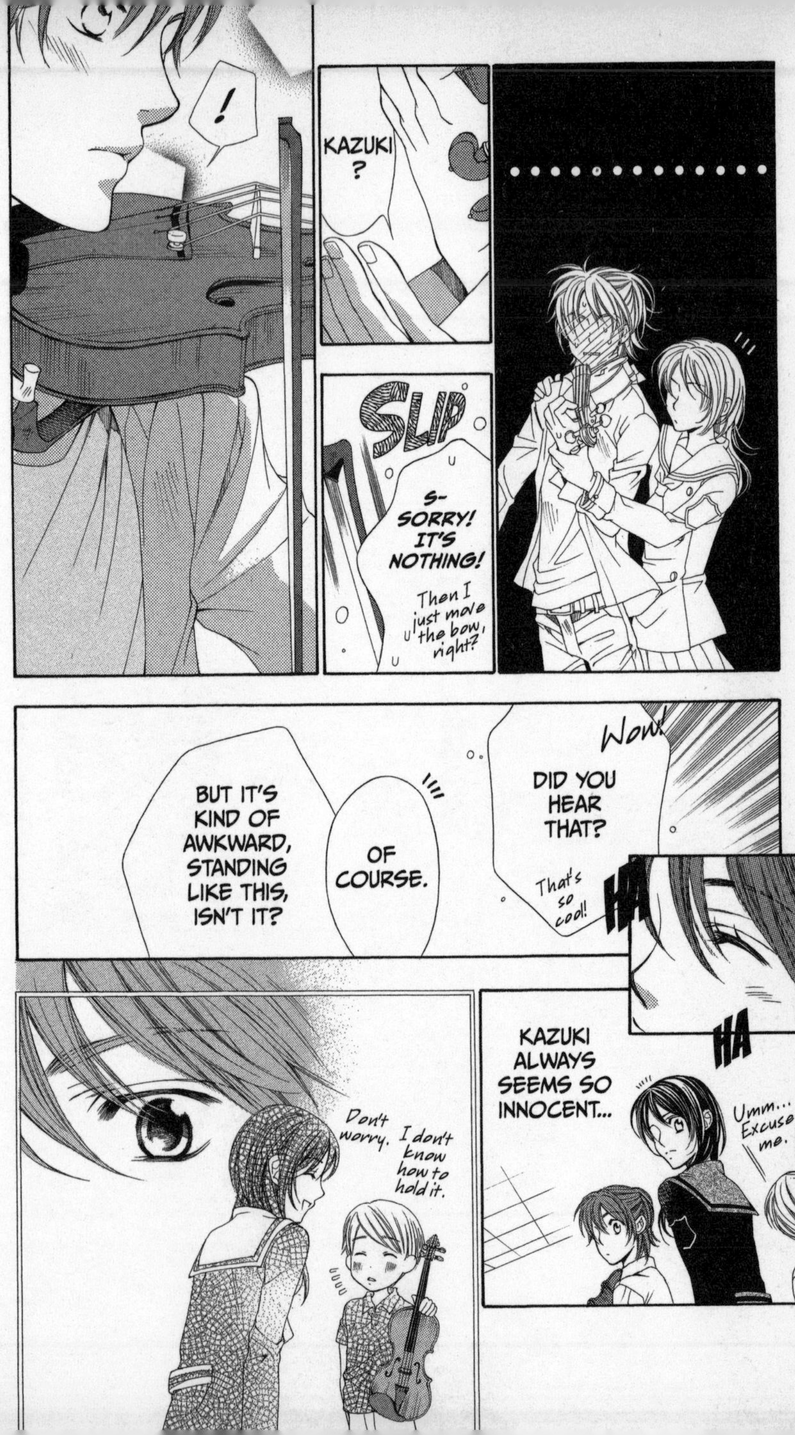

• • • • • • • • • • • • •
KAZUKI?
SLIP
S-SORRY! IT'S NOTHING!
Then I just move the bow, right?
!
Wow!
DID YOU HEAR THAT?
That's so cool!
OF COURSE.
BUT IT'S KIND OF AWKWARD, STANDING LIKE THIS, ISN'T IT?
HA
HA
Umm... Excuse me.
KAZUKI ALWAYS SEEMS SO INNOCENT...
Don't worry.
I don't know how to hold it.

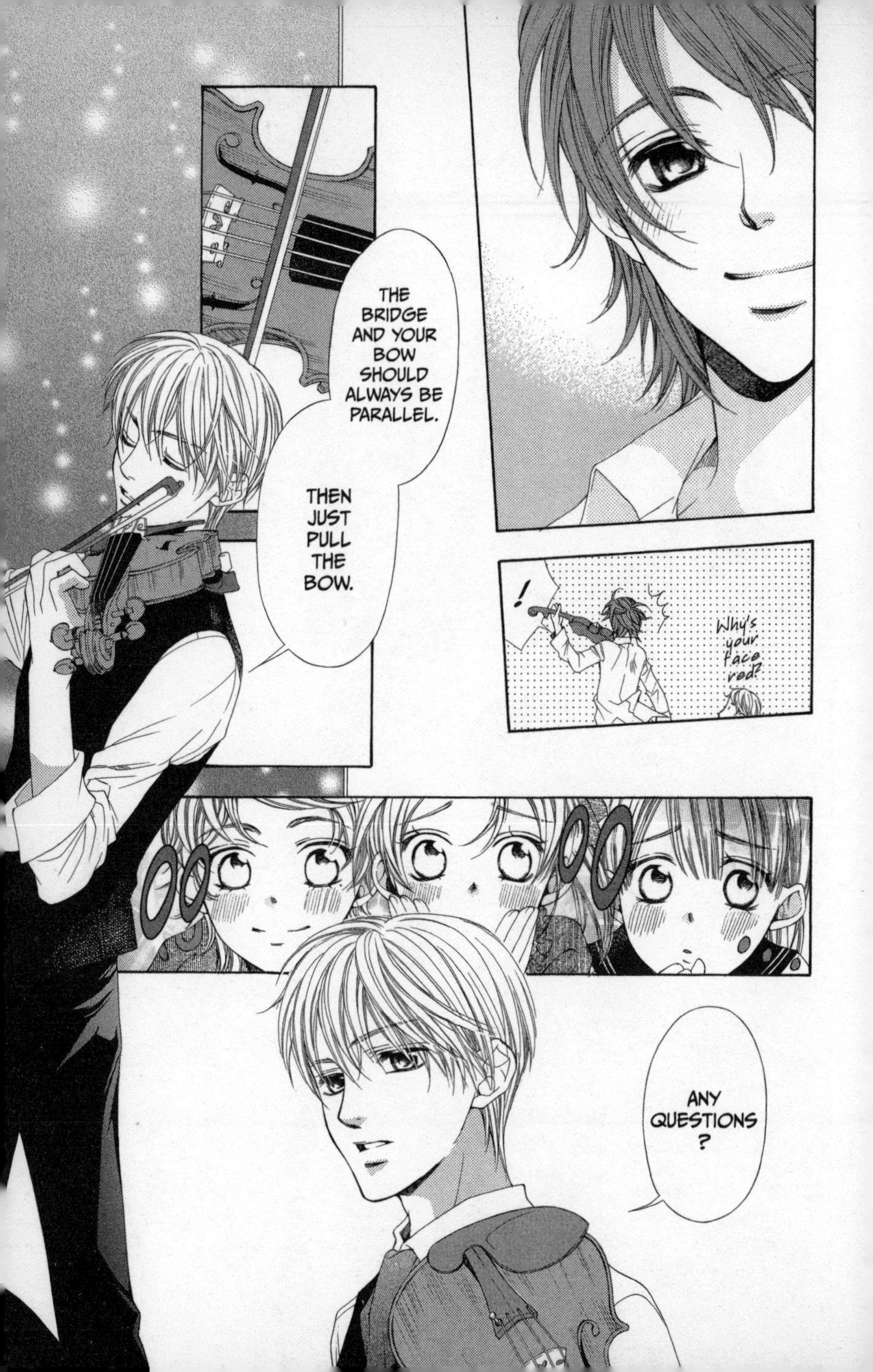
THE BRIDGE AND YOUR BOW SHOULD ALWAYS BE PARALLEL.
THEN JUST PULL THE BOW.
!
Why's your face red?
ANY QUESTIONS?

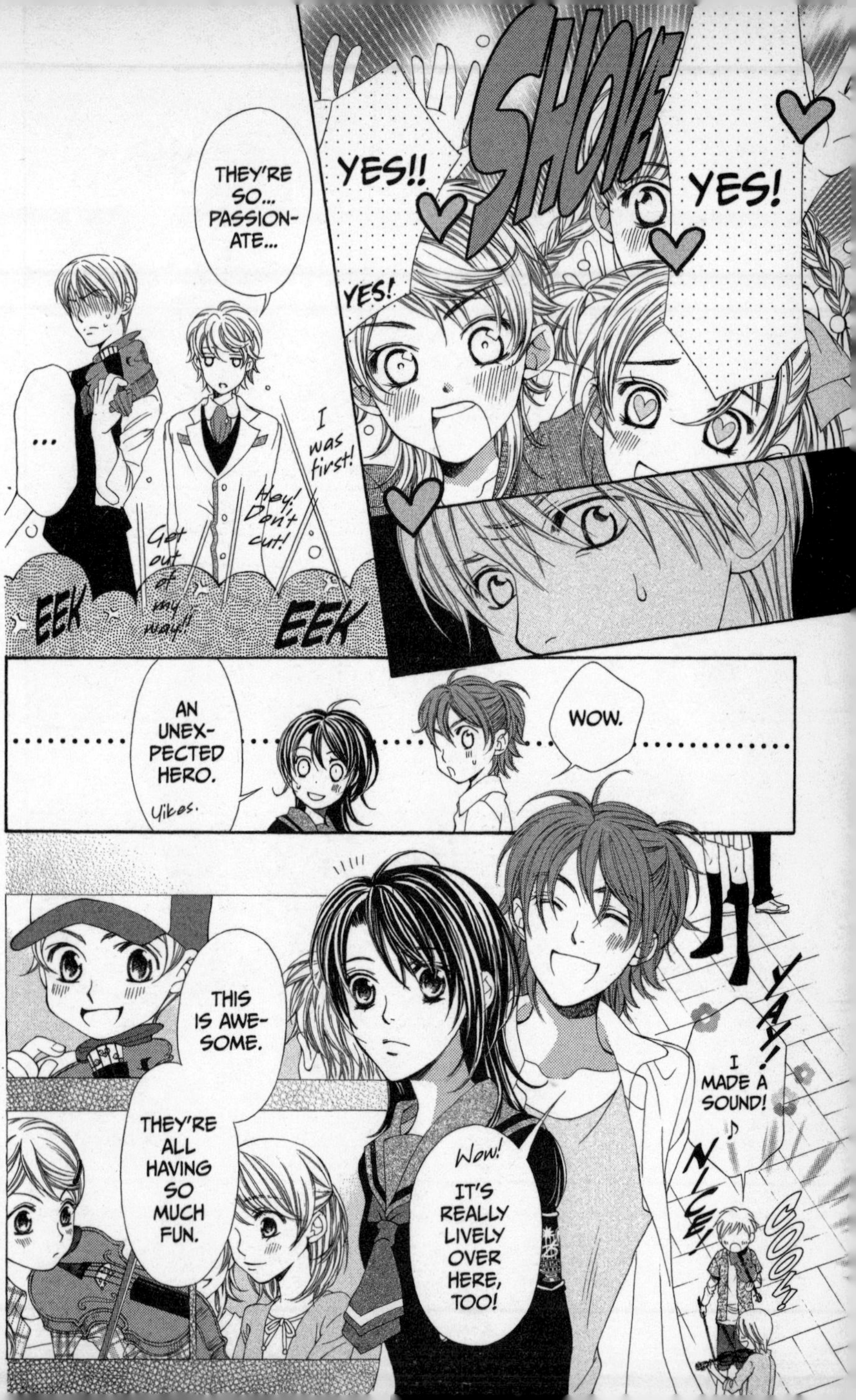
SHOVE
YES!
YES!!
YES!
THEY'RE SO... PASSION-ATE...
I was first!
Hey! Don't cut!
Get out of my way!!
EEK
EEK
...
WOW.
AN UNEXPECTED HERO.
Yikes.
YAY!
I MADE A SOUND! ♪
NICE!
OOOH
Wow!
IT'S REALLY LIVELY OVER HERE, TOO!
THIS IS AWE-SOME.
THEY'RE ALL HAVING SO MUCH FUN.

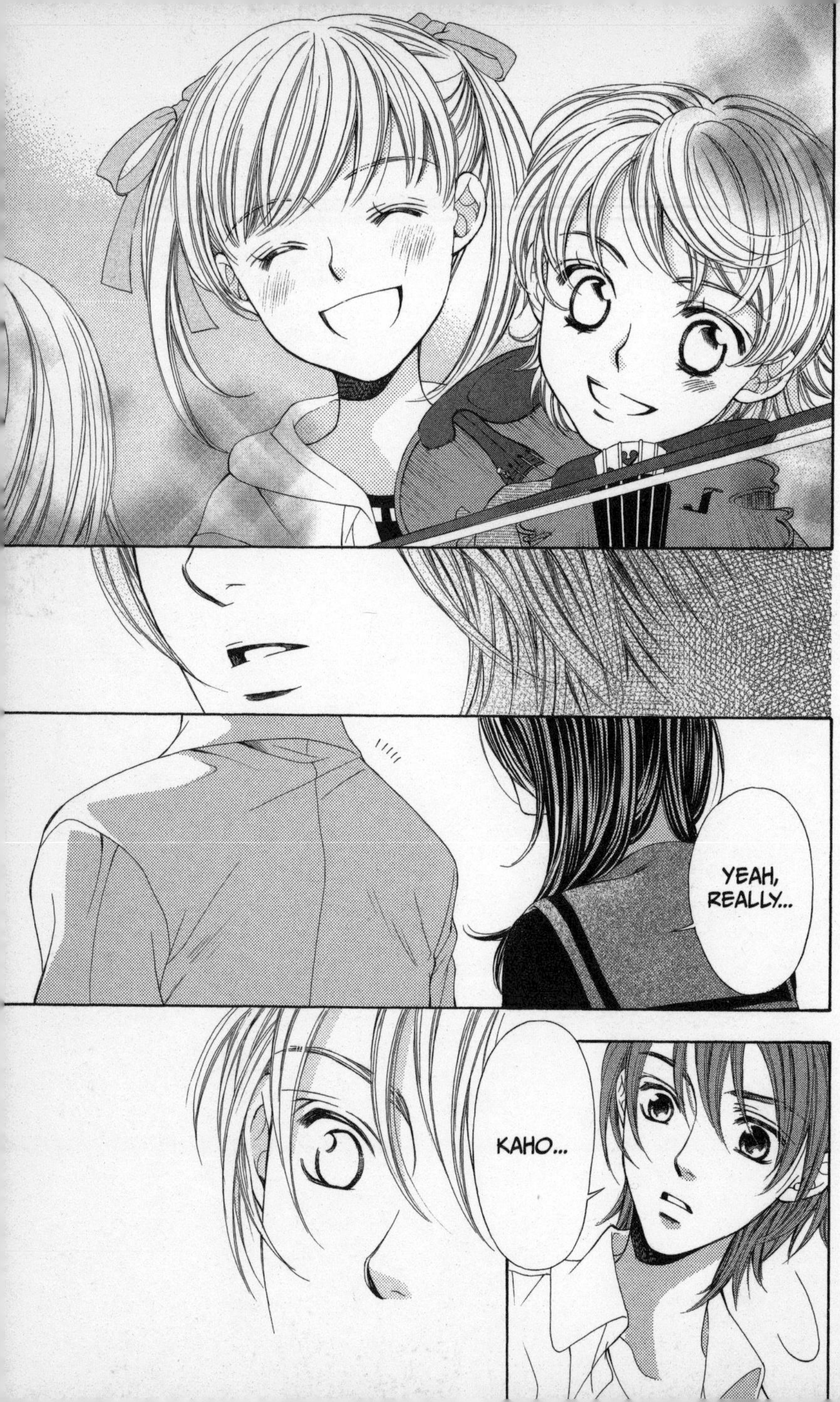
YEAH, REALLY...
KAHO...

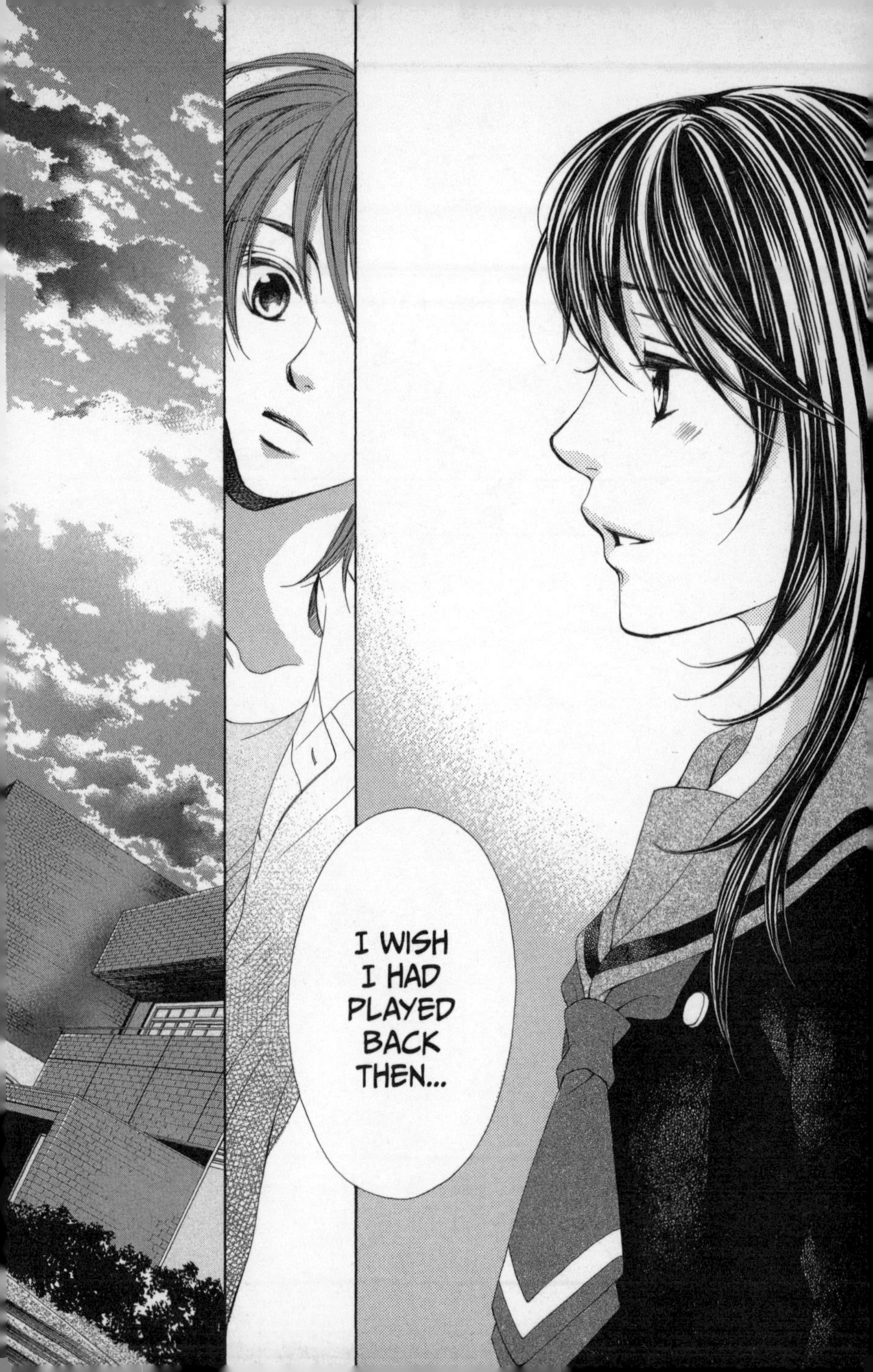
I WISH I HAD PLAYED BACK THEN...

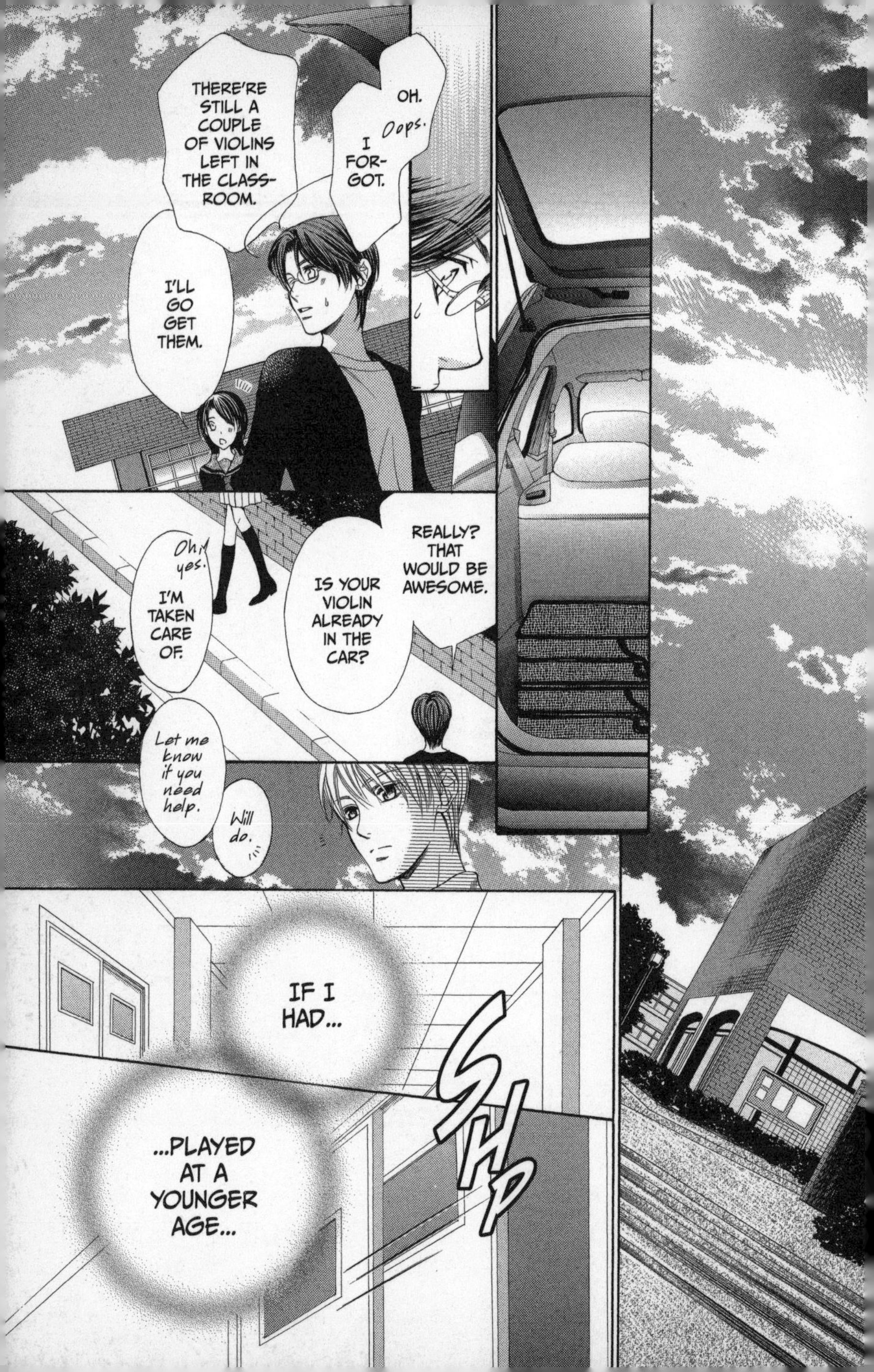
OH.
Oops.
I FOR-GOT.
THERE'RE STILL A COUPLE OF VIOLINS LEFT IN THE CLASS-ROOM.
I'LL GO GET THEM.
REALLY? THAT WOULD BE AWESOME.
IS YOUR VIOLIN ALREADY IN THE CAR?
Oh, yes.
I'M TAKEN CARE OF.
Let me know if you need help.
Will do.
IF I HAD...
...PLAYED AT A YOUNGER AGE...
SHP

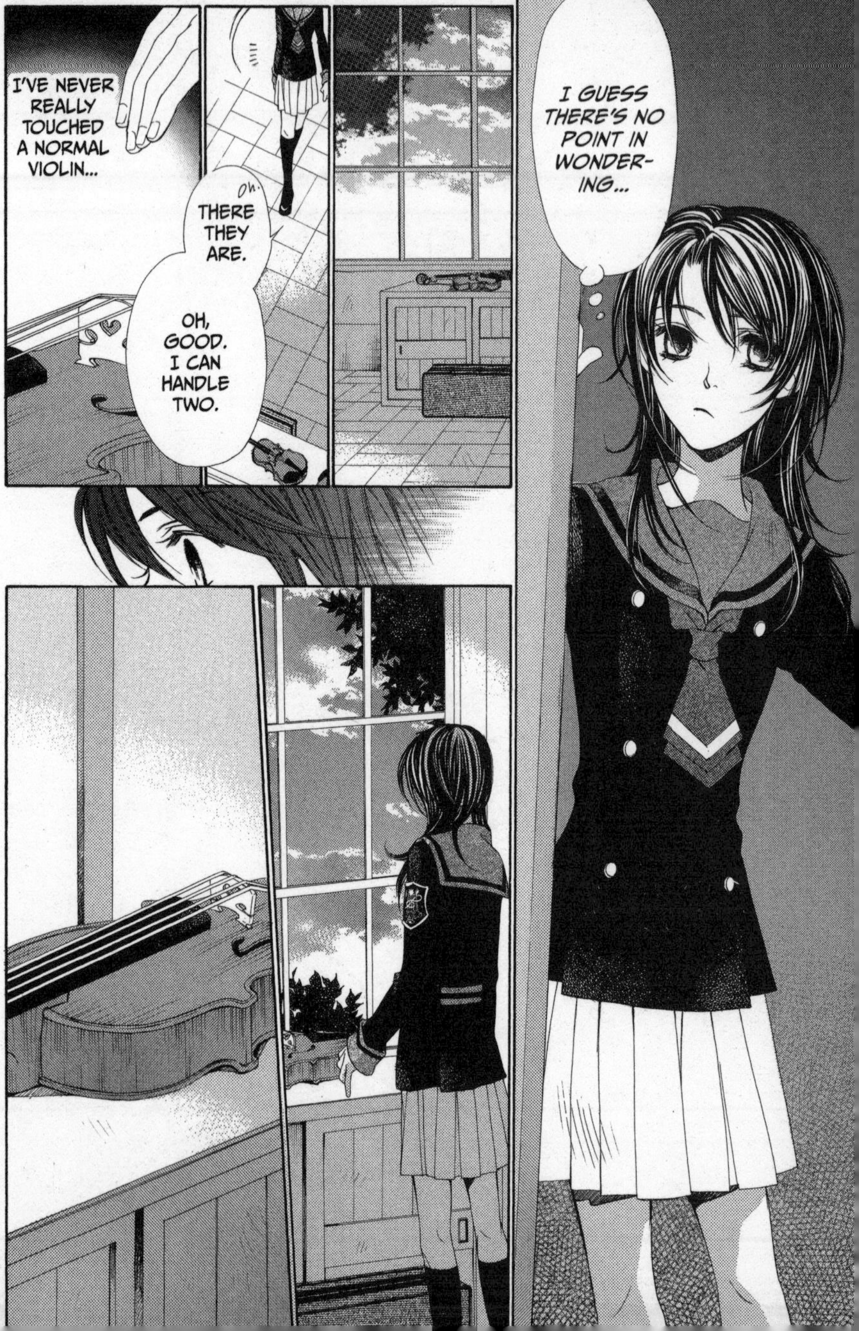
I GUESS THERE'S NO POINT IN WONDER-ING...
Oh.
THERE THEY ARE.
OH, GOOD. I CAN HANDLE TWO.
I'VE NEVER REALLY TOUCHED A NORMAL VIOLIN...

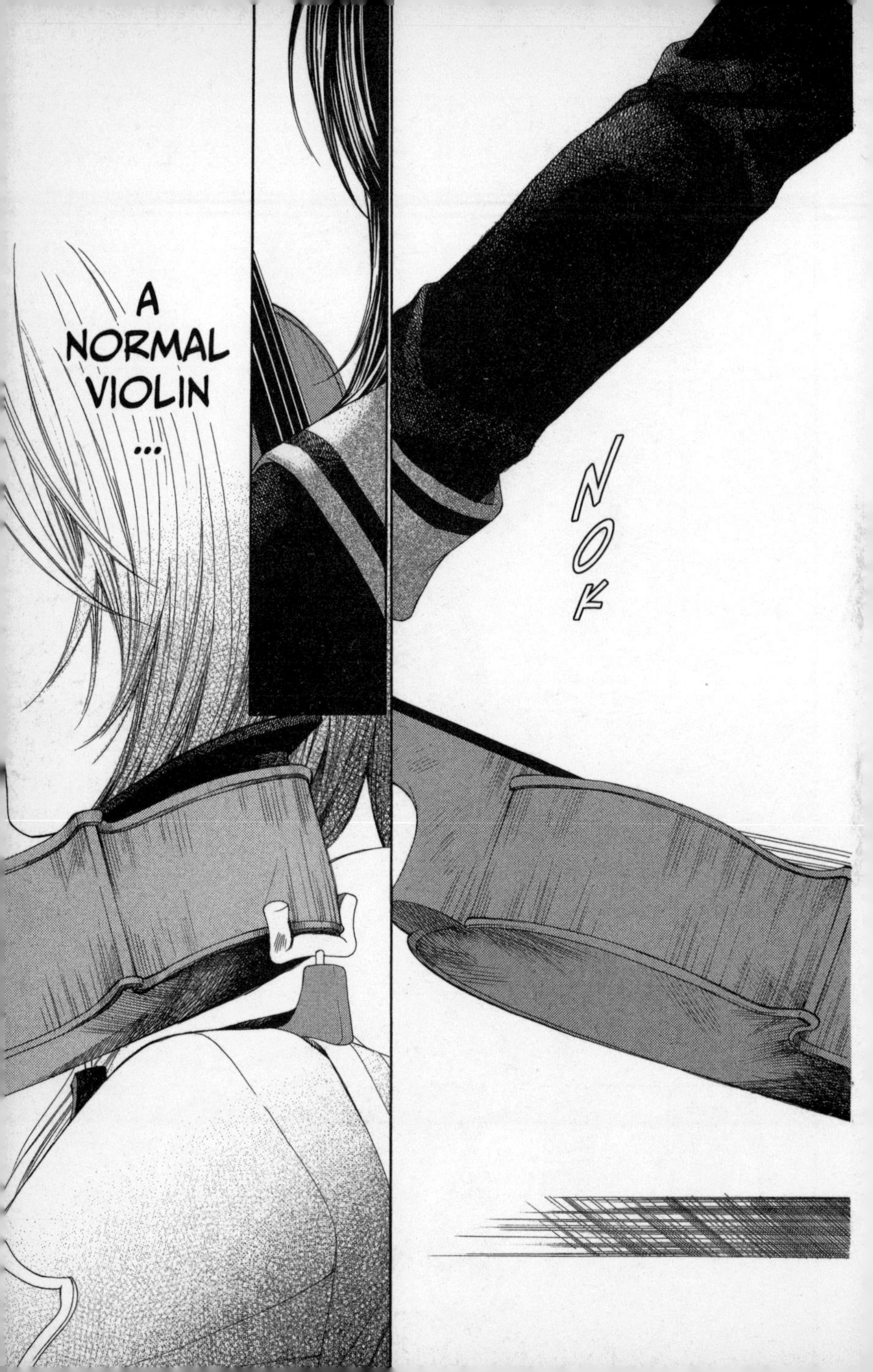
NOK
A NORMAL VIOLIN ...

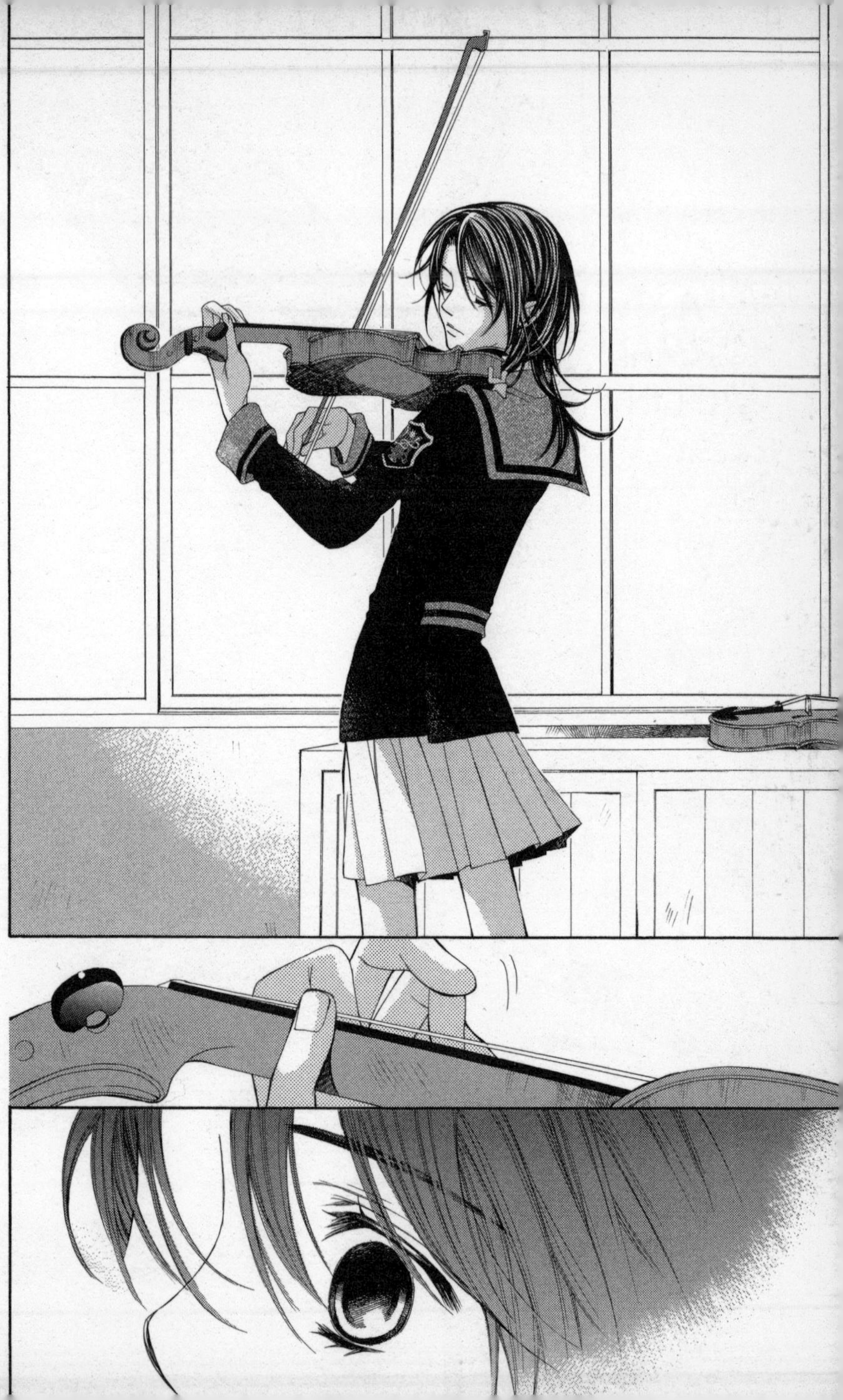

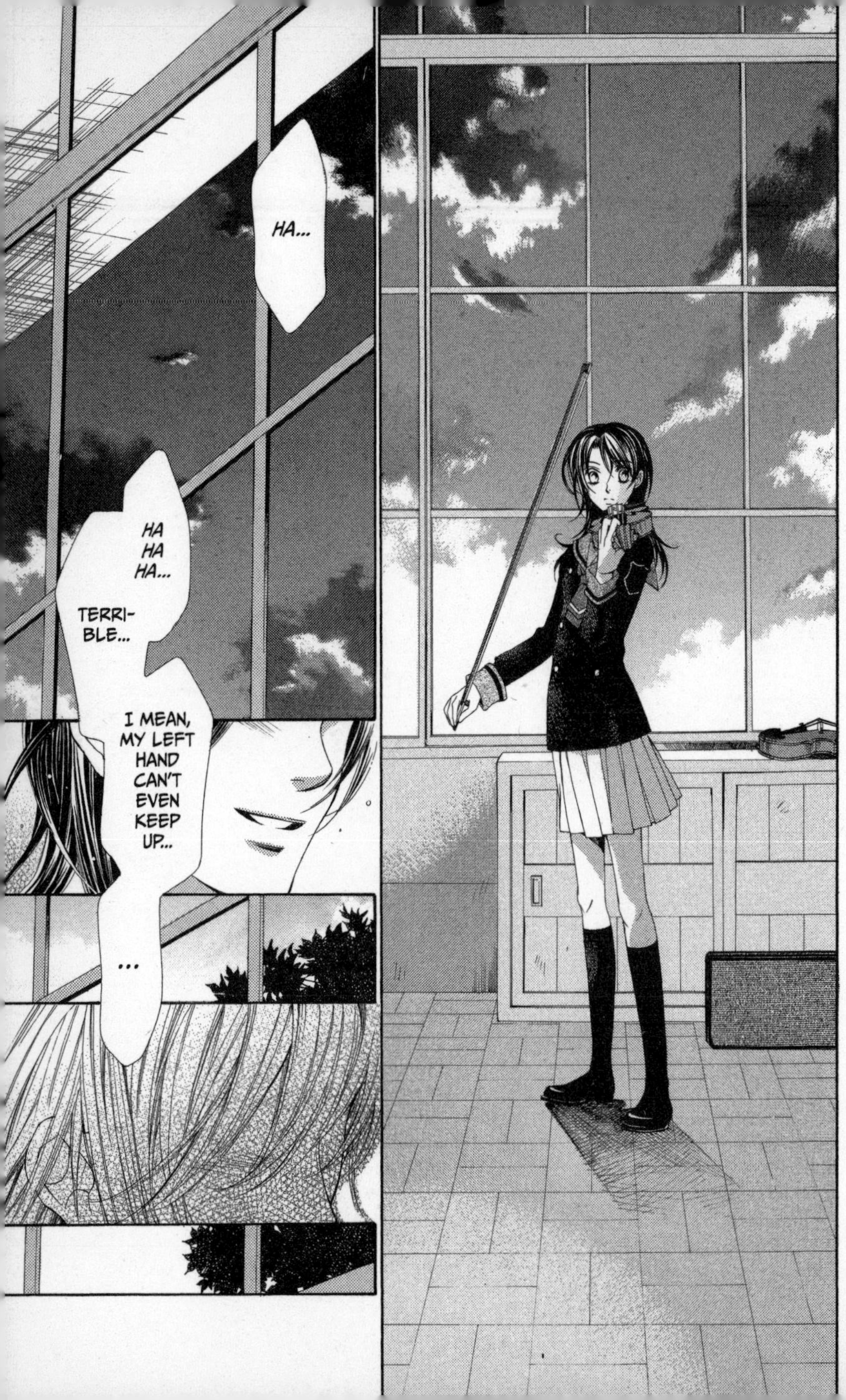
HA...
HA HA HA...
TERRI-BLE...
I MEAN, MY LEFT HAND CAN'T EVEN KEEP UP...
...

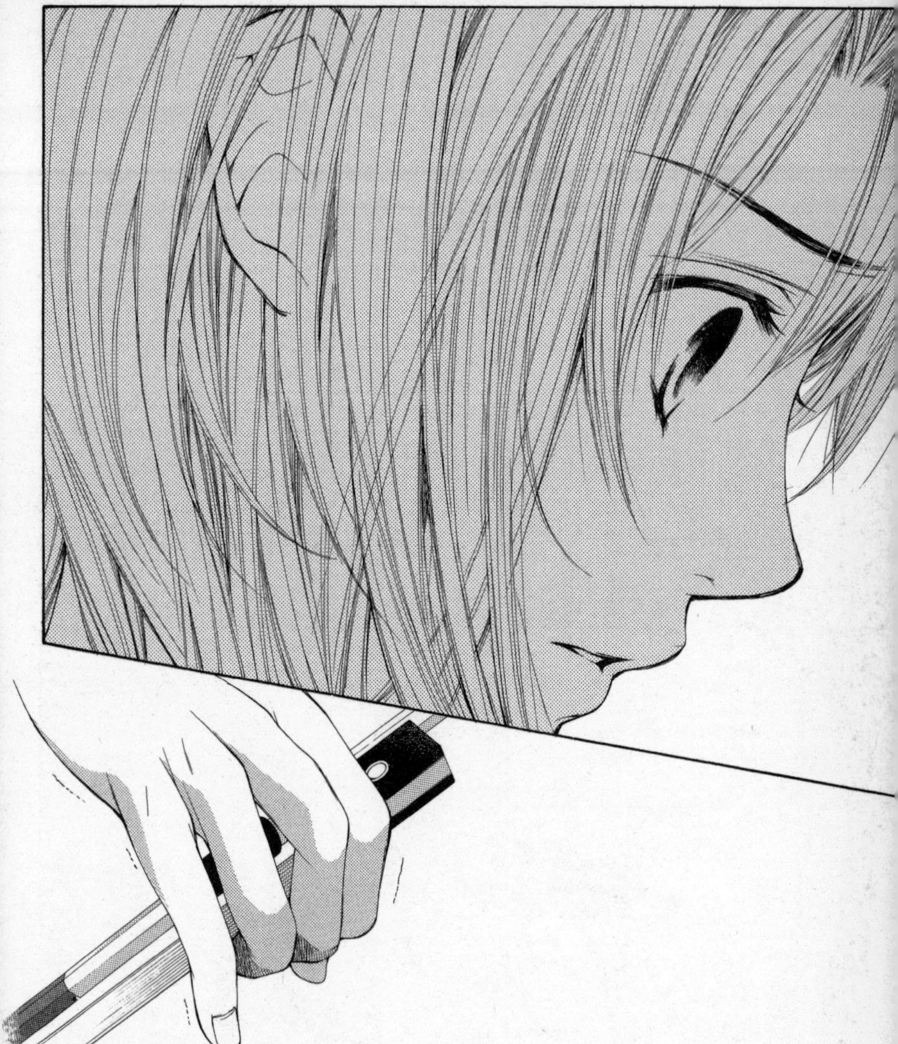

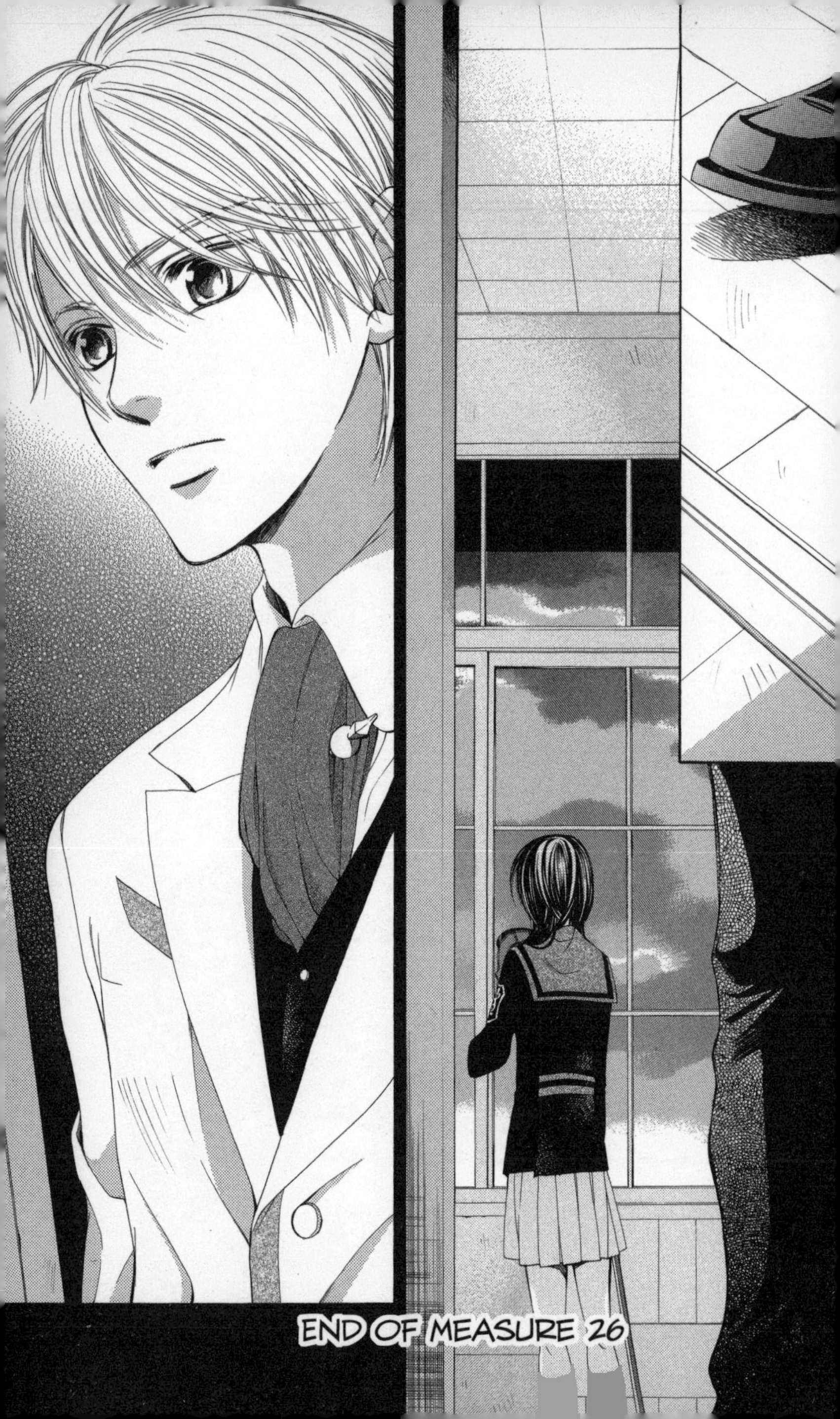
END OF MEASURE 26

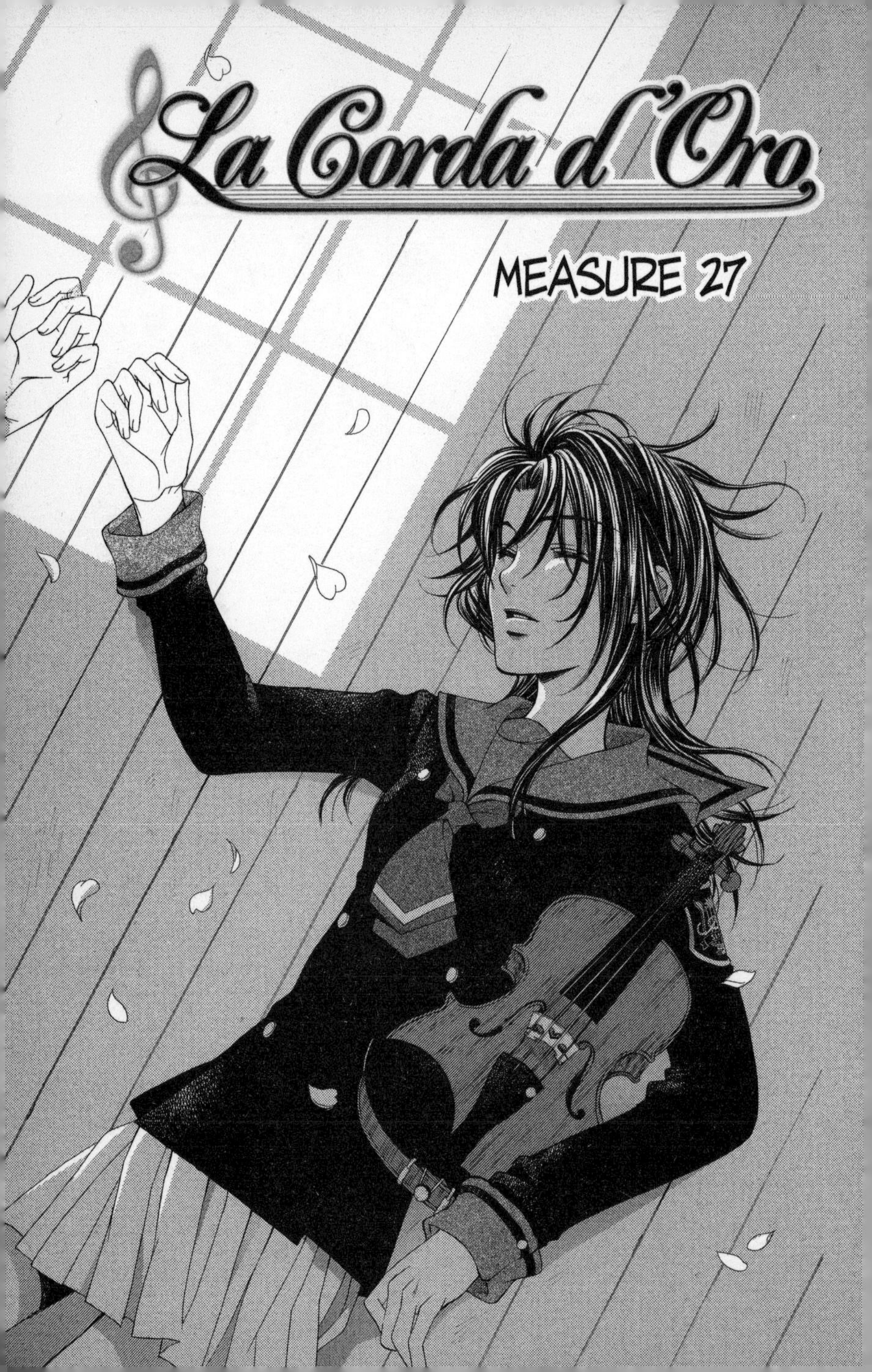
La Corda d'Oro
MEASURE 27

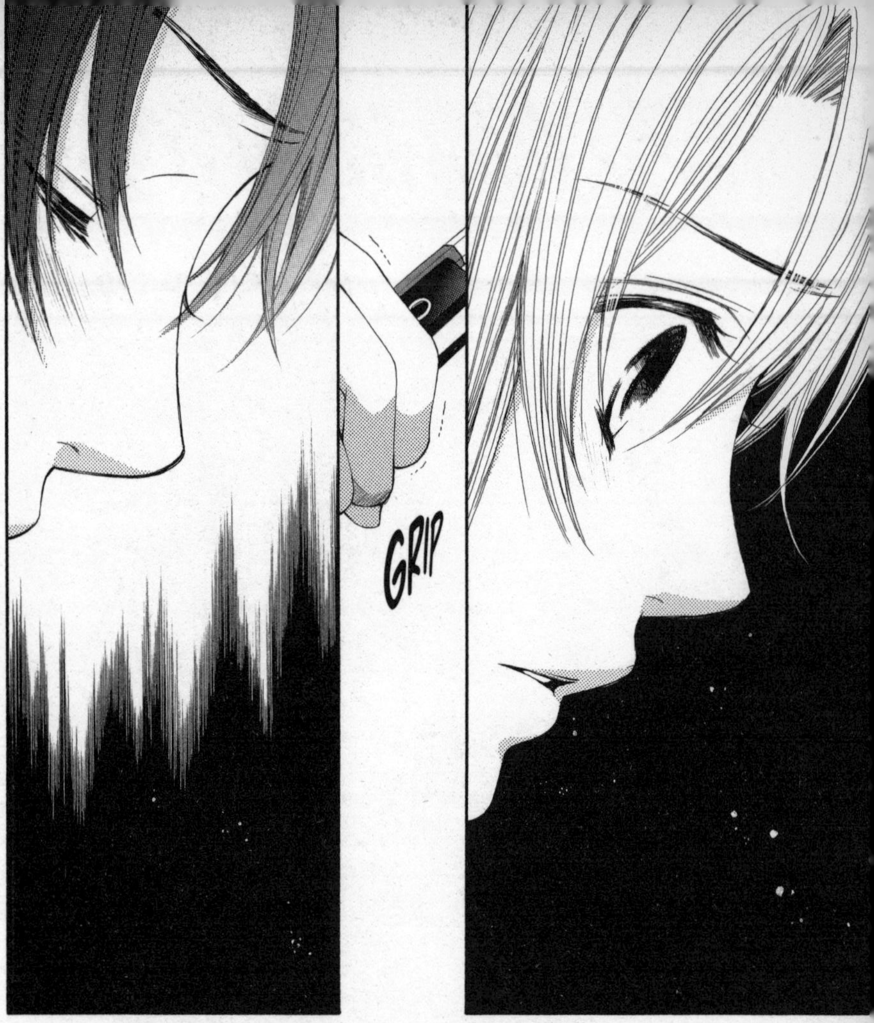
GRIP

Daily Happenings ⑲

Things I hate, part two...

The day after the deadline for Measure 27, I escaped the Kanto region for the first time in three years. I went to Kyushu. I had an insane schedule of hopping on an afternoon flight and coming back on a flight at noon the next day, but I had a lot of fun. I hadn't been to Kyushu since a class trip in high school. Wow. That was a long time ago. So... what I actually want to complain about are planes. The speeding up and taking off and waiting for the seatbelt sign to turn off...I just do not fare well. My whole face tenses up. Add some bad weather and turbulence to the mix and you've got me in tears. (I have only myself to blame...) However, I love bullet trains and trains in general! With my iPod in hand, I could ride forever! But I admit subways aren't much fun. This is all so irrelevant...I'm sorry.

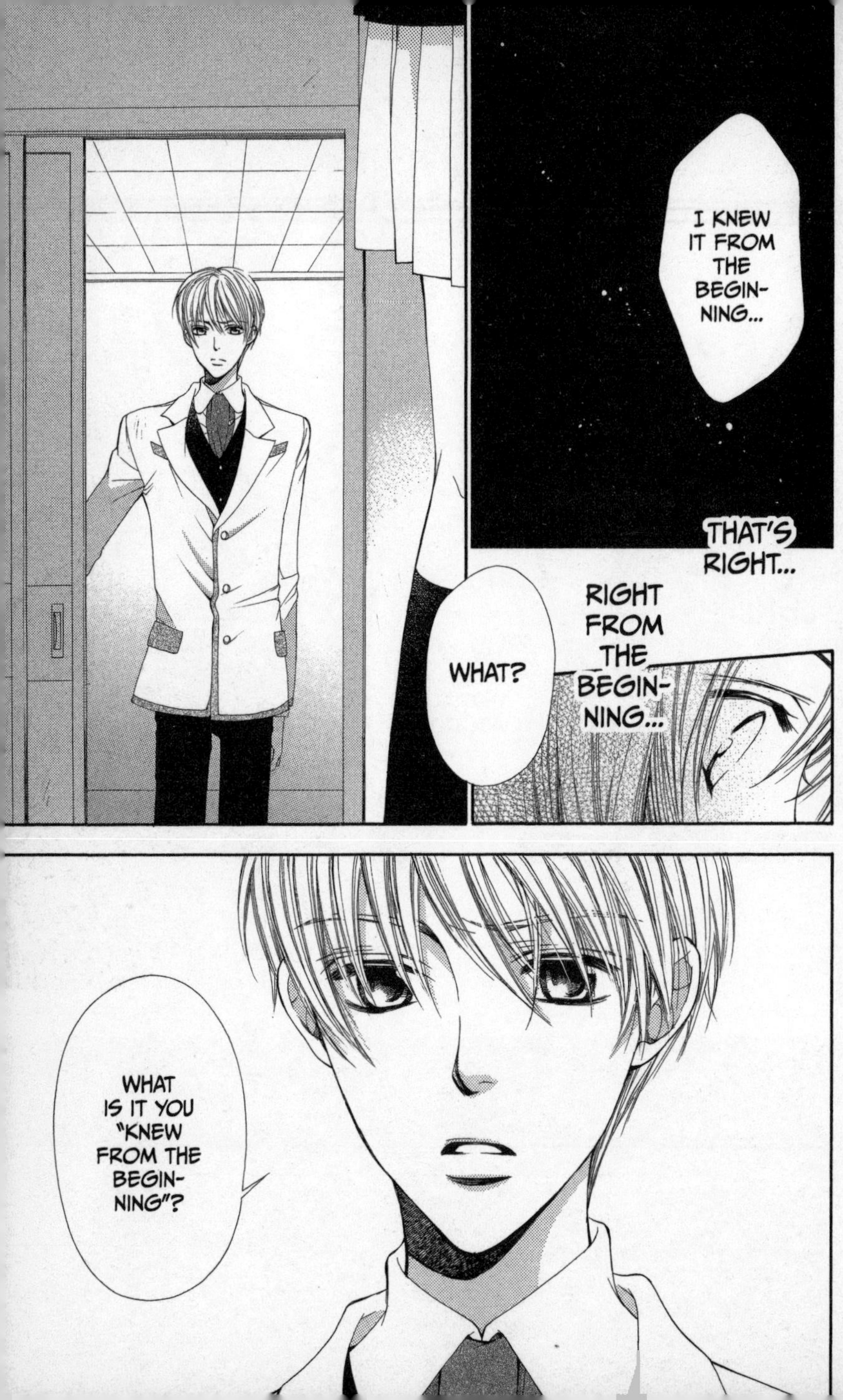
I KNEW IT FROM THE BEGIN-NING...
THAT'S RIGHT...
RIGHT FROM THE BEGIN-NING...
WHAT?
WHAT IS IT YOU "KNEW FROM THE BEGIN-NING"?

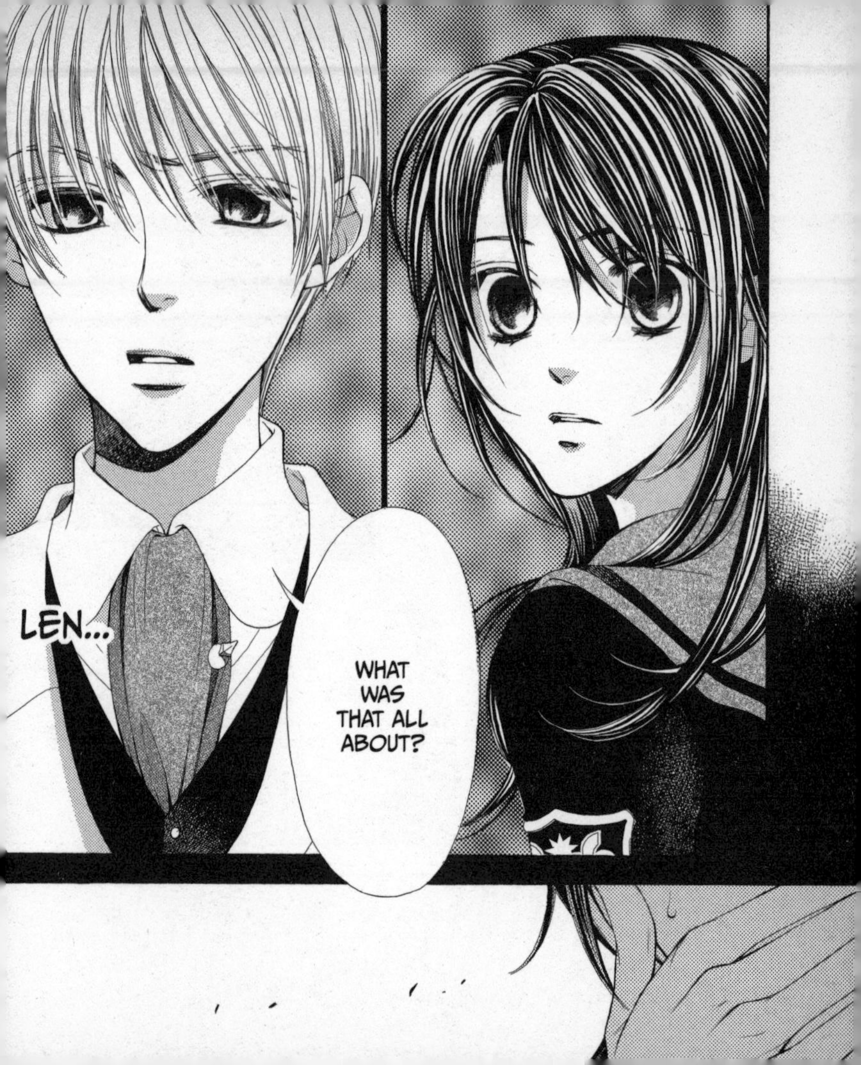
WHAT WAS THAT ALL ABOUT?
LEN...

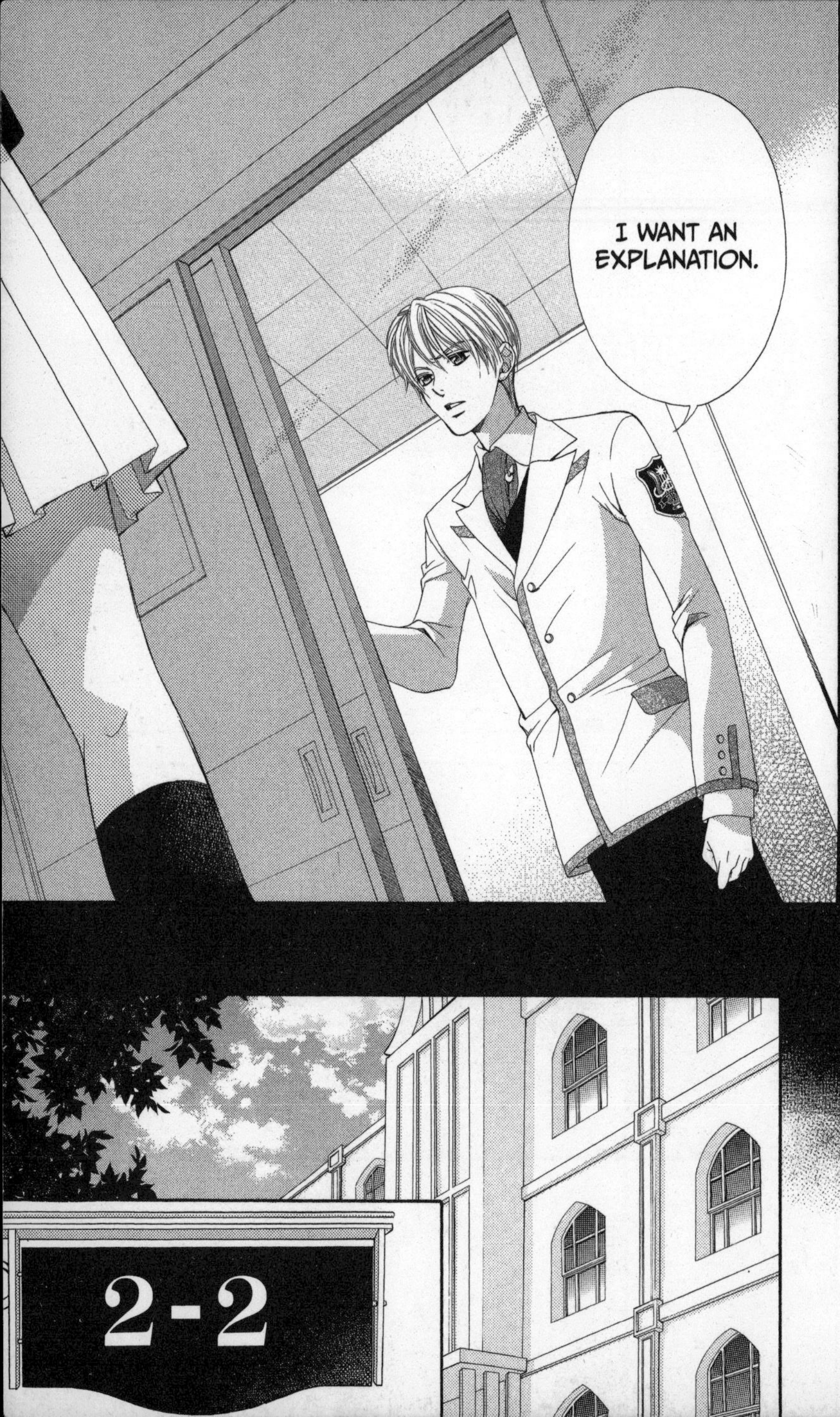
I WANT AN EXPLANATION.
2-2

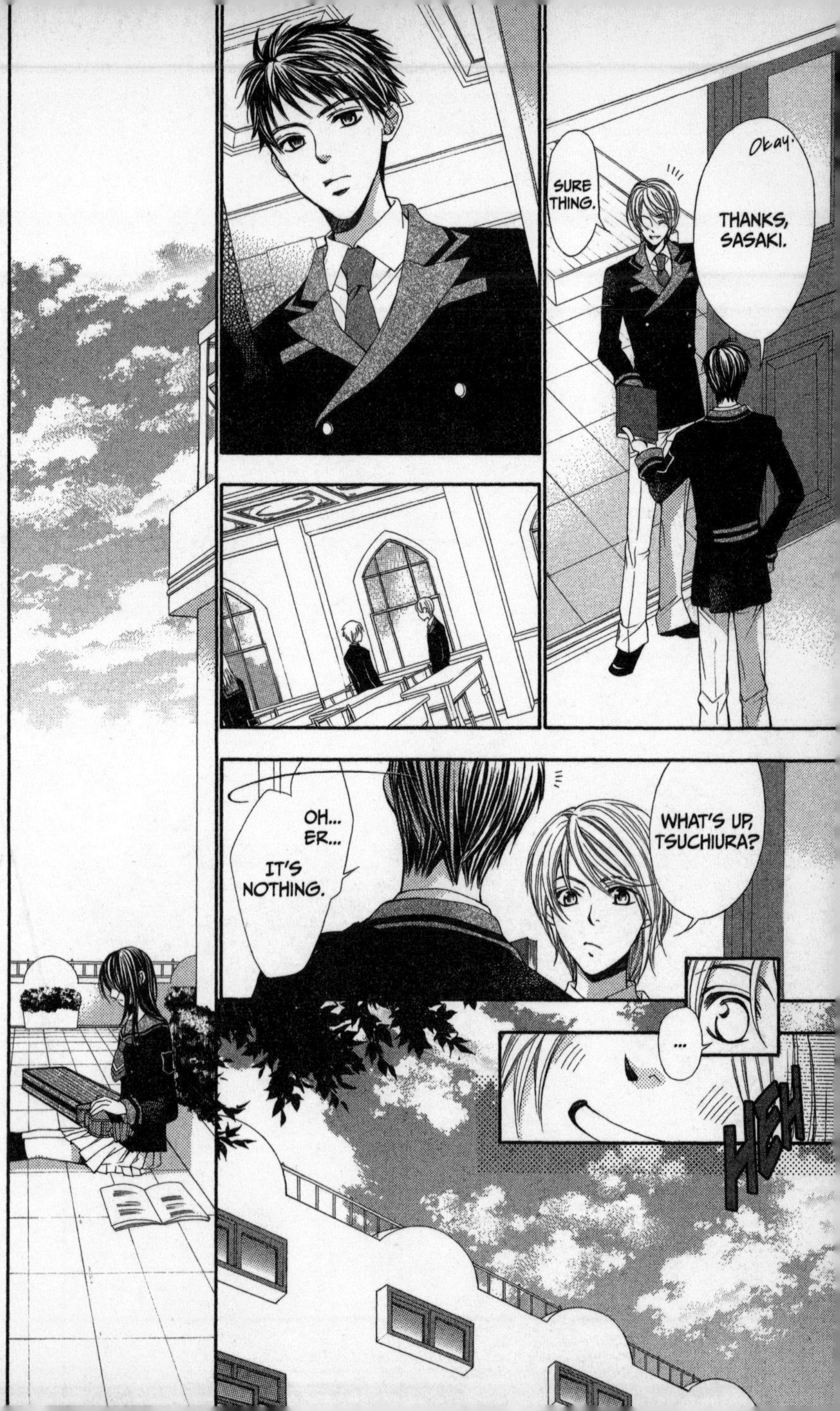
Okay.
THANKS, SASAKI.
SURE THING.
WHAT'S UP, TSUCHIURA?
OH... ER...
IT'S NOTHING.
...
HEH

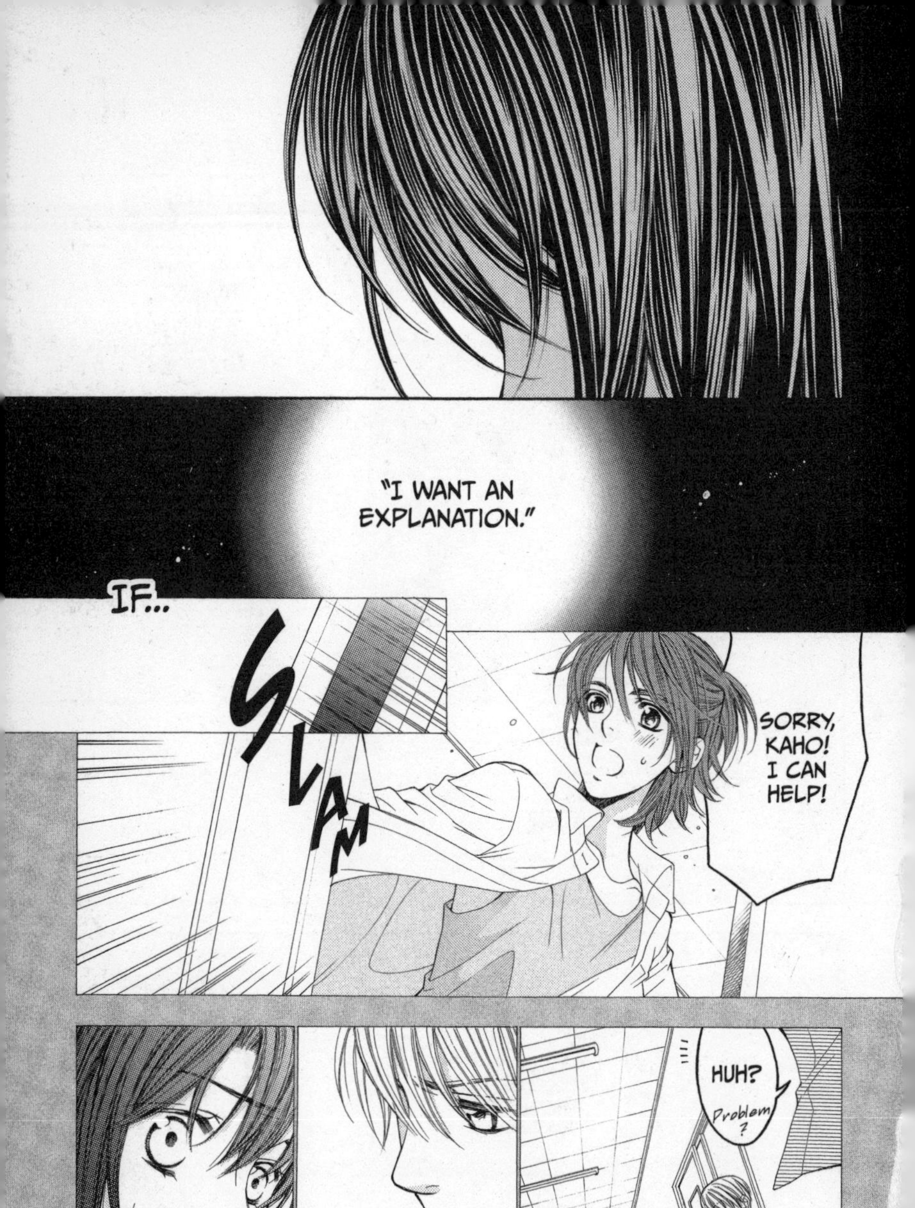
"I WANT AN EXPLANATION."
IF...
SLAM
SORRY, KAHO! I CAN HELP!
!!!
HUH?
Problem?

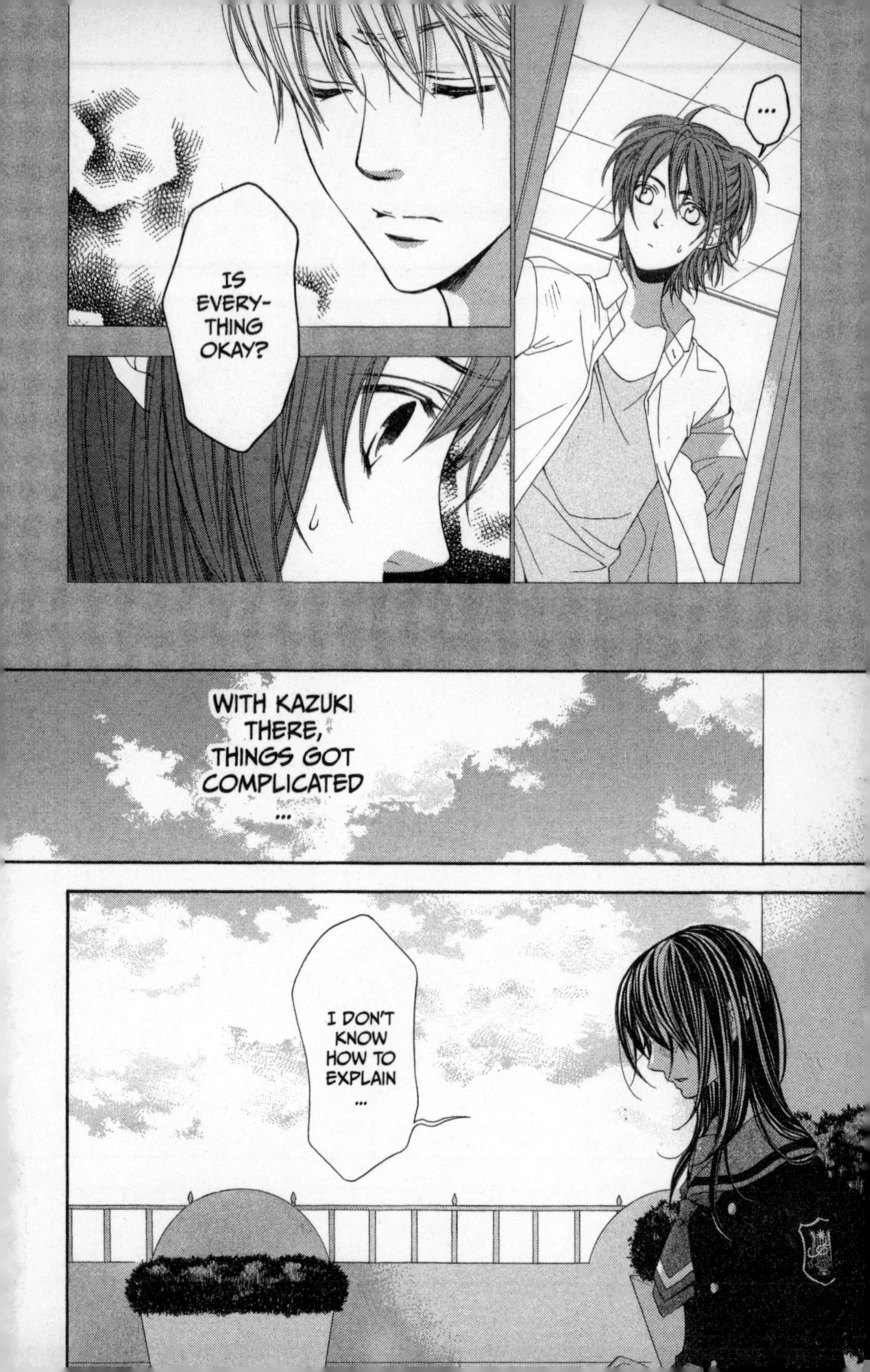
...
IS EVERYTHING OKAY?
WITH KAZUKI THERE, THINGS GOT COMPLICATED ...
I DON'T KNOW HOW TO EXPLAIN ...

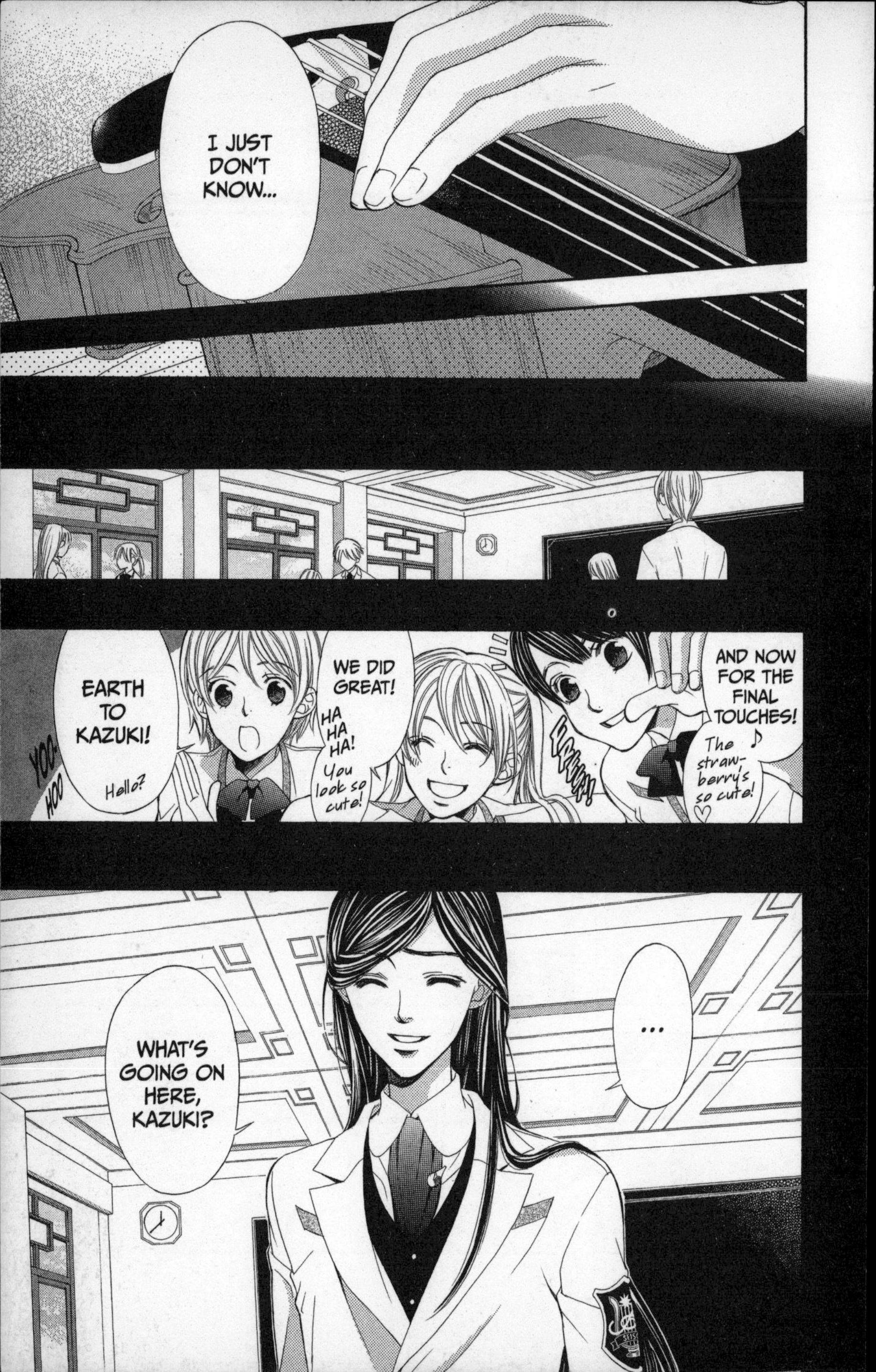
I JUST DON'T KNOW...
AND NOW FOR THE FINAL TOUCHES!
The straw-berry's so cute! ♡
WE DID GREAT!
HA HA HA!
You look so cute!
EARTH TO KAZUKI!
Hello?
YOO-HOO
...
WHAT'S GOING ON HERE, KAZUKI?

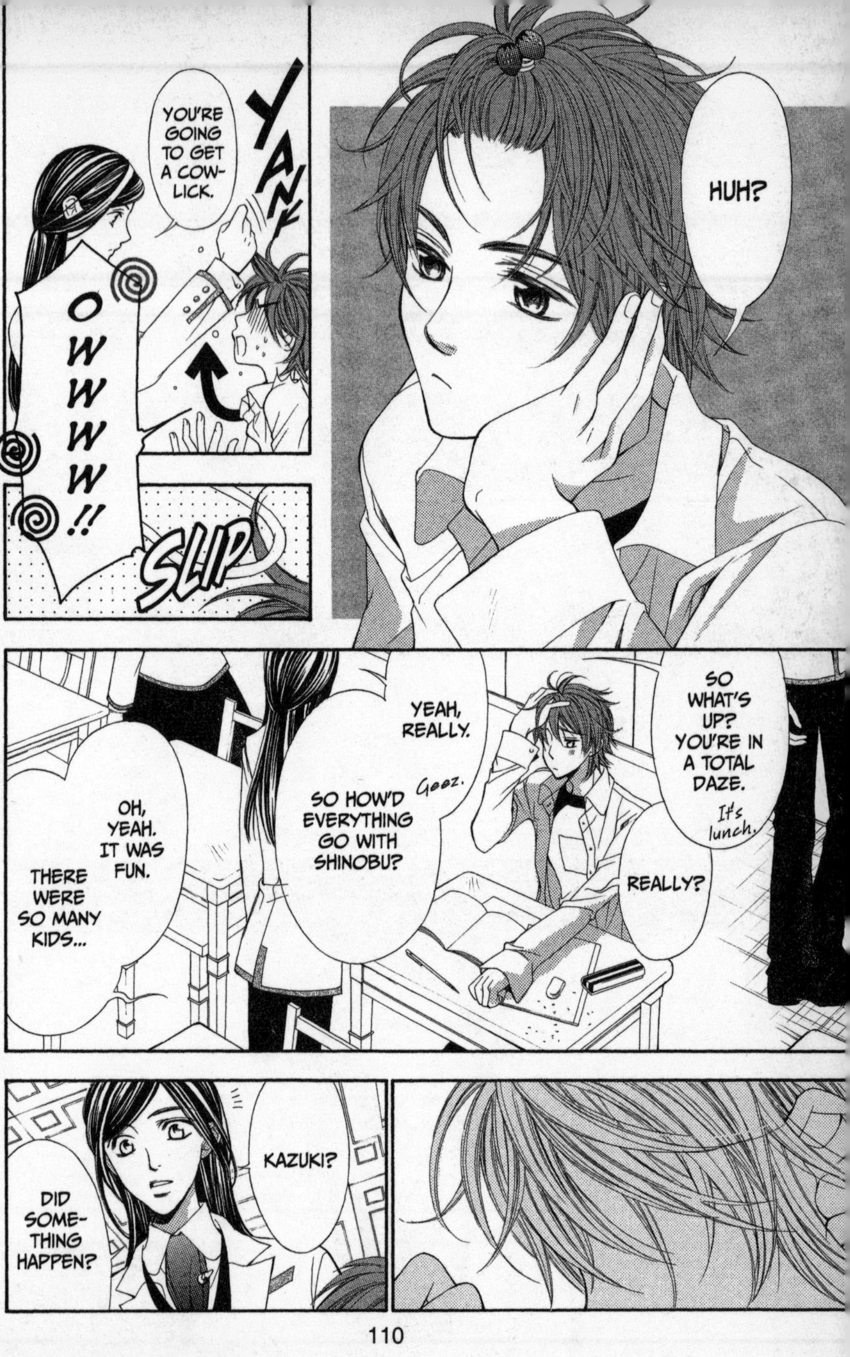
HUH?
YOU'RE GOING TO GET A COW-LICK.
YANK
OWWWWW!!
SLIP
SO WHAT'S UP? YOU'RE IN A TOTAL DAZE.
It's lunch.
REALLY?
YEAH, REALLY.
Geez.
SO HOW'D EVERYTHING GO WITH SHINOBU?
OH, YEAH. IT WAS FUN.
THERE WERE SO MANY KIDS...
KAZUKI?
DID SOMETHING HAPPEN?

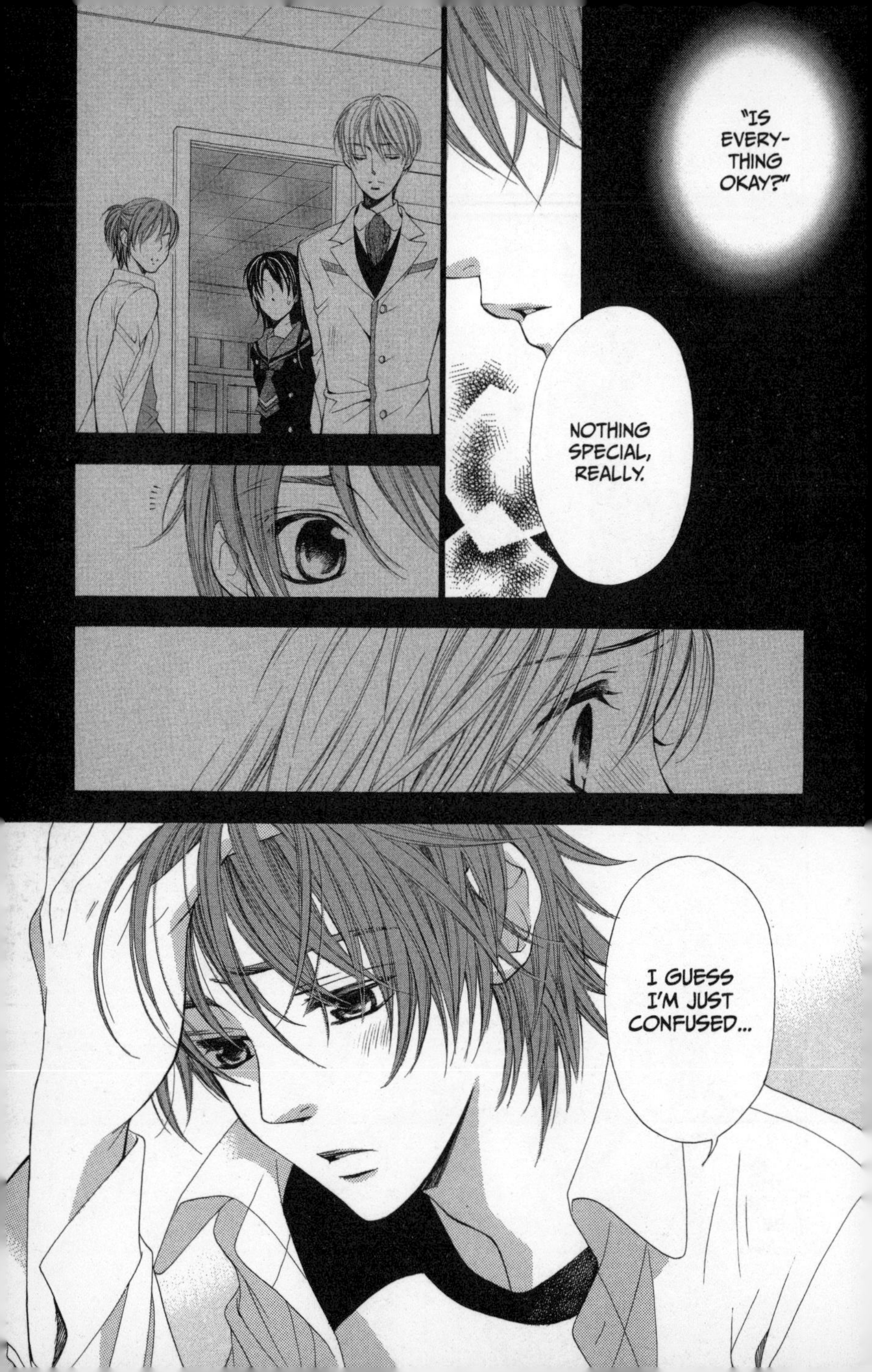
"IS EVERY-THING OKAY?"
NOTHING SPECIAL, REALLY.
I GUESS I'M JUST CONFUSED...

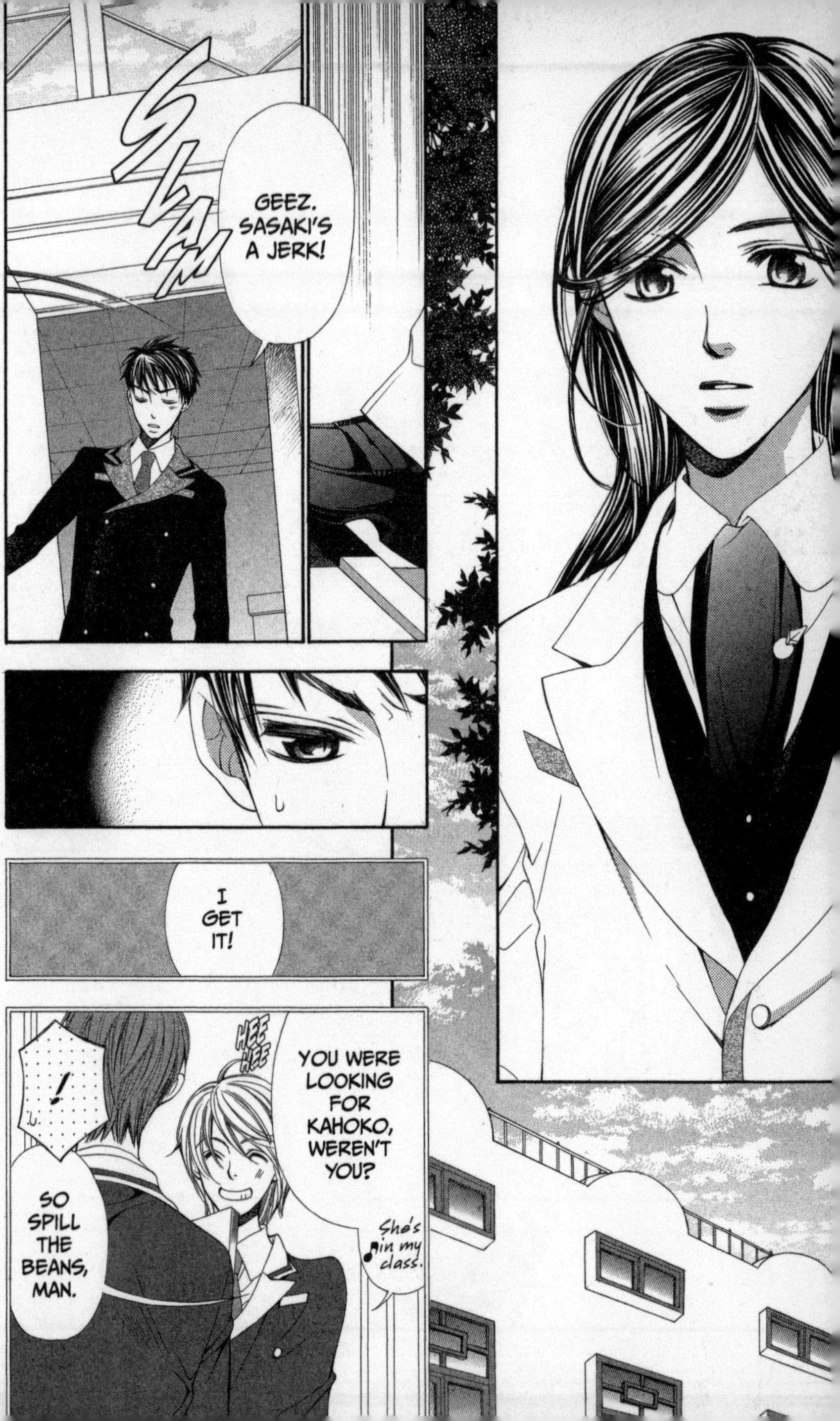
SLAM
GEEZ. SASAKI'S A JERK!
I GET IT!
HEE HEE
YOU WERE LOOKING FOR KAHOKO, WEREN'T YOU?
She's in my class.
!
SO SPILL THE BEANS, MAN.

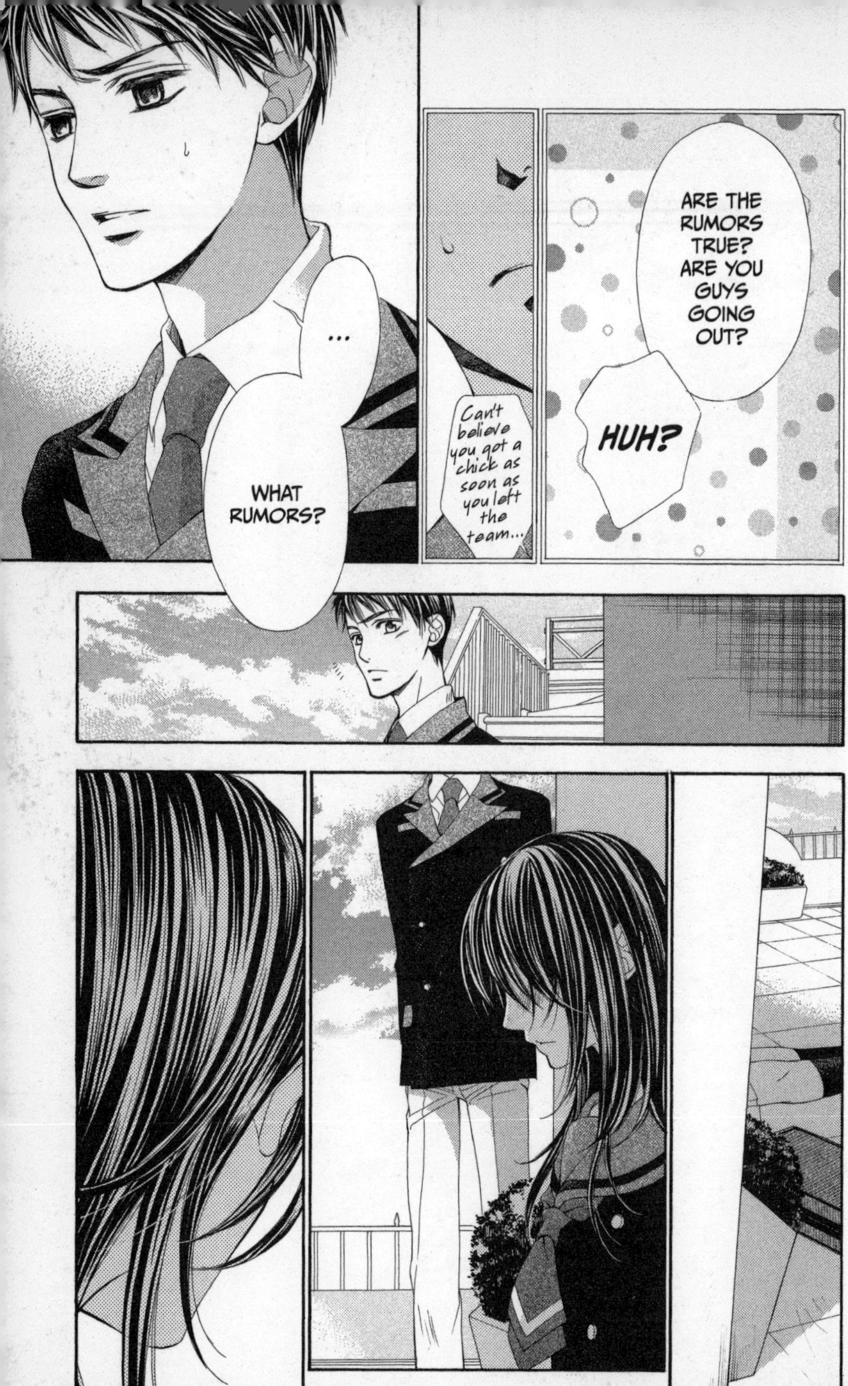
ARE THE RUMORS TRUE? ARE YOU GUYS GOING OUT?
HUH?
Can't believe you got a chick as soon as you left the team...
...
WHAT RUMORS?

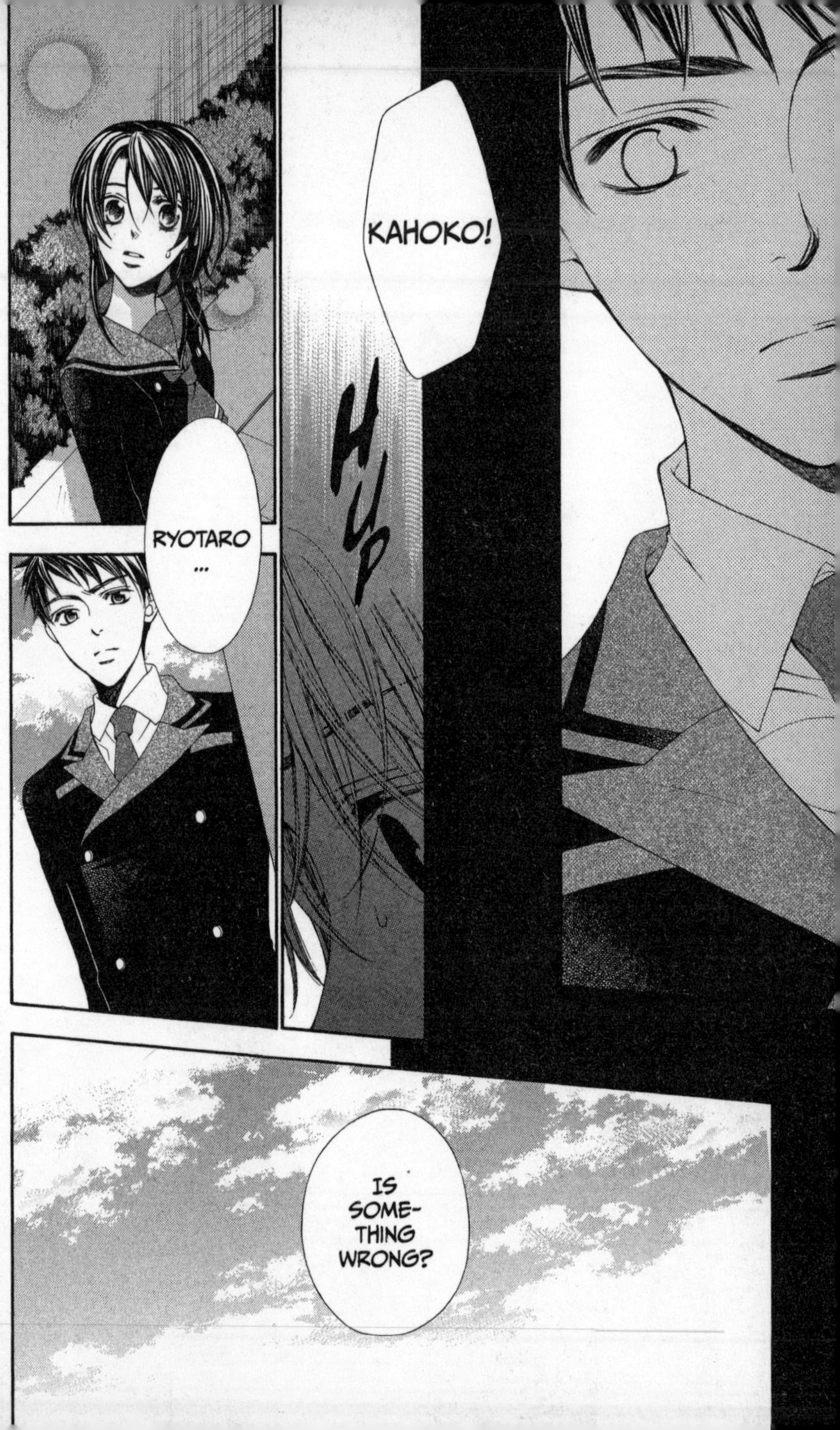
KAHOKO!
HUP
RYOTARO ...
IS SOME-THING WRONG?

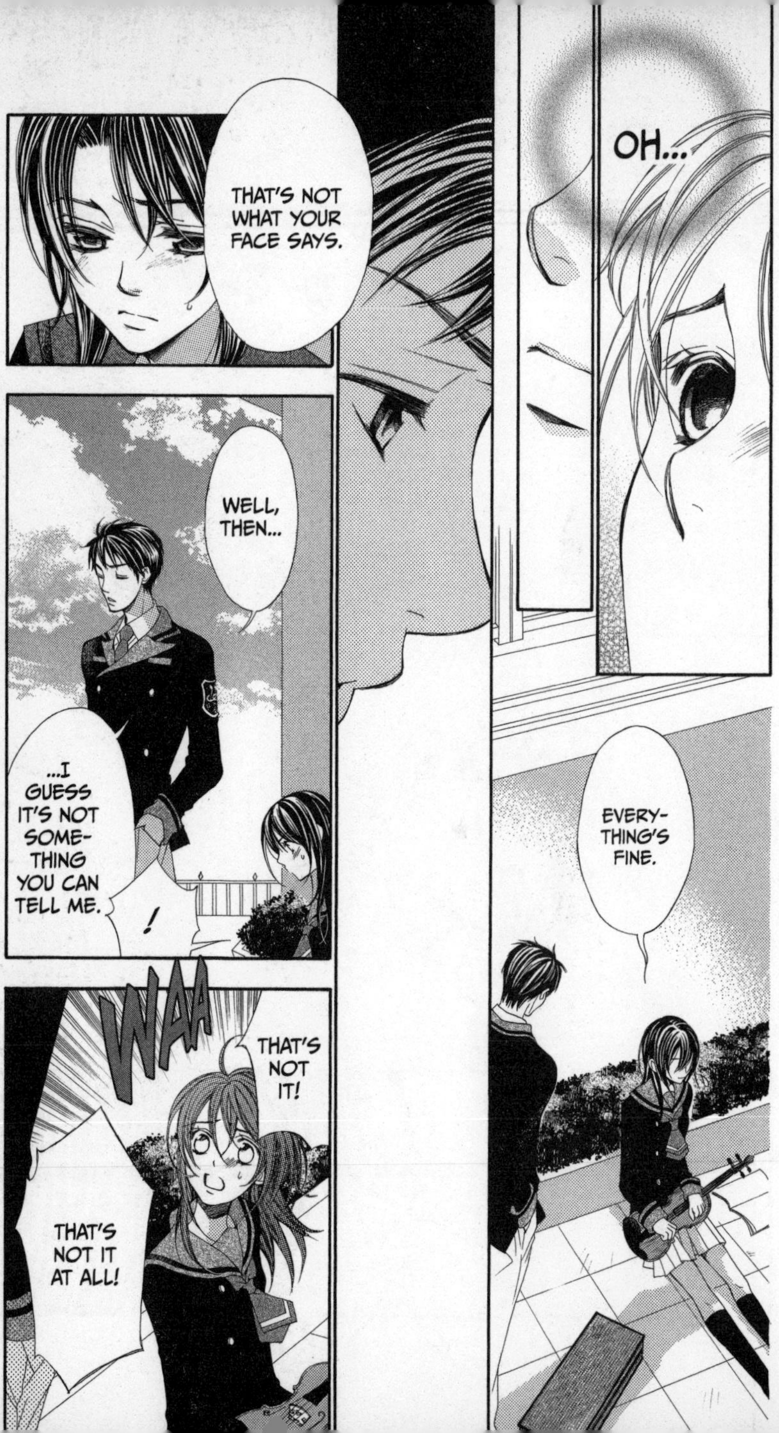
OH...
EVERYTHING'S FINE.
THAT'S NOT WHAT YOUR FACE SAYS.
WELL, THEN...
...I GUESS IT'S NOT SOMETHING YOU CAN TELL ME.
!
WAA
THAT'S NOT IT!
THAT'S NOT IT AT ALL!

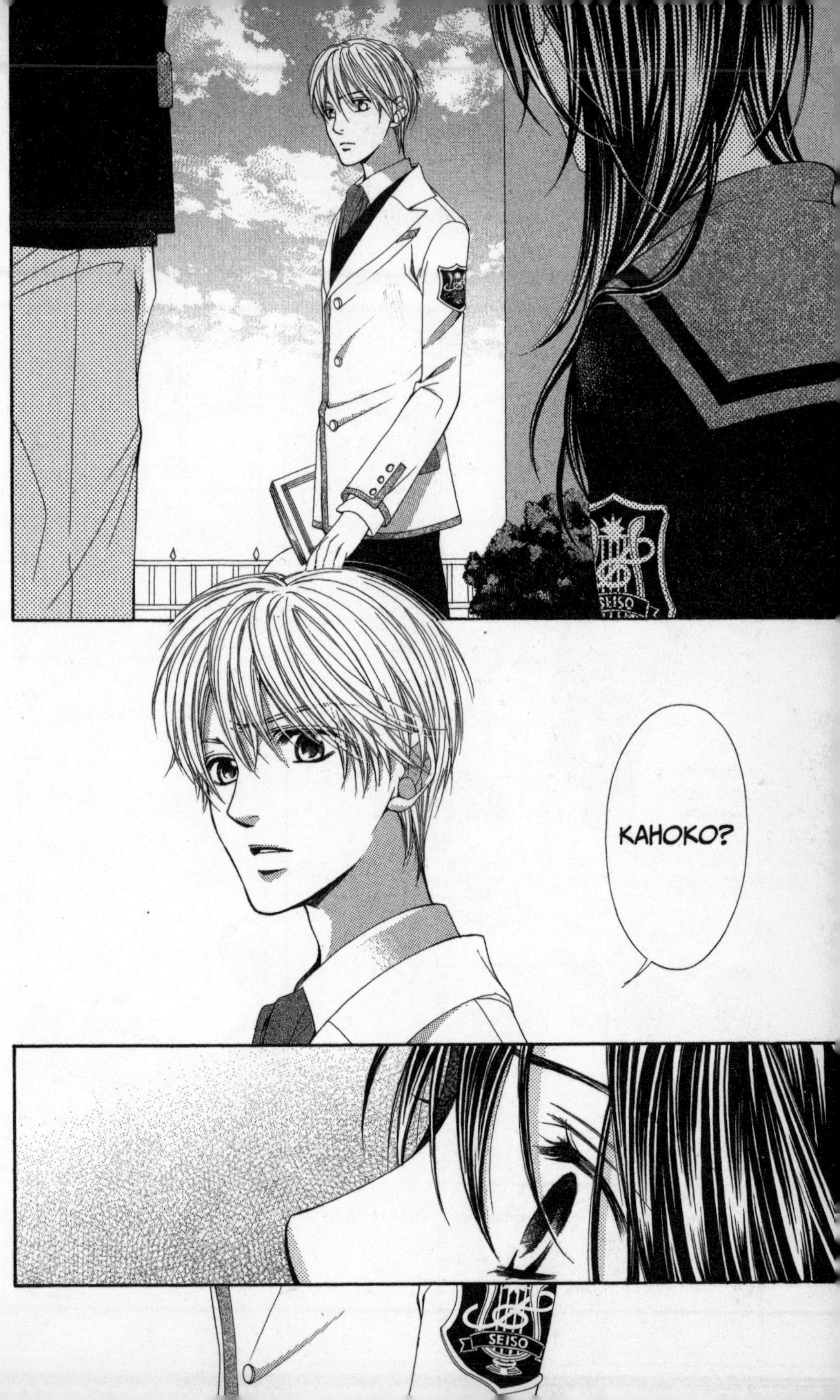
KAHOKO?
SEISO
SEISO

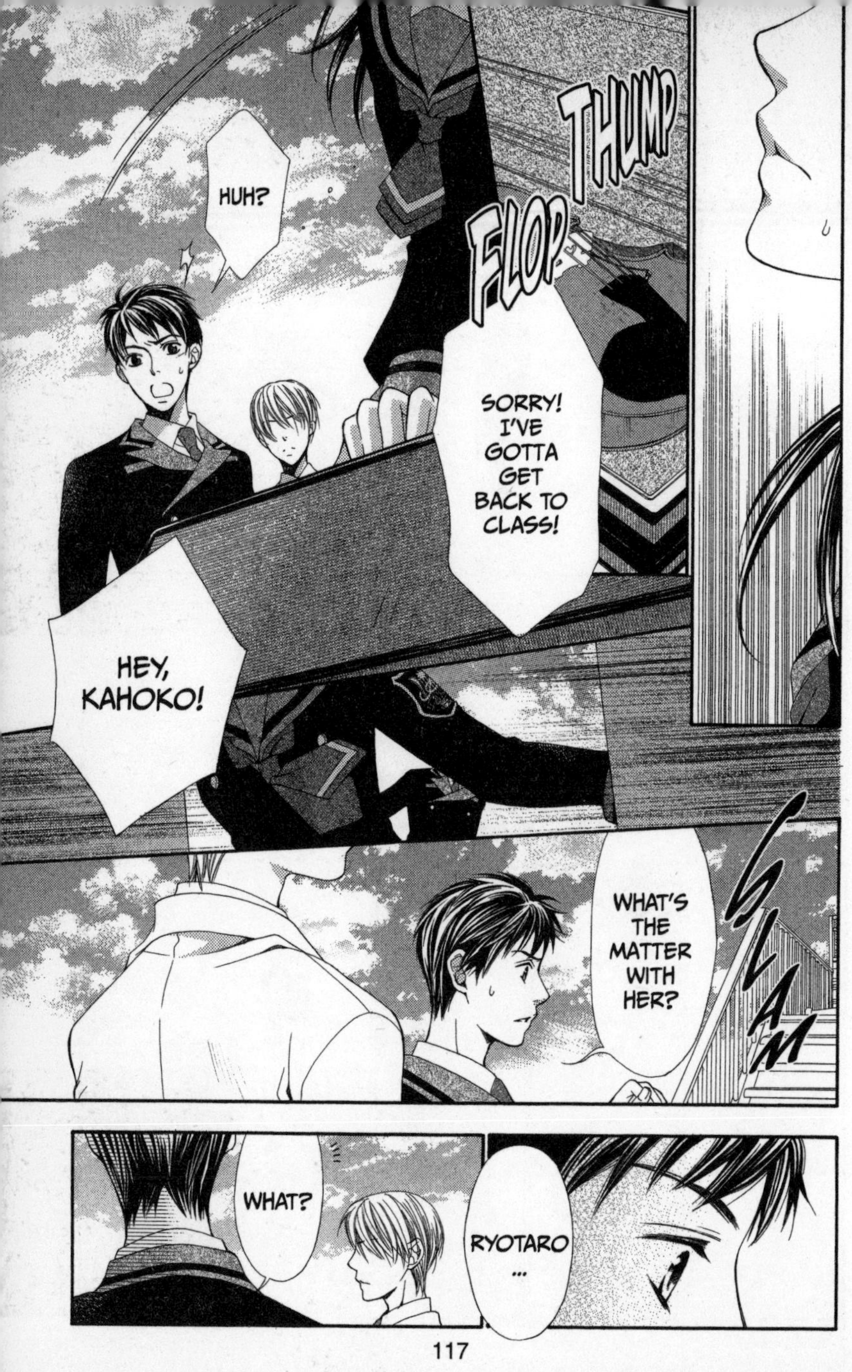
THUMP
FLOP
SORRY! I'VE GOTTA GET BACK TO CLASS!
HUH?
HEY, KAHOKO!
SLAM
WHAT'S THE MATTER WITH HER?
RYOTARO ...
WHAT?

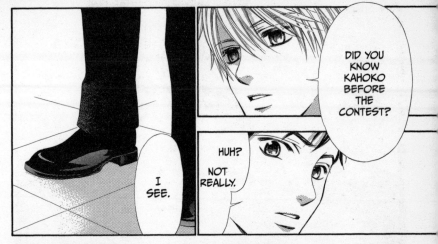

DID YOU KNOW KAHOKO BEFORE THE CONTEST?

HUH? NOT REALLY.

I SEE.

HEY.

LEN?

DID SOME-THING HAPPEN TO HER?

THE MINUTE YOU SHOWED UP, SHE RAN.

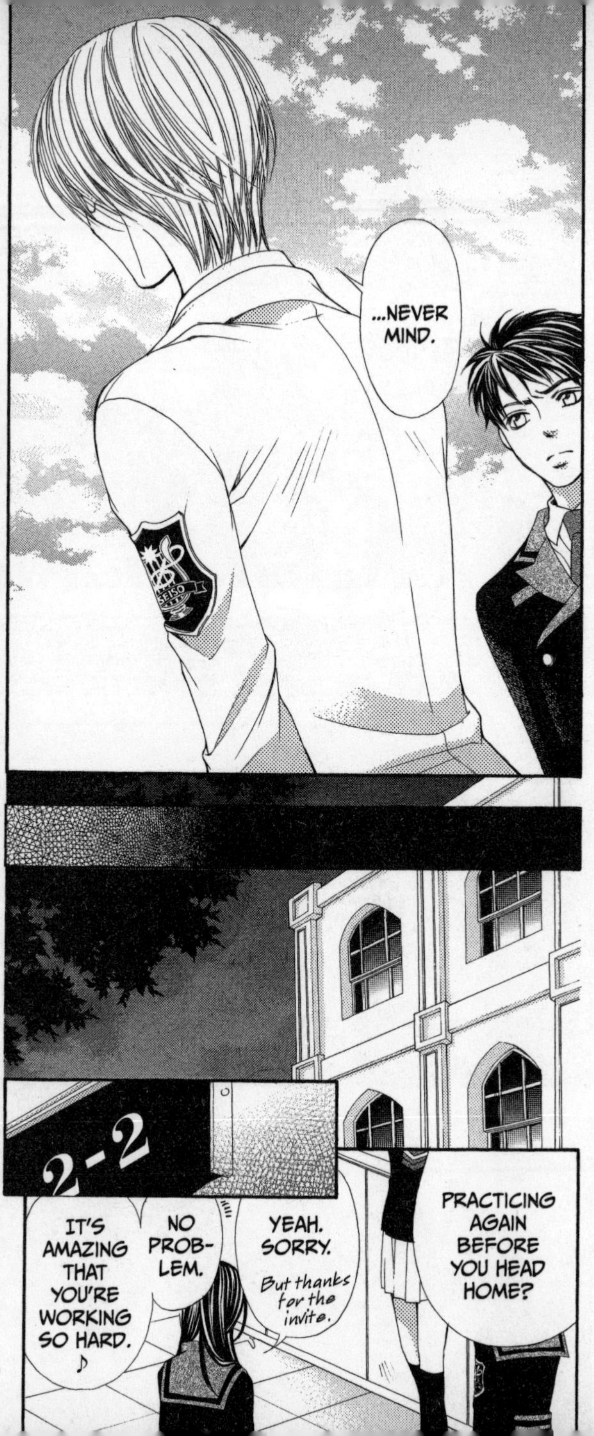
...NEVER MIND.
2-2
PRACTICING AGAIN BEFORE YOU HEAD HOME?
YEAH. SORRY.
But thanks for the invite.
NO PROB-LEM.
IT'S AMAZING THAT YOU'RE WORKING SO HARD. ♪

FOUR

Measure 27... *hmm*...Well, there's Sasaki from Gen Ed...Let's call him Junosuke Sasaki. (I'm just stalling now...)

Actually, his first appearance in print was in the bonus story in this volume.

I gave him another appearance here.
Just felt like it.

I randomly named him Sasaki while I was working on him. I figured I'd change it to a name that came up in the game, but I ended up just going with it. It wasn't particularly well thought out...pretty typical for me.

He might appear again if I feel like it.

He's in Kahoko's class and is on the soccer team.

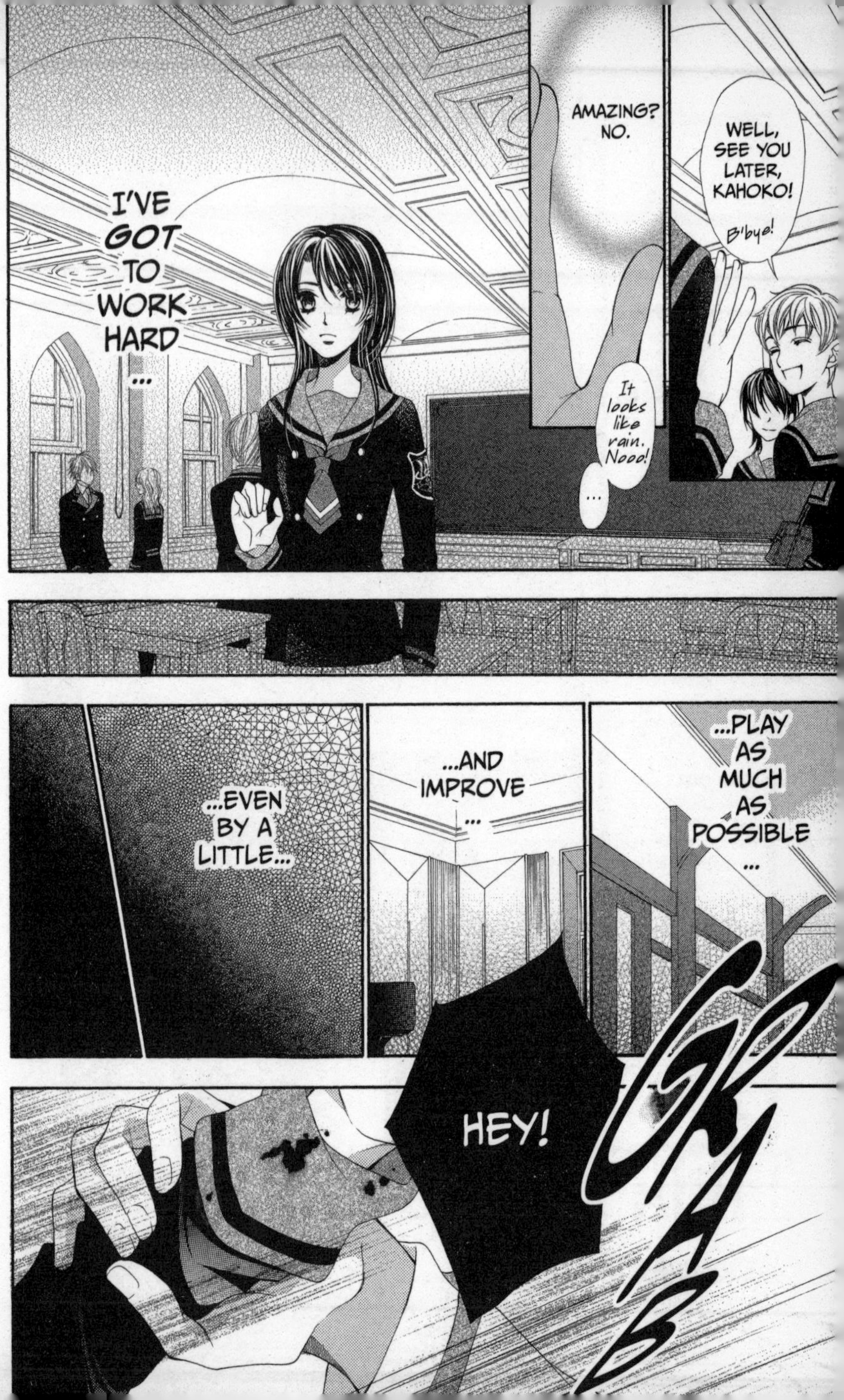
WELL, SEE YOU LATER, KAHOKO!
B'bye!
AMAZING? NO.
It looks like rain. Nooo!
...
I'VE GOT TO WORK HARD...
...PLAY AS MUCH AS POSSIBLE...
...AND IMPROVE...
...EVEN BY A LITTLE...
GRAB
HEY!

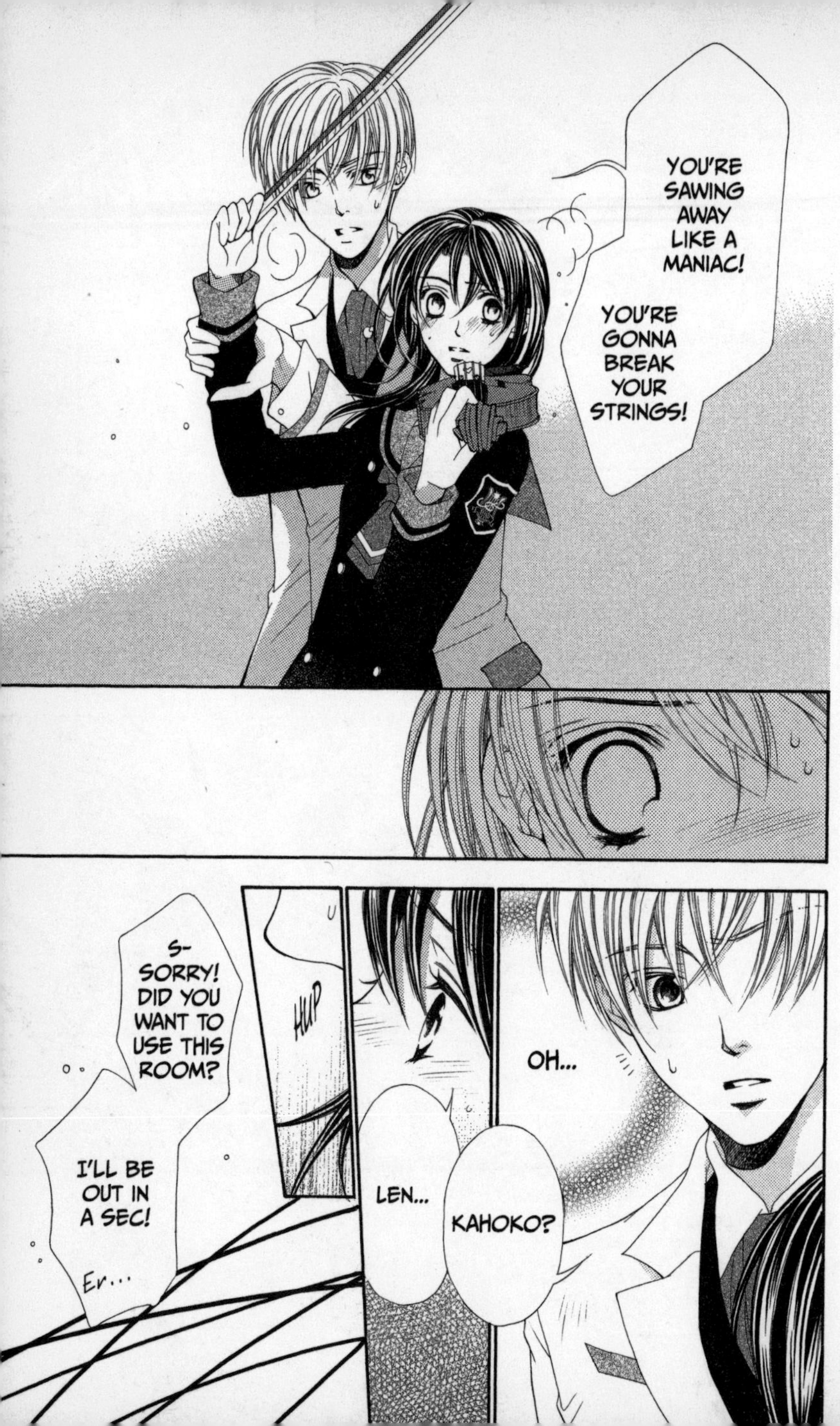
YOU'RE SAWING AWAY LIKE A MANIAC!
YOU'RE GONNA BREAK YOUR STRINGS!
OH...
KAHOKO?
HUP
LEN...
S-SORRY! DID YOU WANT TO USE THIS ROOM?
I'LL BE OUT IN A SEC!
Er...

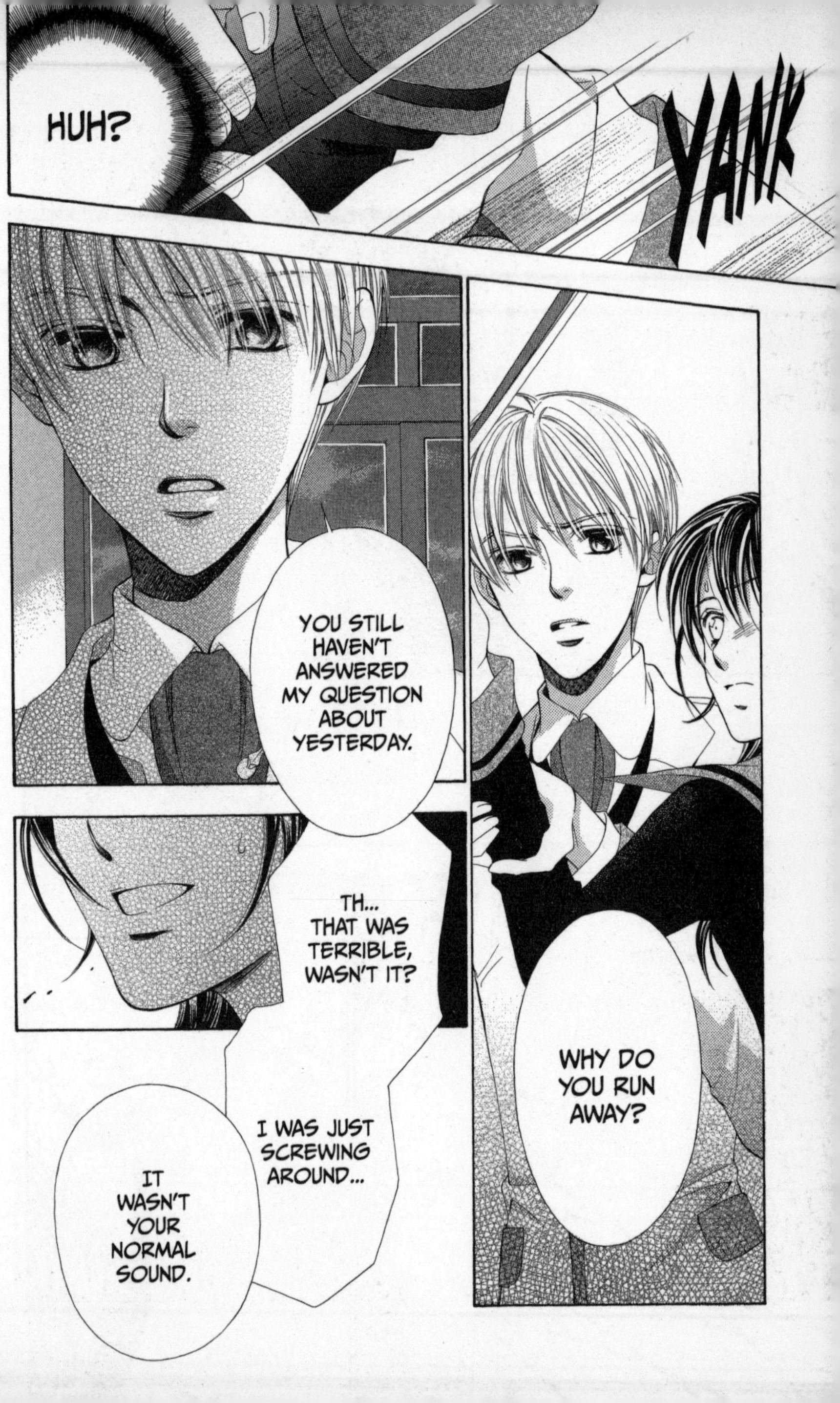
YANK
HUH?
WHY DO YOU RUN AWAY?
YOU STILL HAVEN'T ANSWERED MY QUESTION ABOUT YESTERDAY.
TH... THAT WAS TERRIBLE, WASN'T IT?
I WAS JUST SCREWING AROUND...
IT WASN'T YOUR NORMAL SOUND.

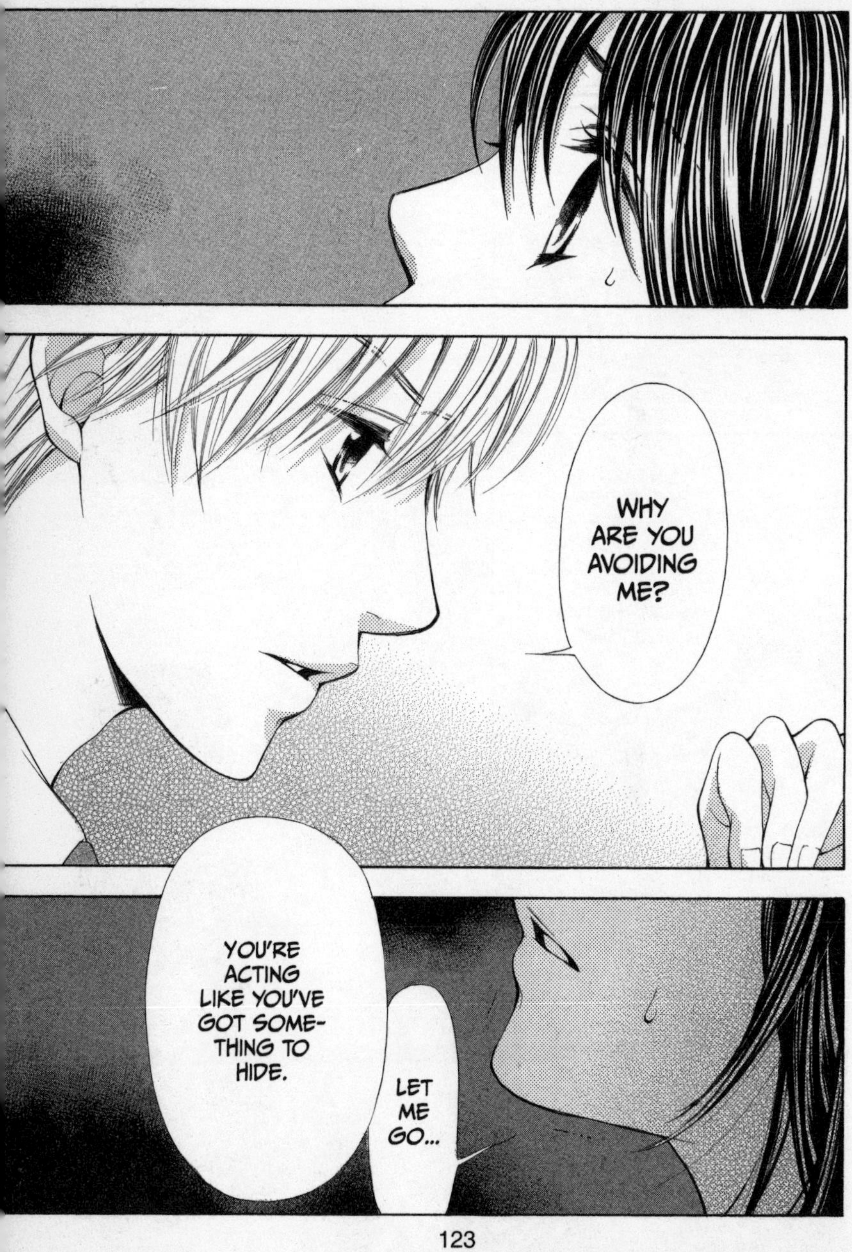
WHY ARE YOU AVOIDING ME?
LET ME GO...
YOU'RE ACTING LIKE YOU'VE GOT SOME-THING TO HIDE.

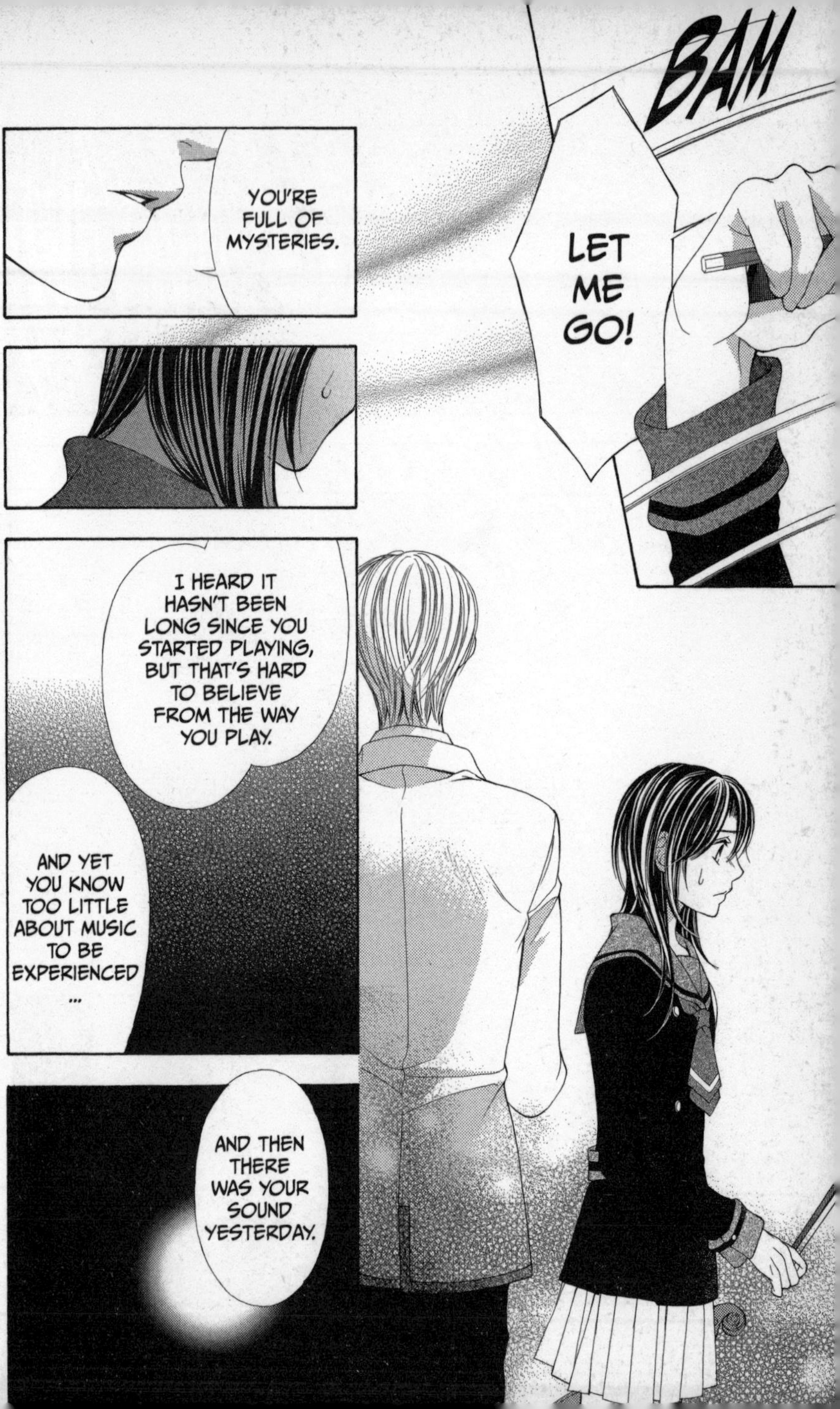
BAM
LET ME GO!
YOU'RE FULL OF MYSTERIES.
I HEARD IT HASN'T BEEN LONG SINCE YOU STARTED PLAYING, BUT THAT'S HARD TO BELIEVE FROM THE WAY YOU PLAY.
AND YET YOU KNOW TOO LITTLE ABOUT MUSIC TO BE EXPERIENCED ...
AND THEN THERE WAS YOUR SOUND YESTERDAY.

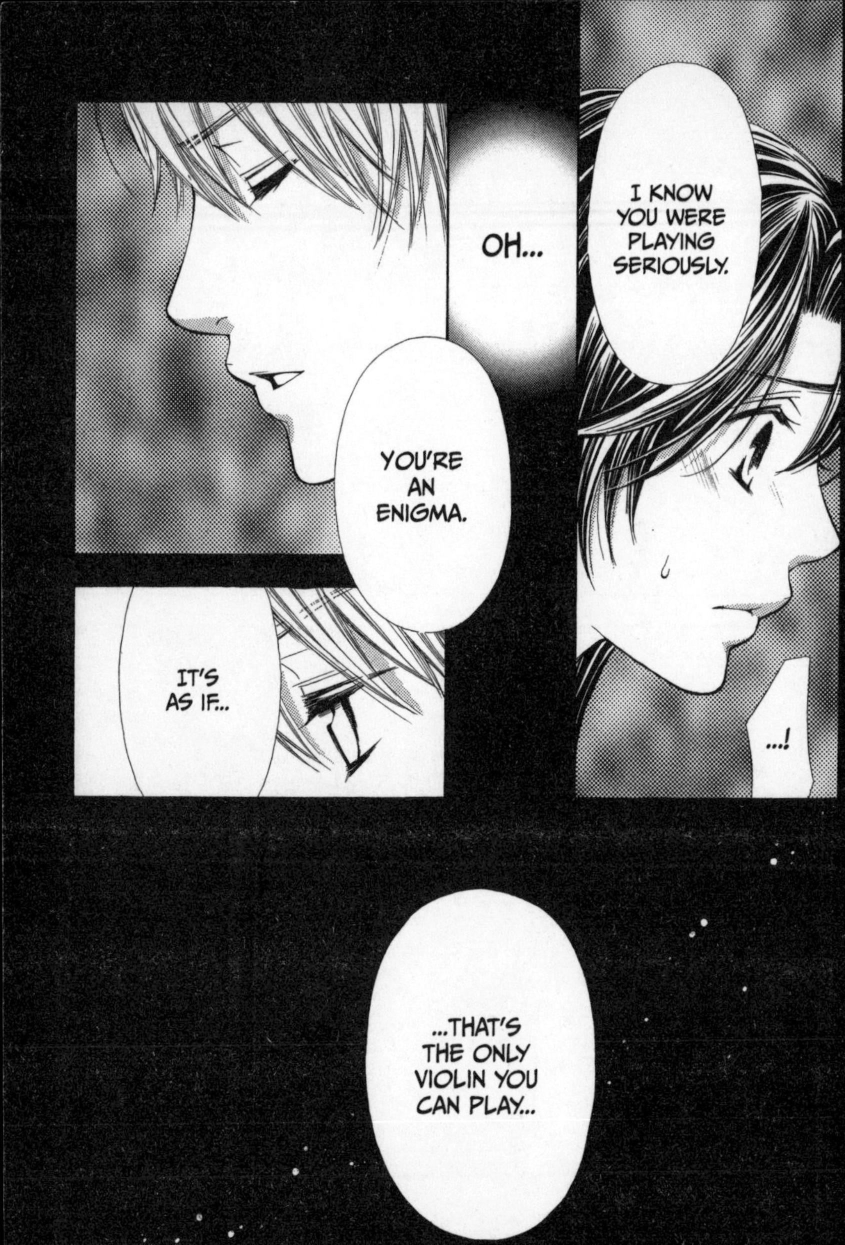
I KNOW YOU WERE PLAYING SERIOUSLY.
...!
OH...
YOU'RE AN ENIGMA.
IT'S AS IF...
...THAT'S THE ONLY VIOLIN YOU CAN PLAY...

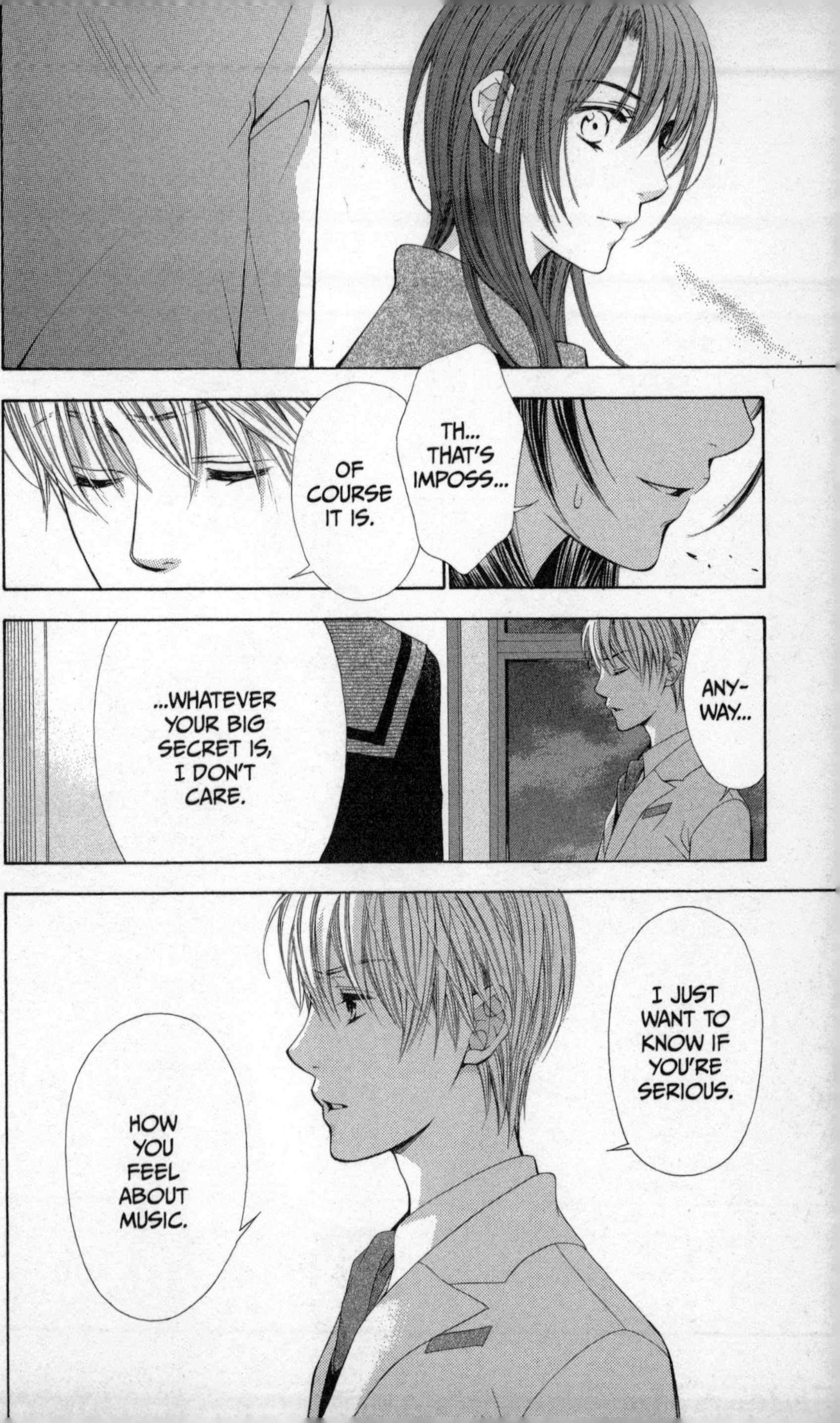
TH... THAT'S IMPOSS...
OF COURSE IT IS.
ANY-WAY...
...WHATEVER YOUR BIG SECRET IS, I DON'T CARE.
I JUST WANT TO KNOW IF YOU'RE SERIOUS.
HOW YOU FEEL ABOUT MUSIC.

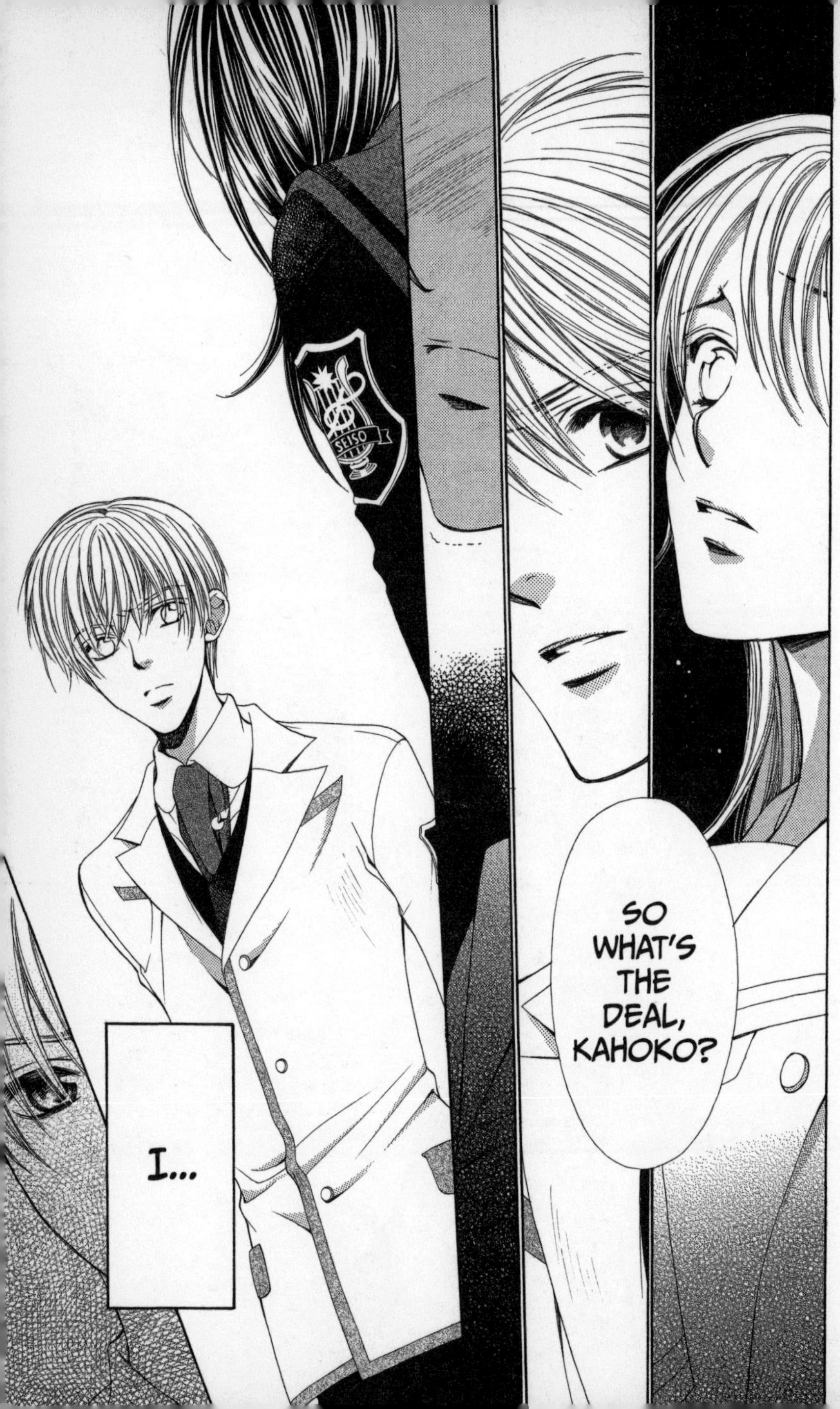
SO WHAT'S THE DEAL, KAHOKO?
SEISO
I...

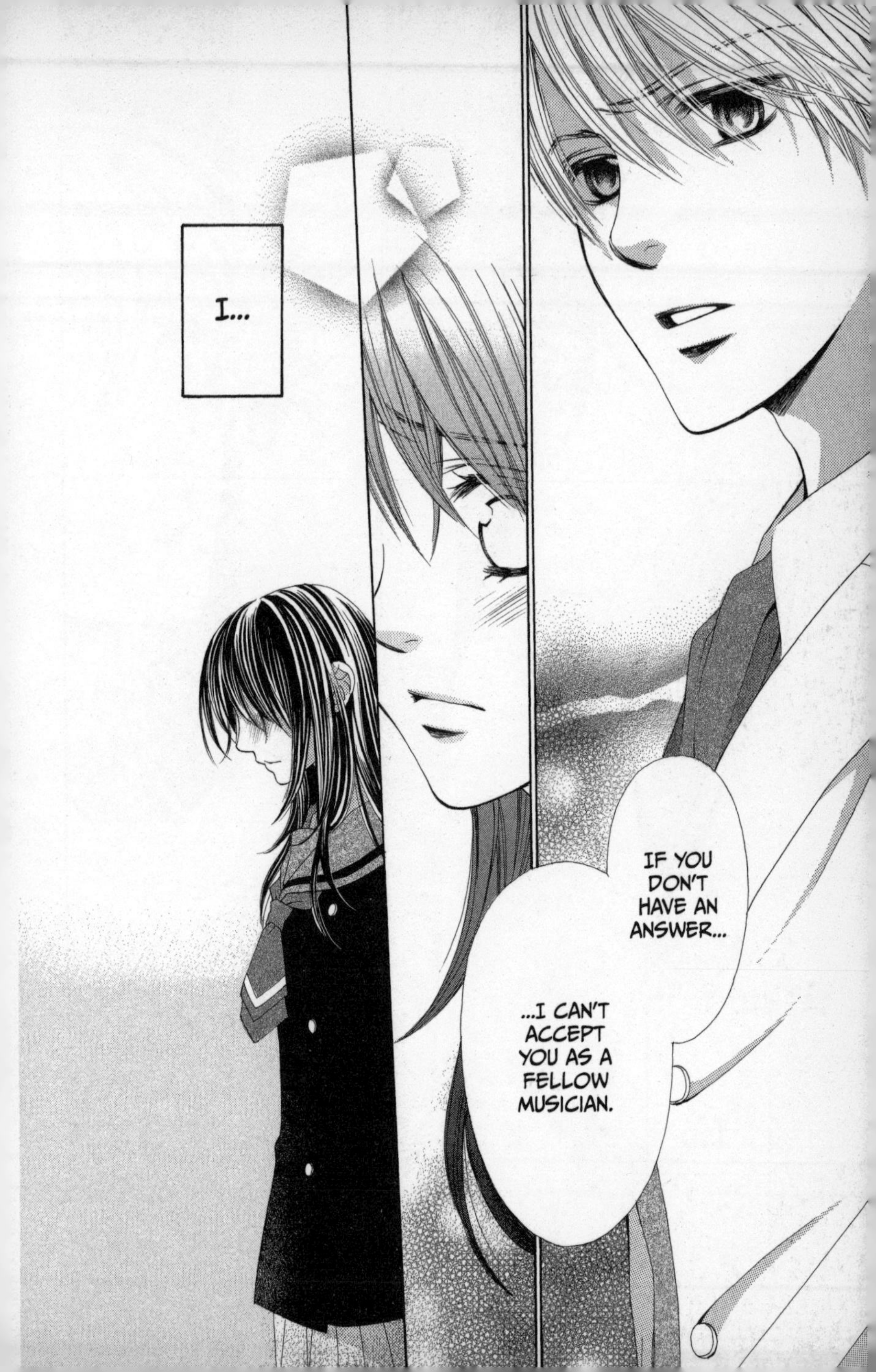
IF YOU DON'T HAVE AN ANSWER...
...I CAN'T ACCEPT YOU AS A FELLOW MUSICIAN.
I...

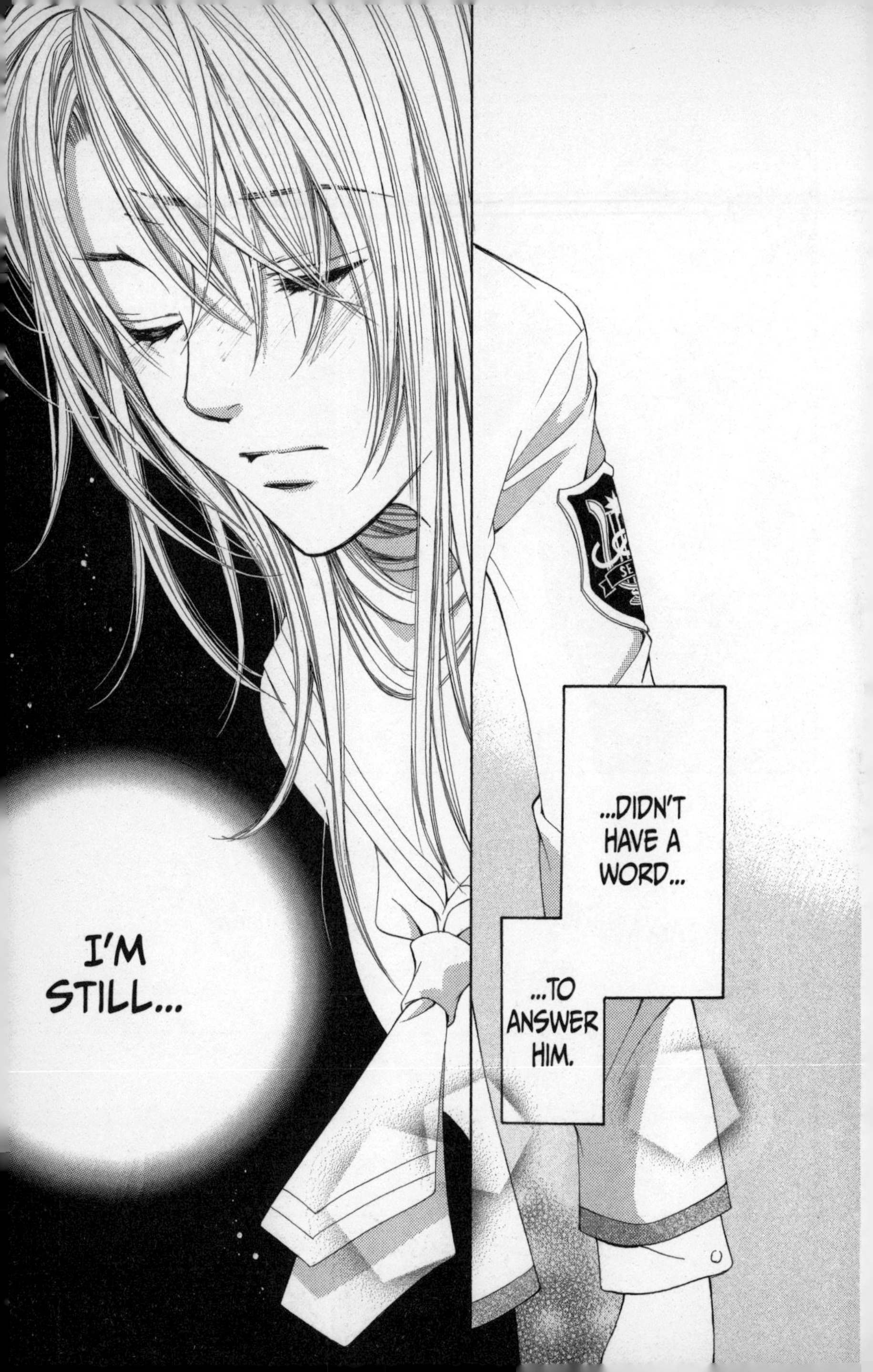
...DIDN'T HAVE A WORD...
...TO ANSWER HIM.
I'M STILL...

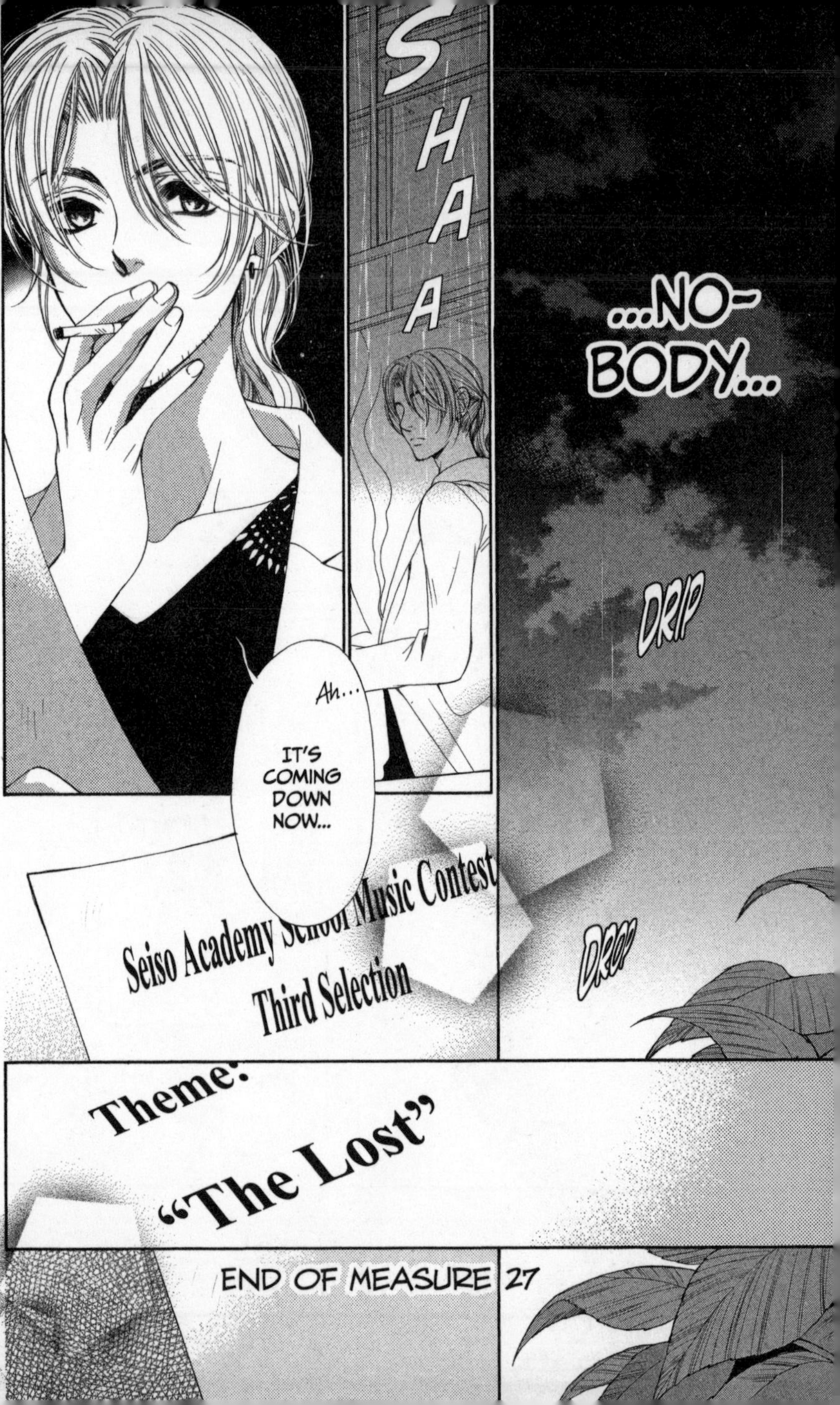
...NO-BODY...
DRIP
DROP
SHAA
Ah... IT'S COMING DOWN NOW...
Seiso Academy School Music Contest
Third Selection
Theme:
"The Lost"
END OF MEASURE 27

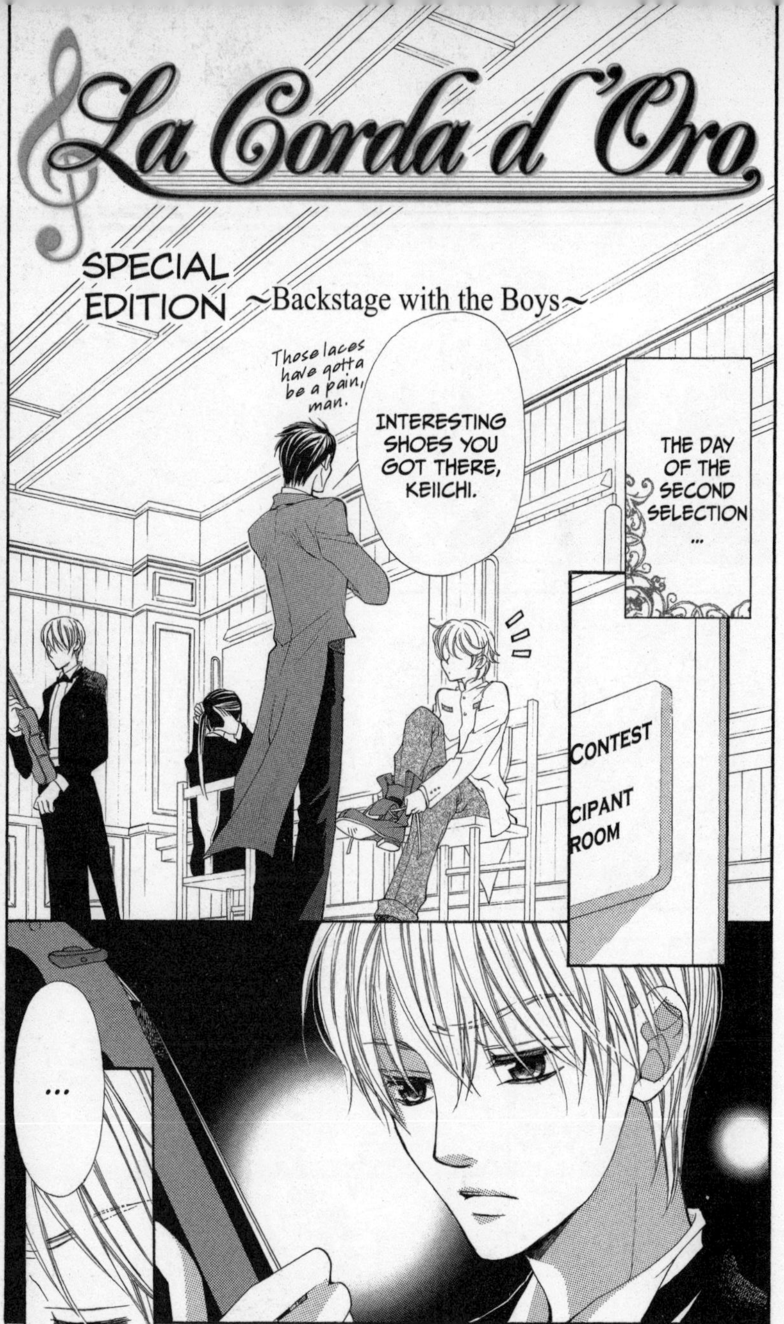
La Corda d'Oro
SPECIAL EDITION ~Backstage with the Boys~
THE DAY OF THE SECOND SELECTION ...
INTERESTING SHOES YOU GOT THERE, KEIICHI.
Those laces have gotta be a pain, man.
CONTEST
CIPANT ROOM
...

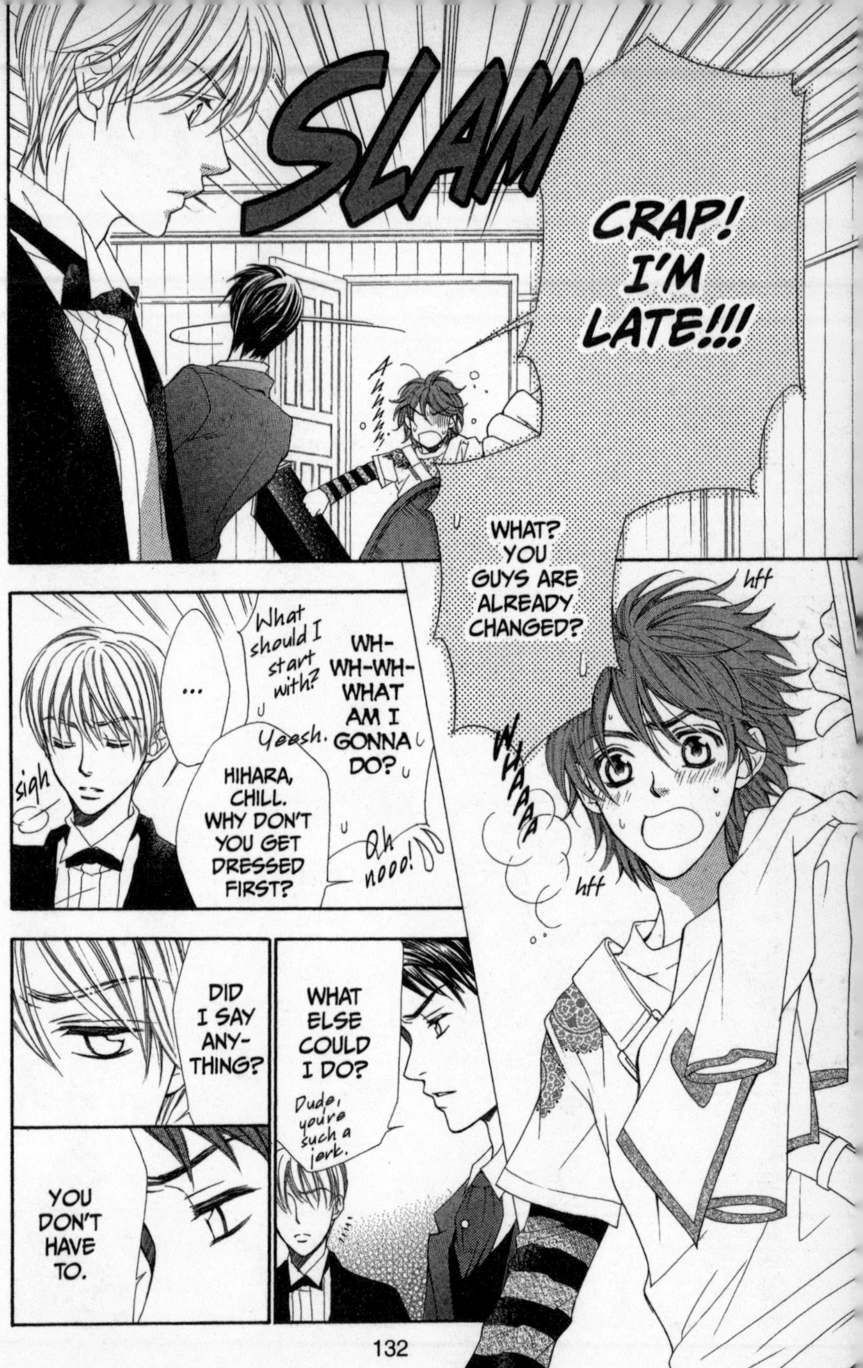
SLAM
CRAP! I'M LATE!!!
WHAT? YOU GUYS ARE ALREADY CHANGED?
hff
WHAAAA
hff
WH-WH-WH-WHAT AM I GONNA DO?
What should I start with?
Oh nooo!
...
Yeesh.
HIHARA, CHILL. WHY DON'T YOU GET DRESSED FIRST?
sigh
WHAT ELSE COULD I DO?
Dude, you're such a jerk.
DID I SAY ANYTHING?
YOU DON'T HAVE TO.

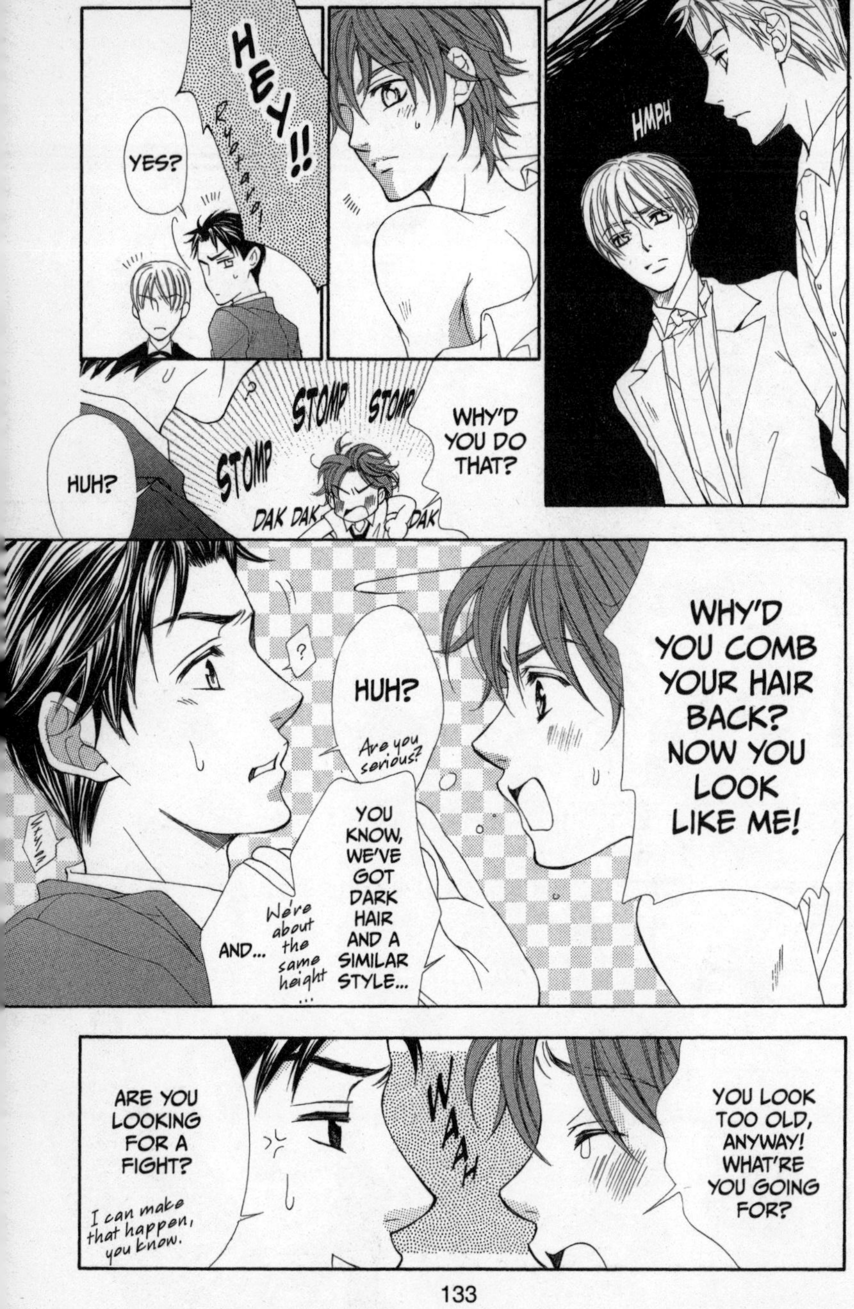
HMPH
HEY!!
YES?
WHY'D YOU DO THAT?
STOMP STOMP
STOMP
DAK DAK DAK
HUH?
WHY'D YOU COMB YOUR HAIR BACK? NOW YOU LOOK LIKE ME!
HUH?
Are you serious?
YOU KNOW, WE'VE GOT DARK HAIR AND A SIMILAR STYLE...
We're about the same height...
AND...
YOU LOOK TOO OLD, ANYWAY! WHAT'RE YOU GOING FOR?
WAAH
ARE YOU LOOKING FOR A FIGHT?
I can make that happen, you know.

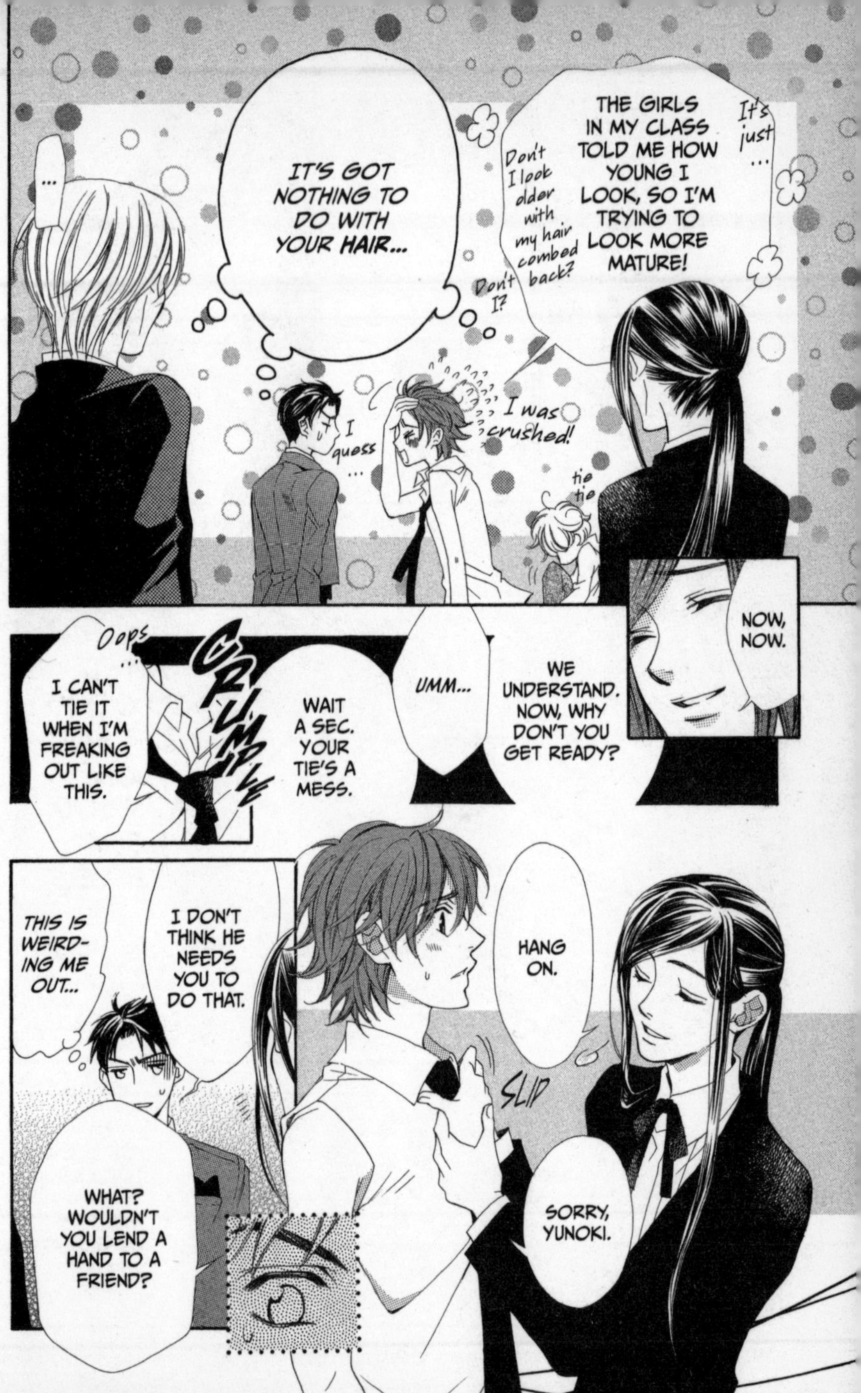
It's just ...
THE GIRLS IN MY CLASS TOLD ME HOW YOUNG I LOOK, SO I'M TRYING TO LOOK MORE MATURE!
Don't I look older with my hair combed back?
Don't I?
I was crushed!
tie tie
I guess ...
IT'S GOT NOTHING TO DO WITH YOUR HAIR...
...
NOW, NOW.
WE UNDERSTAND. NOW, WHY DON'T YOU GET READY?
UMM...
WAIT A SEC. YOUR TIE'S A MESS.
CRUMPLE
Oops...
I CAN'T TIE IT WHEN I'M FREAKING OUT LIKE THIS.
HANG ON.
SLIP
SORRY, YUNOKI.
I DON'T THINK HE NEEDS YOU TO DO THAT.
THIS IS WEIRDING ME OUT...
WHAT? WOULDN'T YOU LEND A HAND TO A FRIEND?

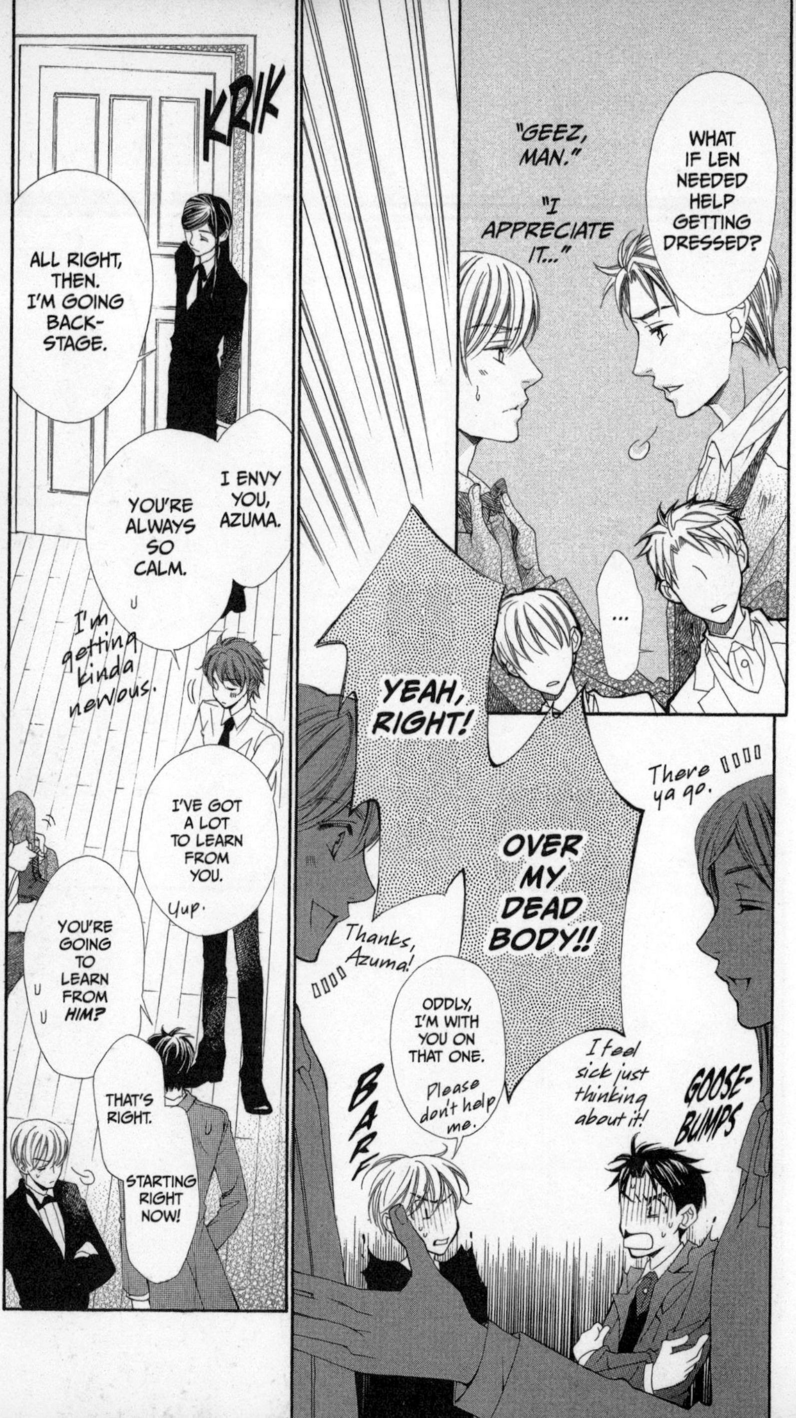
WHAT IF LEN NEEDED HELP GETTING DRESSED?
"GEEZ, MAN."
"I APPRECIATE IT..."
...
There ya go.
GOOSE-BUMPS
I feel sick just thinking about it!
YEAH, RIGHT!
OVER MY DEAD BODY!!
Thanks, Azuma!
ODDLY, I'M WITH YOU ON THAT ONE.
Please don't help me.
BARF
KRIK
ALL RIGHT, THEN. I'M GOING BACK-STAGE.
I ENVY YOU, AZUMA.
YOU'RE ALWAYS SO CALM.
I'm getting kinda nervous.
I'VE GOT A LOT TO LEARN FROM YOU.
Yup.
YOU'RE GOING TO LEARN FROM HIM?
THAT'S RIGHT.
STARTING RIGHT NOW!

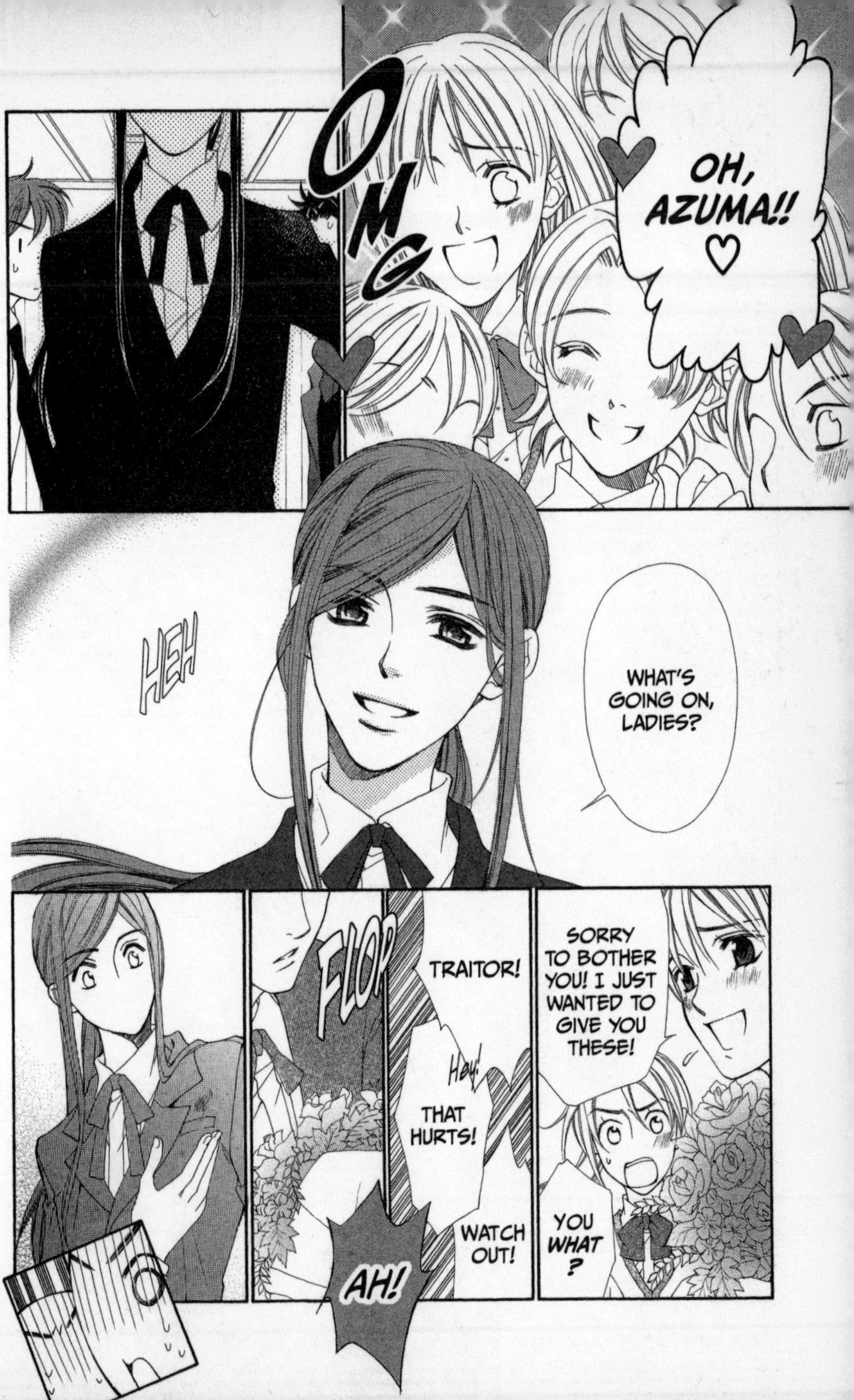
OMG
OH, AZUMA!! ♡
WHAT'S GOING ON, LADIES?
HEH
SORRY TO BOTHER YOU! I JUST WANTED TO GIVE YOU THESE!
YOU WHAT?
TRAITOR!
Hey!
THAT HURTS!
WATCH OUT!
AH!
FLOP

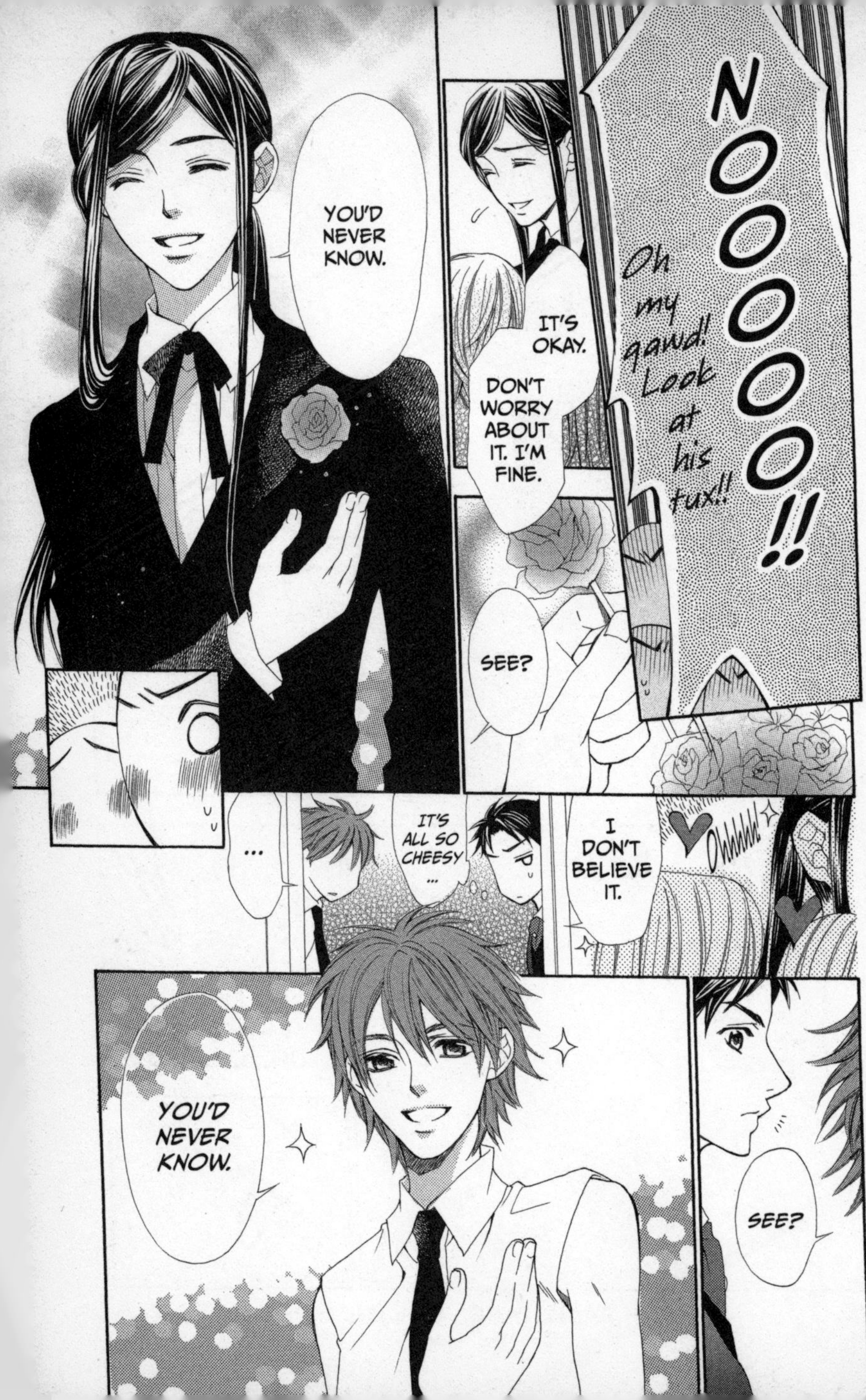
NOOOOOO!!
Oh my gawd! Look at his tux!!
IT'S OKAY.
DON'T WORRY ABOUT IT. I'M FINE.
SEE?
YOU'D NEVER KNOW.
Ohhhhh!
I DON'T BELIEVE IT.
IT'S ALL SO CHEESY...
...
SEE?
YOU'D NEVER KNOW.

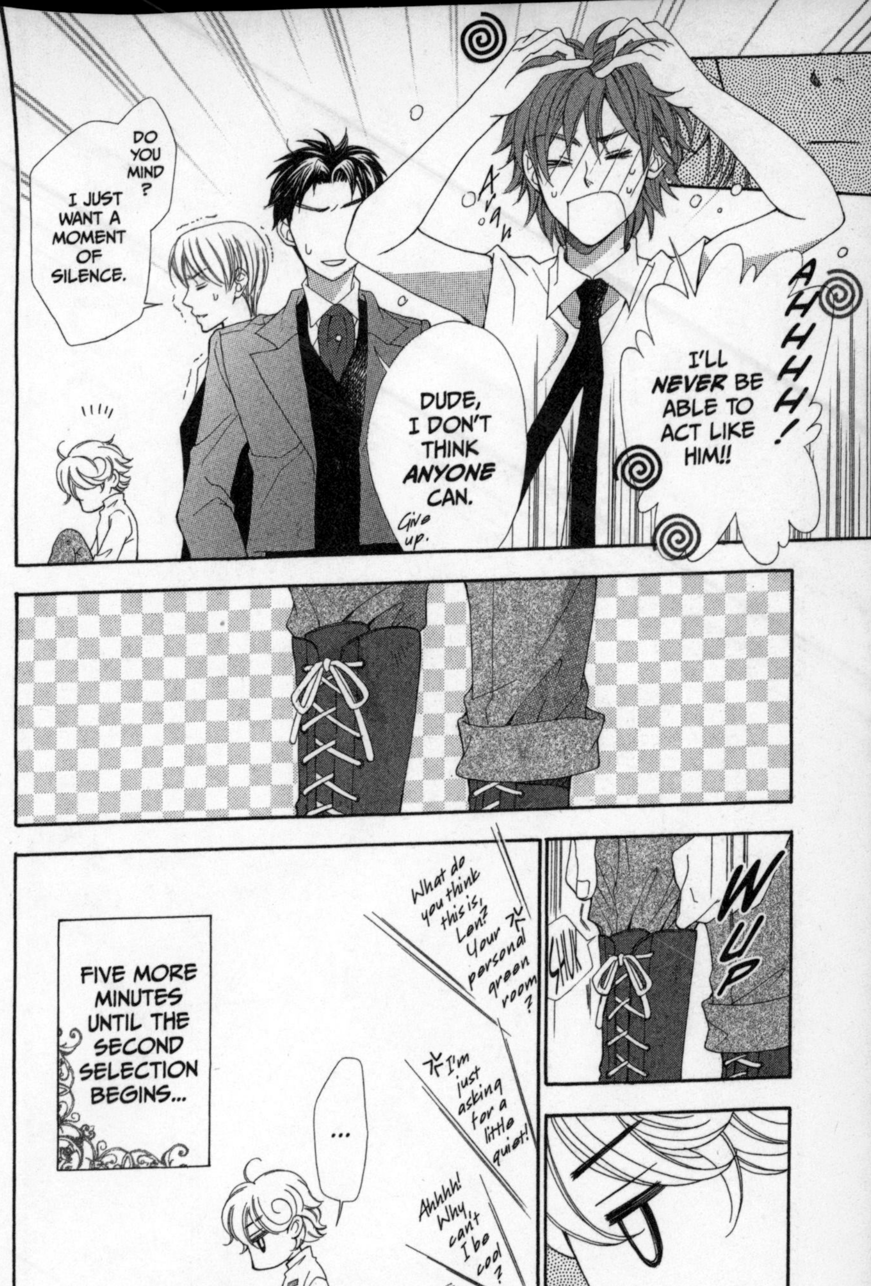
AHHHH!
I'LL NEVER BE ABLE TO ACT LIKE HIM!!
Argh
DUDE, I DON'T THINK ANYONE CAN.
Give up.
DO YOU MIND? I JUST WANT A MOMENT OF SILENCE.
WUP
SHUK
What do you think this is, Len? Your personal green room?
I'm just asking for a little quiet!
Ahhhh! Why can't I be cool?
...
FIVE MORE MINUTES UNTIL THE SECOND SELECTION BEGINS...

END OF BACKSTAGE WITH THE BOYS

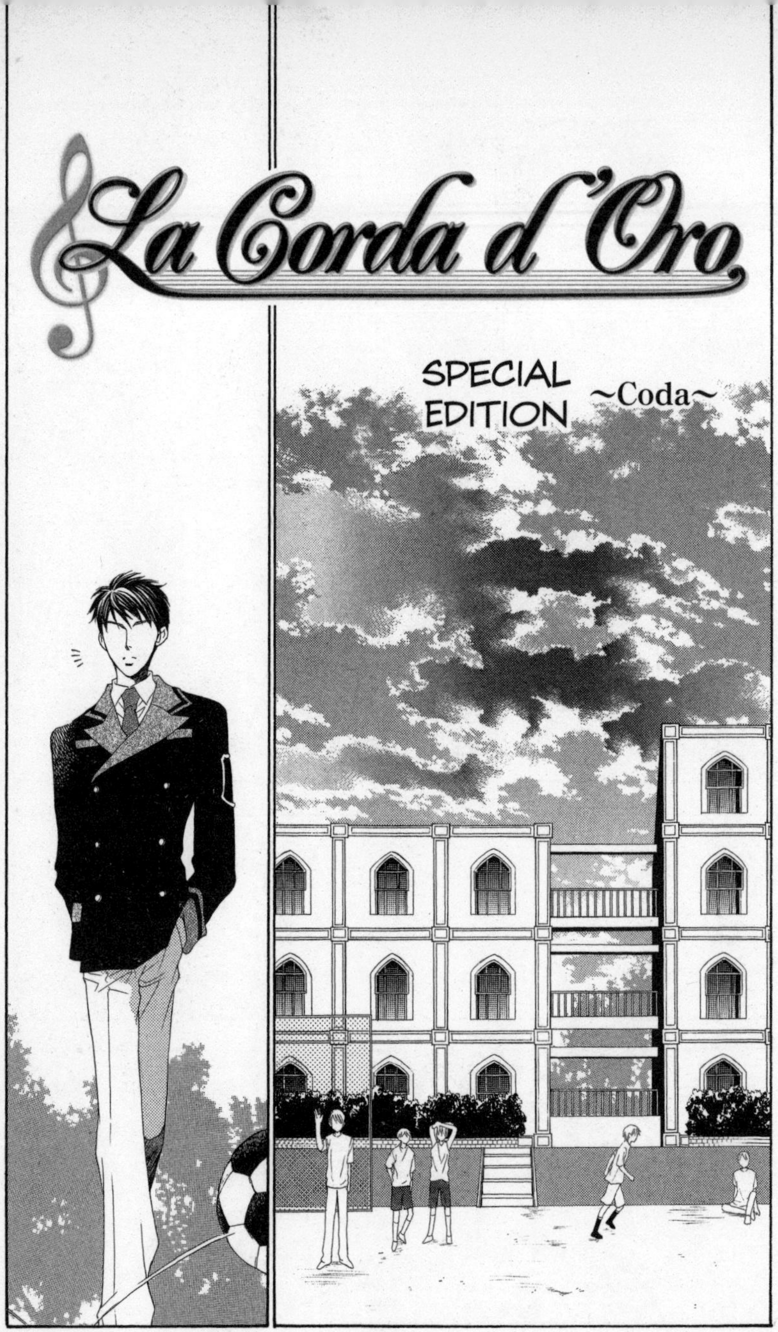
La Corda d'Oro
SPECIAL EDITION
~Coda~

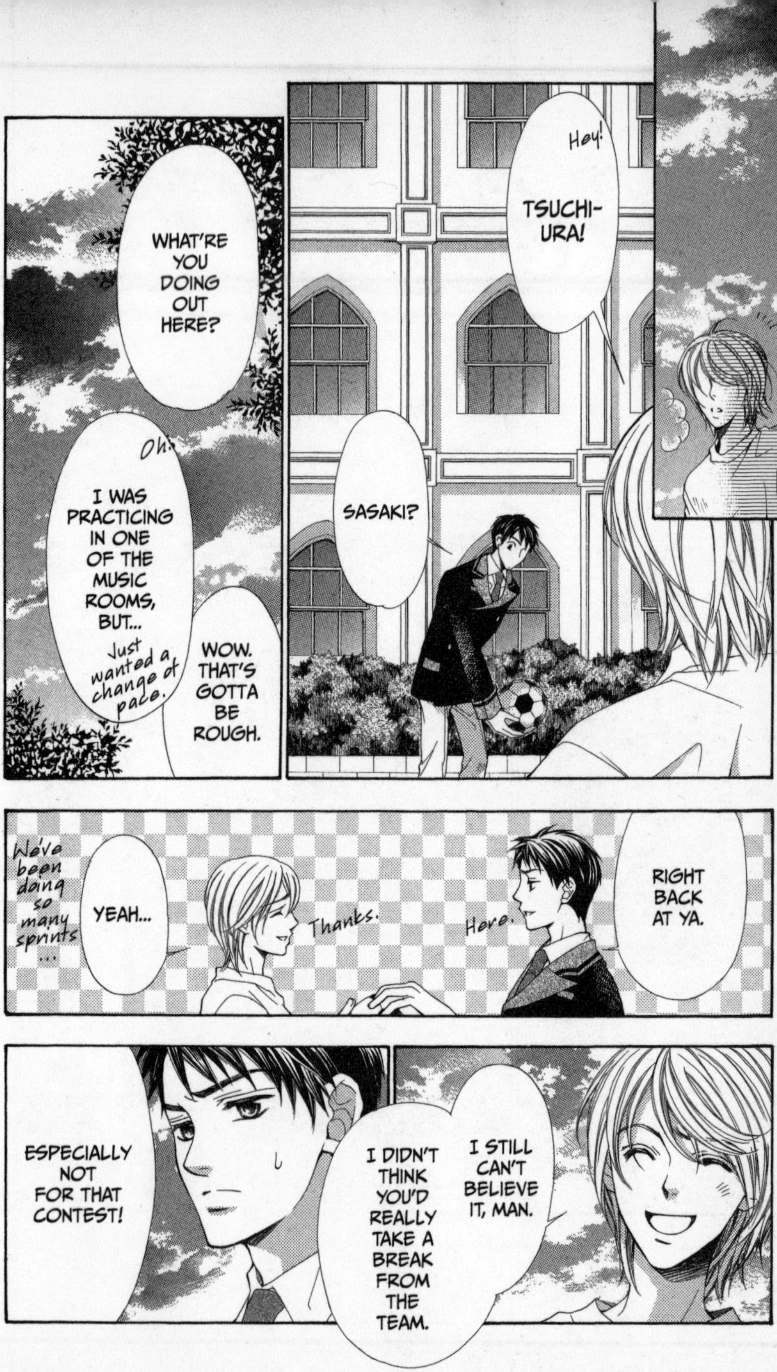
Hey!
TSUCHIURA!
SASAKI?
WHAT'RE YOU DOING OUT HERE?
Oh.
I WAS PRACTICING IN ONE OF THE MUSIC ROOMS, BUT...
Just wanted a change of pace.
WOW. THAT'S GOTTA BE ROUGH.
RIGHT BACK AT YA.
Here.
Thanks.
YEAH...
We've been doing so many sprints...
I STILL CAN'T BELIEVE IT, MAN.
I DIDN'T THINK YOU'D REALLY TAKE A BREAK FROM THE TEAM.
ESPECIALLY NOT FOR THAT CONTEST!

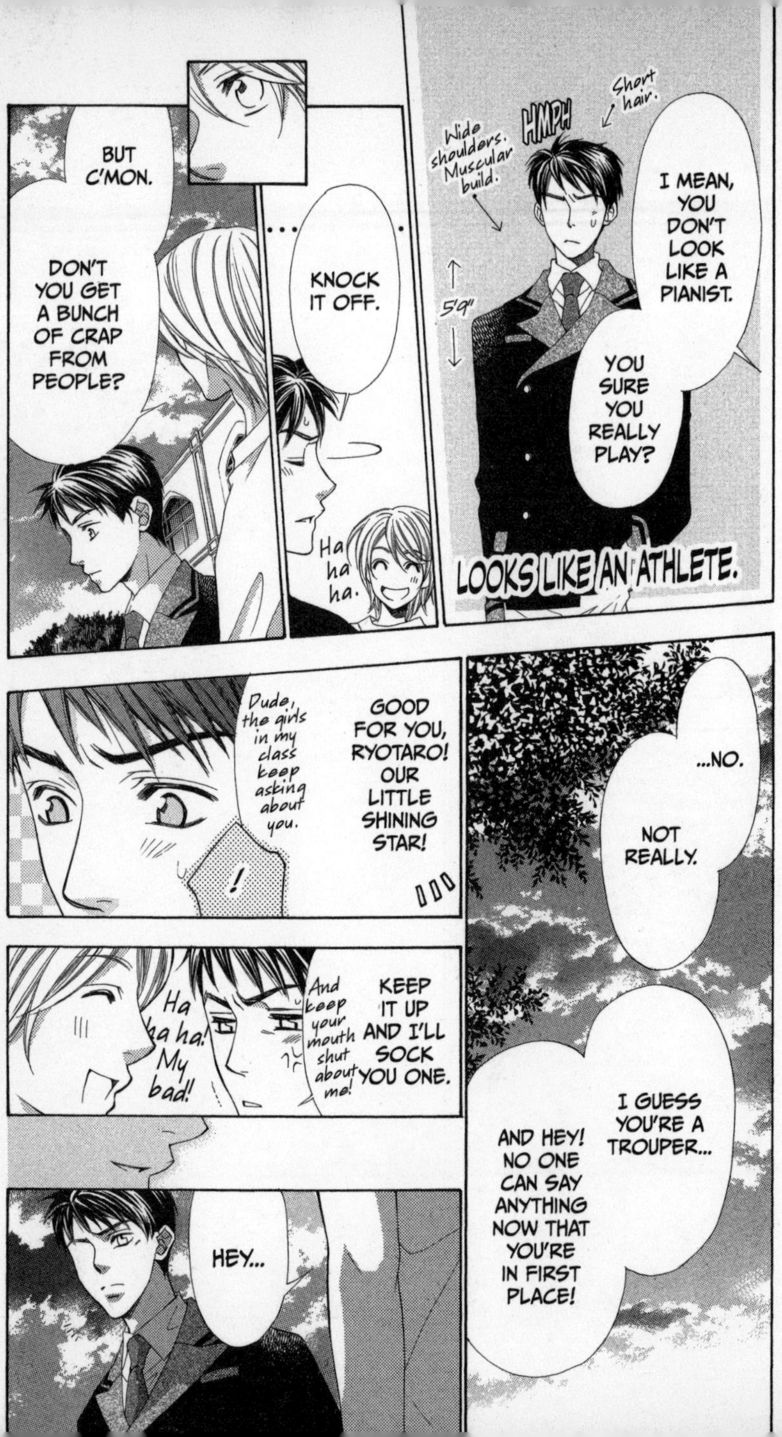
HMPH
Short hair.
Wide shoulders. Muscular build.
5'9"
I MEAN, YOU DON'T LOOK LIKE A PIANIST.
YOU SURE YOU REALLY PLAY?
LOOKS LIKE AN ATHLETE.
......
KNOCK IT OFF.
Ha ha ha.
BUT C'MON.
DON'T YOU GET A BUNCH OF CRAP FROM PEOPLE?
...NO.
NOT REALLY.
I GUESS YOU'RE A TROUPER...
AND HEY! NO ONE CAN SAY ANYTHING NOW THAT YOU'RE IN FIRST PLACE!
GOOD FOR YOU, RYOTARO! OUR LITTLE SHINING STAR!
Dude, the girls in my class keep asking about you.
!
KEEP IT UP AND I'LL SOCK YOU ONE.
And keep your mouth shut about me!
Ha ha ha! My bad!
HEY...

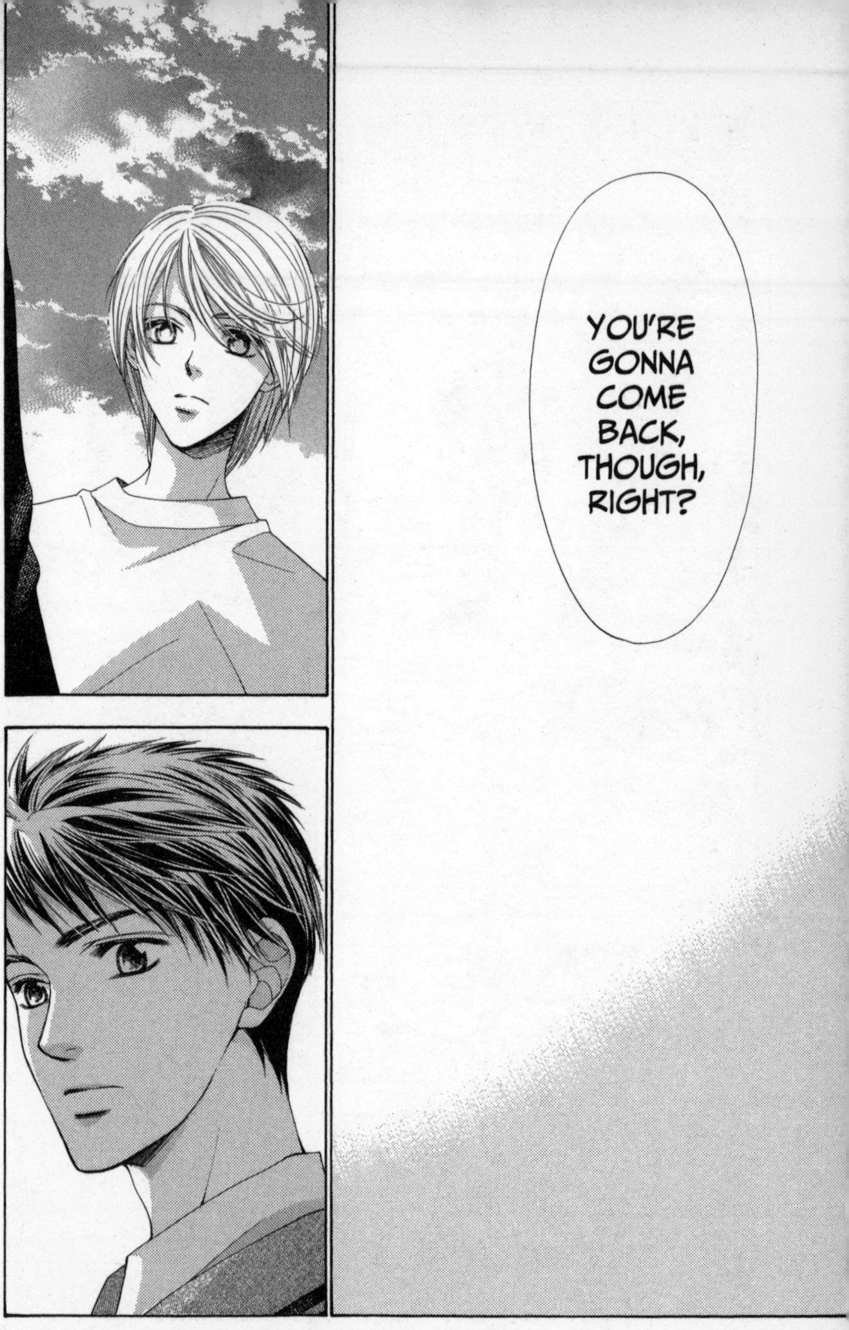
YOU'RE GONNA COME BACK, THOUGH, RIGHT?

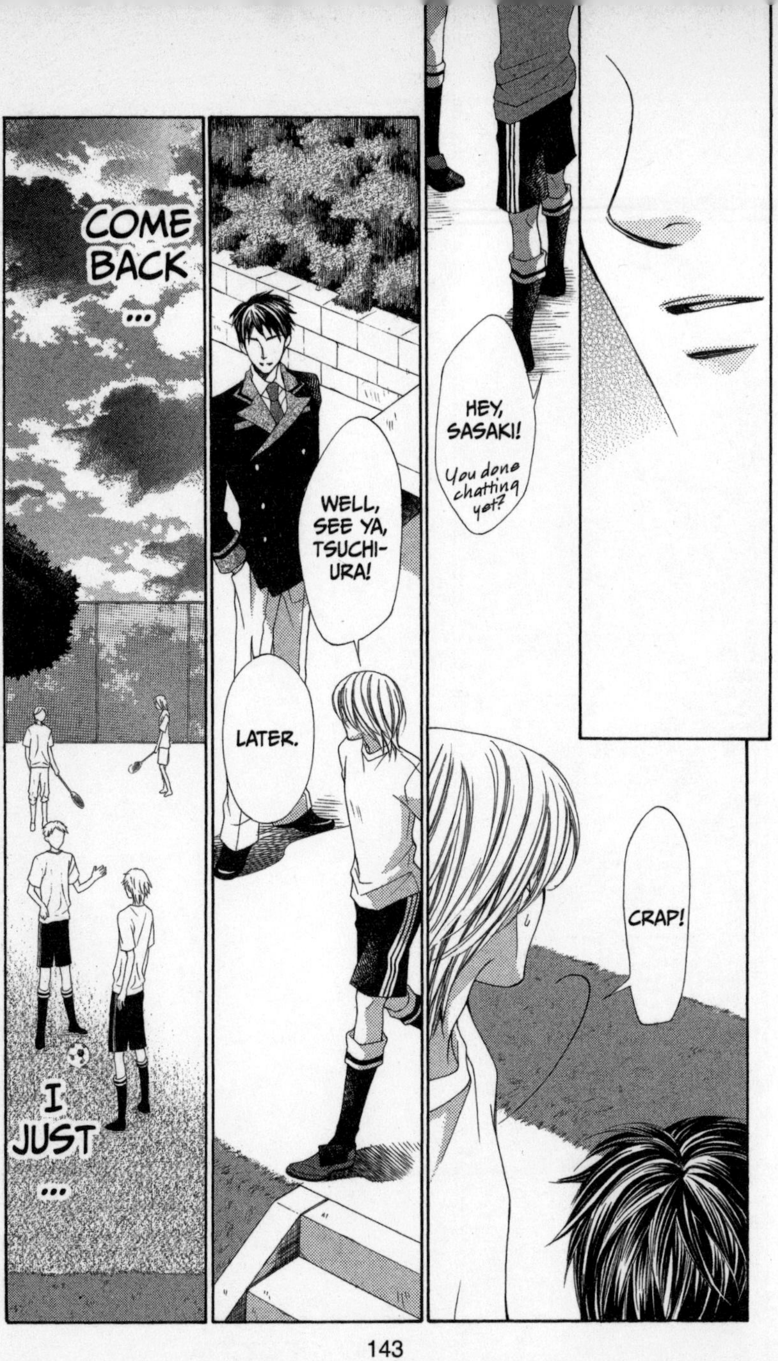
HEY, SASAKI!
You done chatting yet?
CRAP!
WELL, SEE YA, TSUCHI-URA!
LATER.
COME BACK ...
I JUST ...

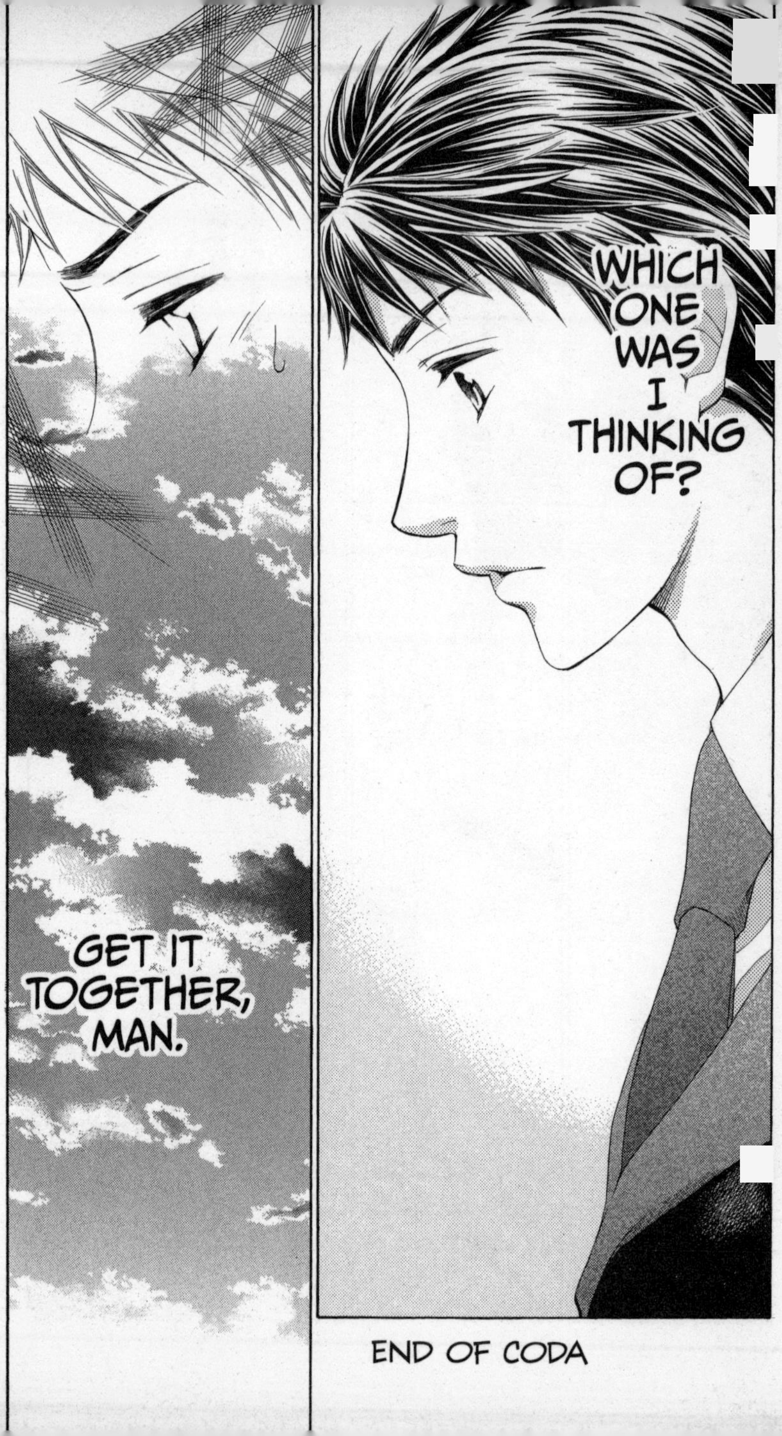
WHICH ONE WAS I THINKING OF?
GET IT TOGETHER, MAN.

END OF CODA

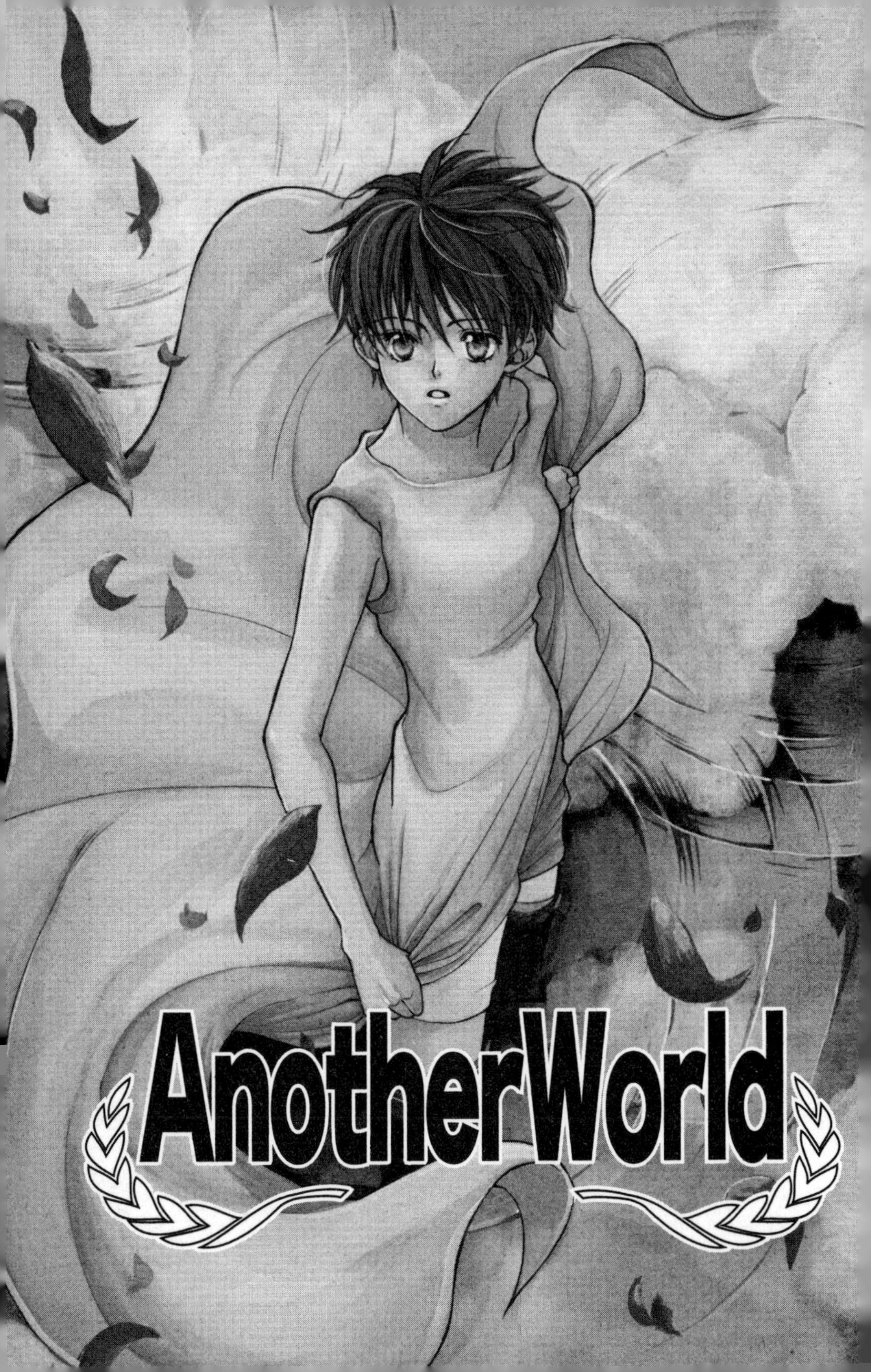
AnotherWorld

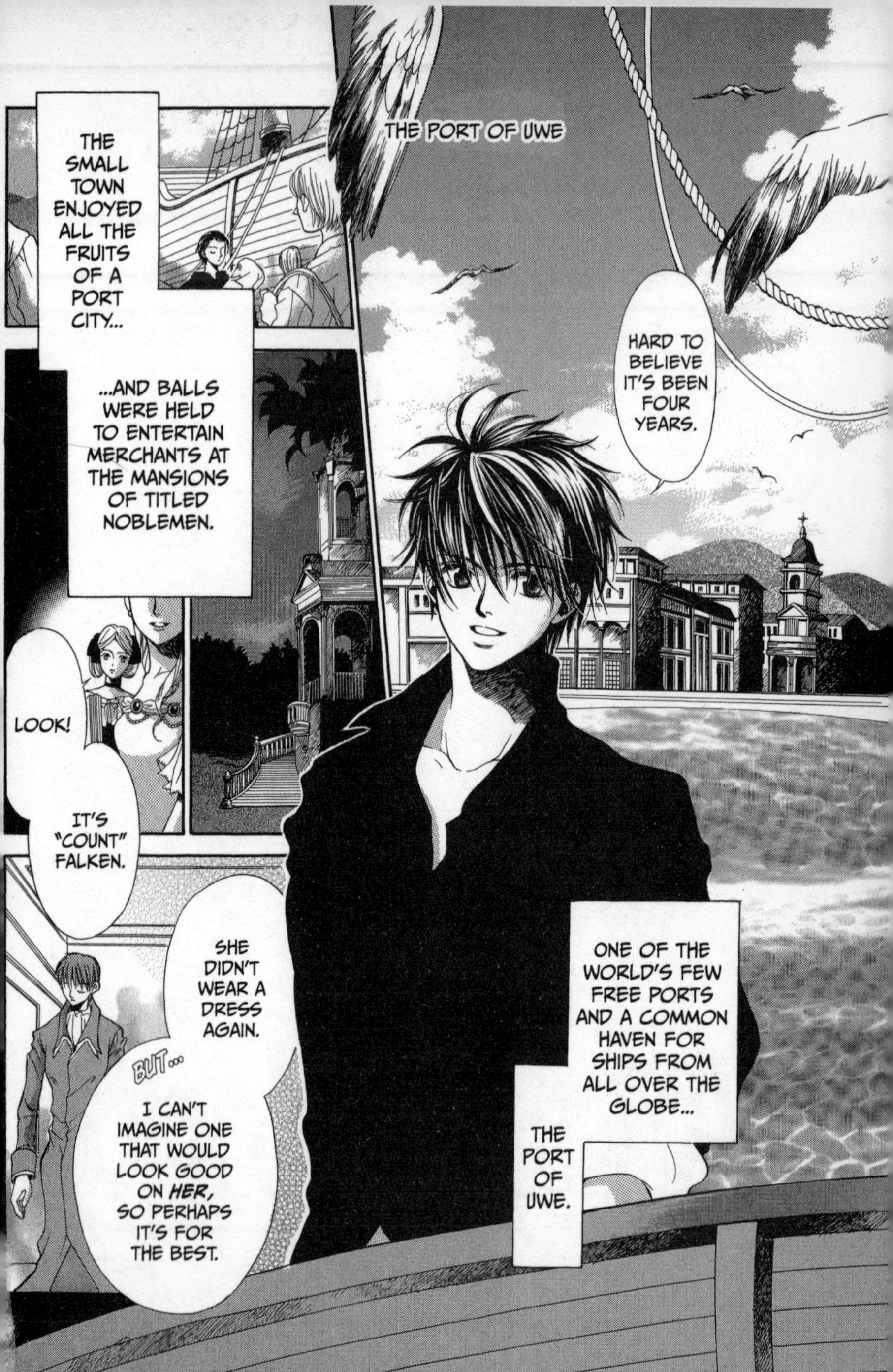
THE PORT OF UWE
HARD TO BELIEVE IT'S BEEN FOUR YEARS.
ONE OF THE WORLD'S FEW FREE PORTS AND A COMMON HAVEN FOR SHIPS FROM ALL OVER THE GLOBE...
THE PORT OF UWE.
THE SMALL TOWN ENJOYED ALL THE FRUITS OF A PORT CITY...
...AND BALLS WERE HELD TO ENTERTAIN MERCHANTS AT THE MANSIONS OF TITLED NOBLEMEN.
LOOK!
IT'S "COUNT" FALKEN.
SHE DIDN'T WEAR A DRESS AGAIN.
BUT...
I CAN'T IMAGINE ONE THAT WOULD LOOK GOOD ON *HER*, SO PERHAPS IT'S FOR THE BEST.

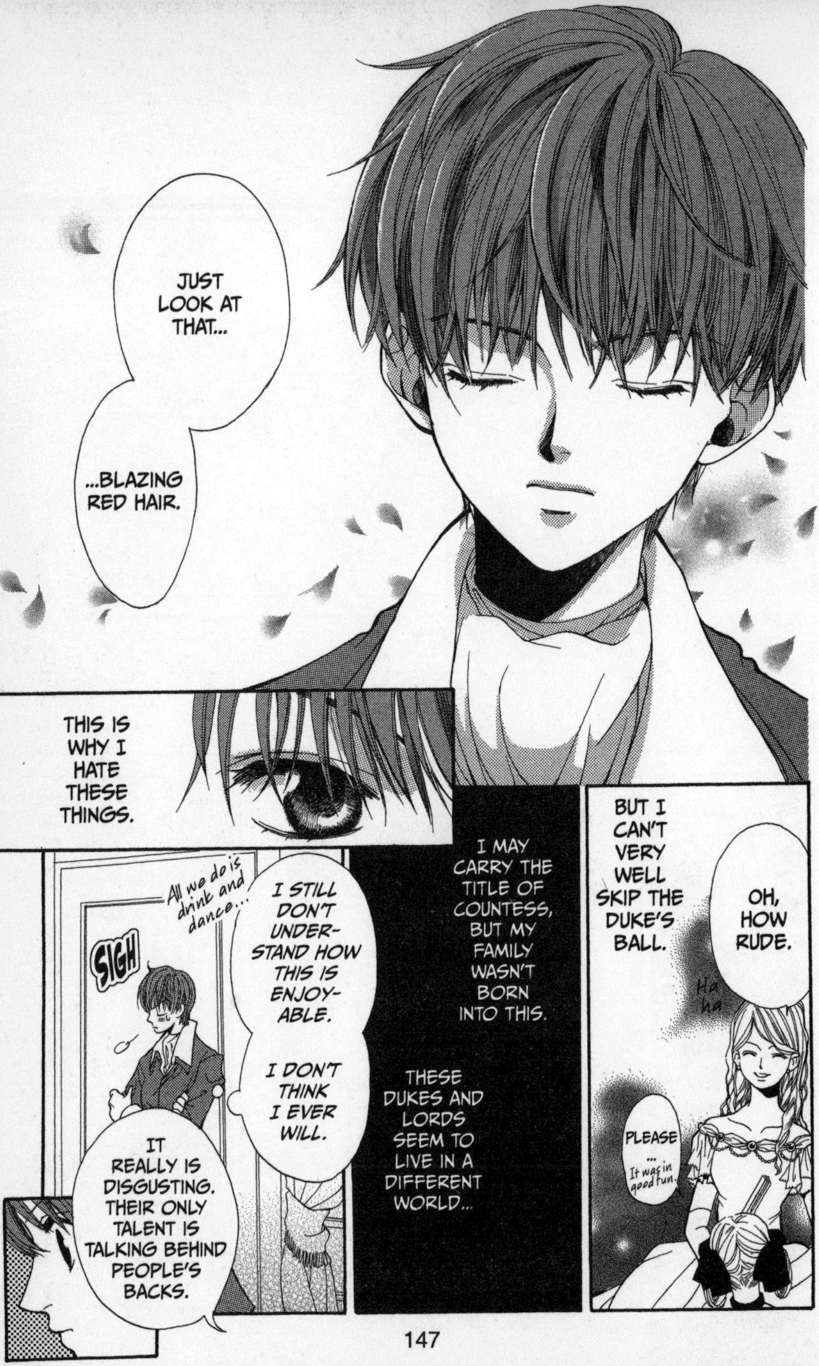

JUST LOOK AT THAT...
...BLAZING RED HAIR.
THIS IS WHY I HATE THESE THINGS.
BUT I CAN'T VERY WELL SKIP THE DUKE'S BALL.
OH, HOW RUDE.
Ha ha
PLEASE ... It was in good fun.
I MAY CARRY THE TITLE OF COUNTESS, BUT MY FAMILY WASN'T BORN INTO THIS.
THESE DUKES AND LORDS SEEM TO LIVE IN A DIFFERENT WORLD...
I STILL DON'T UNDER-STAND HOW THIS IS ENJOY-ABLE.
I DON'T THINK I EVER WILL.
All we do is drink and dance...
SIGH
IT REALLY IS DISGUSTING. THEIR ONLY TALENT IS TALKING BEHIND PEOPLE'S BACKS.

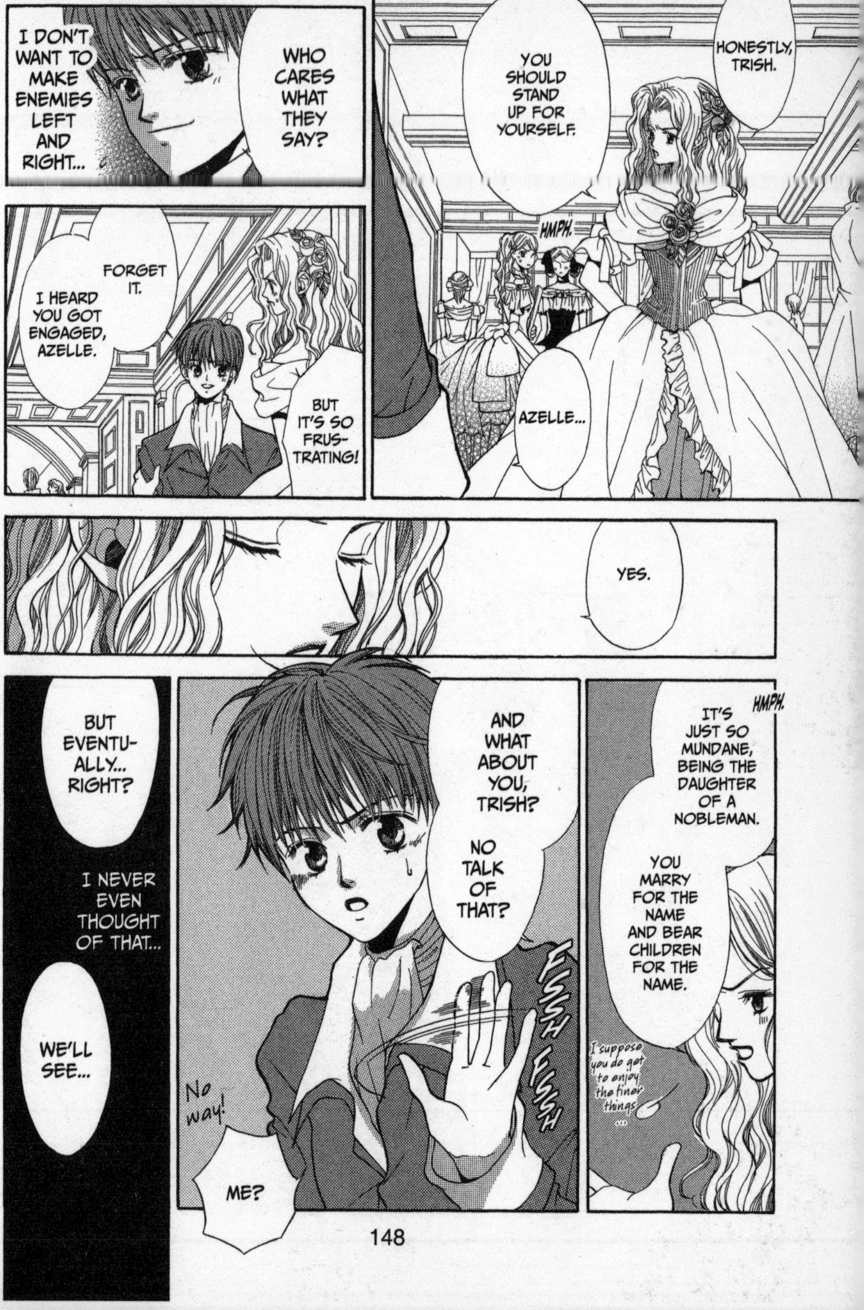
HONESTLY, TRISH.
YOU SHOULD STAND UP FOR YOURSELF.
HMPH.
AZELLE...
WHO CARES WHAT THEY SAY?
I DON'T WANT TO MAKE ENEMIES LEFT AND RIGHT...
BUT IT'S SO FRUS-TRATING!
FORGET IT.
I HEARD YOU GOT ENGAGED, AZELLE.
YES.
HMPH.
IT'S JUST SO MUNDANE, BEING THE DAUGHTER OF A NOBLEMAN.
YOU MARRY FOR THE NAME AND BEAR CHILDREN FOR THE NAME.
I suppose you do get to enjoy the finer things...
AND WHAT ABOUT YOU, TRISH?
NO TALK OF THAT?
FSSH FSSH
No way!
ME?
BUT EVENTU-ALLY... RIGHT?
I NEVER EVEN THOUGHT OF THAT...
WE'LL SEE...

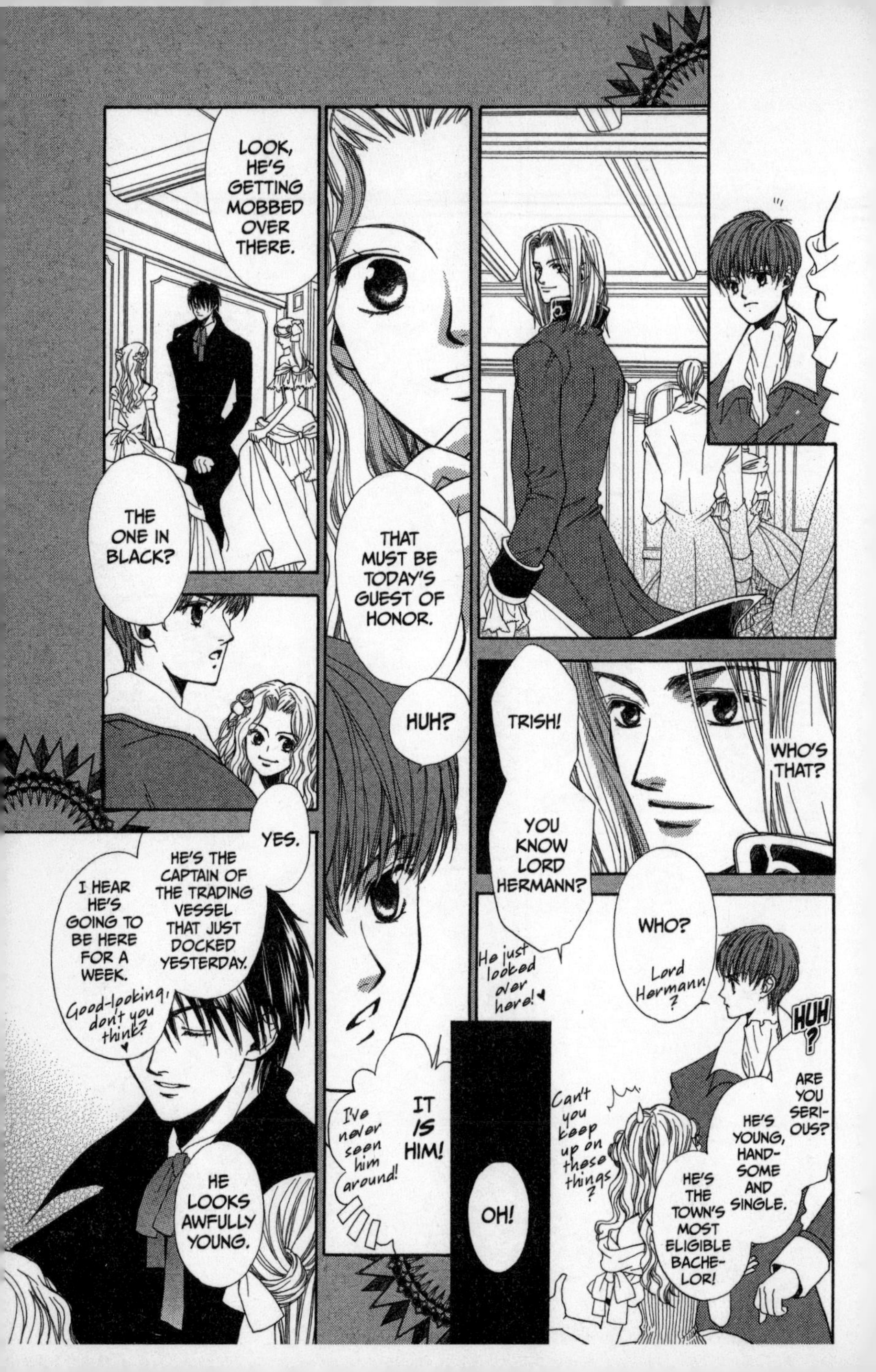
WHO'S THAT?
TRISH!
YOU KNOW LORD HERMANN?
WHO?
Lord Hermann?
He just looked over here!♥
HUH?
ARE YOU SERIOUS?
HE'S YOUNG, HANDSOME AND SINGLE.
HE'S THE TOWN'S MOST ELIGIBLE BACHELOR!
Can't you keep up on these things?
OH!
THAT MUST BE TODAY'S GUEST OF HONOR.
HUH?
IT IS HIM!
I've never seen him around!
LOOK, HE'S GETTING MOBBED OVER THERE.
THE ONE IN BLACK?
YES.
HE'S THE CAPTAIN OF THE TRADING VESSEL THAT JUST DOCKED YESTERDAY.
I HEAR HE'S GOING TO BE HERE FOR A WEEK.
Good-looking, don't you think?♥
HE LOOKS AWFULLY YOUNG.

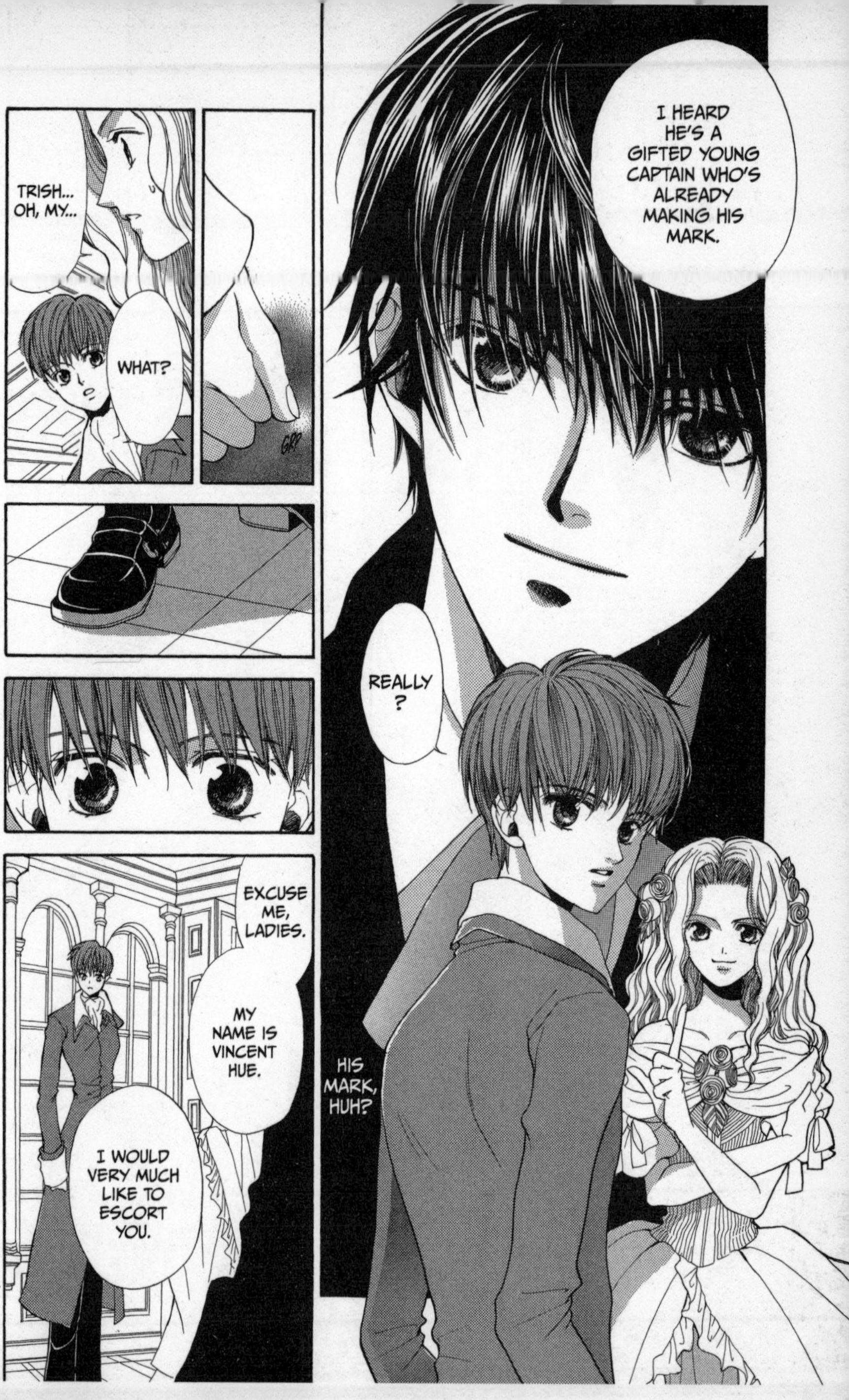
I HEARD HE'S A GIFTED YOUNG CAPTAIN WHO'S ALREADY MAKING HIS MARK.
REALLY?
HIS MARK, HUH?
GRP
TRISH... OH, MY...
WHAT?
EXCUSE ME, LADIES.
MY NAME IS VINCENT HUE.
I WOULD VERY MUCH LIKE TO ESCORT YOU.

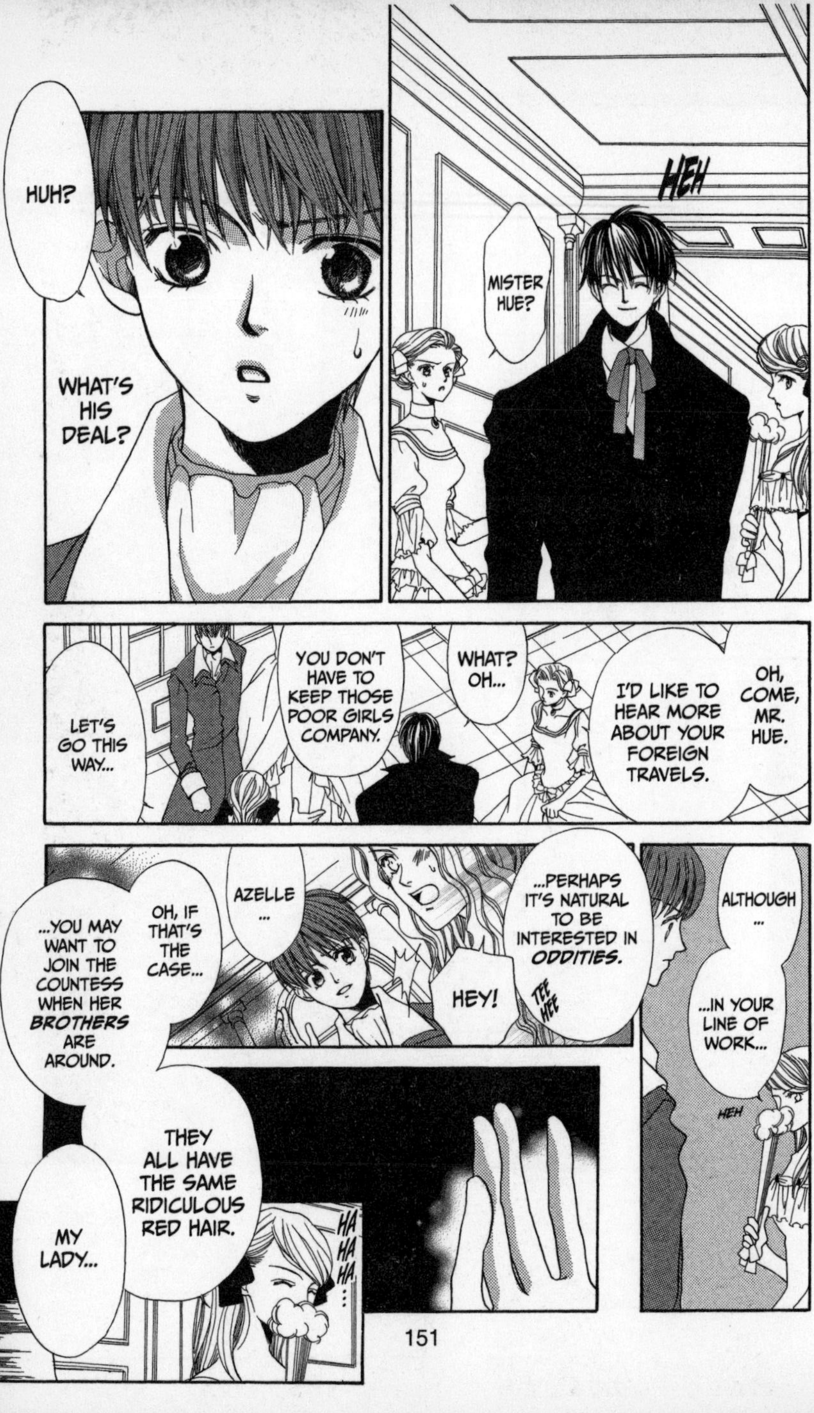
HEH
MISTER HUE?
HUH?
WHAT'S HIS DEAL?
OH, COME, MR. HUE.
I'D LIKE TO HEAR MORE ABOUT YOUR FOREIGN TRAVELS.
WHAT? OH...
YOU DON'T HAVE TO KEEP THOSE POOR GIRLS COMPANY.
LET'S GO THIS WAY...
ALTHOUGH...
...IN YOUR LINE OF WORK...
HEH
...PERHAPS IT'S NATURAL TO BE INTERESTED IN *ODDITIES.*
TEE HEE
HEY!
AZELLE...
OH, IF THAT'S THE CASE...
...YOU MAY WANT TO JOIN THE COUNTESS WHEN HER *BROTHERS* ARE AROUND.
THEY ALL HAVE THE SAME RIDICULOUS RED HAIR.
HA HA HA...
MY LADY...

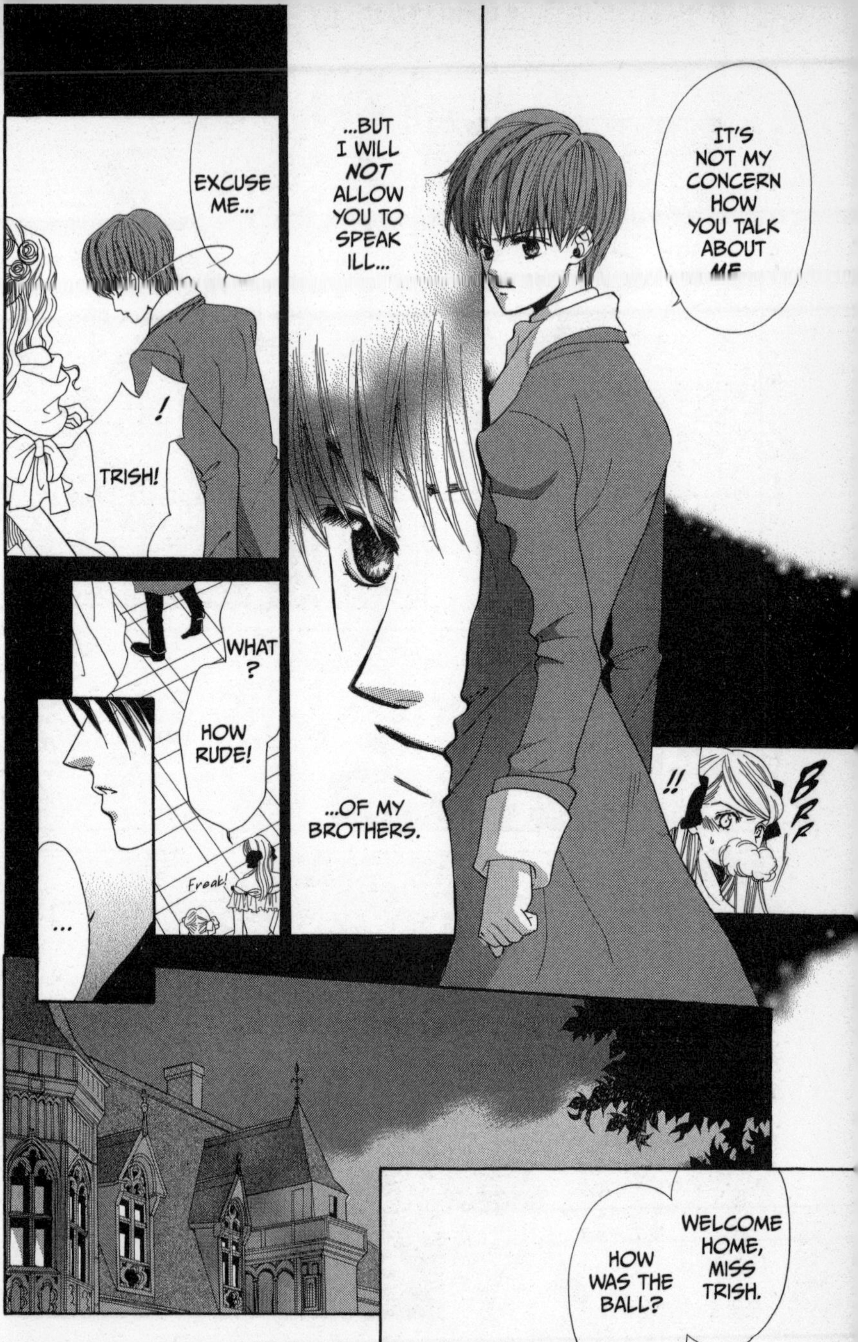
IT'S NOT MY CONCERN HOW YOU TALK ABOUT ME
...BUT I WILL NOT ALLOW YOU TO SPEAK ILL...
...OF MY BROTHERS.
!!
BRR
EXCUSE ME...
!
TRISH!
WHAT?
HOW RUDE!
Freak!
...
WELCOME HOME, MISS TRISH.
HOW WAS THE BALL?

FIVE

"Another World" is a short story from a frighteningly long time ago. Oh, the nostalgia. Frankly, I don't think it's good for one's mental health to look back like this. When I first got these pages back, I couldn't even look at them... *They embarrassed me...*

Old comics are just embarrassing!

I remember I was excited about doing my first color cover, but I had no idea how to color it...

Ha ha ha...

I'd be flattered if you found it even a little enjoyable.

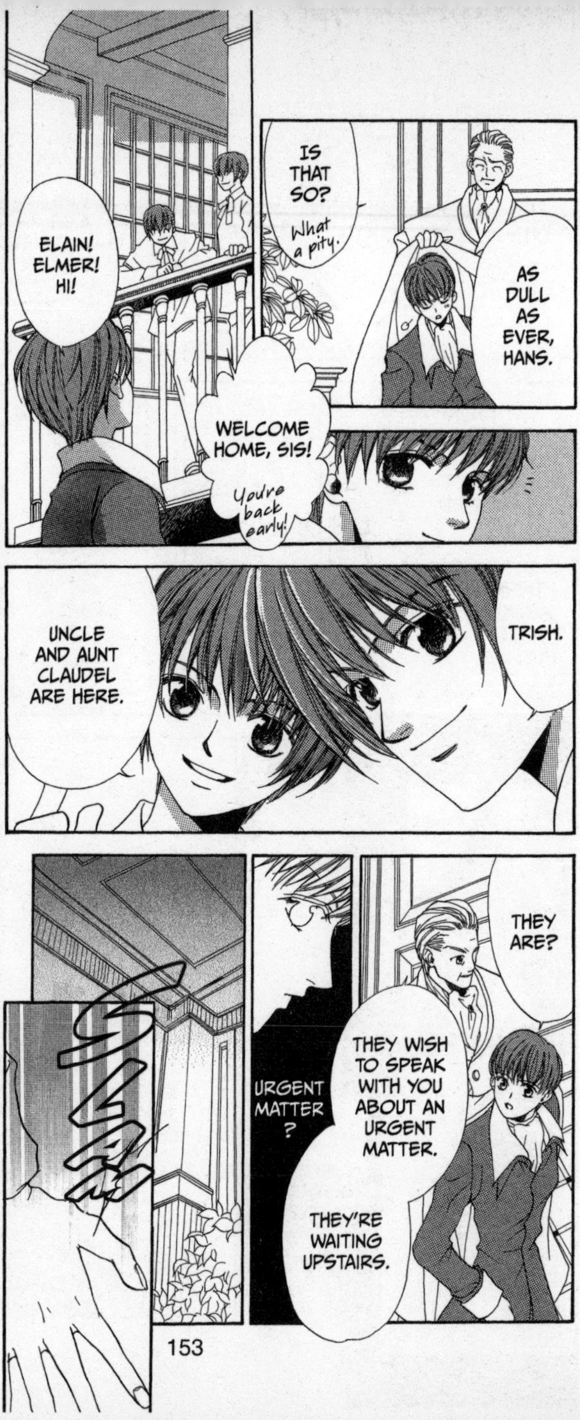
AS DULL AS EVER, HANS.
IS THAT SO? What a pity.
WELCOME HOME, SIS! You're back early!
ELAIN! ELMER! HI!
TRISH.
UNCLE AND AUNT CLAUDEL ARE HERE.
THEY ARE?
THEY WISH TO SPEAK WITH YOU ABOUT AN URGENT MATTER.
THEY'RE WAITING UPSTAIRS.
URGENT MATTER?

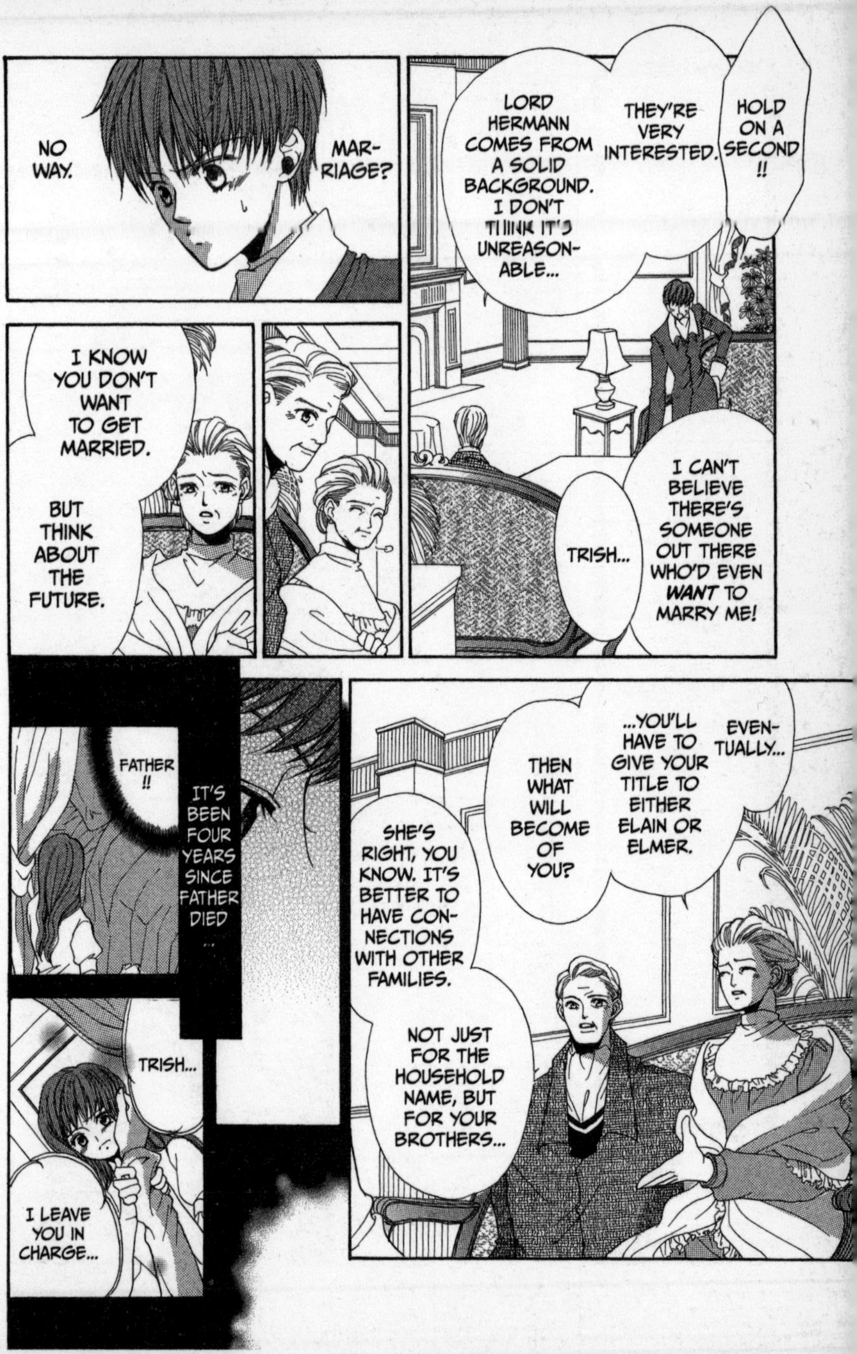
HOLD ON A SECOND !!
THEY'RE VERY INTERESTED.
LORD HERMANN COMES FROM A SOLID BACKGROUND. I DON'T THINK IT'S UNREASONABLE...
I CAN'T BELIEVE THERE'S SOMEONE OUT THERE WHO'D EVEN *WANT* TO MARRY ME!
TRISH...
MARRIAGE?
NO WAY.
I KNOW YOU DON'T WANT TO GET MARRIED.
BUT THINK ABOUT THE FUTURE.
EVENTUALLY...
...YOU'LL HAVE TO GIVE YOUR TITLE TO EITHER ELAIN OR ELMER.
THEN WHAT WILL BECOME OF YOU?
SHE'S RIGHT, YOU KNOW. IT'S BETTER TO HAVE CONNECTIONS WITH OTHER FAMILIES.
NOT JUST FOR THE HOUSEHOLD NAME, BUT FOR YOUR BROTHERS...
IT'S BEEN FOUR YEARS SINCE FATHER DIED...
FATHER !!
TRISH...
I LEAVE YOU IN CHARGE...

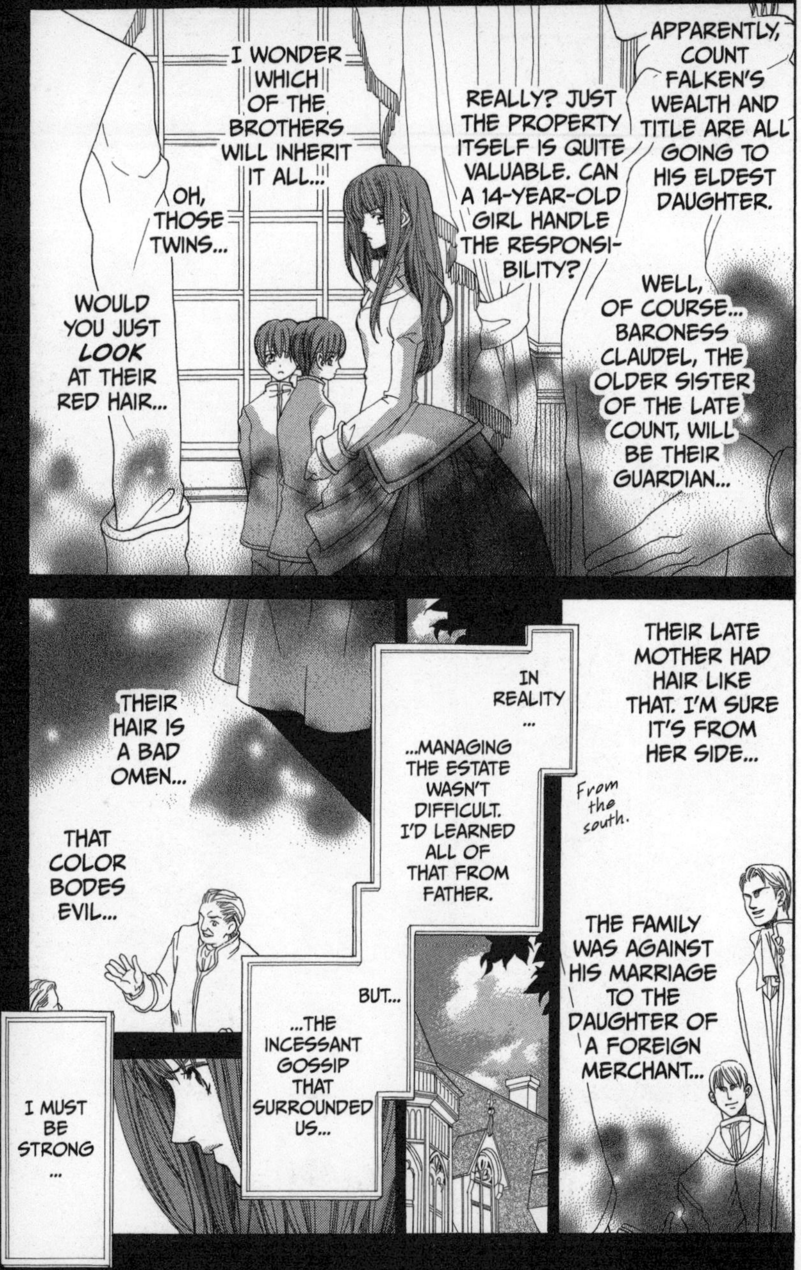
APPARENTLY, COUNT FALKEN'S WEALTH AND TITLE ARE ALL GOING TO HIS ELDEST DAUGHTER.
REALLY? JUST THE PROPERTY ITSELF IS QUITE VALUABLE. CAN A 14-YEAR-OLD GIRL HANDLE THE RESPONSIBILITY?
WELL, OF COURSE... BARONESS CLAUDEL, THE OLDER SISTER OF THE LATE COUNT, WILL BE THEIR GUARDIAN...
I WONDER WHICH OF THE BROTHERS WILL INHERIT IT ALL...
OH, THOSE TWINS...
WOULD YOU JUST *LOOK* AT THEIR RED HAIR...
THEIR LATE MOTHER HAD HAIR LIKE THAT. I'M SURE IT'S FROM HER SIDE...
From the south.
THE FAMILY WAS AGAINST HIS MARRIAGE TO THE DAUGHTER OF A FOREIGN MERCHANT...
IN REALITY...
...MANAGING THE ESTATE WASN'T DIFFICULT. I'D LEARNED ALL OF THAT FROM FATHER.
BUT...
...THE INCESSANT GOSSIP THAT SURROUNDED US...
THEIR HAIR IS A BAD OMEN...
THAT COLOR BODES EVIL...
I MUST BE STRONG...

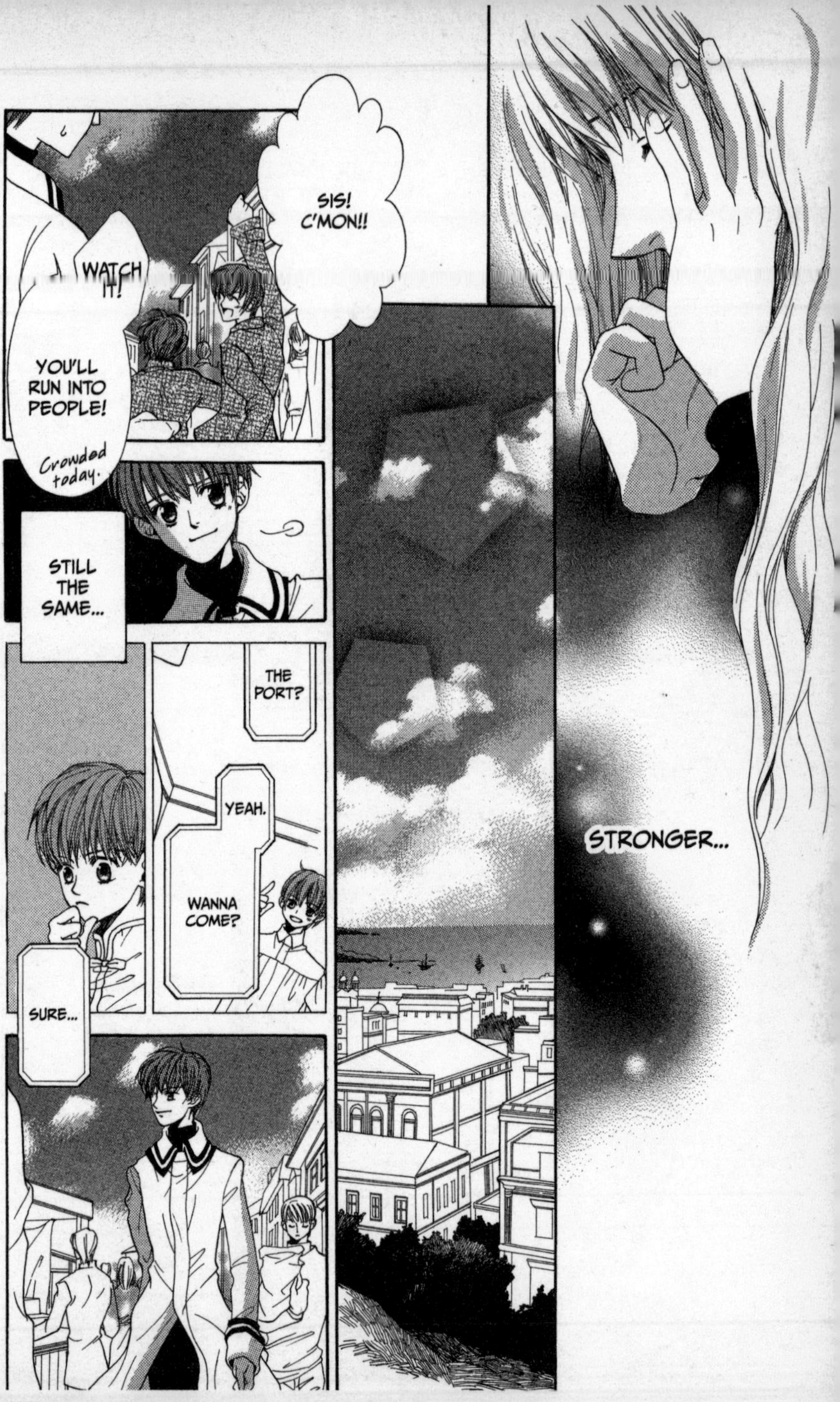
STRONGER...
SIS! C'MON!!
WATCH IT!
YOU'LL RUN INTO PEOPLE!
Crowded today.
STILL THE SAME...
THE PORT?
YEAH.
WANNA COME?
SURE...

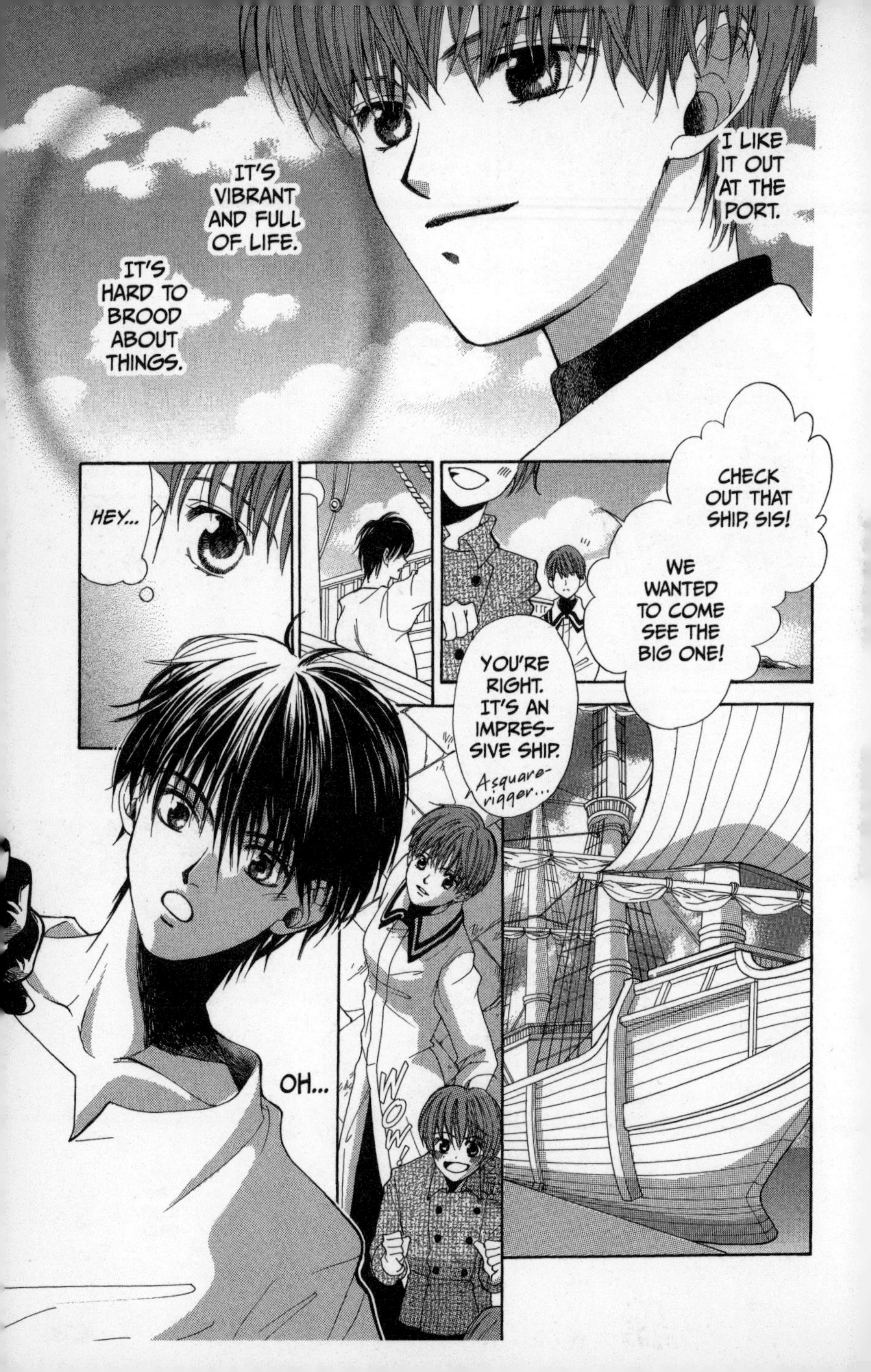
I LIKE IT OUT AT THE PORT.
IT'S VIBRANT AND FULL OF LIFE.
IT'S HARD TO BROOD ABOUT THINGS.
CHECK OUT THAT SHIP, SIS!
WE WANTED TO COME SEE THE BIG ONE!
HEY...
YOU'RE RIGHT. IT'S AN IMPRES-SIVE SHIP.
A square-rigger...
WOW!
OH...

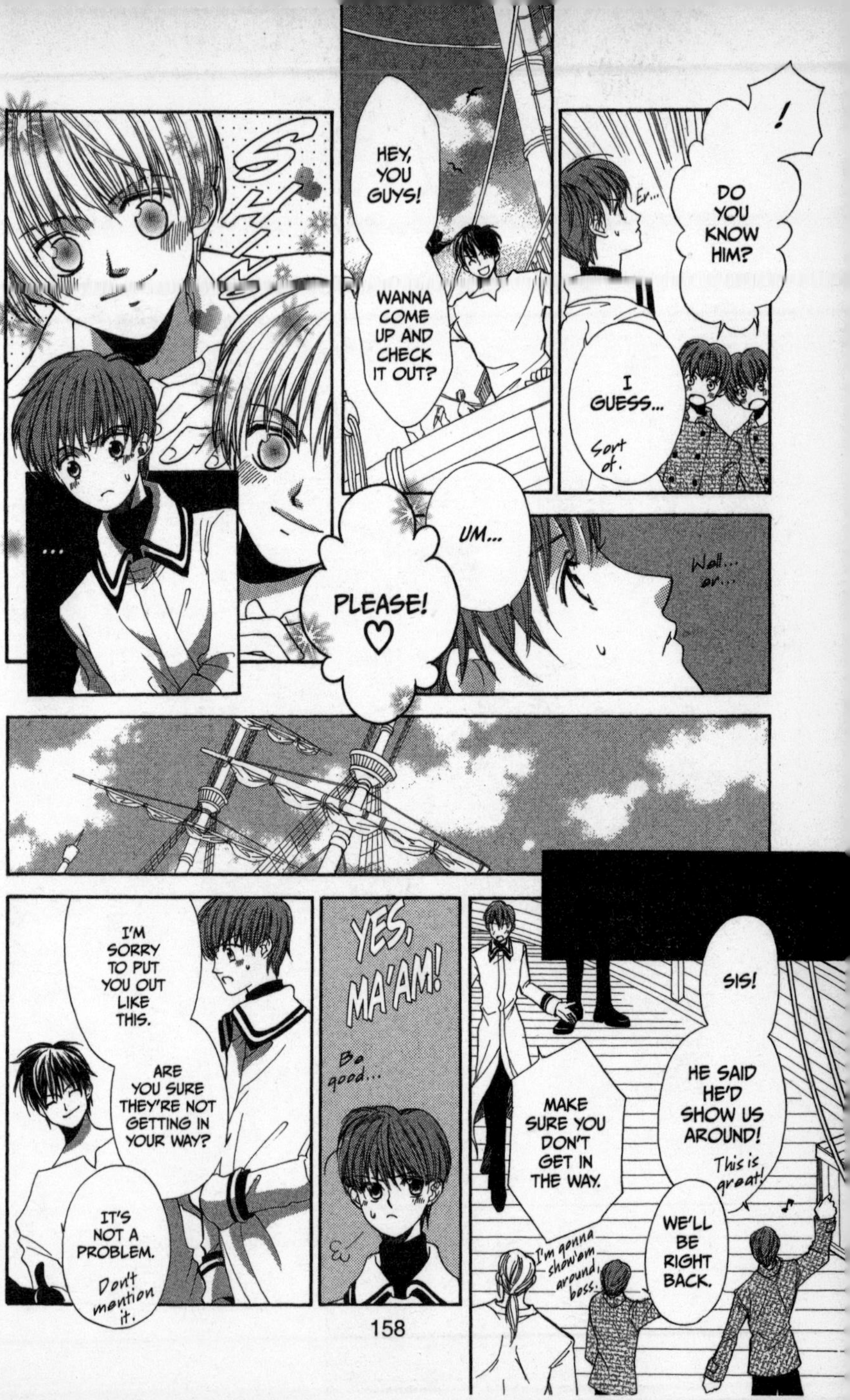
!
DO YOU KNOW HIM?
Er...
I GUESS...
Sort of.
HEY, YOU GUYS!
WANNA COME UP AND CHECK IT OUT?
UM...
Well... er...
PLEASE! ♡
SHIN
...
SIS!
HE SAID HE'D SHOW US AROUND!
This is great!
WE'LL BE RIGHT BACK.
I'm gonna show'em around, boss.
MAKE SURE YOU DON'T GET IN THE WAY.
YES, MA'AM!
Be good...
I'M SORRY TO PUT YOU OUT LIKE THIS.
ARE YOU SURE THEY'RE NOT GETTING IN YOUR WAY?
IT'S NOT A PROBLEM.
Don't mention it.

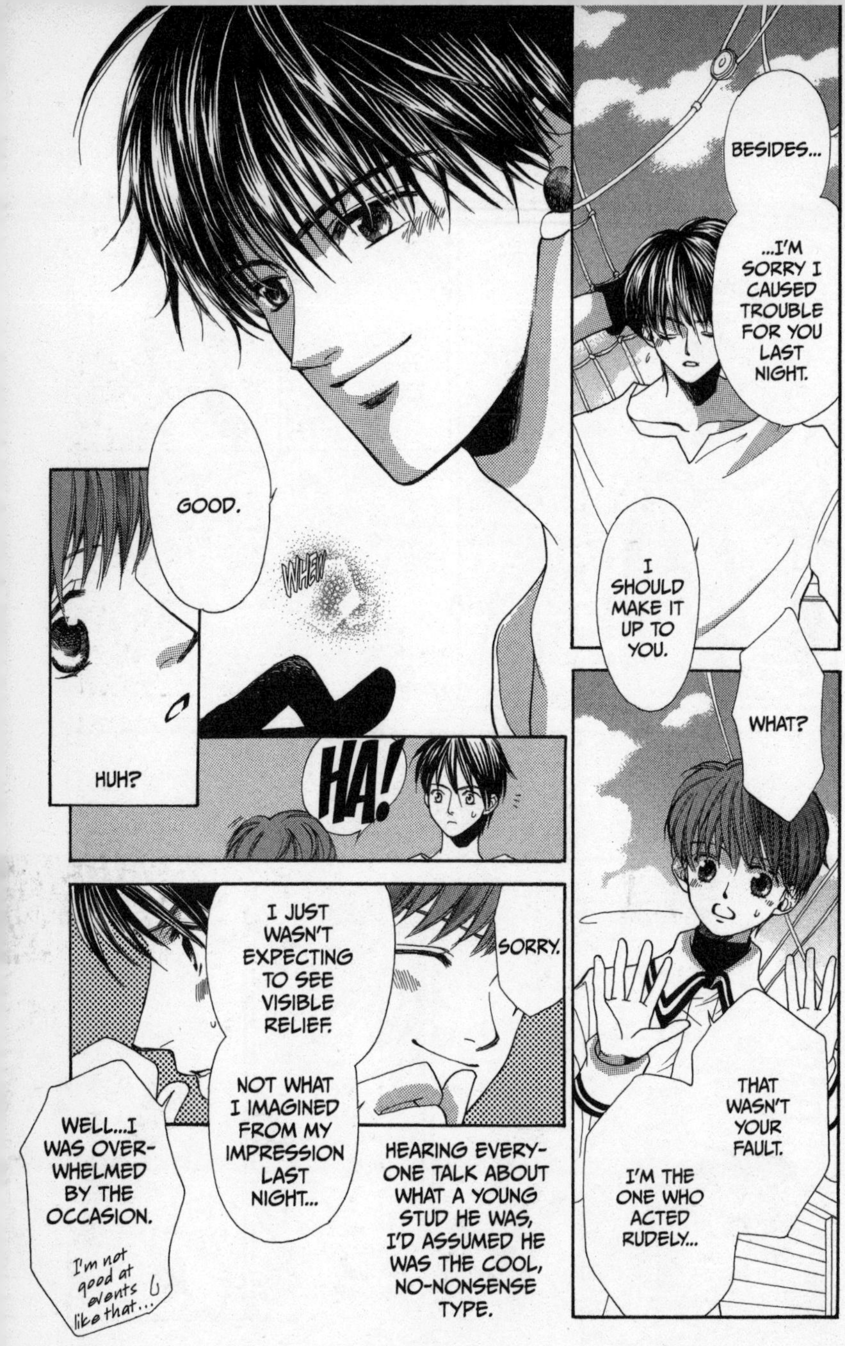
BESIDES...
...I'M SORRY I CAUSED TROUBLE FOR YOU LAST NIGHT.
I SHOULD MAKE IT UP TO YOU.
GOOD.
WHEW
HUH?
WHAT?
THAT WASN'T YOUR FAULT.
I'M THE ONE WHO ACTED RUDELY...
HA!
SORRY.
I JUST WASN'T EXPECTING TO SEE VISIBLE RELIEF.
NOT WHAT I IMAGINED FROM MY IMPRESSION LAST NIGHT...
HEARING EVERY-ONE TALK ABOUT WHAT A YOUNG STUD HE WAS, I'D ASSUMED HE WAS THE COOL, NO-NONSENSE TYPE.
WELL...I WAS OVER-WHELMED BY THE OCCASION.
I'm not good at events like that...

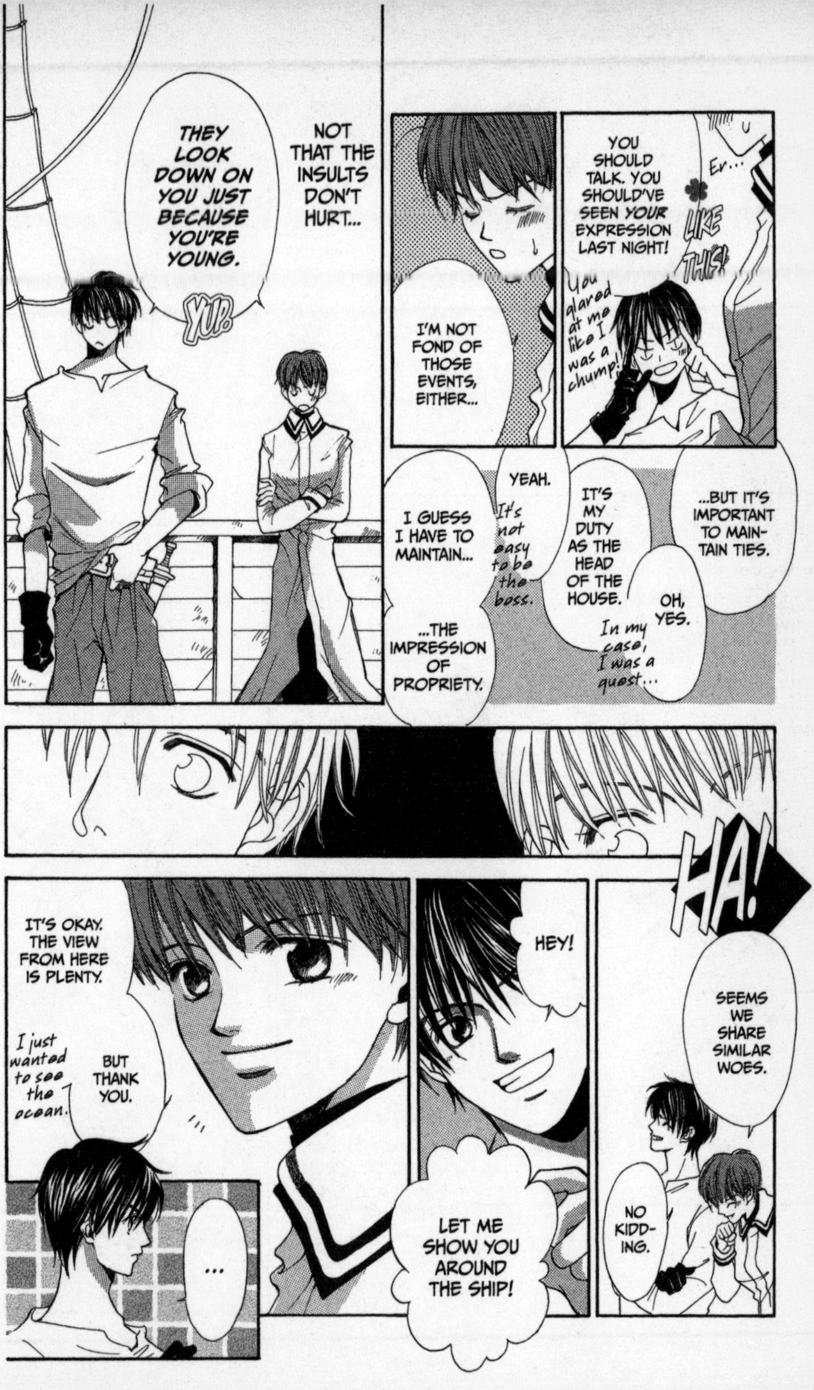
YOU SHOULD TALK. YOU SHOULD'VE SEEN YOUR EXPRESSION LAST NIGHT!
Er...
LIKE THIS!
You glared at me like I was a chump!
I'M NOT FOND OF THOSE EVENTS, EITHER...
...BUT IT'S IMPORTANT TO MAIN-TAIN TIES.
OH, YES.
In my case, I was a guest...
IT'S MY DUTY AS THE HEAD OF THE HOUSE.
YEAH.
It's not easy to be the boss.
I GUESS I HAVE TO MAINTAIN...
...THE IMPRESSION OF PROPRIETY.
NOT THAT THE INSULTS DON'T HURT...
THEY LOOK DOWN ON YOU JUST BECAUSE YOU'RE YOUNG.
YUP.
HA!
SEEMS WE SHARE SIMILAR WOES.
NO KIDD-ING.
HEY!
LET ME SHOW YOU AROUND THE SHIP!
IT'S OKAY. THE VIEW FROM HERE IS PLENTY.
BUT THANK YOU.
I just wanted to see the ocean.
...

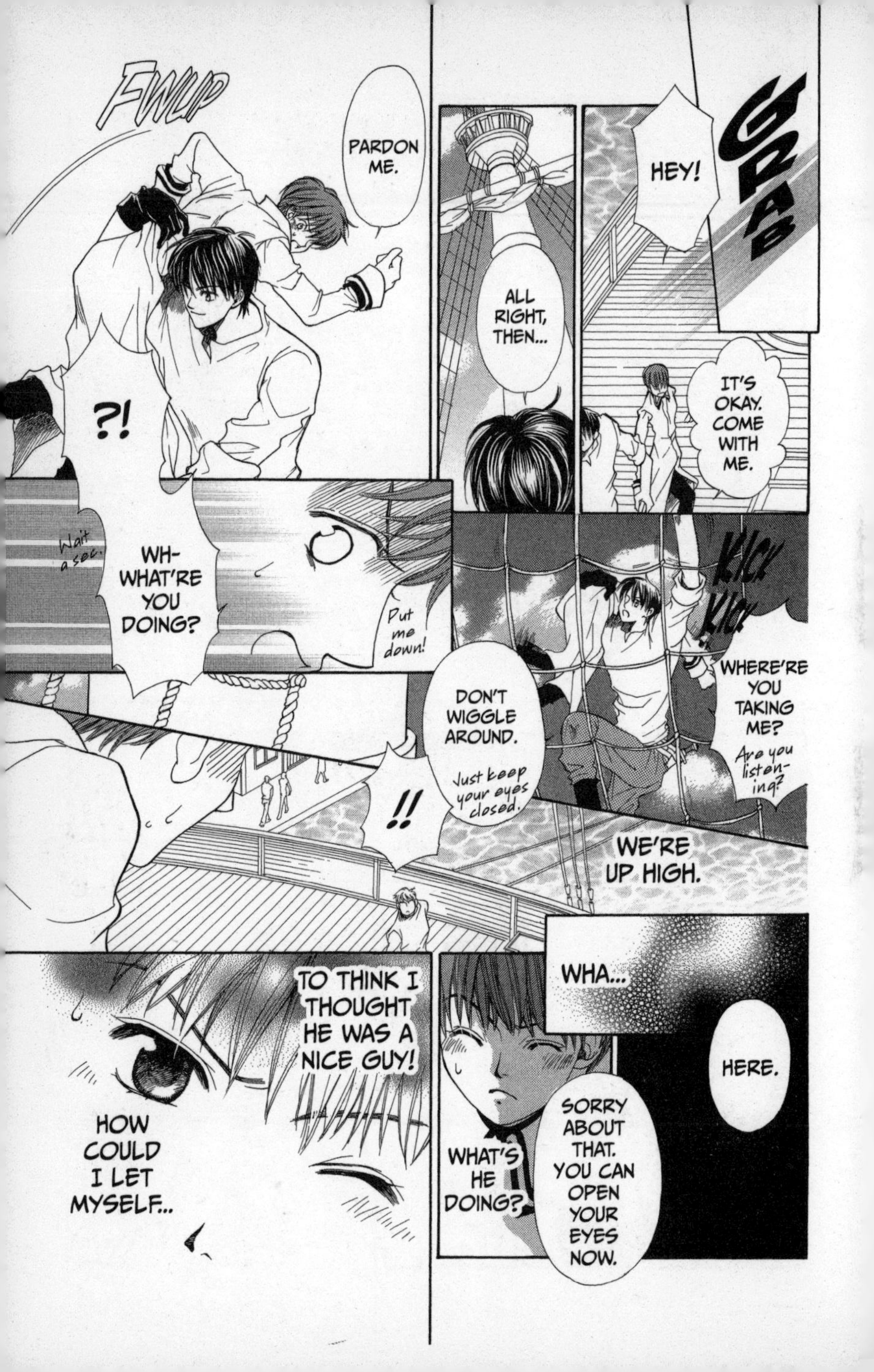
GRAB
HEY!
IT'S OKAY. COME WITH ME.
ALL RIGHT, THEN...
PARDON ME.
FWUP
?!
KICK KICK
WHERE'RE YOU TAKING ME?
Are you listen-ing?
DON'T WIGGLE AROUND.
Just keep your eyes closed.
WH-WHAT'RE YOU DOING?
Wait a sec.
Put me down!
!!
WE'RE UP HIGH.
WHA...
HERE.
SORRY ABOUT THAT. YOU CAN OPEN YOUR EYES NOW.
WHAT'S HE DOING?
TO THINK I THOUGHT HE WAS A NICE GUY!
HOW COULD I LET MYSELF...

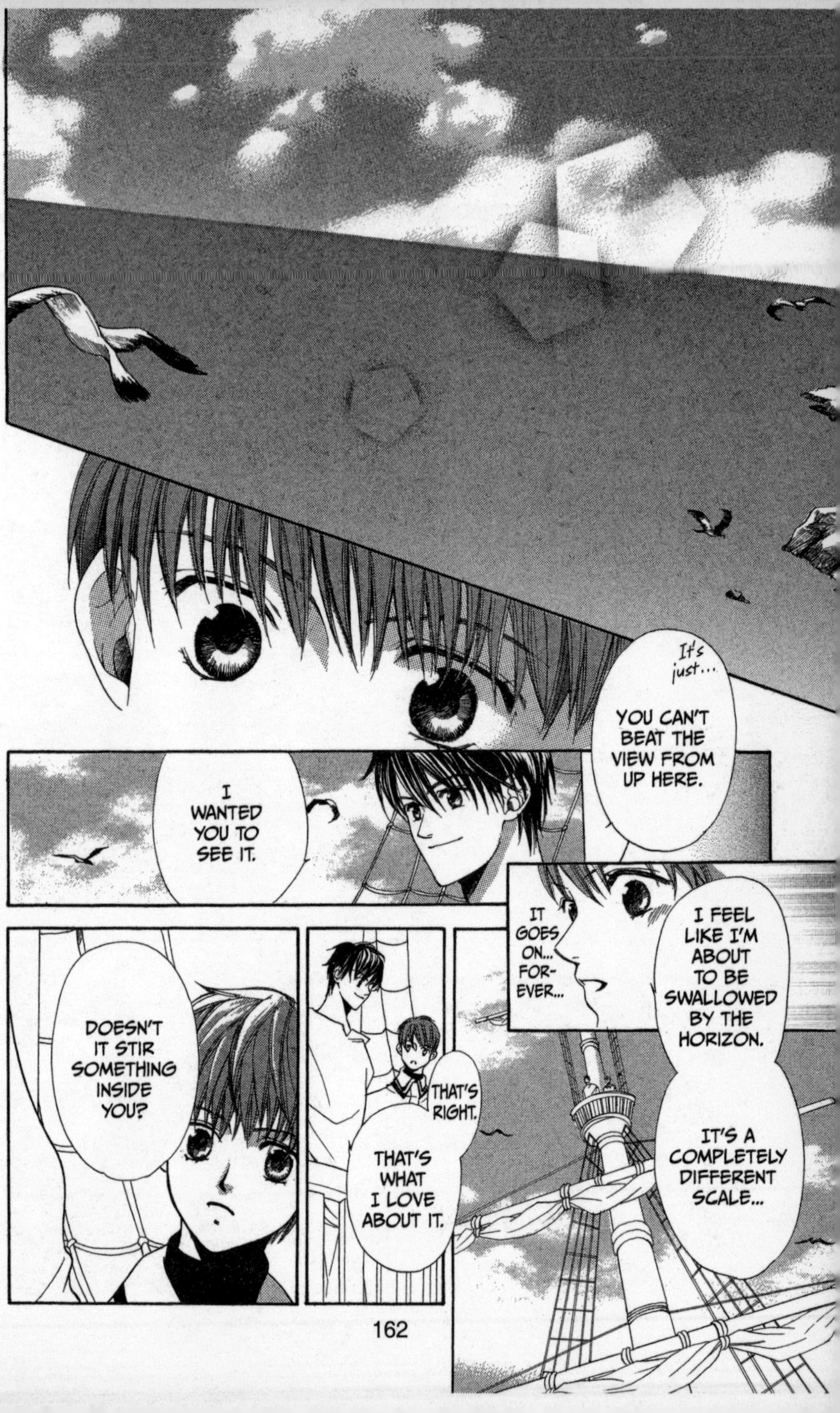

It's just...
YOU CAN'T BEAT THE VIEW FROM UP HERE.
I WANTED YOU TO SEE IT.
I FEEL LIKE I'M ABOUT TO BE SWALLOWED BY THE HORIZON.
IT GOES ON... FOR-EVER...
IT'S A COMPLETELY DIFFERENT SCALE...
THAT'S RIGHT.
THAT'S WHAT I LOVE ABOUT IT.
DOESN'T IT STIR SOMETHING INSIDE YOU?

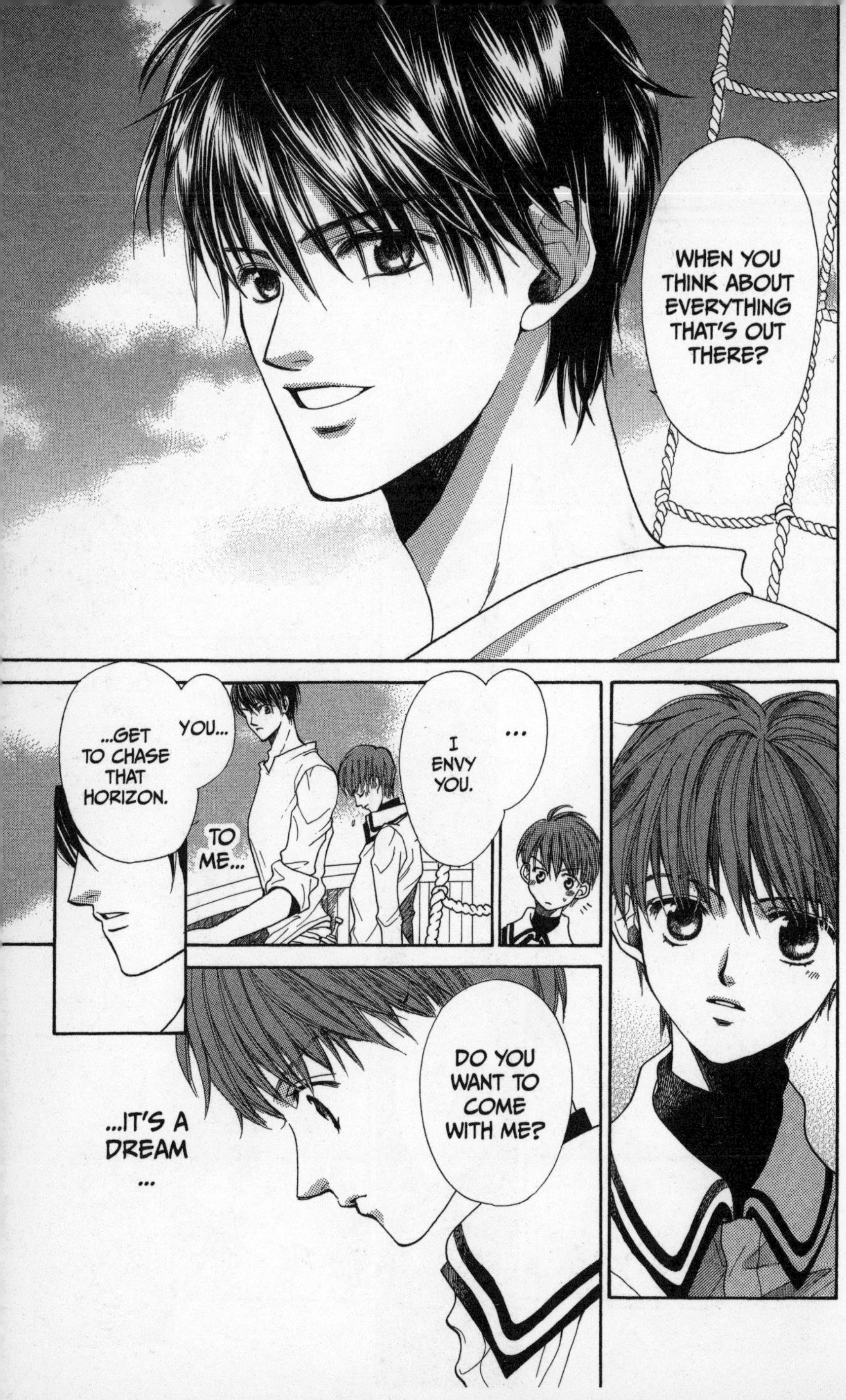
WHEN YOU THINK ABOUT EVERYTHING THAT'S OUT THERE?
...
I ENVY YOU.
YOU...
...GET TO CHASE THAT HORIZON.
TO ME...
DO YOU WANT TO COME WITH ME?
...IT'S A DREAM ...

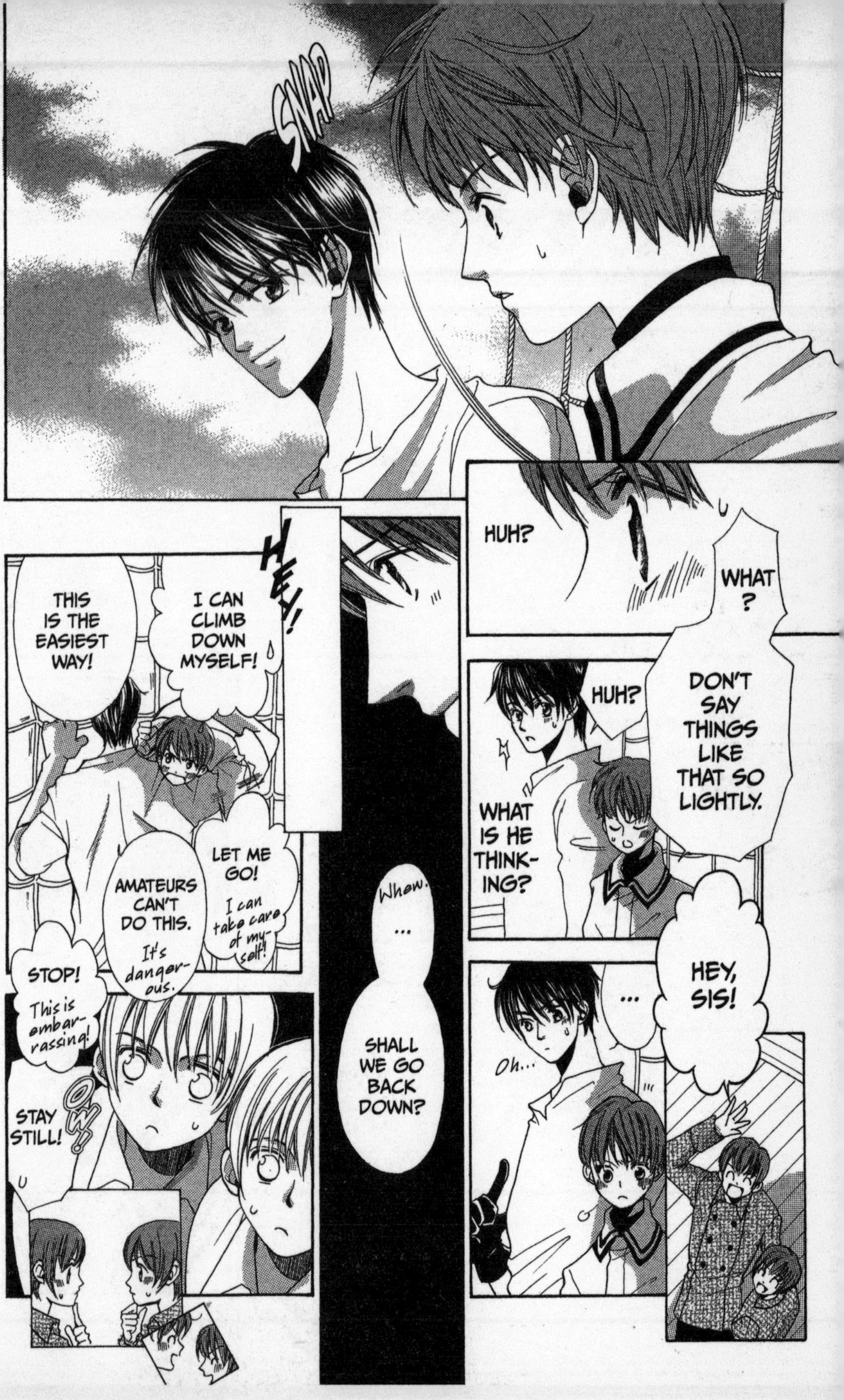
SNAP
HUH?
WHAT?
HUH?
DON'T SAY THINGS LIKE THAT SO LIGHTLY.
WHAT IS HE THINKING?
HEY, SIS!
...
Oh...
HEY!
Whew.
...
SHALL WE GO BACK DOWN?
I CAN CLIMB DOWN MYSELF!
THIS IS THE EASIEST WAY!
LET ME GO!
I can take care of myself!
AMATEURS CAN'T DO THIS.
It's dangerous.
STOP!
This is embarrassing!
OW!
STAY STILL!

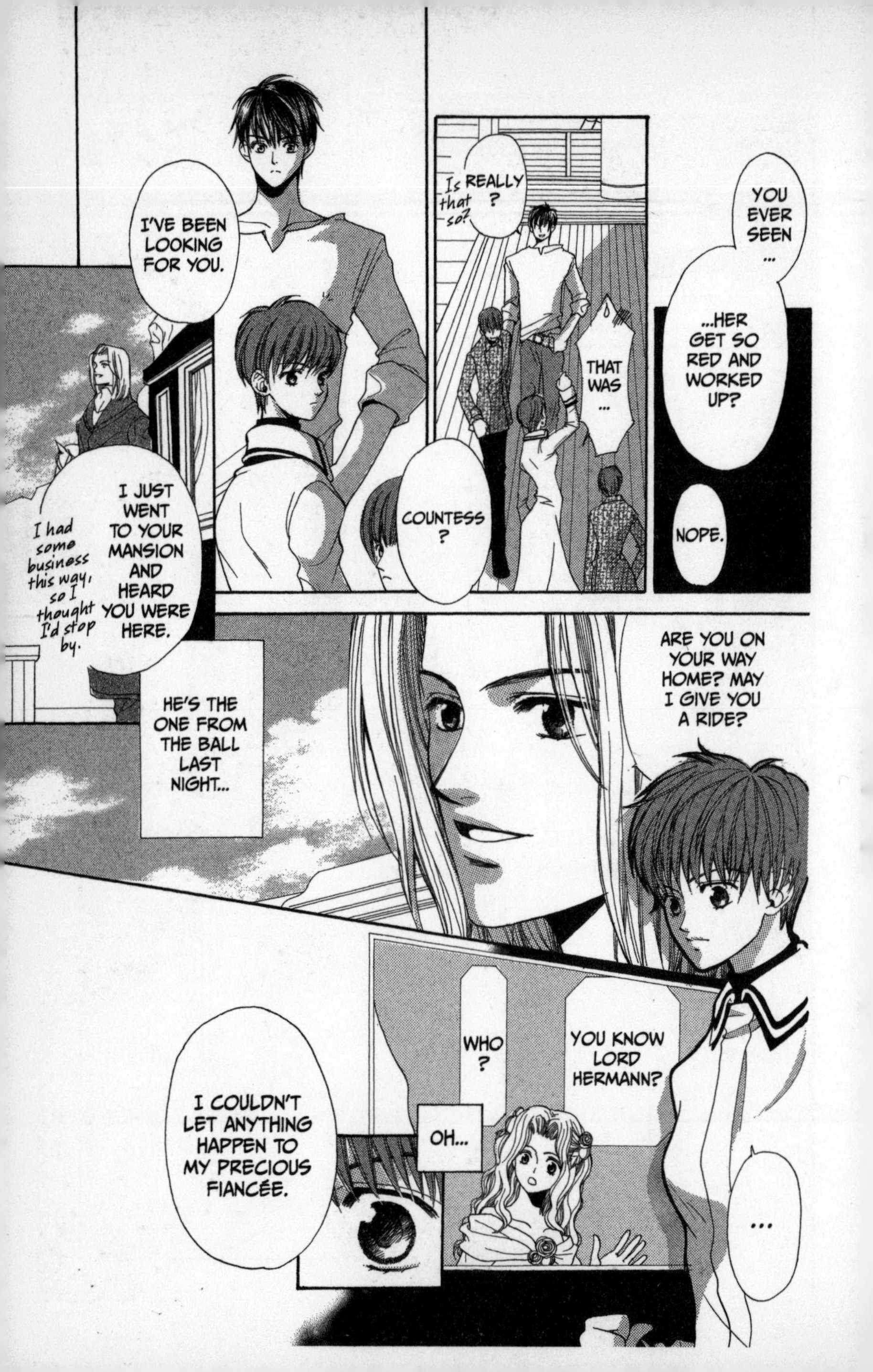
YOU EVER SEEN ...
...HER GET SO RED AND WORKED UP?
NOPE.
REALLY ?
Is that so?
THAT WAS ...
COUNTESS ?
I'VE BEEN LOOKING FOR YOU.
I JUST WENT TO YOUR MANSION AND HEARD YOU WERE HERE.
I had some business this way, so I thought I'd stop by.
HE'S THE ONE FROM THE BALL LAST NIGHT...
ARE YOU ON YOUR WAY HOME? MAY I GIVE YOU A RIDE?
...
YOU KNOW LORD HERMANN?
WHO ?
OH...
I COULDN'T LET ANYTHING HAPPEN TO MY PRECIOUS FIANCÉE.

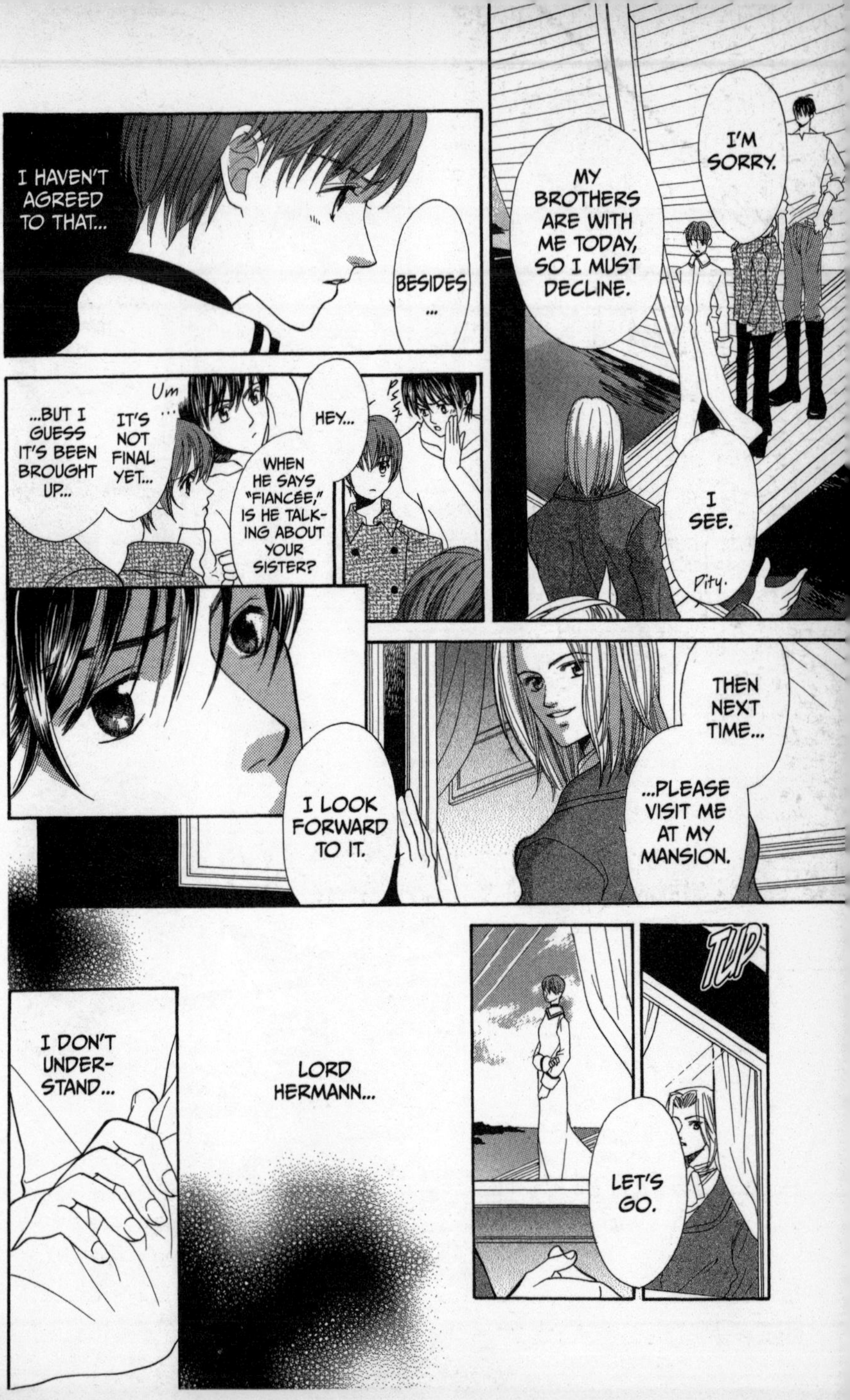
I'M SORRY.
MY BROTHERS ARE WITH ME TODAY, SO I MUST DECLINE.
I SEE.
Pity.
BESIDES...
I HAVEN'T AGREED TO THAT...
Pssst
HEY...
WHEN HE SAYS "FIANCÉE," IS HE TALKING ABOUT YOUR SISTER?
Um...
IT'S NOT FINAL YET...
...BUT I GUESS IT'S BEEN BROUGHT UP...
THEN NEXT TIME...
...PLEASE VISIT ME AT MY MANSION.
I LOOK FORWARD TO IT.
TUP
LET'S GO.
LORD HERMANN...
I DON'T UNDERSTAND...

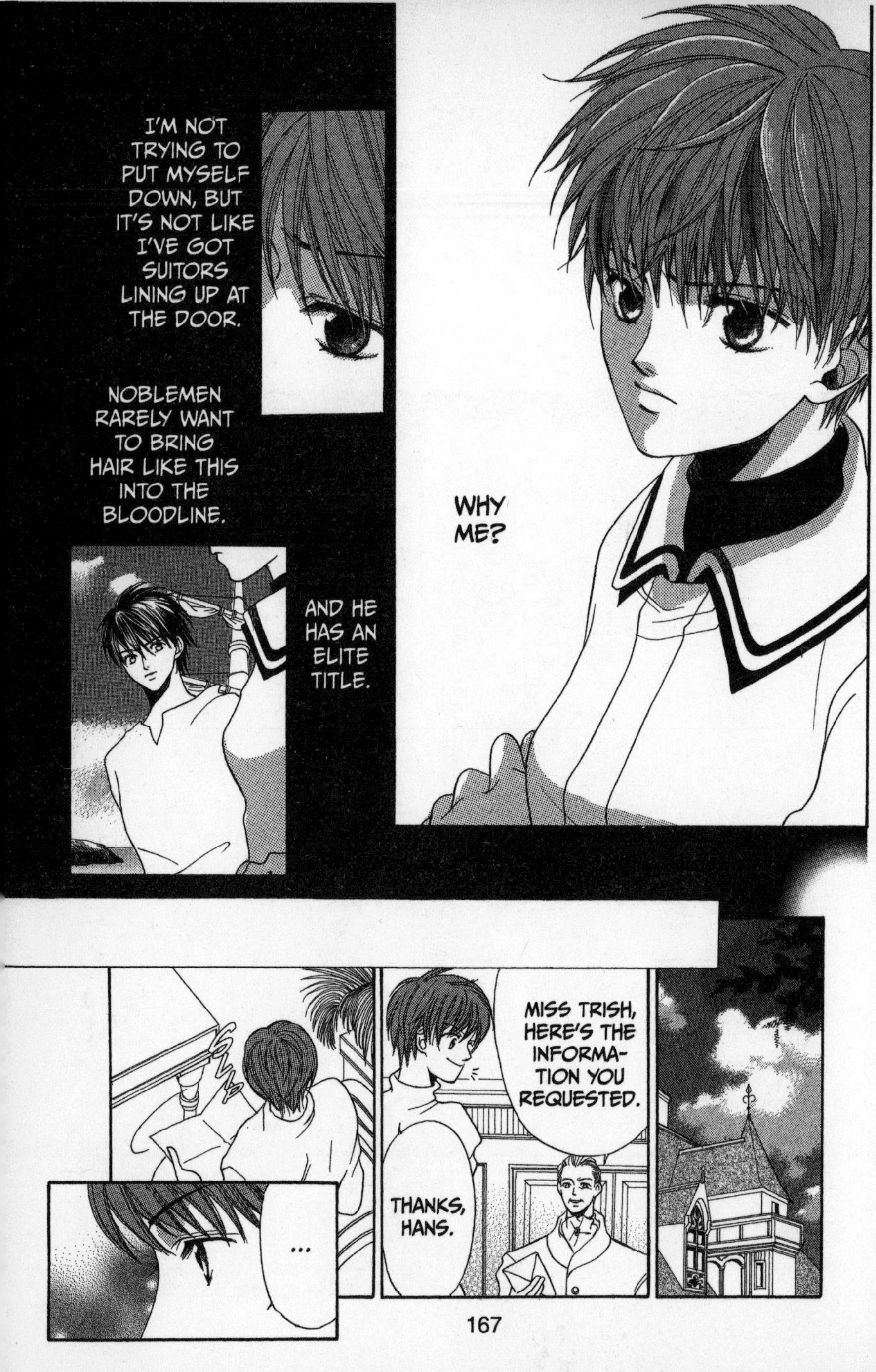
WHY ME?
I'M NOT TRYING TO PUT MYSELF DOWN, BUT IT'S NOT LIKE I'VE GOT SUITORS LINING UP AT THE DOOR.
NOBLEMEN RARELY WANT TO BRING HAIR LIKE THIS INTO THE BLOODLINE.
AND HE HAS AN ELITE TITLE.
MISS TRISH, HERE'S THE INFORMATION YOU REQUESTED.
THANKS, HANS.
...

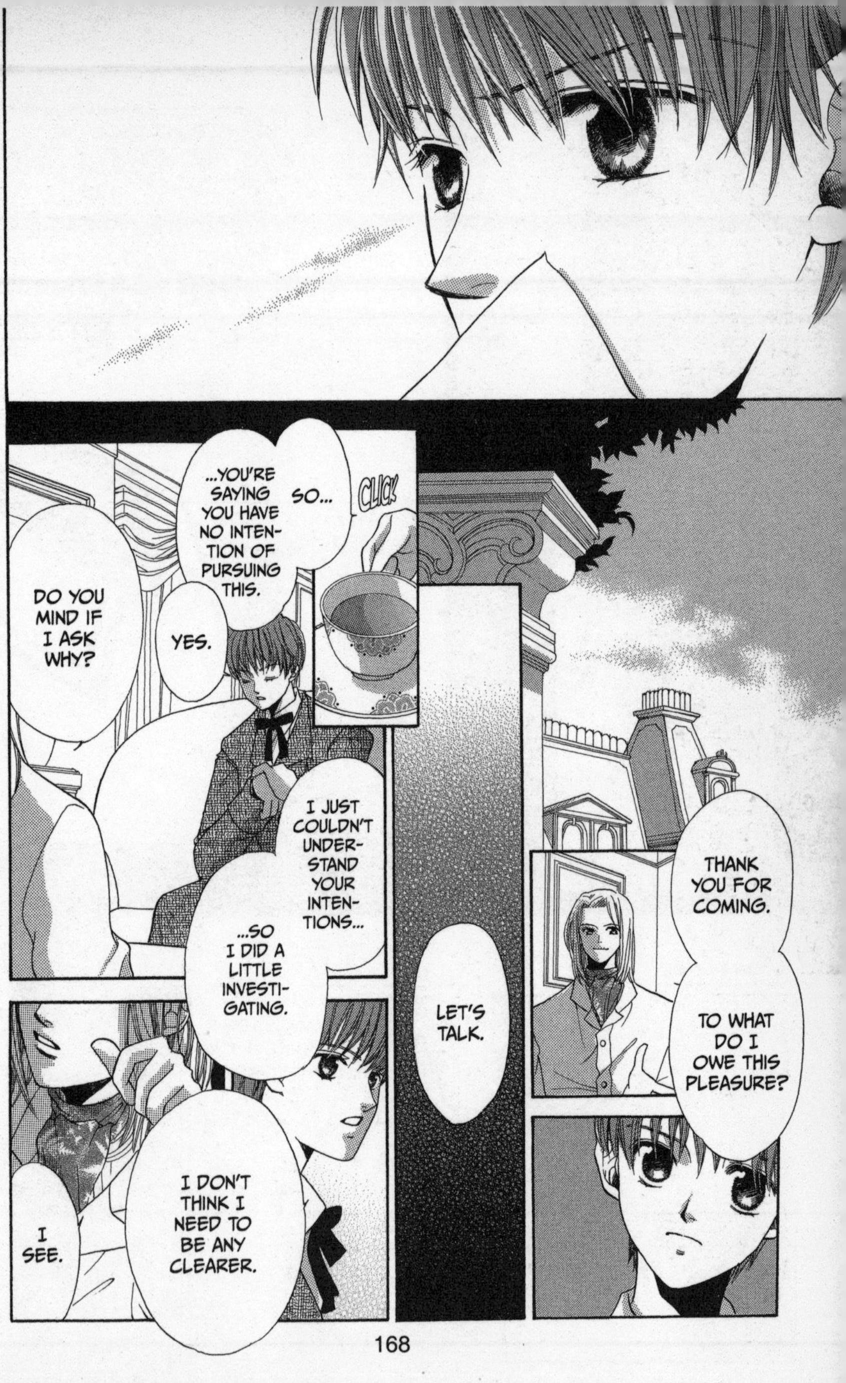
THANK YOU FOR COMING.
TO WHAT DO I OWE THIS PLEASURE?
LET'S TALK.
CLICK
SO...
...YOU'RE SAYING YOU HAVE NO INTENTION OF PURSUING THIS.
YES.
DO YOU MIND IF I ASK WHY?
I JUST COULDN'T UNDERSTAND YOUR INTENTIONS...
...SO I DID A LITTLE INVESTIGATING.
I DON'T THINK I NEED TO BE ANY CLEARER.
I SEE.

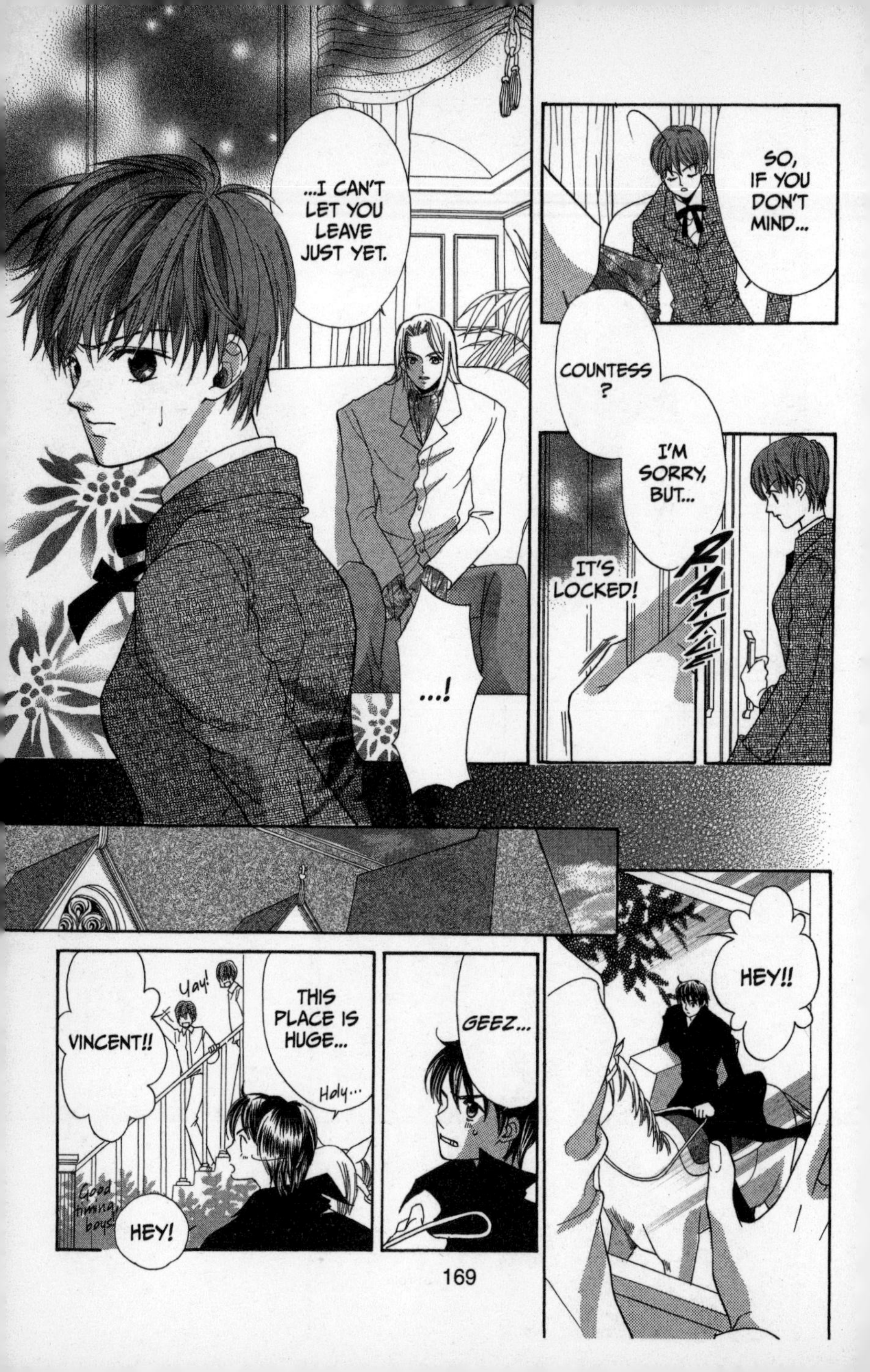
SO, IF YOU DON'T MIND...
COUNTESS?
I'M SORRY, BUT...
RATTLE
IT'S LOCKED!
...I CAN'T LET YOU LEAVE JUST YET.
...!
HEY!!
GEEZ...
THIS PLACE IS HUGE...
Holy...
VINCENT!!
Yay!
Good timing, boys.
HEY!

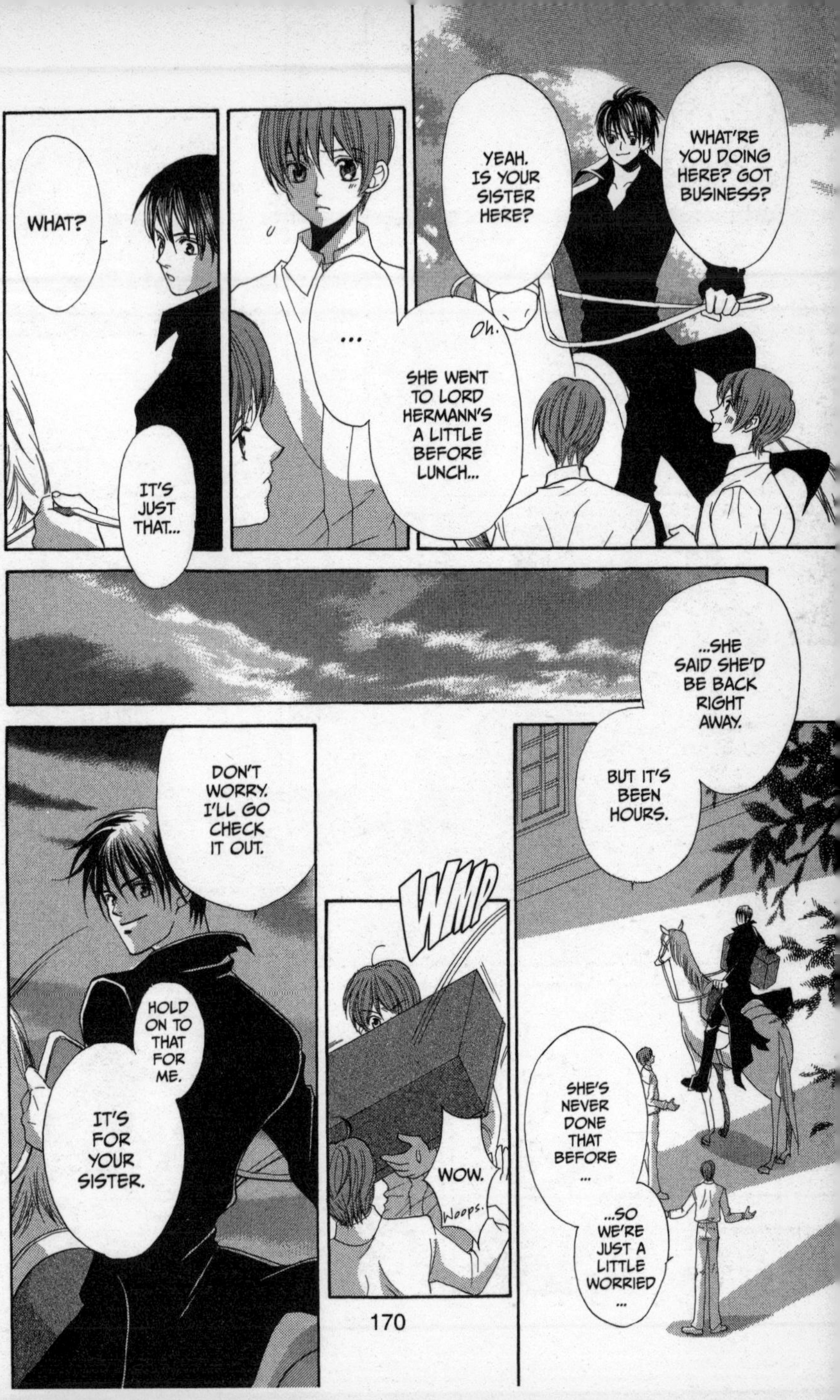

WHAT'RE YOU DOING HERE? GOT BUSINESS?
YEAH. IS YOUR SISTER HERE?
Oh.
SHE WENT TO LORD HERMANN'S A LITTLE BEFORE LUNCH...
...
WHAT?
IT'S JUST THAT...
...SHE SAID SHE'D BE BACK RIGHT AWAY.
BUT IT'S BEEN HOURS.
SHE'S NEVER DONE THAT BEFORE ...
...SO WE'RE JUST A LITTLE WORRIED ...
DON'T WORRY. I'LL GO CHECK IT OUT.
HOLD ON TO THAT FOR ME.
IT'S FOR YOUR SISTER.
WMP
WOW.
Woops.

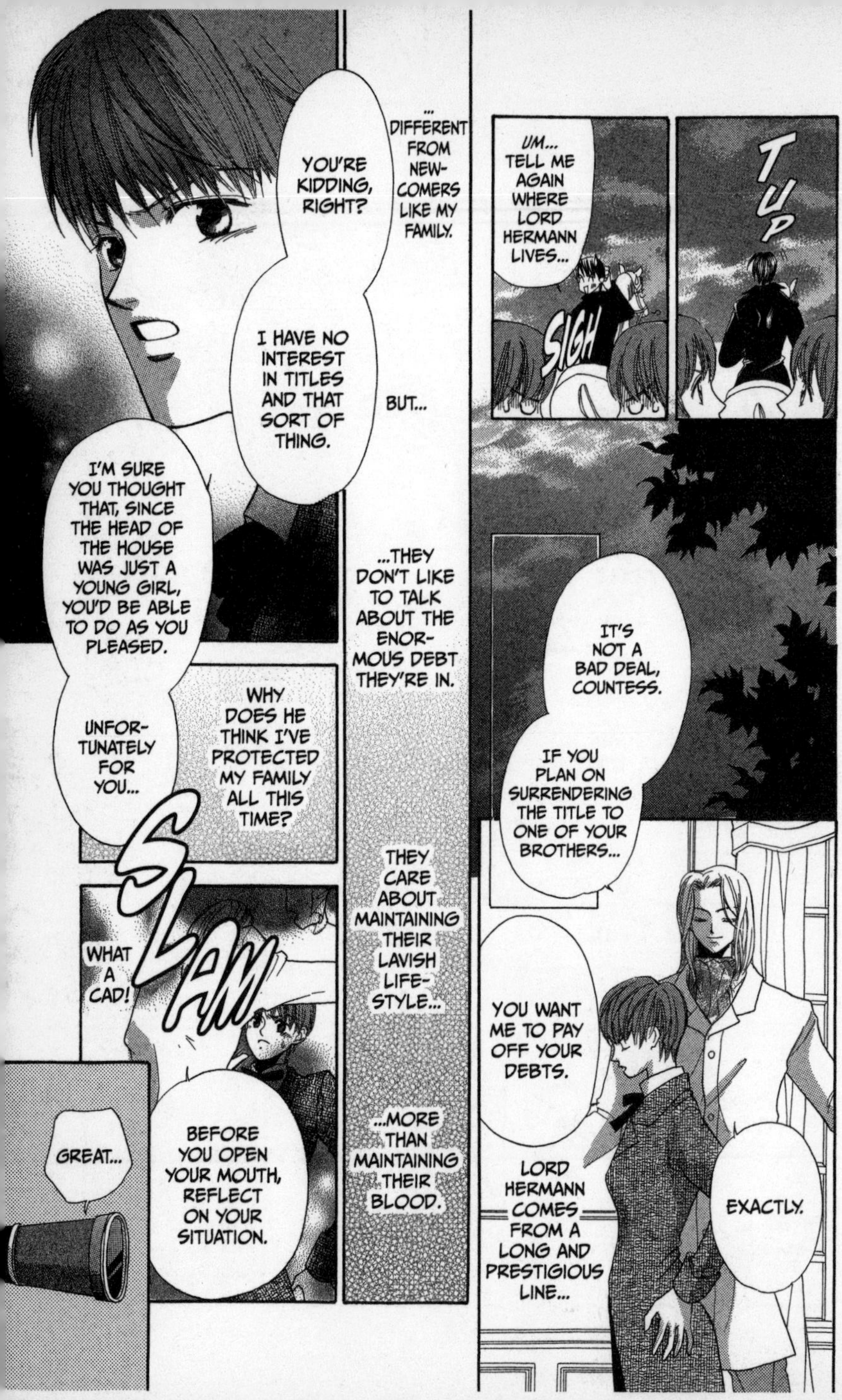
TUP
UM... TELL ME AGAIN WHERE LORD HERMANN LIVES...
SIGH
IT'S NOT A BAD DEAL, COUNTESS.
IF YOU PLAN ON SURRENDERING THE TITLE TO ONE OF YOUR BROTHERS...
YOU WANT ME TO PAY OFF YOUR DEBTS.
EXACTLY.
LORD HERMANN COMES FROM A LONG AND PRESTIGIOUS LINE...
... DIFFERENT FROM NEW-COMERS LIKE MY FAMILY.
BUT...
...THEY DON'T LIKE TO TALK ABOUT THE ENOR-MOUS DEBT THEY'RE IN.
THEY CARE ABOUT MAINTAINING THEIR LAVISH LIFE-STYLE...
...MORE THAN MAINTAINING THEIR BLOOD.
YOU'RE KIDDING, RIGHT?
I HAVE NO INTEREST IN TITLES AND THAT SORT OF THING.
I'M SURE YOU THOUGHT THAT, SINCE THE HEAD OF THE HOUSE WAS JUST A YOUNG GIRL, YOU'D BE ABLE TO DO AS YOU PLEASED.
UNFOR-TUNATELY FOR YOU...
WHY DOES HE THINK I'VE PROTECTED MY FAMILY ALL THIS TIME?
SLAM
WHAT A CAD!
BEFORE YOU OPEN YOUR MOUTH, REFLECT ON YOUR SITUATION.
GREAT...

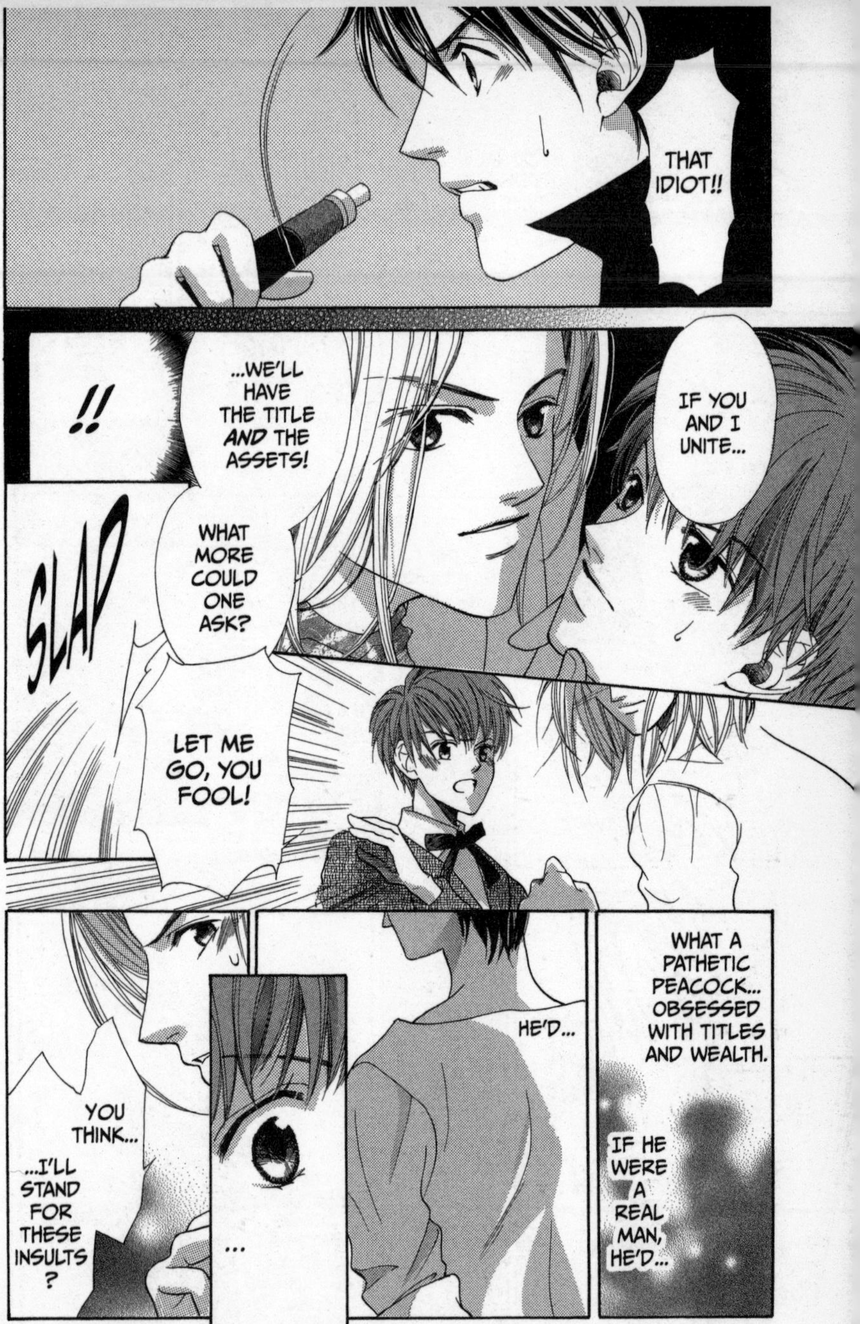
THAT IDIOT!!
IF YOU AND I UNITE...
...WE'LL HAVE THE TITLE AND THE ASSETS!
!!
WHAT MORE COULD ONE ASK?
SLAP
LET ME GO, YOU FOOL!
WHAT A PATHETIC PEACOCK... OBSESSED WITH TITLES AND WEALTH.
IF HE WERE A REAL MAN, HE'D...
HE'D...
...
YOU THINK...
...I'LL STAND FOR THESE INSULTS?

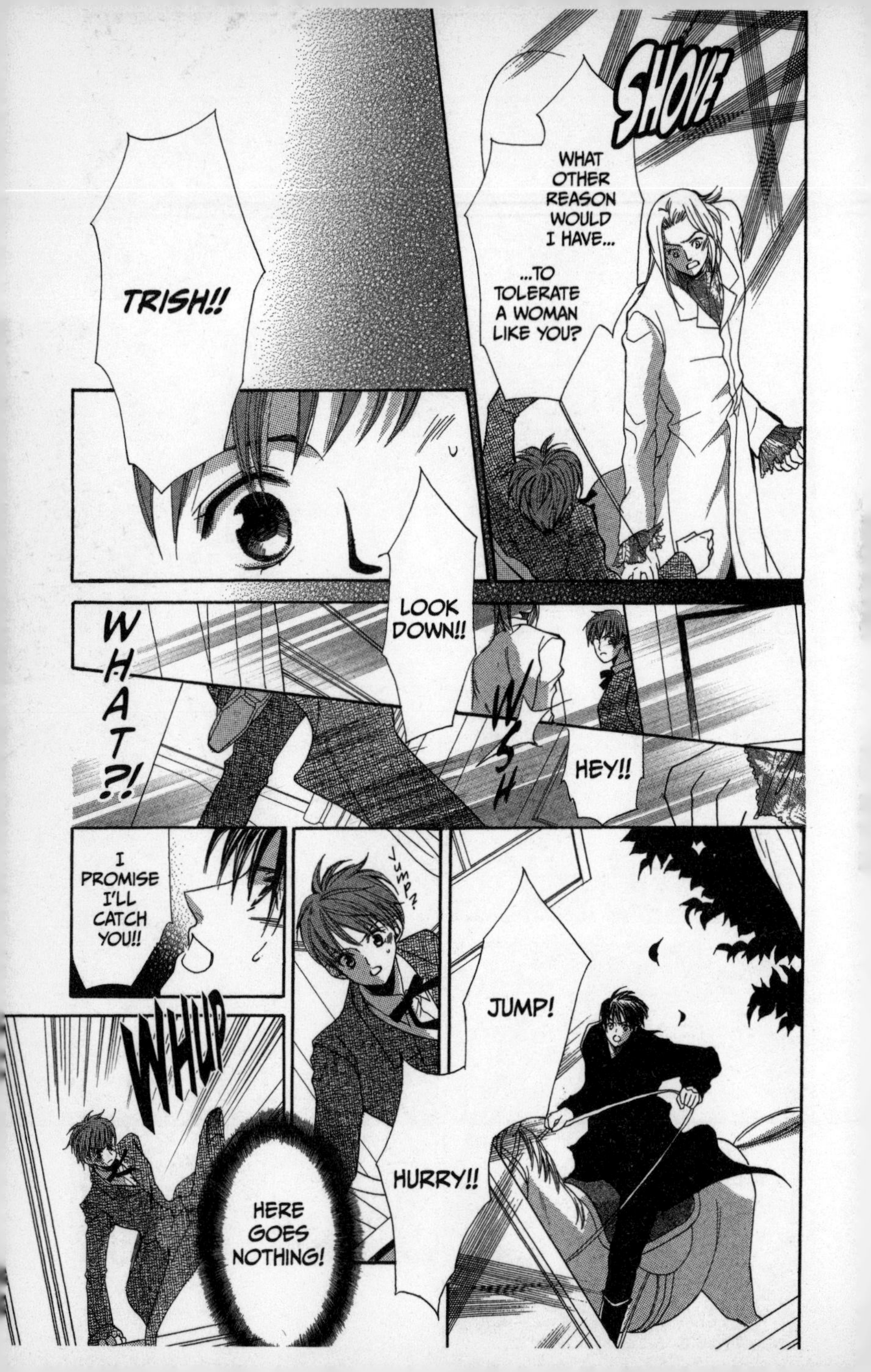
SHOVE
WHAT OTHER REASON WOULD I HAVE...
...TO TOLERATE A WOMAN LIKE YOU?
TRISH!!
LOOK DOWN!!
HEY!!
WSH
WHAT?!
JUMP!
HURRY!!
JUMP?
I PROMISE I'LL CATCH YOU!!
WHUP
HERE GOES NOTHING!

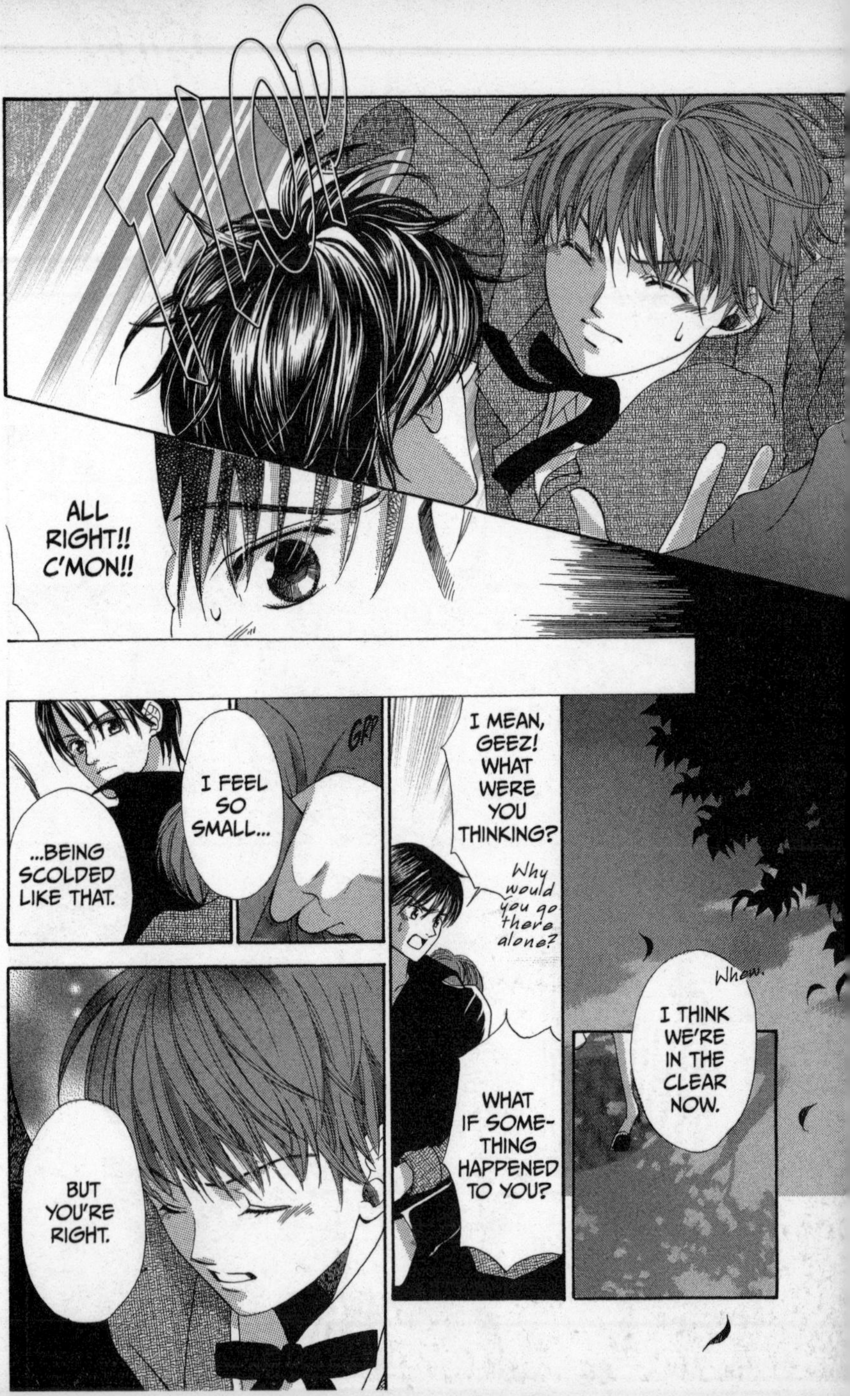
FLOP
ALL RIGHT!! C'MON!!
Whew.
I THINK WE'RE IN THE CLEAR NOW.
I MEAN, GEEZ! WHAT WERE YOU THINKING?
Why would you go there alone?
WHAT IF SOME-THING HAPPENED TO YOU?
I FEEL SO SMALL...
...BEING SCOLDED LIKE THAT.
BUT YOU'RE RIGHT.

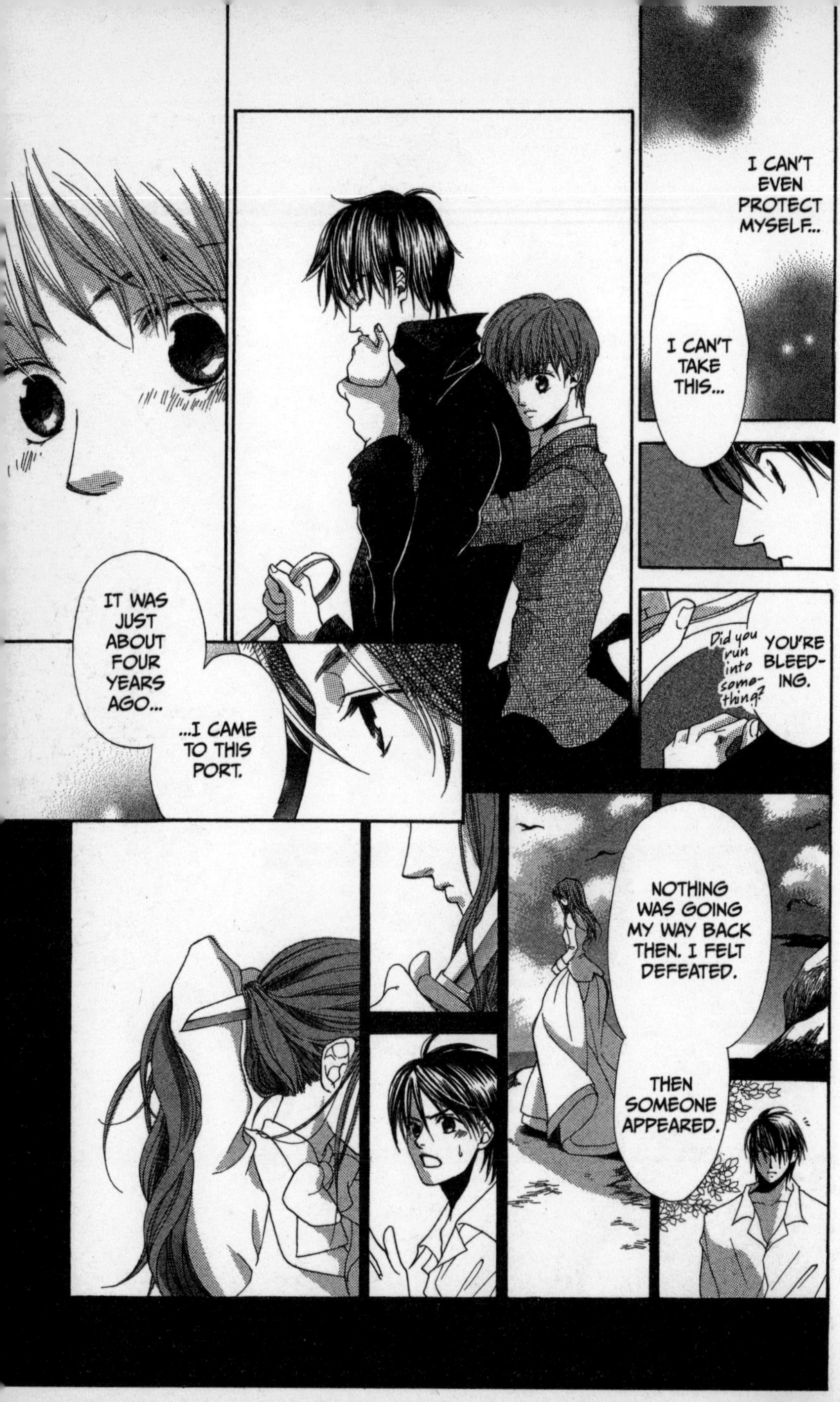
I CAN'T EVEN PROTECT MYSELF...
I CAN'T TAKE THIS...
YOU'RE BLEEDING.
Did you run into something?
IT WAS JUST ABOUT FOUR YEARS AGO...
...I CAME TO THIS PORT.
NOTHING WAS GOING MY WAY BACK THEN. I FELT DEFEATED.
THEN SOMEONE APPEARED.

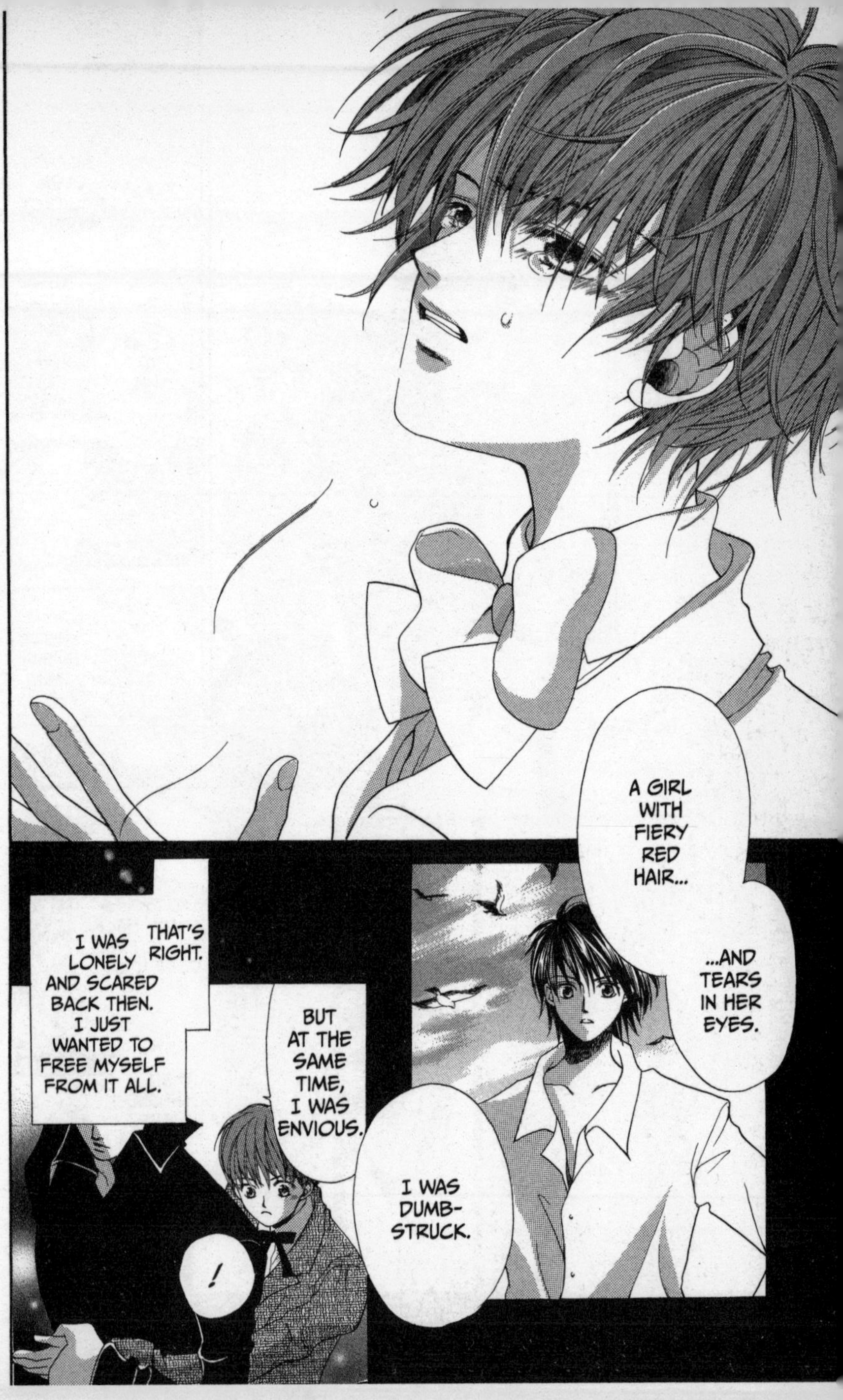
A GIRL WITH FIERY RED HAIR...
...AND TEARS IN HER EYES.
I WAS DUMB-STRUCK.
THAT'S RIGHT.
I WAS LONELY AND SCARED BACK THEN. I JUST WANTED TO FREE MYSELF FROM IT ALL.
BUT AT THE SAME TIME, I WAS ENVIOUS.
!

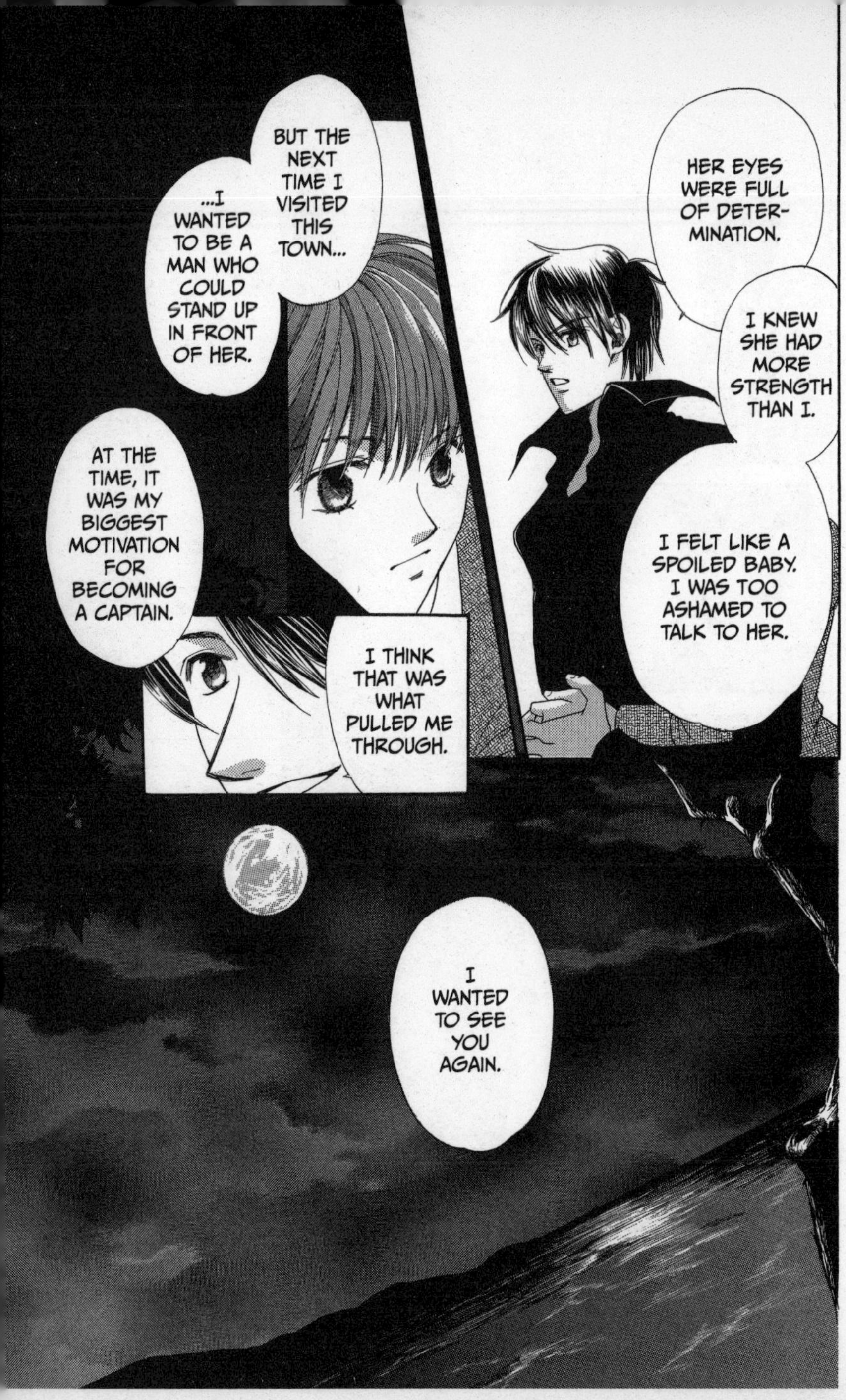
HER EYES WERE FULL OF DETER-MINATION.
I KNEW SHE HAD MORE STRENGTH THAN I.
I FELT LIKE A SPOILED BABY. I WAS TOO ASHAMED TO TALK TO HER.
BUT THE NEXT TIME I VISITED THIS TOWN...
...I WANTED TO BE A MAN WHO COULD STAND UP IN FRONT OF HER.
AT THE TIME, IT WAS MY BIGGEST MOTIVATION FOR BECOMING A CAPTAIN.
I THINK THAT WAS WHAT PULLED ME THROUGH.
I WANTED TO SEE YOU AGAIN.

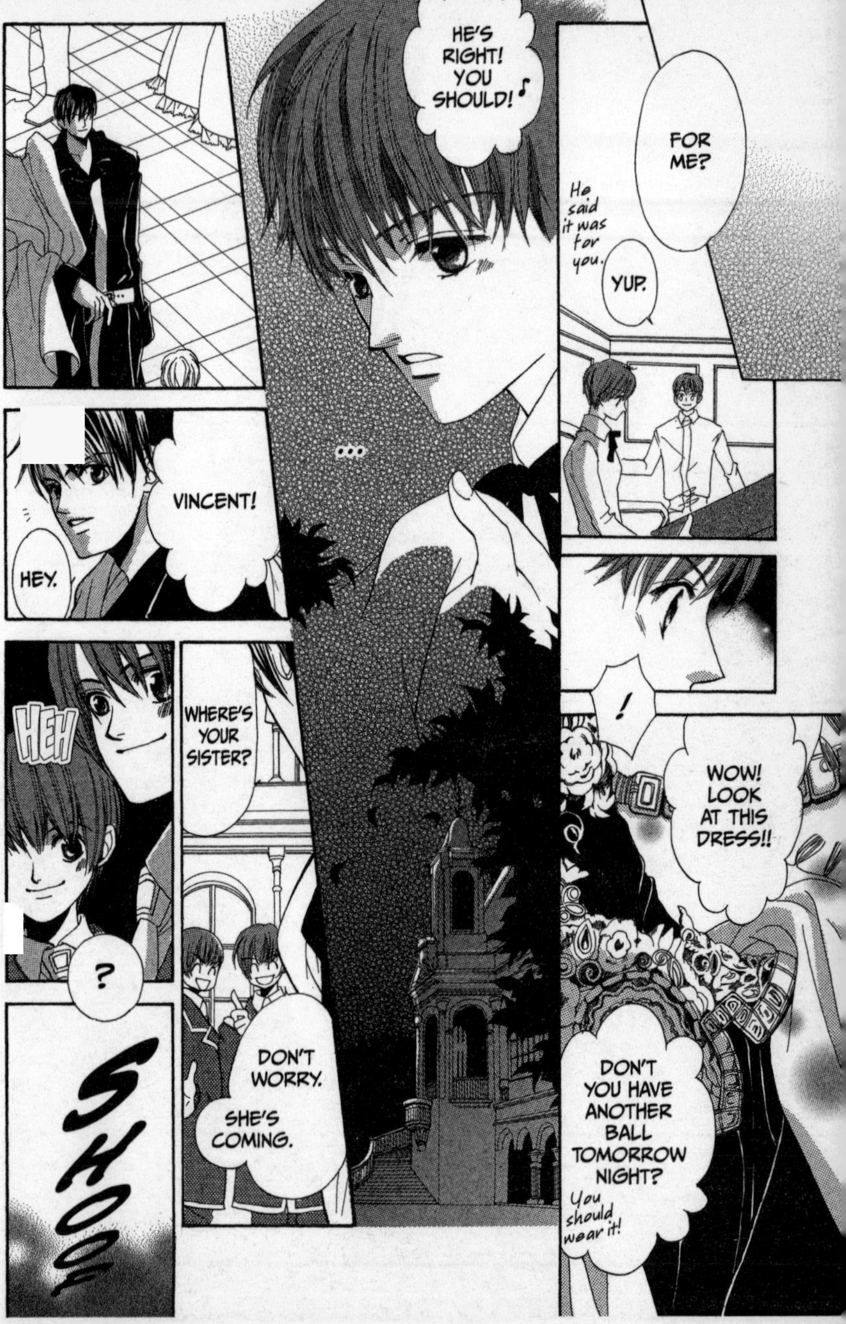
FOR ME?
He said it was for you.
YUP.
!
WOW! LOOK AT THIS DRESS!!
DON'T YOU HAVE ANOTHER BALL TOMORROW NIGHT?
You should wear it!
HE'S RIGHT! YOU SHOULD! ♪
...
VINCENT!
HEY.
WHERE'S YOUR SISTER?
HEH
?
DON'T WORRY.
SHE'S COMING.
SHOO

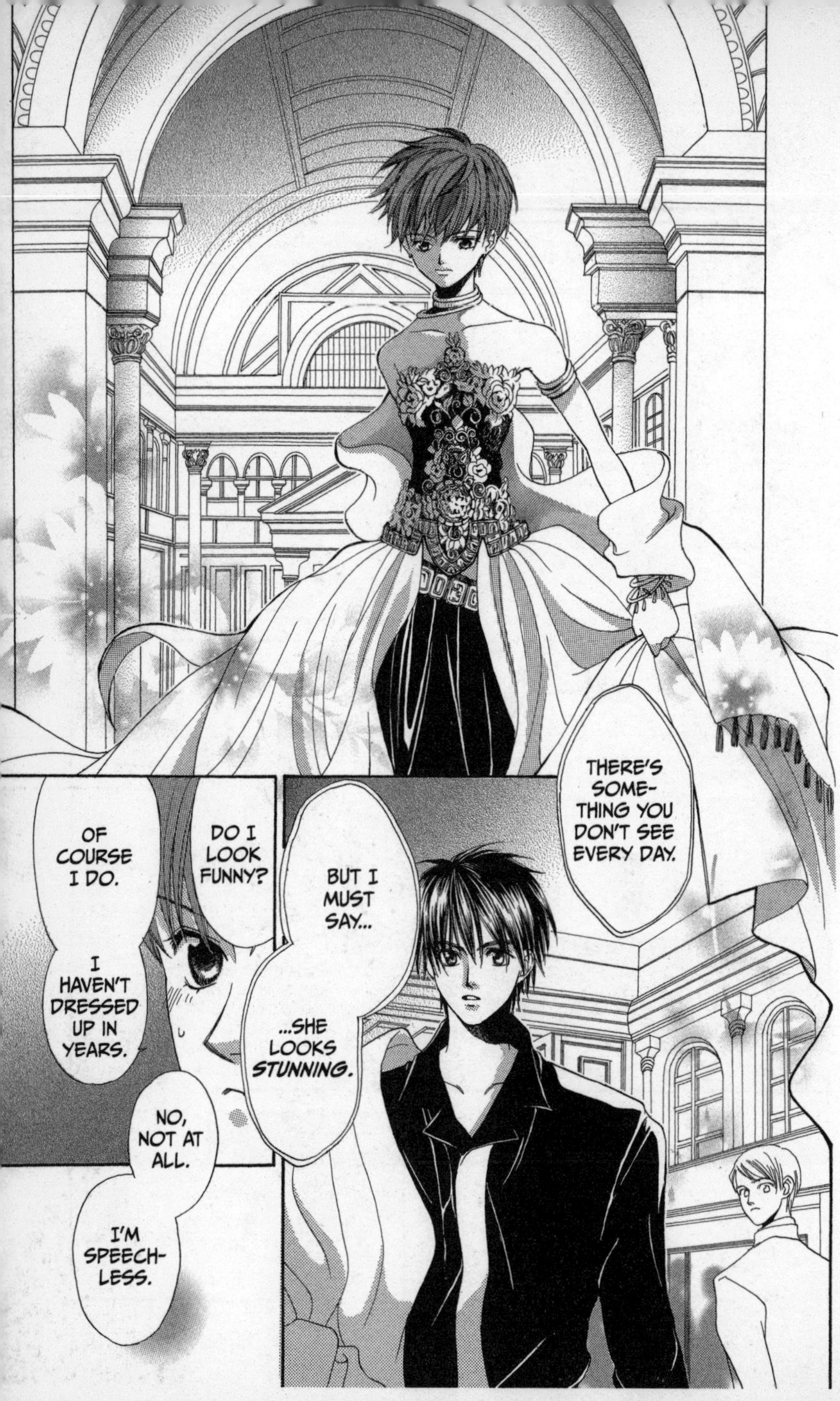
THERE'S SOME-THING YOU DON'T SEE EVERY DAY.
BUT I MUST SAY...
...SHE LOOKS *STUNNING*.
DO I LOOK FUNNY?
OF COURSE I DO.
I HAVEN'T DRESSED UP IN YEARS.
NO, NOT AT ALL.
I'M SPEECH-LESS.

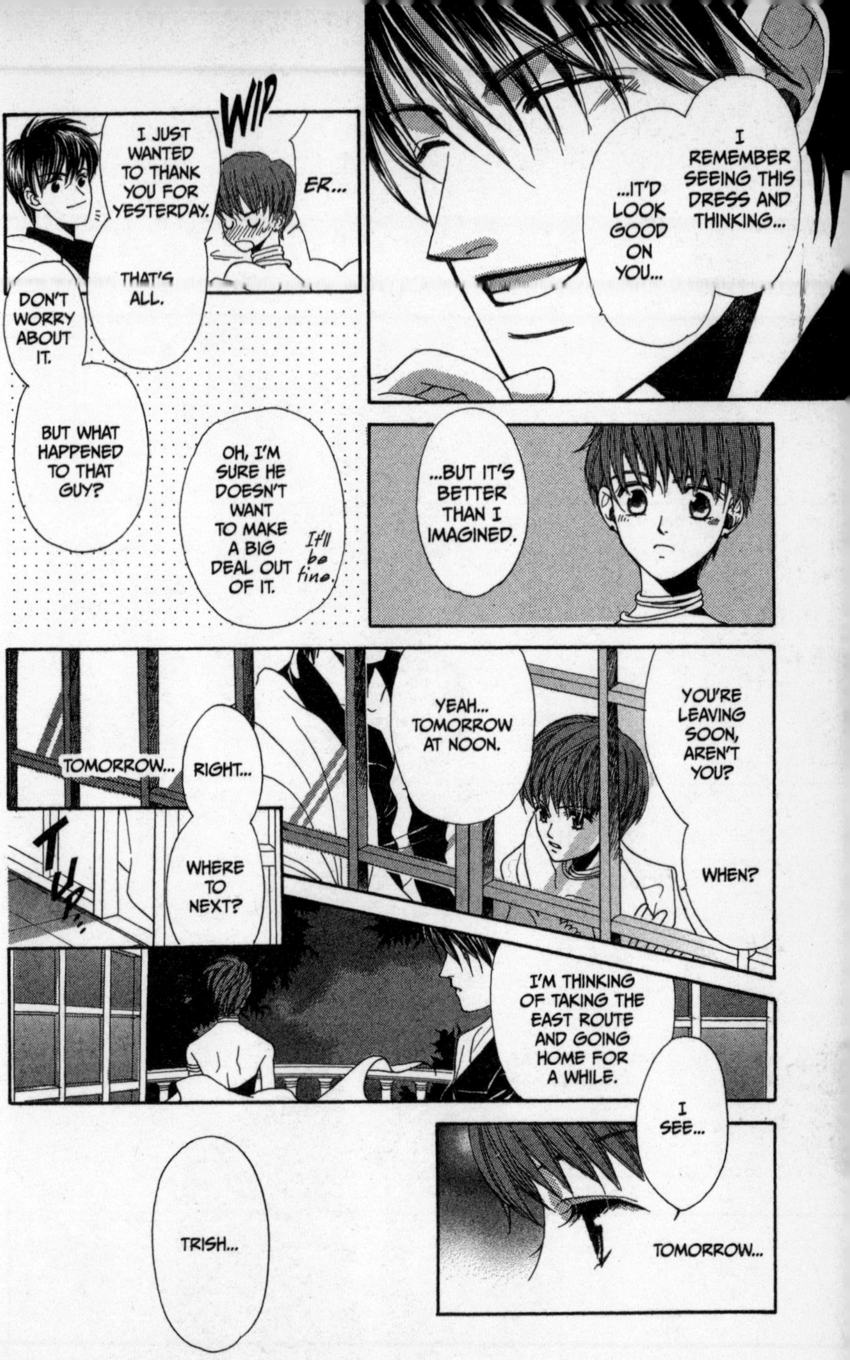
I REMEMBER SEEING THIS DRESS AND THINKING...
...IT'D LOOK GOOD ON YOU...
...BUT IT'S BETTER THAN I IMAGINED.
WIP
ER...
I JUST WANTED TO THANK YOU FOR YESTERDAY.
THAT'S ALL.
DON'T WORRY ABOUT IT.
BUT WHAT HAPPENED TO THAT GUY?
OH, I'M SURE HE DOESN'T WANT TO MAKE A BIG DEAL OUT OF IT.
It'll be fine.
YOU'RE LEAVING SOON, AREN'T YOU?
WHEN?
YEAH... TOMORROW AT NOON.
RIGHT...
TOMORROW...
WHERE TO NEXT?
TUP
I'M THINKING OF TAKING THE EAST ROUTE AND GOING HOME FOR A WHILE.
I SEE...
TOMORROW...
TRISH...

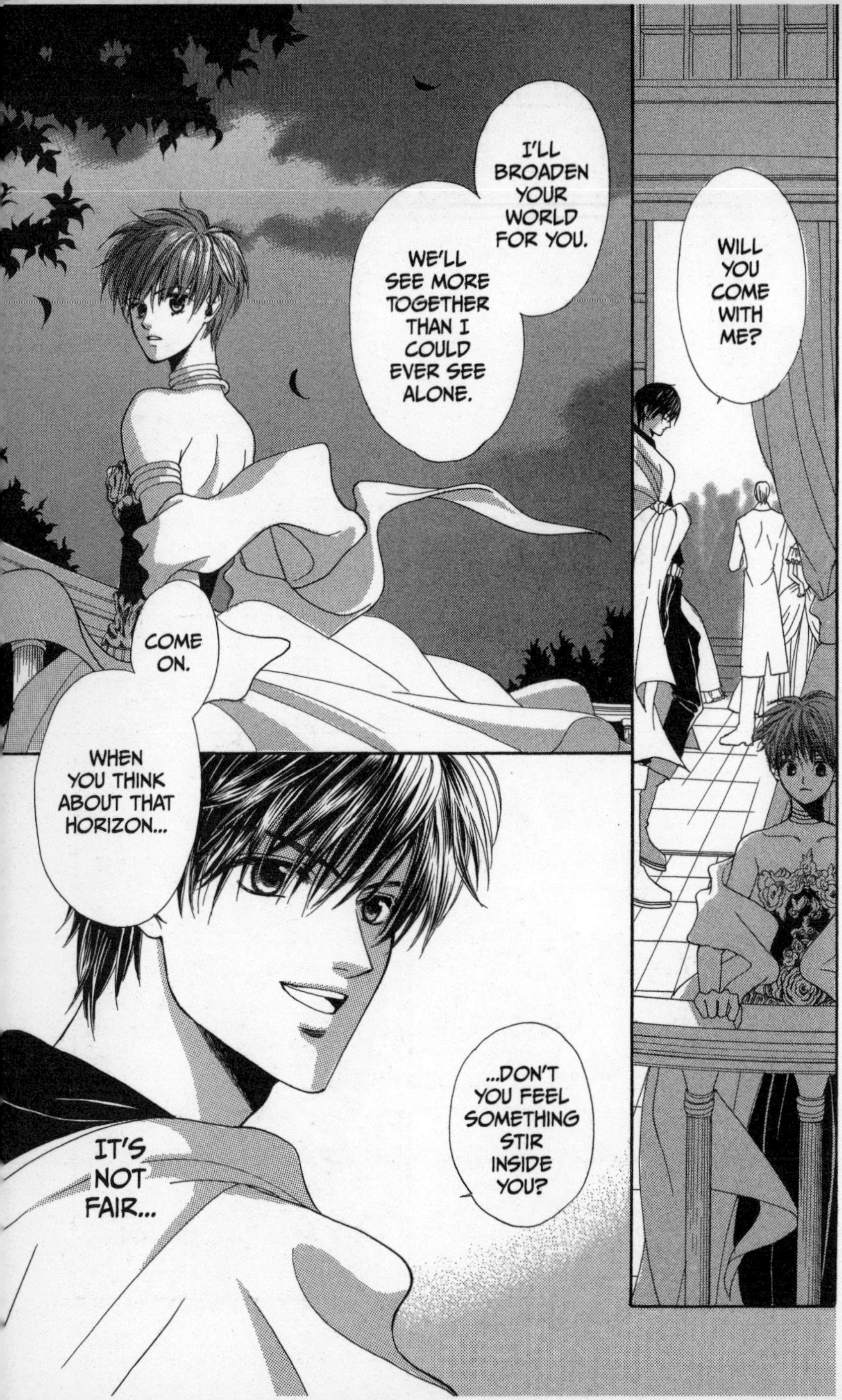
WILL YOU COME WITH ME?
I'LL BROADEN YOUR WORLD FOR YOU.
WE'LL SEE MORE TOGETHER THAN I COULD EVER SEE ALONE.
COME ON.
WHEN YOU THINK ABOUT THAT HORIZON...
...DON'T YOU FEEL SOMETHING STIR INSIDE YOU?
IT'S NOT FAIR...

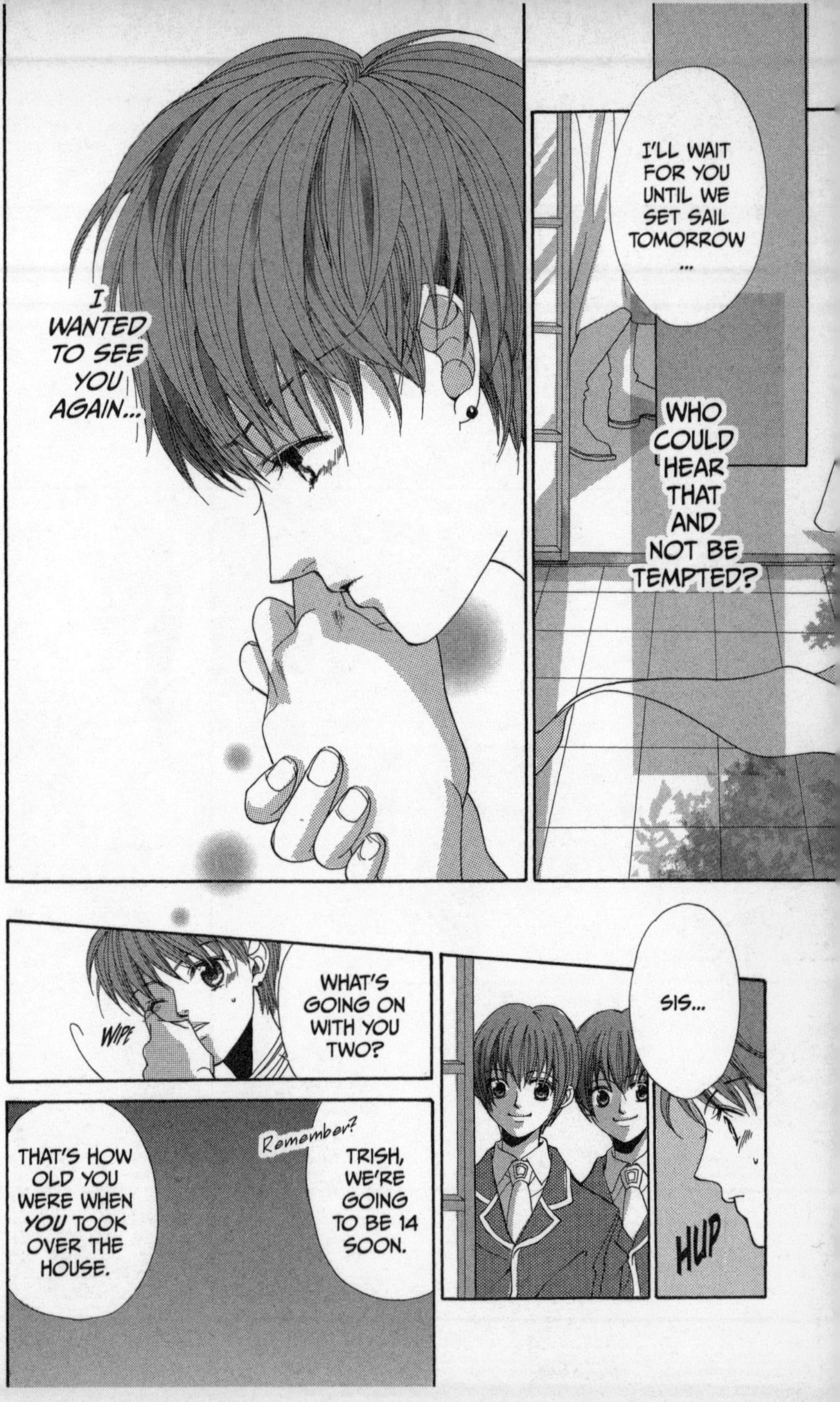
I'LL WAIT FOR YOU UNTIL WE SET SAIL TOMORROW ...
WHO COULD HEAR THAT AND NOT BE TEMPTED?
I WANTED TO SEE YOU AGAIN...
SIS...
HUP
WHAT'S GOING ON WITH YOU TWO?
WIPE
TRISH, WE'RE GOING TO BE 14 SOON.
Remember?
THAT'S HOW OLD YOU WERE WHEN YOU TOOK OVER THE HOUSE.

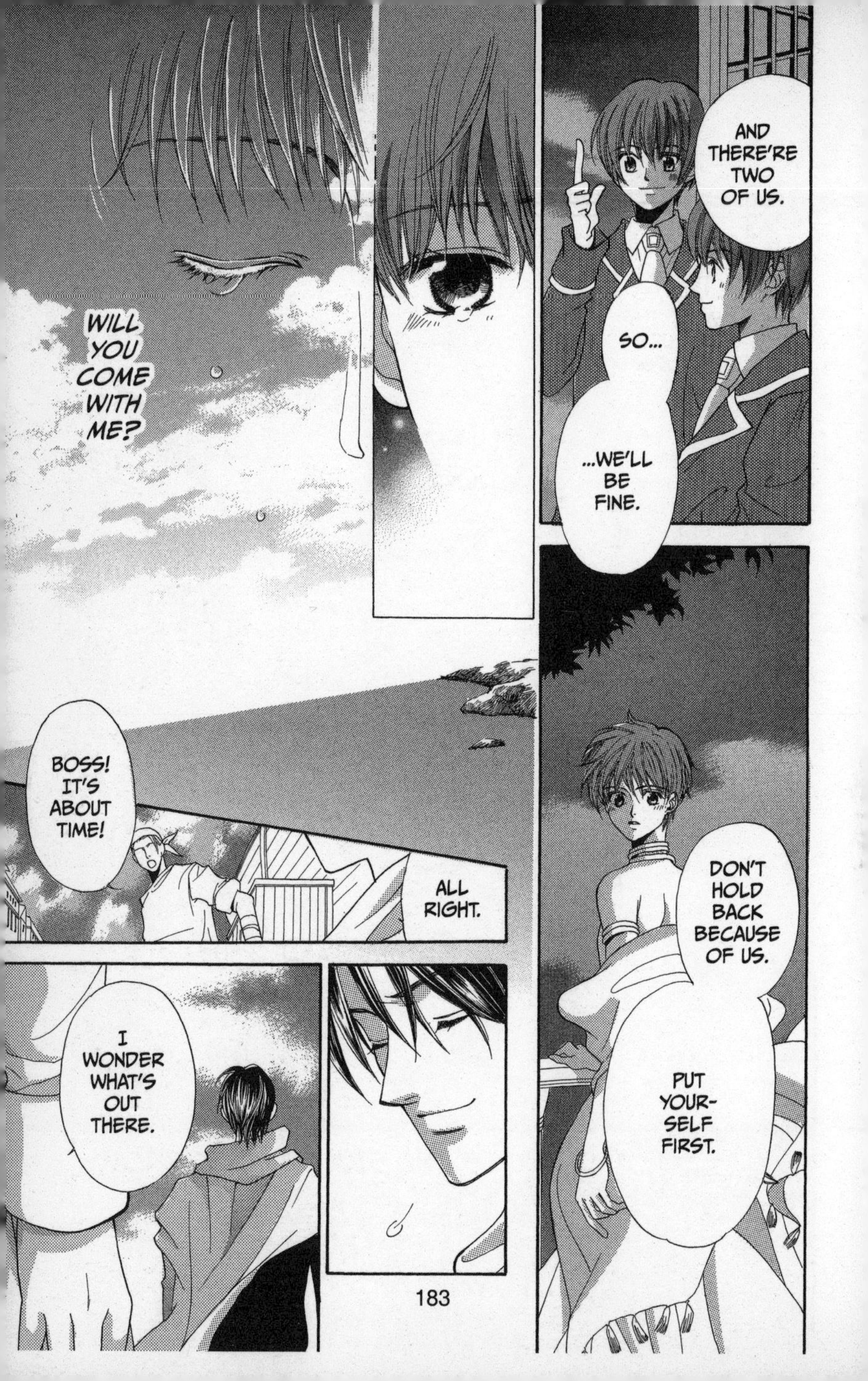
AND THERE'RE TWO OF US.
SO...
...WE'LL BE FINE.
WILL YOU COME WITH ME?
DON'T HOLD BACK BECAUSE OF US.
PUT YOUR-SELF FIRST.
BOSS! IT'S ABOUT TIME!
ALL RIGHT.
I WONDER WHAT'S OUT THERE.

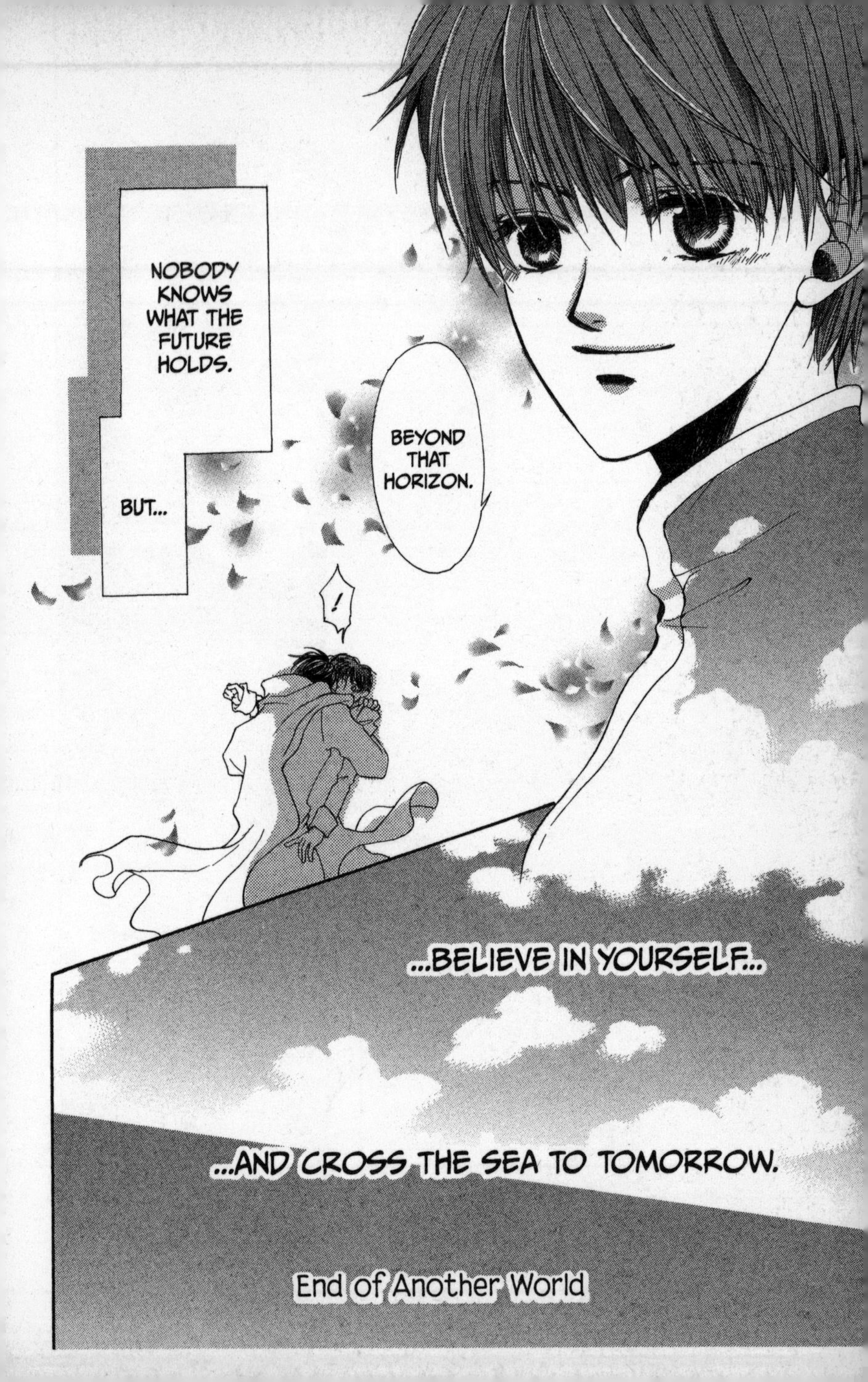
BEYOND THAT HORIZON.
NOBODY KNOWS WHAT THE FUTURE HOLDS.
BUT...
!
...BELIEVE IN YOURSELF...
...AND CROSS THE SEA TO TOMORROW.
End of Another World

BACKSTAGE WITH THE JOURNALISM CLUB #5

I KNOW I HAVEN'T BEEN AROUND MUCH LATELY.

...

YES.

SO HERE GOES NOTHING...

...

金澤　紘人

HIROTO KANAZAWA

MUSIC TEACHER

BIRTHDAY:	MARCH 1
ZODIAC SIGN:	PISCES
BLOOD TYPE:	A
HEIGHT:	6'
FAMILY:	PARENTS, 1 YOUNGER SISTER, BROTHER-IN-LAW (SISTER'S HUSBAND)
HOBBIES:	COOKING, FISHING, WATCHING BASEBALL
FAVORITE FOOD:	RAMEN

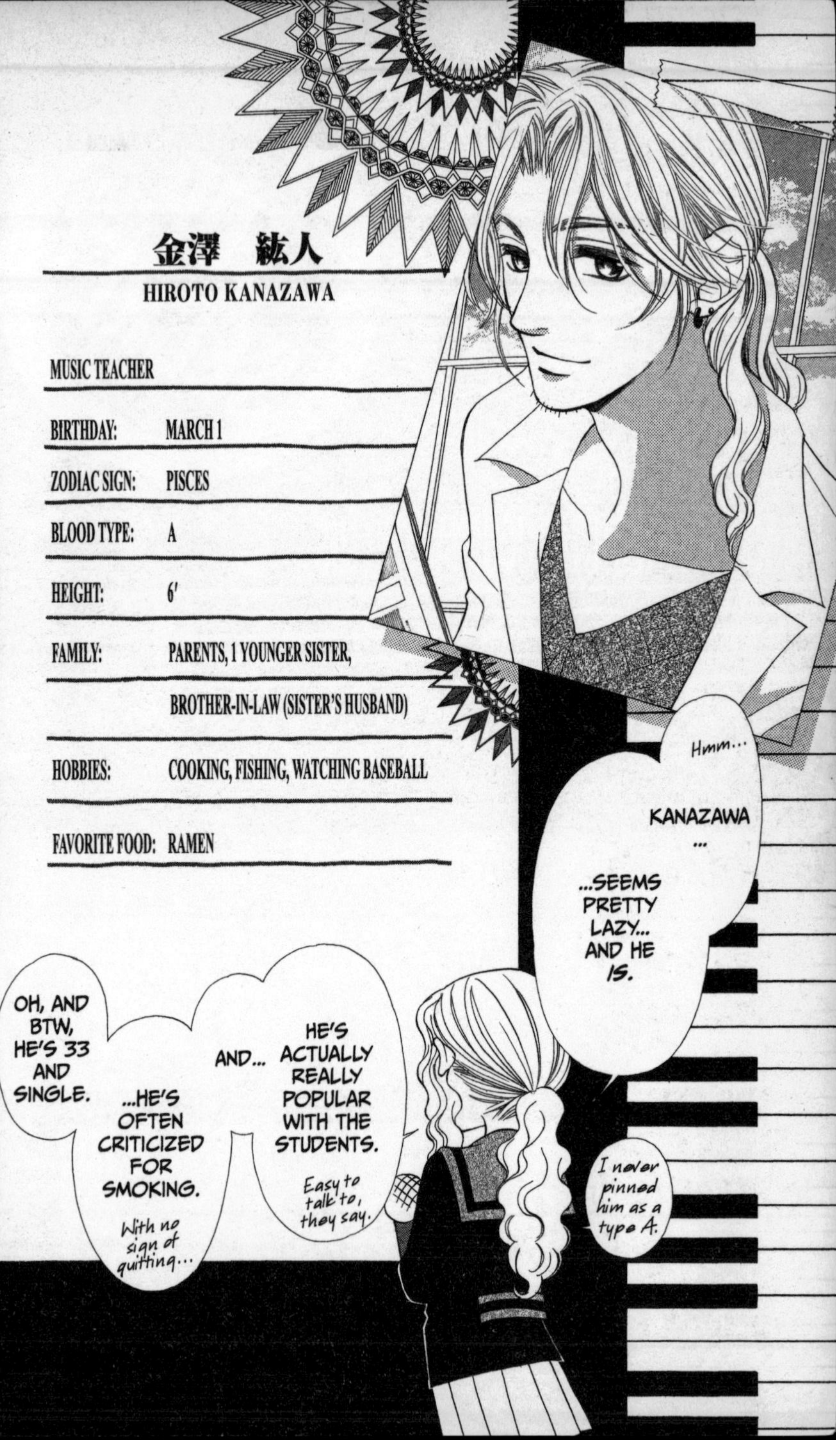
Hmm...
KANAZAWA ...
...SEEMS PRETTY LAZY... AND HE IS.
I never pinned him as a type A.
AND... HE'S ACTUALLY REALLY POPULAR WITH THE STUDENTS.
Easy to talk to, they say.
...HE'S OFTEN CRITICIZED FOR SMOKING.
With no sign of quitting...
OH, AND BTW, HE'S 33 AND SINGLE.

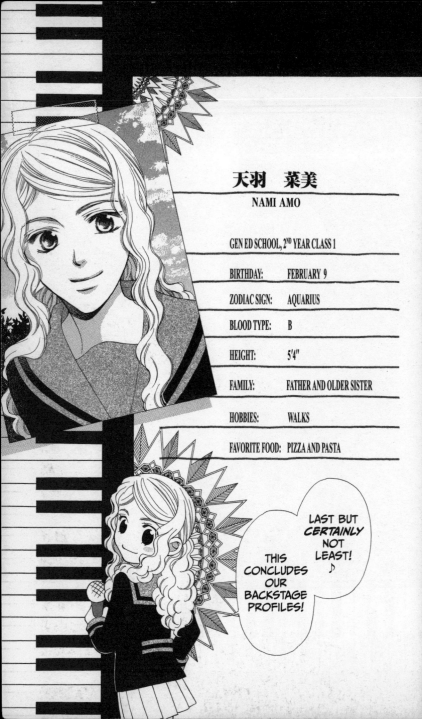

天羽　菜美

NAMI AMO

GEN ED SCHOOL, 2ND YEAR CLASS 1

BIRTHDAY:	FEBRUARY 9
ZODIAC SIGN:	AQUARIUS
BLOOD TYPE:	B
HEIGHT:	5'4"
FAMILY:	FATHER AND OLDER SISTER
HOBBIES:	WALKS
FAVORITE FOOD:	PIZZA AND PASTA

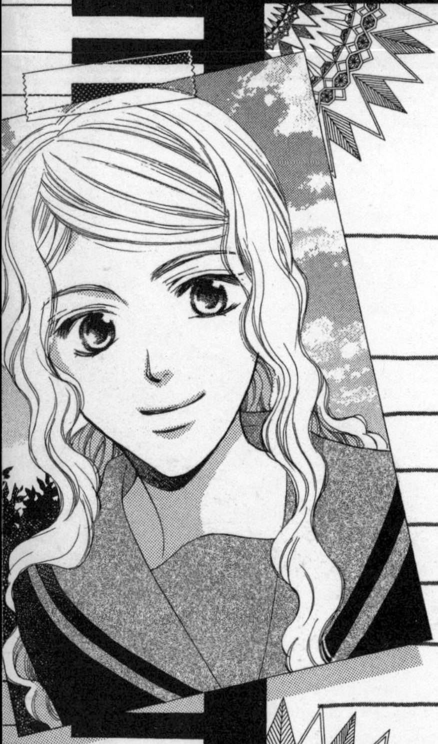

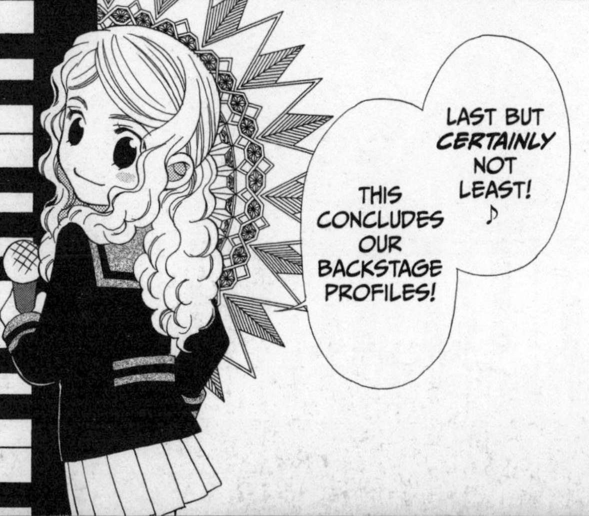

LAST BUT *CERTAINLY* NOT LEAST! ♪
THIS CONCLUDES OUR BACKSTAGE PROFILES!

POSTSCRIPT

Hello again. Yuki here. Thank you again for being such loyal readers. There's usually about six months between volumes, but volume 6 came out just four months after volume 5 in Japan! It was quick... for me, at least. Maybe that's why they included that extra story from years ago ... I think I'm being punished.

Last but not least, thanks to my readers, Koei, and everybody who helped me: family, friends and my editor. Thanks a bunch.

Well, I hope to see you in the next volume! (I can't believe it's already volume 7!)

Yuki Kure

SPECIAL THANKS

A.Kashima
M.Shiino
N.Sato
W.Hibiki
K.Hashiba

La Corda d'Oro End Notes

You can appreciate music just by listening to it, but knowing the story behind a piece can help enhance your enjoyment. In that spirit, here is background information about some of the topics mentioned in *La Corda d'Oro*. Enjoy!

Page 76, panel 1: *Eine Kleine Nachtmusik*
One of Mozart's best-known compositions, originally written for a chamber ensemble of two violins, viola and cello. Its formal title is *Serenade for Strings in G Major*, but it's much better known by this name, which means "a little night music."

Page 77, panel 1: Boccherini
Luigi Boccherini (1743-1805), a classical composer from Italy, was a prolific writer of chamber music, including almost 100 pieces for string quartet. His reputation diminished after his death, with some 19th-century critics dismissively calling him "Haydn's wife." In recent decades, however, he has regained some popularity. His famous *String Quintet in C Major* was featured in the movie *Master and Commander: The Far Side of the World*.

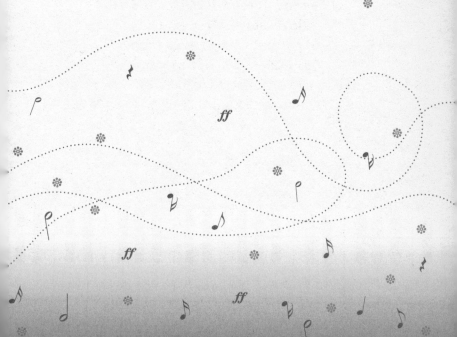

Yuki Kure made her debut in 2000 with the story *Chijo yori Eien ni* (Forever from the Earth), published in monthly *LaLa* magazine. *La Corda d' Oro* is her first manga series published. Her hobbies are watching soccer games and collecting small goodies.

LA CORDA D'ORO
Vol. 6
The Shojo Beat Manga Edition

STORY AND ART BY
YUKI KURE
ORIGINAL CONCEPT BY
RUBY PARTY

English Translation & Adaptation/Mai Ihara
Touch-up Art & Lettering/Gia Cam Luc
Design/Yukiko Whitley
Editor/Shaenon K. Garrity

Editor in Chief, Books/Alvin Lu
Editor in Chief, Magazines/Marc Weidenbaum
VP of Publishing Licensing/Rika Inouye
VP of Sales/Gonzalo Ferreyra
Sr. VP of Marketing/Liza Coppola
Publisher/Hyoe Narita

Printed in Canada

Published by VIZ Media, LLC
P.O. Box 77010
San Francisco, CA 94107

Shojo Beat Manga Edition
10 9 8 7 6 5 4 3 2 1
First printing, January 2008

store.viz.com

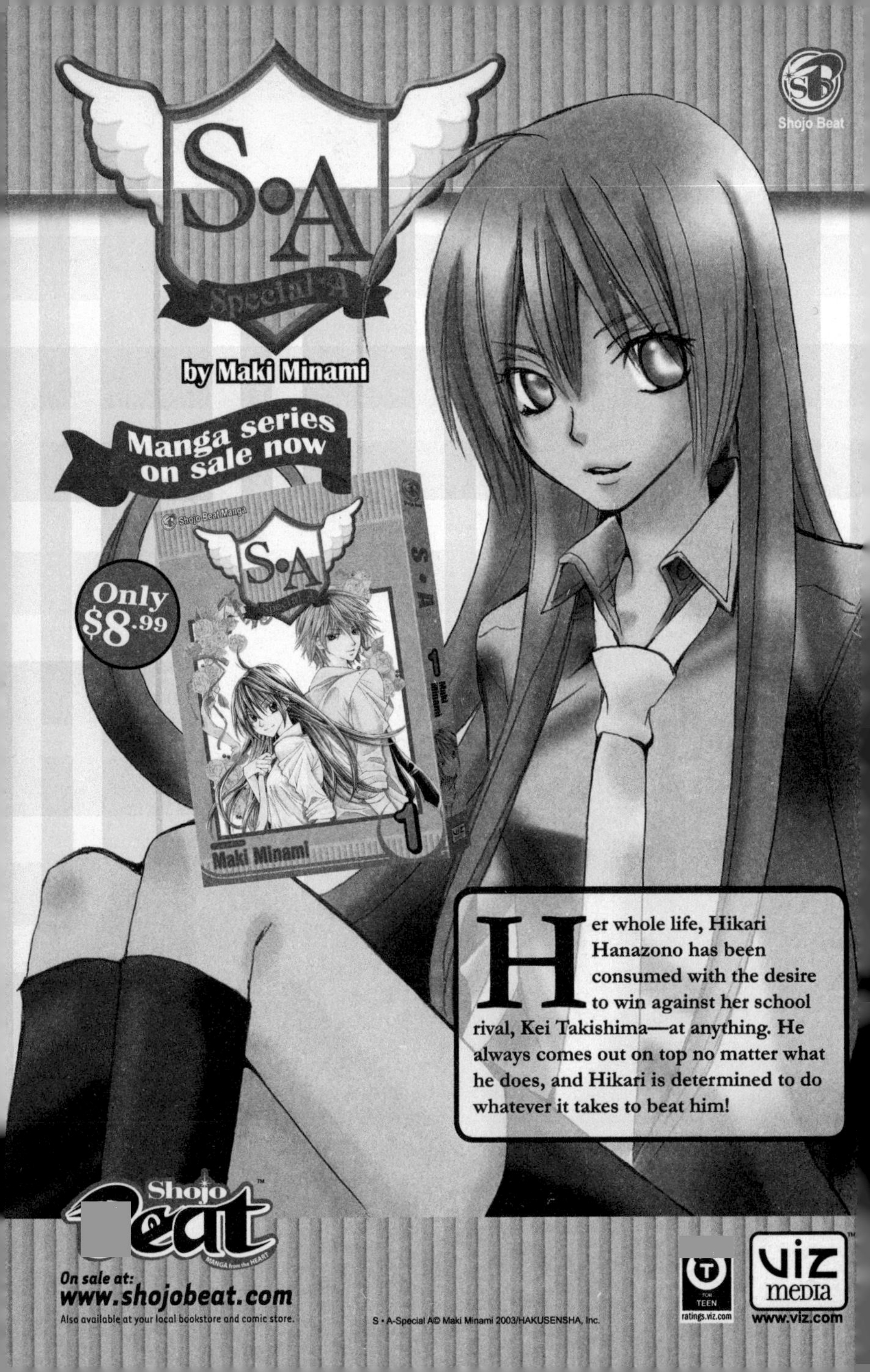

Shojo Beat
S•A
Special A
by Maki Minami
Manga series on sale now
Shojo Beat Manga
S•A
Maki Minami
Only $8.99
Her whole life, Hikari Hanazono has been consumed with the desire to win against her school rival, Kei Takishima—at anything. He always comes out on top no matter what he does, and Hikari is determined to do whatever it takes to beat him!
Shojo Beat
MANGA from the HEART
On sale at:
www.shojobeat.com
Also available at your local bookstore and comic store.
S • A-Special A© Maki Minami 2003/HAKUSENSHA, Inc.
T
TEEN
ratings.viz.com
VIZ media
www.viz.com

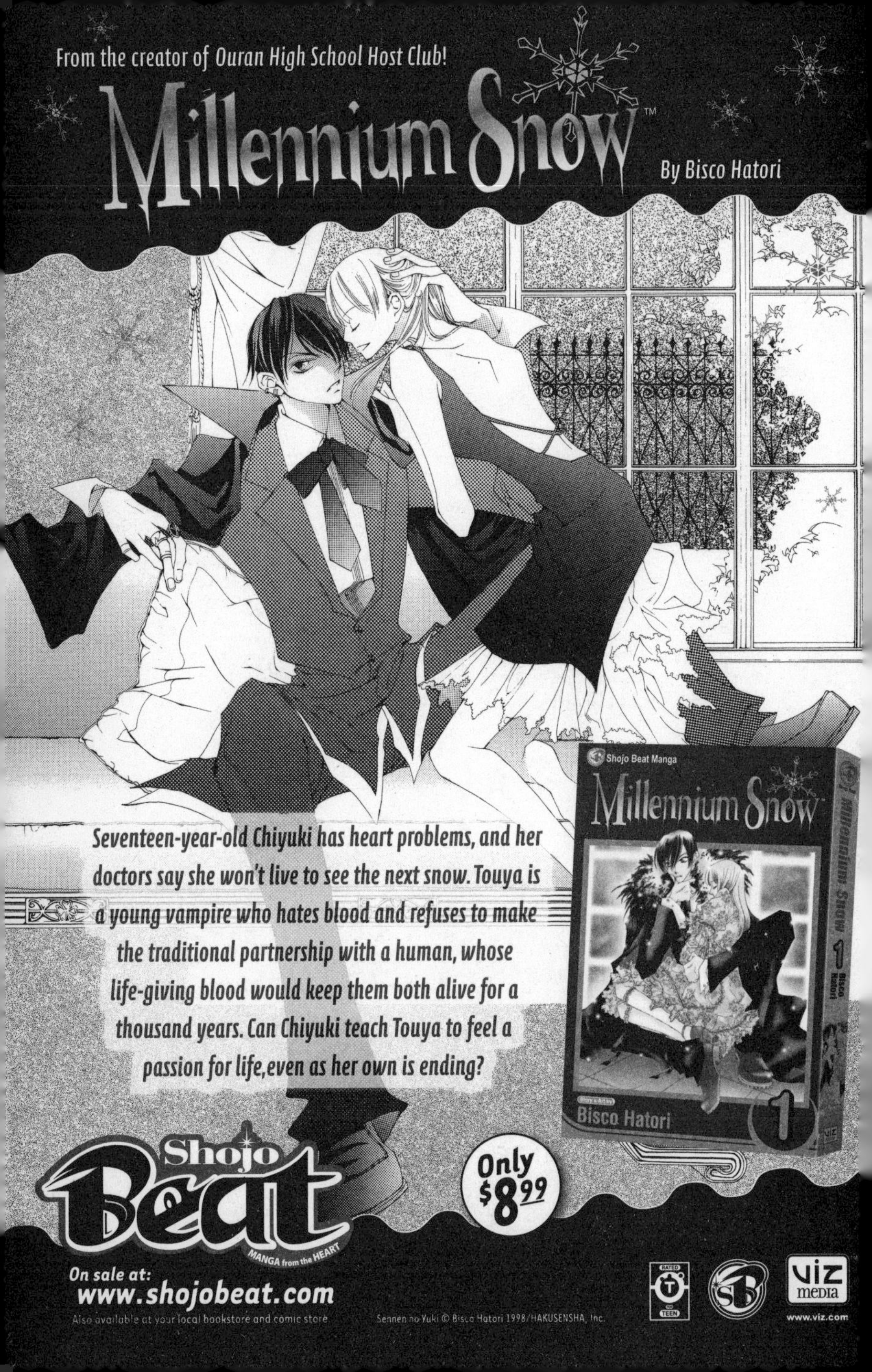
From the creator of Ouran High School Host Club!
Millennium Snow™
By Bisco Hatori
Seventeen-year-old Chiyuki has heart problems, and her doctors say she won't live to see the next snow. Touya is a young vampire who hates blood and refuses to make the traditional partnership with a human, whose life-giving blood would keep them both alive for a thousand years. Can Chiyuki teach Touya to feel a passion for life,even as her own is ending?
Shojo Beat Manga
Millennium Snow
Bisco Hatori
1
Only $8.99
Shojo Beat
MANGA from the HEART
On sale at:
www.shojobeat.com
Also available at your local bookstore and comic store.
Sennen no Yuki © Bisco Hatori 1998/HAKUSENSHA, Inc.
RATED T TEEN
VIZ MEDIA
www.viz.com

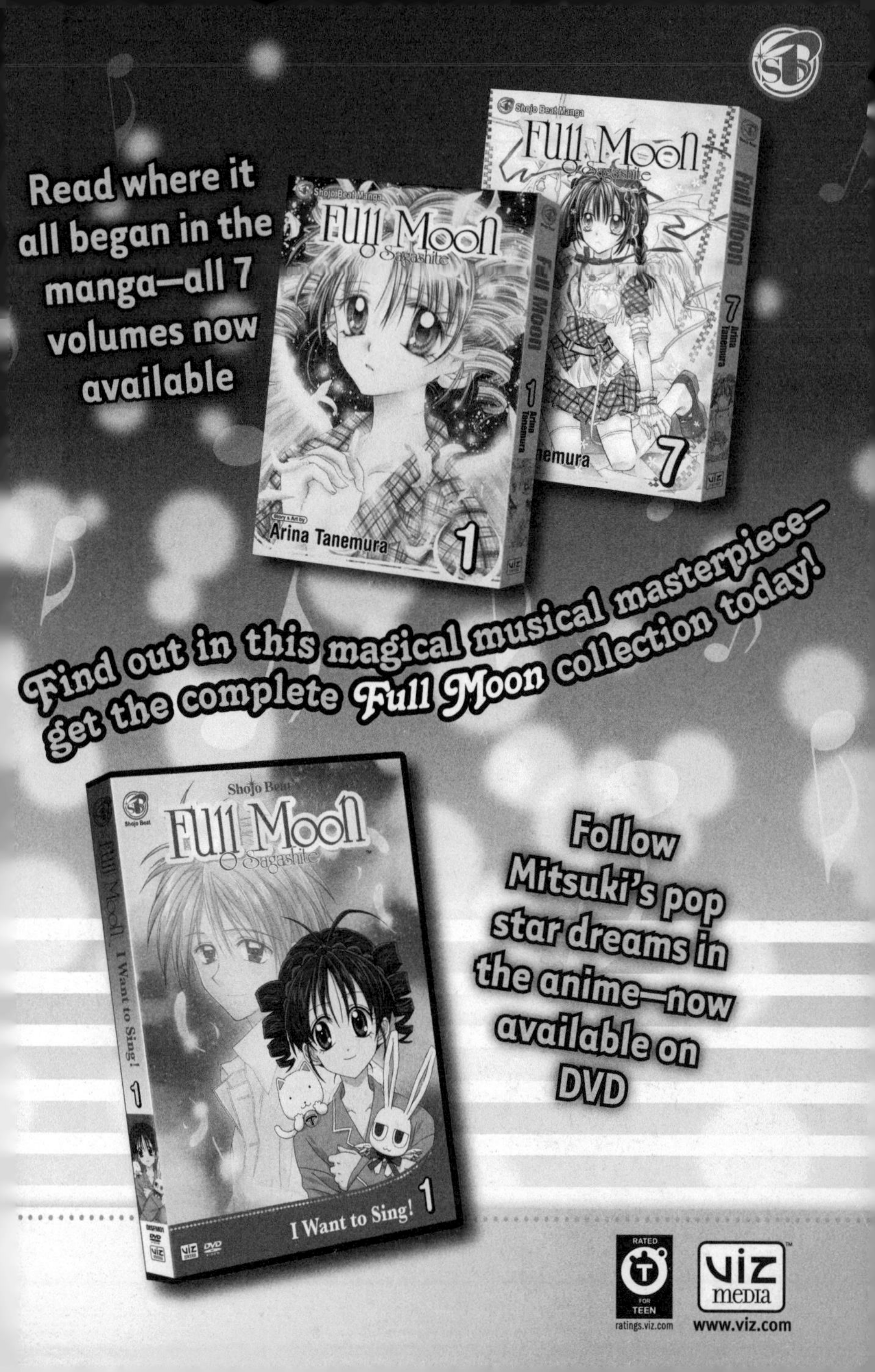
Read where it all began in the manga—all 7 volumes now available
Shojo Beat Manga
Full Moon O Sagashite
Story & Art by Arina Tanemura
1
7
Find out in this magical musical masterpiece—get the complete Full Moon collection today!
Shojo Beat
Full Moon O Sagashite
I Want to Sing! 1
Follow Mitsuki's pop star dreams in the anime—now available on DVD
RATED T FOR TEEN
ratings.viz.com
VIZ media
www.viz.com

Full Moon

O Sagashite

By Arina Tanemura

creator of *The Gentlemen's Alliance †*

Mitsuki loves singing, but a malignant throat tumor prevents her from pursuing her passion.

Can two fun-loving Shinigami give her singing career a magical jump-start?

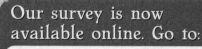